AF538350

Democracy Assistance Bypassing Governments in Recipient Countries

This book addresses important and under-researched issues such as, the role of young people in democratization processes, the role of new democracies in sharing their transition experience, and the effectiveness of aid. A major theme of the book is democracy assistance efforts by the NGOs from Central and Eastern Europe to support young people in Eastern Europe, the Western Balkans, and Central Asia. It examines this theme in a comparative perspective and with a deeper analysis of reasons and ways to support young people, the need to support them and the effectiveness of these efforts.

Bringing together a wide range of material on democracy assistance of Central and Eastern European countries that includes surveying the providers and beneficiaries of aid and looking for better methods of impact evaluation, the book advances a framework for assessing democracy assistance efforts. It concludes with implications of the impact of democracy assistance on young people and democracy diffusion from Central and Eastern European democracies to other countries.

This text will be of key interest to scholars and students of democracy, democratization, Central and Eastern Europe, Post-Soviet studies, and European and Comparative Politics, as well as for practitioners (donors, NGOs) who want to know *what* works best, and *why* and *when* in aid provision.

Paulina Pospieszna is Assistant Professor at Adam Mickiewicz University in Poznań, Poland.

Democratization Studies
(Formerly Democratization Studies, Frank Cass)

Democratization Studies combines theoretical and comparative studies with detailed analyses of issues central to democratic progress and its performance, all over the world.

The books in this series aim to encourage debate on the many aspects of democratization that are of interest to policy-makers, administrators and journalists, aid and development personnel, as well as to all those involved in education.

Democratization in the 21st Century
Reviving Transitology
Edited by Mohammad-Mahmoud Ould Mohamedou and Timothy D. Sisk

Democratizing Public Governance in Developing Nations
With Special Reference to Africa
Edited by M. Shamsul Haque, Anastase Shyaka, Gedeon M. Mudacumura

Political Participation, Diffused Governance, and the Transformation of Democracy
Patterns of Change
Yvette Peters

When Democracies Collapse
Assessing Transitions to Non-Democratic Regimes in the Contemporary World
Luca Tomini

Challenges of Democracy in the 21st Century
Concepts, Methods, Causality and the Quality of Democracy
Edited by Luca Tomini and Giulia Sandri

The Legitimacy of Citizen-led Deliberative Democracy
The G1000 in Belgium
Didier Caluwaerts and Min Reuchamps

Democracy Assistance Bypassing Governments in Recipient Countries
Supporting the "Next Generation"
Paulina Pospieszna

Democracy Assistance Bypassing Governments in Recipient Countries

Supporting the "Next Generation"

Paulina Pospieszna

LONDON AND NEW YORK

First published 2019
by Routledge
2 Park Square, Milton Park, Abingdon, Oxon OX14 4RN

and by Routledge
711 Third Avenue, New York, NY 10017

Routledge is an imprint of the Taylor & Francis Group, an informa business

British Library Cataloguing-in-Publication Data
A catalogue record for this book is available from the British Library

Library of Congress Cataloging-in-Publication Data
A catalog record has been requested for this book

ISBN: 978-1-138-89506-5 (hbk)
ISBN: 978-1-315-17968-1 (ebk)

Typeset in Times New Roman
by Wearset Ltd, Boldon, Tyne and Wear

For all pro-democratic NGOs engaged in democracy promotion

Contents

Figures

Tables

Acknowledgments

There are many important individuals, organizations and institutions that made the realization of this book possible. First and foremost, this book emerges out of an extensive research project that was undertaken during 2013–2017 and funded by the National Science Center (NCN) in Poland (grant number UMO-2013/09/D/HS5/04381). Without the generous support of this granting institution, this project would not be possible, for which I am very grateful. I am also indebted to Aleksandra Galus for her work on this research grant. I was lucky to have such an outstanding PhD student with exceptional organization skills, dedication, independence in research and confidence in acting and performing difficult tasks. Without her commitment to science and excellence in the pursuit of knowledge, this research grant would not have gone that far.

I also would like to thank two wonderful devoted civic activists with great experience and knowledge in aiding civil society in partner countries who inspired me, and who allowed me to understand the opportunities and threats that NGOs are facing, especially Ewa Romanowska (Borussia Foundation), and Lena Prusinowska (the Leaders for Change). In fact, this book idea began when I took part, as a participant observer, in the activities put on by these organizations for young people from Belarus, Moldova, Russia and Ukraine. I am also grateful to Renata Koźlicka-Glińska and Agnieszka Mazur from the donor organization, the Polish American Freedom Foundation, for being open to my ideas and for allowing the social experiment to be conducted to perform impact evaluation of the youth program. It has been a very rewarding experience for me, as a researcher, to see that practitioners and scholars can meet somewhere in the middle and benefit from mutual collaboration.

I would like to thank many representatives of governmental and non-governmental organizations from the four CEE countries, as well as from Bosnia-Herzegovina, Georgia, and Ukraine interviewed for this study, without whome I would also not have been able to undertake such a great task to conduct surveys among the young people. These organizations allowed me to observe that much democracy assistance work is done by civil society organizations that collaborate with partners in recipient countries within a specific project, and to expand my earlier research to explore how these projects impact the beneficiaries, how effective they are in changing opinions and behaviors of the target groups, and whether they contribute to diffusing democratic ideas and behaviors.

However, before the idea of evaluating democracy assistance from non-state actors in Central and Eastern Europe was finalized in the form of the research project, it underwent many modifications. I would like to thank Henrik Urdal for his inspiration as well as constructive criticism of the methodology as well as very helpful and down-to-earth comments on the first draft of the research proposal during my short-term scientific mission at the Peace Research Institute in Oslo (PRIO), and Sabine Carey for allowing me to develop this idea during my post-doctoral research at the University of Mannheim.

There have been also many other people and institutions that have been supportive over the last few years of my research that contributed to this book. First, many thanks to the following individuals and universities that invited me to give talks: Simone Dietrich (the Essex Lab), Britta Weiffen (University of São Paulo/the Martius Chair for German and European Studies), Alice Freifeld and Michael Berhnhard (University of Florida), as well as Serhii Plokhii (Harvard Ukrainian Research Institute—HURI). Moreover, special thanks are due to members of the European Consortium for Political Research (ECPR) "Citizenship" standing group for the inspiration and comments on the early stage of my work. Other three very valuable conference meetings were: "Democracy and Authoritarianism: Rethinking the Boundary" organized by ENS-Triangle, Lyon (many thanks to Dorota Dakowska), "Deliberating Democratization: Examining Democratic Change and the Role of International Democracy Support," organized by the Westminster Foundation for Democracy, and the "Experiments in Foreign Aid Research" Workshop organized by the University of California, Washington Center. Having an opportunity meet prominent scholars and get authoritative comments on my research, has been a very valuable experience during the research phase and the development of the book project.

I am convinced that the breakthrough in writing process of my book was a short stay as a visiting scholar at the IFES at the Frankfurt Viadrina University. Many thanks to Timm Beichelt for the invitation, Estela Schindel for being a good host and Susann Worschech for inspiring discussion about social networks, democracy promotion and Eastern European politics. It was a special time and location, which was very needed while writing a book.

I would also like to thank the former Dean of the Political Science Department at Adam Mickiewicz University in Poznań Professor Tadeusz Wallas for offering me a position at my *alma mater* after nine years of education and research abroad and for a great opportunity to begin a new stage in my academic career. My thanks also go to the current Dean, Professor Andrzej Stelmach, for allowing me to balance my work as a lecturer and career as a researcher, and for allowing me to take a semester break to focus on writing this book. I would also like to thank my colleagues in the Political Science Department at Adam Mickiewicz University in Poznań as well as the research team of the Beethoven grant, especially Gerald Schneider, Patrick Weber, Joanna Skrzypczyńska, and Beata Stępień. I am grateful for their collegiality, support and understanding especially in the final stage of writing a book. I feel I also ought to thank the administrative staff (especially Maria Lutomska) for service and for helping me to tackle bureaucratic regulations and procedures.

Finally, I must thank my family and friends. Marysia Galbraith for her comments on the book proposal and invaluable suggestions. It is a blessing to have a mentor and a big sister like her. My husband, Marcin, for being a patient and dedicated partner, for listening to all of my concerns over the previous year regarding my work, and for helping me with data late at night after work and during precious weekends. Thanks are also due to my parents and parents-in-law for giving me much appreciated support support during busy times by providing childcare and all the possible help that the family needed, assuring me that I "do not have to worry about anything and can focus on writing a book." I would also like to thank to my two sons, Maks and Aleks, who kept me sane during the writing process and who reminded me of what is most important in life. Also, I could not have seen this project through without the support of many friends. Thank you.

Introduction

This research considers some of the opportunities for democracy promotion in difficult and uncertain times for liberal democracy. Among many actors that constitute the democracy promotion community, there is multiplicity of non-governmental organizations that play an increasingly important role at the international level. Although there is a lot of research about NGOs as recipients, there is not much about the NGOs as providers of democracy assistance. This research continues to fill this gap. It focuses on NGOs from Central and Eastern Europe (CEE NGOs) that while promoting democracy do not facilitate the hegemony of certain model of democracy and open up space to broaden the way democracy is supported and maintained (Pospieszna, 2014).

Scholars and practitioners agree that democracy assistance has to be continued but should no longer just be generous—it must be smart. Thus, funding itself cannot be credited with the democratic breakthrough. Today, the words by former UN Secretary-General Kofi Annan on rule-of-law promotion, which can be applied to the promotion of any type of international norms and standards, become even more relevant: "We must learn as well as to eschew one-size-fits-all formulas and the importance of foreign models, and instead, base our support on national assessments, national participation and national needs and aspirations" (UN Security Council, 2004). I argue that bypass democracy assistance offers this opportunity to understand the needs of the recipients, since it is the way to provide assistance to civil society actors omitting governments. It is also about the network of NGOs that crosses borders. Bypassing uncooperative or corrupt governments, and channeling aid through non-state actors in recipient countries might be the only form of democracy promotion that is suitable and effective in times when authoritarianism is staging a comeback (Burrows and Stephan, 2015).

The goal of this research is to generate a larger body of knowledge that is needed in democracy promotion literature, to offer something fresh and to initiate deeper reflection on what exactly these non-state actors are doing when they engage in democracy promotion. When examining democracy assistance, it also is important to engage with the discussion how the idea of democracy is defined by different actors in order to better understand and explain the dynamics and effects of democracy promotion (Hobson and Kurki, 2012). Therefore, this research focuses on *what* exactly the actors are doing when they engage in democracy promotion, *what type of democracy* they promote, and *how*. Democracy assistance should also be designed in ways that will produce meaningful change. Therefore, I examine *whether* and *how* democracy assistance works on the ground, what is the *impact* of these efforts, thus helping to build knowledge why, under what conditions democracy assistance works. In most recent studies, scholars have examined a variety of potential relationships by depicting circumstances under which democracy assistance promoted democracy (Bermeo, 2016; Kalyvitis and Vlachaki, 2012). However, as observed by Wright and Winters (2010) as well Dietrich (2013) in evaluating the aid effectiveness, the studies tend to assume that governments are the sole recipients, and senders of foreign aid (Bermeo, 2016; de Mesquita and Smith, 2009; Svensson, 2000), whereas aid is also delivered through non-state actors.

It is not to say that NGOs are the central actor in democracy promotion. Still without the support of the donors, NGOs engagement would be less apparent, but would draw attention to the important role of bypassing democracy assistance in reaching civil society in recipient countries and in influencing those who are the major protagonists of change. It is also to show that the strength of democracy promotion lies in building networks, inclusion and achieving synergy. The coalitions that might turn out to be only a bastion of liberal democracy norms,[1] which in the case of the post-communist region,[2] would contribute to the perseverance of democratic values. This raises the question why we should be looking at democracy assistance when the trend—especially in the post-Soviet space—has been a backlash against democracy promotion.

"Democracy empowers individuals, provides space, but it can give you a kick into teeth" as one of the keynote speakers said during the conference on democracy promotion bringing together practitioners and scholars organized by the Westminster Foundation for Democracy.[3] This is the example of the Central and Eastern European (CEE) countries (the Czech Republic, Hungary, Poland and Slovakia) today, often called the Visegrád Four countries or the new members of the EU. Since 1989, they have experienced a relatively successful transformation to democracy and capitalism (Pridham, 2005; Ekiert, Kubik, and Vachudova, 2007). By the end of the 1990s, they were considered consolidated and stable democracies whose membership of NATO (since 1999) and the EU (since 2004) has been viewed as an important democratically stabilizing factor (Pridham, 2006; Schimmelfennig, 2007). Today, Central and Eastern European politics is once again back on front pages of newspapers. Some scholars point to a recent "democratic fatigue" in these countries (Rupnik and Zielonka, 2013; Ekiert and Ziblatt, 2013; Dawson and Hanley, 2016) or even de-democratization (Ágh, 2015). They are certainly facing populist threats (Tomini, 2015), and are seen as the core of the "EU's illiberal democracies" (Applebaum, 2016).

The rise and success of populists presents a direct challenge to the role of the civil society sector, however, it should be noticed that NGOs from Central and Eastern Europe that are the focus of this book, were embedded in this liberal trend themselves as recipients of aid, as well as being very active during the democratization processes contributing to important changes in their countries. These two important experiences as well as openness of partner countries towards cooperation explain the NGOs' involvement in sharing (transition) experience. They also developed their own models of democracy assistance programs by targeting predominantly non-state actors, instead of governments (Horký-Hluchář and Lightfoot, 2013; Petrova, 2014; Pospieszna, 2014; Szent-Iványi, 2012, 2014; Tolstrup, 2014), even in countries that restrict space for civil society. Thus, the CEE NGOs provide good material for studying the effectiveness of such democracy assistance programs.

A thorough knowledge of non-state actors in CEE countries and their know-how in delivery of bypass democracy assistance, even in times of crackdown, is an important feature of CEE democracy assistance. In fact, NGOs in CEE serve as a conduit of democratic norms, which is important especially in the current situation when some new democracies in the region (Poland and Hungary) are experiencing democratic crises or even democratic "backsliding." More importantly, without the engagement of NGOs, which are able to use their networks to reach civil society, CEE countries' democracy assistance, which since 2004 became the most important pillar of bilateral aid delivered within development cooperation, especially in the Czech Republic, the Slovak Republic, and Poland, would not be possible. Given the fact that democracy assistance is driven by non-states actors in CEE countries, this adds credibility and legitimacy to this process. I also believe that challenges of democratization in the EU's Eastern neighborhood and autocratic influences and a resurgence from Russia and in post-Soviet Eurasia (Obydenkova and Libman, 2015) further increases the timeliness and potential relevance of this study.

This book contributes not only to the emergent literature focusing on NGOs as senders of aid, as well as the role of non-state actors from the Central and Eastern European states in democracy aid, but it is also one of the first studies to focus on youth as a target of democracy assistance programs. As compared to other areas of democracy assistance, such as election assistance, human rights assistance, and media assistance, youth support has received little attention; therefore, this book adds to our understanding by showing the efforts to support young people in Eastern Europe, the Western Balkans and Georgia. A major target group in democracy assistance in these countries has been youth, the "next generation" (Diuk, 2012). However, little is known about the reasons for foreign engagement in supporting young people abroad within democracy assistance as well as the nature and the impact of these efforts, and there have been no evaluations that do this in a systematic way.

There also are other reasons to focus on youth democracy assistance. First, youth participation plays a special role in building and developing civil society and thus democracy—can be advocates for democratic change and contestants of non-democratic regimes through mobilizing protests, uprisings and peaceful demonstrations. Participation is important for political change as well as economic development, for building social skills crucial for political engagement (Almond and Verba, 1963; Brady, Verba and Schlozman, 1995; Putnam, 2000;

Putnam, Leonardi and Nanetti, 1993; Walzer, 2002). Active, aware, informed and determined citizens are important not only for building and maintaining democracy (Checkoway, 2010; Ekiert, Kubik and Vachudova, 2007). The youth groups played a crucial role in the protests in Ukraine during the Orange Revolution, like *Pora*, as well as during Euromaidan (Diuk, 2014a) or during the Arab Spring (Honwana, 2013; Mulderig, 2013). This democratizing potential of young people is also motivating more thorough investigation of the opinions and attitudes of young people in countries that are struggling with democracy. By doing this, I hope also to contribute to the link between youth participation and engagement and democratization discussed in the literature (Crawford and Lijphart, 1995).

There is also another reason for choosing democracy assistance directed toward young people, which corresponds to the concerns regarding the timelessness of the book and current trend in democratization in the post-Soviet space: young people also become an important civil society group to work with, especially in authoritarian countries, where cooperation with the government is ineffective and where civil society organizations are restricted. Interestingly, young donors from CEE recognize the support for young people as one of the main targets in democracy assistance and the goal of many youth programs implemented by the NGOs from CEE is to activate young people to be more socially responsible for their local community, region and country, believing that a democratic country requires such active participation. I have found that many programs targeted at these groups aim to educate them—about the citizens' rights and the role they can play in society, and about the functioning of democratic institutions and authorities' responsibilities (Pospieszna and Galus, 2018). Whereas the aim is to activate and educate young people, little is known about the effectiveness of this type of democracy assistance.

Following the recent trend in aid effectiveness literature to focus on aid programs (Norris, 2017), this project also concentrates on youth programs with the aim of demonstrating the reasons for, as well as the efforts of, supporting young people in recipient countries by CEE donors, and also by evaluating the effectiveness of the programs by measuring perceptions of recipient actors regarding democracy, the role of the state and citizens, and their knowledge of democratic standards. I contribute to building theory of democratic change in which agent empowerment plays a crucial role. In this empowerment process, the third actor, a neighboring country, plays an important role, because of a shared common past and similar socio-cultural features or simply because of a transition experience that is relevant. Democratization literature is clear that democratization can be influenced by external factors, however, the question if this can promote meaningful change still remains a matter of scholarly and public debate. The book contributes to the better understanding of intra-region diffusion, understood as a process by which an idea, institution, policy, model is diffused through certain channels to the members of the social system, that may result in political similarities specific to the post-Soviet region (Bunce and Wolchik, 2006b; Deutsch and Welzel, 2016; Inglehart and Welzel, 2005, 2009; Jahn, 2006; Simmons,

Dobbin and Garrett, 2008; Wejnert, 2014). This contribution and conceptual clarity related to democracy and democratization (including the definition of democracy and democratization) is included in the theoretical chapter of this book.

The book answers four questions: *Why do NGOs from the CEE countries choose to target youth abroad when offering democracy assistance? How is the youth in target countries being supported? Do young people in target countries need this support? Finally, what is the impact of bypass democracy assistance projects on the direct beneficiaries, namely young people—are these efforts effective in terms of their capacity to diffuse democratic norms and practices?* Given that, the empirical material results from the combination of different methods. Specifically, the results are based not only on the social experiments, which help to establish the impact of the democracy assistance program on young people, but also on surveying young people in recipient countries in order to determine whether there is a need to support them, as well as on content analysis and interviews to answer first two research questions.

Argument in brief

Democracy assistance is a specific type of aid which aims to support democracy through promoting human rights, the rule of law, elections and political processes, civil society, and democratic institutions in a target country. In times when authoritarianism is staging a comeback, donors prefer to bypass uncooperative or corrupt governments, and, instead of government-to-government aid, they channel aid through non-state actors. Recent studies seem to acknowledge that democracy assistance bypassing governments is important for the better understanding what works, and what does not, in democracy aid and why (Bush, 2015; Dietrich, 2013; Pospieszna, 2014). It should be noted, nevertheless, that most of our knowledge is lost since we do not have information and data on programs involving civil society actors in donor and recipient countries which are not only funded from the government sources, and the aim of this book is to fill this gap. Although there has been substantial increase in research on evaluating democracy aid, surprisingly little is known about the effectiveness of bypass democracy assistance.

Democracy assistance that bypasses a government dominates aid delivery coming from the new EU member states in the Central and Eastern Europe (CEE). CEE countries find democracy assistance an effective way of sharing their transition experience with their neighbors (Szent-Iványi, 2012, 2014) and to exert a positive influence on civil society actors and thus democratization (Petrova, 2014; Pospieszna, 2014). My previous study contributed to investigating how a former democracy assistance recipient country goes about assisting other states in their struggles for democracy and this study unveiled the key role of donor-country-based non-governmental organizations (NGOs) in shaping the state's democracy assistance and their unique ability to reach civil society groups in recipient countries (Pospieszna, 2014). My earlier research project also demonstrated that although donor states provide funding, donor-country-based NGOs as well as target country-based non-state actors because of their knowledge and expertise are behind designing and implementing democracy assistance programs. In this study, I present research on democracy assistance driven by non-state actors believing that state-based explanations give an incomplete picture of how democracy assistance works on the ground.

I argue that CEE NGOs were embedded in liberal thinking and promote liberal democracy among civil society actors in other post-communist countries. Specifically, I argue that CEE NGOs that were established in the 1990s were embedded by the liberal concept of democracy that shaped their understanding of the type of democracy that should be promoted in other post-communist countries. I demonstrate the beginning of civil society organizations in the region, how the confidence in liberal democracy prevailed within the democracy promotion community of non-state actors, as well as how the belief in internalization of these norms led to the emergence of active citizens willing to engage with the state directly and/or through organized civil society. Transnationally allied CEE non-state actors promote liberal democracy norms because the goal is "freeing of the people" and empowering them. It is expected that CEE endorses the emergence of liberal democracy norms, collective understandings, and active citizenship participation, and promotes these principles in their youth programs. Citizens' participation and involvement in politics is central to the study of political systems and liberal democracy.

I believe that there is a need to support young people in post-communist countries. The region is well known for a political culture that is conservative and patriarchal and the culture of active participation is weak often because of co-optation, forceful connection between the ruling elites and the population (national government are other actors, who regard civil society as an object of their policies and political action) (Diuk, 2012; Roberts, 2009). I expect to find differences in citizens' evaluations of democracy between young people in post-communist countries, also in the levels of social trust, which is a cultural dimension (Norris, 2011). I also expect to find differences in the level of political and civic engagement, which might be connected with the way young people value citizenship norms (Bolzendahl and Coffé, 2013), since citizenship norms is a wide concept which is linked to people's active participation in society (Delanty, 2000; Dwyer, 2000). Although young people may believe in the desirability of democracy, they might have little confidence in some key democratic institutions; thus they need to be socialized into the values of engaged citizenship, human empowerment, because this will lead to changes in political culture, and will influence politics and foster the demand for liberal democracy, as expressed by Inglehart and Welzel (2005). Youth projects that are supported by governments are usually financially unsustainable, because they often receive short-term support (Kovacheva, 2005).

My argument is that CEE NGOs utilize bypass democracy assistance. As the recipients of similar assistance in the past, they developed their own way of sharing their experience and passed the best practice developed in their own countries to civil society organizations in the target countries. Thus, these organizations are bypassing the governments in recipient countries, and often in their own countries as well, in order to form linkages and networks with civil society organizations in target countries or directly reach beneficiaries. This form of assistance in practice means that CEE NGOs and non-state actors share responsibility and tasks over implementation of the programs. Although such partners are mainly organizations in recipient countries, sometimes, especially in authoritarian states, the beneficiaries are reached directly, and these are schools, teachers, young people, women, etc. The logic behind such designed CEE NGOs' support (financial, technical, and logistical) to the society in recipient countries, is that these efforts translate into greater support for democracy and participation, which in turn can lead to pressuring governments.

The partnership also means greater local ownership of the project as the partner in the target country communicates the needs; thus avoiding ready-made solutions when sharing their knowledge. I situate discussion in a literature that explores the role of CEE NGOs as local actors in reshaping existing beliefs and practices as well as in adjusting foreign norms into the local context (Acharya, 2004, 2011). Given their close linkages and knowledge on the ground, they developed the ability to respond to the needs of recipient countries. Because of the strengths of bypass democracy assistance *I argue that this from of democracy promotion in the long-term is an effective form of influencing changes in target societies.*

Bypass democracy assistance has a chance of being effective in diffusing the norms of democracy, because: (1) it avoids governments and allows for the continuation of democracy promotion in difficult times for democracy (authoritarianism staging come back, closing space for civil society and democracy promoters etc.); (2) cooperation respects the cultural specificity of countries, thanks to which implemented changes better meet specific needs; (3) the support goes not only via NGOs but also directly through various beneficiaries (youth, women, teachers, etc.), which can empower them vis-à-vis state; (4) it involves networks, social ties, long-term cooperation, and thus is more likely to create social capital; (5) a diffusion of knowledge and "feedback loops with partner countries" is more likely to take place.

According to this model of democracy assistance aid delivery, not only uncooperative and corrupt governments in recipient countries can be bypassed (Dietrich, 2013), but also governments in home countries can be omitted. The CEE NGOs consider themselves liberal and pro-democratic actors, and are thus found nowadays to be in opposition to the governments in these countries. The fact that they continue implementing programs in post-communist countries adds the credibility to democracy assistance coming from this region. Nevertheless, it requires them to be creative in securing funding for their projects. Bypassing governments means being independent of government sources, but does not mean relying on foreign funding alone. Overreliance on foreign funds may undermine NGOs' autonomy and flexibility of action and ultimately NGOs' comparative advantage may suffer; therefore, it is about limiting donor influence by diversifying their sources of income. Also, NGOs can be also perceived as intermediary institutions through which funding goes to non-state actors in target countries to protect them from excessive donor influence.

Given the fact that the civil society has to face nowadays this global trend resulting in the reduction of freedom and space for democratic activities and the backlash against promoting democratic development (Carothers and Brechenmacher, 2014), scholars observed that the nature of Western democracy assistance has been changing and that what is known as "good governance" has been an increasing proportion of democracy assistance (Bush, 2015). However, bypass democracy assistance offers an opportunity for not punishing civil society whose governments are uncooperative or even enact restrictive NGOs laws with reduced aid flow, but rather allows non-state actors to find different channels and tactics to deliver democracy aid regardless, for example through reaching civil society groups directly—young people, teachers, parents, writers, and so-called leaders in their local communities. When targeting direct beneficiaries, which in times of backlash against democracy promotion is important, it allows for the continuation of democracy assistance efforts. This is a very important contribution to democracy assistance literature as well as to broader democratization literature.

Bypass democracy assistance that reaches direct beneficiaries (youth, women, teachers, etc.) is effective through empowering them, which in turn can be an efficient tool for democratic change—the diffusion of democratic norms depends on the local actors who directly benefit from funding channeled through these projects and norms promotion. By targeting the direct beneficiaries in recipient countries (youth), democracy assistance efforts of CEE NGOs can be more effective, namely by diffusing the democratic norms more successfully as well as by empowering individuals and democratic groups, thus leading to possible changes in recipient countries.

The theoretical frame that guides the analysis is grounded in the theory of change and focuses on agent empowerment mechanism as an efficient tool for democratic change. My approach to democratization is bottom-up and people-centered, and focuses on the contributions of citizens to the political system, which differs from the top-down approach in focusing on improving the quality of democracy or democratization process through citizens' participation. The role of youth for democratization as agents of change and the growth of individual matter for democratization and for democratic sustainability. Therefore, this book contributes to building a theory of how non-state actors can be empowered by foreign means (Crawford and Lijphart, 1995; Ekiert and Hanson, 2003; Haerpfer *et al.*, 2009; Kopstein and Reilly, 2000; Tilly, 2007).

Following Finkel, Pérez-Liñán and Seligson's (2007) "the empowerment of agents" I believe that *democracy assistance bypassing governments is effective through empowering democratic groups.* Assistance can empower the democratic groups, which receive aid—NGOs and other civil society actors—or those that are affected by the results of democracy assistance programs, so-called direct beneficiaries (youth, women, teachers, etc.), and help them articulate their interest to policymakers (Cohen and Rogers, 1992). Moreover, democracy aid can create financial independence of the non-state actors, developed by democracy aid, and may empower these groups to make pro-democratic changes in their countries and to recruit the others. By empowering pro-democratic groups in recipient countries, however, democracy assistance attempts to affect these groups' power and to alter the power relationship among the incumbent government, as well as other societal actors, thus potentially to facilitate liberalization and democratization.

In recent literature on democracy assistance, scholars (Finkel, Pérez-Liñán and Seligson, 2007; Pérez-Liñán, Finkel and Seligson, 2016), are theorizing about an agent empowerment mechanism; however, they have not been able yet to test it. I believe that in my study on democracy assistance delivered to young people, which takes a micro perspective in evaluating the role of local actors, I am able to demonstrate whether civil society actors are empowered and able to introduce changes into the society. By empowering civil society, this can change the power relations in countries, as youth becomes the agent of change, actors that may eventually be capable of exerting influence on the preferences of their own states. Such opportunities are embedded in networks (Keck and Sikkink, 1998). Through transnational activism, recipients become global citizens rather than national citizens (Oxley and Morris, 2013; Tarrow, 1998).

Thus, *bypass democracy assistance restores the value of civil society as a core component of liberal democracy*. However it is more than a support to civil society, since it involves networks, social ties, and creating social capital. Bypass is, in fact, about social networks. What is novel about my approach is that I study the topic from the perspective of social networks that impact the democracy change in the recipient country in an indirect way through allowing individuals and organizations in recipient countries to obtain access to the social capital of these networks. Fundamental issues in social science form the relationship between the individual and society, the relationship between micro and macro. Actors' identities, goals and aspirations are themselves subject to change. They arise and are sustained through interaction, and that the human subject must be regarded as an ongoing developmental process. The agency and structure interpenetrate one another. Namely, CEE NGOs embedded in international networks together with civil society actors create an agency that affects structure, which in turn leads to gradual change (democratic transition). Structure determines, and it is, in turn, determined by the actions of the individuals. Thus, networks play a role as protagonists of democracy.

Democracy promotion through networks rather than direct donor-beneficiary should works better which can be explained through social network and social capital theories. The transnational networks link with groups bypassing the governments both in their countries as well as in recipient countries. However, the purpose of this network is not to put pressure on government (often inefficient and often corrupt) in recipient countries directly, but rather to put pressure on governments indirectly through empowered civil society groups themselves, which are equipped with information, often also money by transnationally operating CEE NGOs. Through their networks they can be an effective instrument of democracy promotion across territorial boundaries, linking civil society organizations and individuals. Scholars believe that supporting links between citizens and other groups of civil society is of fundamental importance both for building and strengthening civil society (Henderson, 2002; McMahon, 2000; Richter, 2002; Wilde, 2002).

Researchers recognize that building a sustainable civil society requires continuity in financing and maintaining long-term cooperation.[4] I argue that one of the main benefits resulting from bypass democracy assistance is that it builds lasting ties both within and between the state and citizens, and cooperation of non-governmental organizations with civil society in target countries is its long-term aim. The relations of CEE non-governmental organizations with NGOs or civil society groups in other post-communist countries have been ongoing for many years and thus in their opinion can contribute to the development of civil society and can bring about the intended results. Finally, scholars also highlight the importance of improving the impact of knowledge sharing through better definitions of what constitutes transition experience,and call for establishing clear "feedback loops with partner countries," and involving non-state actors more systematically (Mariyasin, 2013; Szent-Iványi and Végh, 2018). The bypass democracy assistance allows for feedback loops and it engages non-state actors on both sides, requiring implementation of projects in cooperation, thus actors are not only social entrepreneurs who are willing to share their vision with others, but also mediate between the global and the local (Nicholls, 2006).

Bypass democracy assistance not only includes the benefits of partnering and networking among groups of civil society, but also the experience ("peer-to-peer learning") that neighboring partners can share and which can affect individuals in target countries. An extensive knowledge of non-state actors in CEE countries and their know-how in delivering bypass democracy assistance to neighboring countries, even in the times of a backlash against democracy assistance especially in the post-Soviet space, is another aspect that should be taken into account if we want to study aid effectiveness. Exploring these efforts adds also to our knowledge of how with the help of external support, namely democracy assistance coming from the neighbors, democratic norms and practices are being diffused. In case of CEE countries, the engagement of non-state actors in democracy assistance and their willingness to share transition experience increases the CEE countries' credibility as democracy promoters in times when their state of democracy and governments are subject to criticism (Sedelmeier, 2014). I believe that what we really should expect from bypass democracy assistance is the ability to reach civil society in recipient countries through their civil society networks, as well as good knowledge of local circumstances and needs of the recipient societies, which geographical as well as cultural proximity facilitates.

If we are able to observe the impact of bypass democracy assistance through its impact on individuals—for example if they become active and also willing to spread this activeness to others in society, we can better understand the diffusion mechanism of democratic norms and practices between civil society. Democratization literature is clear that democratization can be influenced by external factors. However, the question of whether this can promote meaningful change still remains a matter of scholarly and public debate. Diffusion itself can be defined as a process by which an idea, institution, policy, model, or the like, is spread through certain channels to the members of the social system (e.g., within a state or across states) (Bunce and Wolchik, 2006a; Deutsch and Welzel, 2016; Inglehart and Welzel, 2009; Inglehart and Welzel, 2005; Jahn, 2006; Simmons, Dobbin, and Garrett, 2008; Wejnert, 2014).

Today's world map shows that regimes are similar within regions and scholars find significant effects for regional diffusion (Brinks and Coppedge, 2006; Jacoby, 2006; O'Loughlin *et al.*, 2007; Starr, 1991). Also, recently there has been some effort to explain observable processes of diffusion in the post-communist world that could be the result of cross-national collaboration including US democracy promoters as well as regional democracy promoters and dedicated local activists (Bunce and Wolchik, 2006b). Therefore, this research contributes to this literature by taking a look at the impact of CEE funded projects to support young people in neighboring EU countries and by evaluating these efforts, which may help determine whether democratic norms and practices are being diffused.

To sum up, arguing that bypass democracy assistance is effective through empowering local democratic groups, specifically young people, an agent empowerment model will be used to refine the theoretical argument. Young people became an important civil society group to work with, especially where cooperation with the government is ineffective and where the activity of civil society organizations is limited or restricted. It is believed that CEE NGOs, while recognizing the support for young people as one of the main targets in democracy assistance, activate young people to be more socially responsible for their local community, region, and country, believing that a democratic country requires such active participation. This book determines whether the youth democracy assistance programs implemented by CEE non-state actors indeed change opinions and views of young people in recipient countries and empower them to become more active and aware citizens. By investigating the impact of bypass democracy assistance, this research will contribute to better awareness of different types of channels through which democracy assistance can take place and the efforts to keep civil society space open.

Research design and methodology

The findings contained in this book result from the research carried out in the years 2010–2017. My methodological approach is diverse and encompasses mixed methods: (1) the content analysis of materials and documents collected on various CEE NGOs democracy assistance projects targeting young people in Eastern Europe, the Western Balkans and Georgia; (2) public opinion polling among young people from Bosnia-Herzegovina, Georgia and Ukraine on the attitudes, knowledge and participation of young people; (3) in-depth interviews conducted during fieldwork with the representatives of ministerial aid programs that engage in democracy assistance as well as with representatives of non-governmental organizations in the Czech Republic, Slovakia, Hungary and in Poland involved in development assistance, and in particular in the promotion of democracy; (4) social experiments in order to evaluate the influence of youth democracy assistance projects.

In order to better understand what kind of youth assistance is given to young people in recipient countries, and what kind of attitudes, behaviors and norms are being promoted for young people through the programs of CEE NGOs, as well as whether bypass democracy assistance delivery mechanism is used in youth projects, I have collected NGO youth project data from projects conducted in CEE between 2000 and 2017 in Belarus, Bosnia-Herzegovina, Georgia, Moldova, Russia and Ukraine. In a systematic way, I provide types of youth projects implemented in target countries. A collection of programs and their analysis also allows the following question to be answered: To what extent are the actions of the CEE NGOs in promoting democratic norms and behavior among young people legitimate in the specific recipient countries?

There are two reasons for examining youth programs directed towards these countries. First, all countries are major recipients of aid coming from Poland, the Czech Republic, Slovakia, and Hungary. Hungarian organizations due to geographical proximity, as well as historical reasons, and cultural similarity prefer to cooperate with the organizations from the Western Balkan countries. The Czech Republic as well as Slovakia has a number of well-known NGOs operating in the Eastern neighborhood and in the Western Balkans. Polish NGOs, however, are engaged in Ukraine and Belarus, since these countries are foreign policy priority countries. Second, they are located in three different regions of Europe: the Western Balkans, Eastern Europe, and the Caucasus region, and although they had all experienced communism, their transition periods from authoritarianism have been shaped by different political developments as well as influenced by different external factors. What they have in common is that they all struggle to democratize and lock-in democratic norms and institutions. The different political situations in Bosnia-Herzegovina, Ukraine, and Georgia are discussed using secondary literature as well as popular indicators of democracy compiled by Freedom House or Varieties of Democracy (V-Dem).

In order to answer questions regarding the reason for CEE NGOs' engagement to target youth abroad within their democracy assistance efforts, I draw on extensive interviews with non-state actors. The role of domestic non-state actors is also supported by the interviews conducted with the NGO activists and representatives from the Polish Aid, Slovak Aid, the Czech Transition Promotion Program, or the Department for International Development and Humanitarian Aid at the Ministry of Foreign Affairs and Trade of Hungary. The insights from both sectors, allow me to present the reasons for supporting youth and to what extent CEE countries' own experience with both transition and receiving aid, shaped their view on how to support young people in other countries. In addition to interviews and material collection, I also employ participant observation methodology in order to understand better the requirements, procedures and implementation of youth programs.

Democracy assistance works best where recipient groups are in greatest need (Pérez-Liñán, Finkel and Seligson, 2016). Therefore, by exploring the recipient side in the democracy assistance equation, this book shows whether young people in countries targeted by CEE NGOs are in demand for support. By demonstrating young people's attitudes toward institutions, their political preferences, views on democracy and their participation in the three target countries, Bosnia-Herzegovina, Georgia, and Ukraine, using public opinion polling data, conducted and compiled for this study, this book not only provides fascinating results whether recipient groups are indeed in need of external support but also shows the nature of the future systems in these countries, which in turn makes important implications for democracy aid.

Specifically, the aim is to investigate in the comparative perspective the interest, knowledge, and opinion of young people regarding public affairs, the political system, and democracy as well as their level of participation. For this purpose, the Youth Participation Survey was constructed and conducted in 2016 among 600 young people aged 18–21 in Bosnia-Herzegovina, Georgia, and Ukraine in 2016. Civil society is important for democratization and young people can be drivers of change. However, they have to be well informed, motivated, and empowered to introduce changes in their countries. Are they aware citizens? Are they interested in public affairs? What are their opinions about the political system, their roles, performance, and the role of a citizen? Are they active through membership or voting? These are the questions that the public opinion polling data, conducted and compiled specially for this study, can answer. The survey questions were inspired by existing surveys, such as the International Social Survey Program and the World Values Survey as well as literature by Parsons and Shils (1951), Almond and Verba's (1963) civic culture, and most the recent study by Diuk (2012) on youth in Azerbaijan, Russia and Ukraine.

The same questionnaire is used in order to be able to draw comparisons. The questions covering political attitudes, participation and other issues have been included in surveys of young people Poland, the Czech Republic, Slovakia, and Hungary. Such comparative perspective shows how knowledge and participation differs across countries given different political settings as well as whether there is a difference in youth knowledge and attitudes regarding democracy and their overall engagement in democratizing versus consolidated democracies.

Being aware that impact comes not from the efforts of individual organizations, and that in order to assess the impact one should take the multiplier effect of many NGOs both CEE NGOs and civil society in recipient countries that are working together and exerting pressure from many different nodes. However, at the same time following the recent trend to evaluate the democracy aid programs (Norris, 2017), I believe that randomized evaluations can shed light not only on the impact of specific programs, but also on behavioral parameters and questions of more general theoretical interest (Kremer, 2003). The goal is to answer the following questions: How do we know that their efforts work? How do the democracy assistance projects impact youth who are beneficiaries of the project? How effective are these projects in changing opinions and behaviors of the target groups? Finally, do they contribute to diffusing democratic ideas and behaviors? If we want to find answers, it is recommended to adopt a micro perspective, and thus in my study, I examine the micro-foundations of the relationship between the bypass democracy assistance programs and their outcomes on beneficiaries through conducting randomized social experiments.

I believe this method solves the problem of attribution; i.e., how we can attribute the changes to the impact of the project. Often, how practitioners and how researchers see the change. result from the fact that they operate at different levels: practitioners at micro level, and scholars at macro-level.[5] I believe that the literature and practice can benefit if we take a theoretical position or number of theoretical sub-positions and narrow the focus of the work to achieve the best

Literature motivation	Research questions	Data collection and analysis
The role of external actors in supporting democratization processes Effectiveness of democracy promotion	Why do CEE NGOs choose to target youth abroad within their democracy assistance efforts? What are the obstacles that CEE NGOs are facing in promoting democracy today?	Interviews with NGOs activists engaged in democracy promotion and governmental representatives in the Czech Republic, Hungary, Poland, and Slovakia.
The role of civil society in democratization and democratic consolidation	How is youth being supported?	The database of youth projects
Political participation Micro-macro link	Is there a need to support young people in recipient countries? How do the democracy assistance projects impact the youth, the beneficiaries of the project?	Polling among young people (beneficiaries of the democracy assistance programs) from Bosnia-Herzegovina, Georgia, and Ukraine on the attitudes, knowledge and participation of young people
Theory of change Agent empowerment Human development	How effective are these projects in changing opinions and behaviors of the target groups? Do they contribute to diffusing democratic ideas and behaviors?	Social experiment (randomized control trials) Qualitative methods: interviews with the participants/focus group discussions

Figure I.1 An analytical framework and methodologies.

way to test theory. The aim of this book is to evaluate democracy assistance efforts directed towards young people at the micro level, that is at the impact of democracy assistance programs on beneficiaries' opinions, perceptions, capabilities to participate, etc.

The method of social experiments, also known as randomized controlled trials (RCTs) (Morton and Williams, 2008) or random assignment studies, which is the most credible and accurate form of impact evaluation extensively used in development assistance, is employed to evaluate the impact of one of the youth projects. There is still much to learn about where, why, and how democracy promotion is most effective. Undoubtedly, it is difficult to measure the effects of a democracy and governance programs unlike developmental programs in the areas of health, for example, where evaluation is more straightforward, but not impossible.

For NGOs' democracy assistance efforts to be effective, they should be able to measure their success and learn from their failures. However, NGOs are making an effort to gain greater expertise in their areas of interest, and are conducing regular self-evaluations and are learning from mistakes. Within cooperation with one of the CEE NGOs I was able to convince the organization to implement a new methodology of assessing the impact of their civic education program, which I believe can be promoted among other organizations. I show how this method was employed and whether it was useful to determine the project's impact. With this novel method, this study is a breakthrough in research on democracy assistance effectiveness, and provides an important contribution not only to the scholarly literature but also practitioners (donors, NGOs), who want to know what works best in democracy aid provision (Bollen, Paxton and Morishima, 2005; National Research Council, 2008).

With these methodologies applied, the study makes four important contributions to theory and practice. First, by showing young democracies' efforts to influence youth participation in other countries, I demonstrate that youth activism is, and can be, influenced from outside. Second, by demonstrating how CEE NGOs support youth participation abroad through different programs, we learn how these non-state actors share their experience with democracy, how they conceptualize democracy and the importance they attach to the role of participation in building and maintaining a democratic regime. Third, by surveying potential beneficiaries of the democracy assistance programs, the study shows the opinions, perceptions as well as level of social and political engagement of young people from the target countries. Fourth, the study shows the usefulness of experimental method in evaluating democracy assistance given a growing trend among both scholars and practitioners toward experimental analyses and studying how democracy assistance should work. There is also surprisingly little systematic and comparative evidence on what works in democracy assistance among NGOs and donors.[6] This is mainly because there are no good impact evaluation methods employed. NGOs and donors are more likely to use before-and-after comparisons. However, this method cannot rigorously determine whether key outcomes can be attributed to NGOs' democracy assistance project.

Only recently there is a greater interest among national and international assistance agencies in better understanding "what works and what does not and why" but mainly in case of programs supporting economic development, health and environment.[7] If practitioners know which projects work best and why and when, scarce resources for democracy may be used more effectively.

Outline of the study

In Chapter 1, I present the theoretical framework and argument. It starts with defining democracy assistance, which comprises funding for ensuring human rights, rule of law, elections and political processes, civil society (civic education, free media), establishing democratic political institutions, and supporting civil liberties. The idea of democracy assistance projects is to boost the democratic potential in target countries rather than providing external incentives or pressure for pro-democratic changes. Then, I show the gap in the democracy assistance literature regarding the youth activism, as well as contributions of the book to theory and practice. It is followed by the research questions that will be answered in subsequent chapters: Why do CEE countries choose to target youth abroad within their democracy assistance efforts and how is the youth in other countries being supported? (Chapter 3); Is there is a need to support young people in recipient countries? (Chapter 4); Are these efforts effective in empowering the youth in recipient countries? (Chapter 5); What are the obstacles that CEE NGOs are facing in promoting democracy today? (Chapter 6).

Recognizing the importance of the civil society, the CEE countries engaged financially to support civil society in EU neighboring countries in 2003/2004 through establishing separate departments at the Ministries of Foreign Affairs. From the beginning of these programs' existence, it became clear that a great portion of bilateral aid coming from these countries would go for democratizing purposes in other post-communist countries in order to fulfill foreign policy goals of having democratic and peaceful neighbors. There is also another feature of CEE democracy assistance that makes it unique: the major domestic partners in democracy assistance are donor-country-based NGOs who were recipients of democracy aid in the past and played an important role in CEE countries' transition. These entities established links with other civil society actors in neighboring countries already in the 1990s and with national or foreign funding, implement projects often in cooperation with their counterparts in recipient countries. It is well acknowledged that civil society is important for democratization and sustainability of democracy, and thus the great potential of young people in these processes cannot be neglected. The goal of Chapter 2 is to present how CEE NGOs were embedded into liberal thinking and how they became non-state actors involved in democracy promotion in the post-communist region. I explore whether CEE NGOs that were established in the 1990s were embedded by the liberal concept of democracy that shaped their understanding of the type of democracy that should be promoted in other post-communist countries. I demonstrate the beginning of civil society organizations in the region based on the Polish example. Also, given their close linkages and knowledge on the ground, I test whether they developed the ability to respond to the needs of recipient countries. This chapter also explores the engagement of organizations in supporting young people. The arguments are supported by the interviews, collection of materials and the youth projects.

CEE NGOs perceive democracy assistance as a way to share their transition experience, which refers to their knowledge of how to make economic and political reforms, and how to make them with the engagement of civil society. As an important component of civil society, they perceive young people, the generation that is the future of the target countries. Therefore, in Chapter 3 I explore projects in Central and Eastern European countries directed toward youth in democratizing countries in Eastern Europe, such as Ukraine, Moldova, Russia, the Western Balkan countries, and in Georgia as well as in an authoritarian country, like Belarus. Specifically, I show, based on the programs what type of democracy is being promoted among young people, what kinds of norms, what kind of youth assistance is given to young people in recipient countries and what kind of attitudes, behaviors, and norms are being promoted to young people through the programs implemented by CEE NGOs. By investigating these programs, we can also learn how non-state actors involved in democracy promotion actually understand democracy. Relying on the interviews conducted with representatives of NGOs who worked on these democracy assistance programs directed toward young people in Eastern Europe, as well as the database of youth projects compiled for this project, I group youth assistance programs into the classification already used by practitioners.

After demonstrating the efforts of CEE countries to support young people in Eastern Europe, the Western Balkans and in Georgia, the question is whether young people indeed require such support. In order to empower young people, it is necessary to understand how young people participate in civic and political lives and what being citizens means to them, as well as how satisfied they are with the political system they have and whether they trust political authorities and institutions. After the collapse of the Soviet Union, the societies in the post-communist region experienced the revolutions, political and economic instability, measures that are well-known in Putin's Russia were also emulated in their countries. They also experienced war in Bosnia-Herzegovina, and currently in Ukraine. In young people's mind-set, elections have been unfair and a change of government through elections not considered as legitimate. However, in many places in Europe, there is evidence that young people are excluded from social and political life, which is expressed as a kind of "political apathy." This is demonstrated by low voter turnout, low interest in joining political parties and lack of knowledge enabling them to make conscious electoral decisions. Thus, the goal of Chapter 4 is to demonstrate conventional and non-conventional forms of political engagement of young people, interest in politics, whether they share information and contact people and how, whether they participate in social life. As the result, this chapter offers some fascinating findings about eighteen- to twenty-one-year-olds in three countries: attitudes toward and confidence in institutions, political preferences, how youth view their political system and democracy and whether they participate or aspire to change anything (in their local community as well as at the national level). To anyone interested in the political situation of these countries this chapter provides some insights into "next generation" that may lead to political change. Also, by looking at characteristics or values in the society, the study may help to determine some important trends and the nature of the future systems in these countries. By reviewing three examples of youth in specific political environments, we can assess the channels that are available to them to participate, also in politics. All results are being presented in comparison with young people from Central and Easter European countries.

After identifying the need to support young people, and demonstrating various programs, the next step, which is undertaken in Chapter 5, is to evaluate the impact of democracy assistance programs. First, I provide some practical recommendations on how we can go about measuring the impact of the youth projects. These suggestions are drawn from the experience with one of the CEE youth projects aimed at educating and activating young people in Eastern Europe. The chapter begins with the demonstration of popular methods of programs' impact evaluations, such as "before-and-after comparisons," in order to show why the commonly adopted methods are insufficient to determine the impact. Next, I show the merits of the randomized control trails method by presenting the results from the experiment set up with one of the collaborating NGOs. I demonstrate the findings based on the experiment conducted with the civic education program directed towards young people from Belarus, Moldova, Russia and Ukraine, the aim of which is to educate for democracy, i.e., they include activities aimed to teach citizens in target countries basic values, knowledge, and skills related to democracy and to empower young people to engage into civic participation. I situate and justify my study in relation to previous experiments in the research field and in relation to the broader literature on the impact of democracy assistance. I discuss the usefulness of this method as well as its limitations.

Chapter 6 demonstrates the current developments introduced by the governments of Poland and Hungary that constrain their activity in the field of democracy assistance both at home and abroad. I demonstrate civil society's reaction to governments' efforts to shrink civil society space, and to undermine division of powers. Also, with the example of a new law limiting the access of foreign funds, I show how NGOs in Poland and Hungary struggle to prolong their activity. The chapter concludes with the statement that perhaps those organizations that are in networks developed through bypass democracy assistance are more likely to survive and adapt to the new situation, which opens the door to future research on the analysis of networks through which survival of liberal democracy norms is possible.

In the concluding chapter, I briefly revisit the puzzle that stimulated my inquiry and remind the reader why solving this puzzle was important for the greater body of political science (democracy promotion literature, democratization, aid effectiveness) and practitioners (donors, NGOs) in general. I discuss the project's contribution by providing answers to four research questions (why and how the young people in Eastern Europe, the Western Balkans, and Georgia are supported by the CEE countries, whether they need to be supported, and whether the youth support provided by CEE countries is effective) as well as identifying strengths and weaknesses of this study. Then, I discuss where this research might be taken subsequently.

Notes

1 The liberal democracy is based on the ingredients of an electoral democracy. However it also includes additional rights and liberties for example, minority rights, regardless of cultural, ethnic or religious features; multiple channels for political expression (beyond parties and elections); multiple sources of information (media pluralism) as well as a wide range of freedoms including freedom of expression (belief, opinion, discussion, speech, publication), assembly, demonstration; as well as the rule of law, securing human rights and protecting citizens from discriminatory judiciary, unjustified detention and terror as well as torture (Diamond, 2003, 35–36; Ferrin and Kriesi, 2016, 47).

2 Post-communist countries include the EU's new member states, and candidate countries in the Eastern Neighborhood, the Western Balkans, and in post-Soviet Central Asia.

3 A conference "Deliberating Democratization: Examining Democratic Change and the Role of International Democracy Support," organized by Westminster Foundation for Democracy, March 7 and 8, 2017.

4 Short-term foreign funding can help in the development of NGOs, but it is not enough to ensure the widespread democratic values of the community and the rapid development of civil society. A similar point is made by Siegel and Yancey (1992), Ottaway and Chung (1999), Quigley (2000), Henderson (2003, p. 153), Jarábik (2006, p. 86), Tudoroiu (2007, p. 340).

5 Expressed by Marina Ottaway during the conference organized by Westminster Foundation for Democracy entitled "Deliberating Democratization: Examining Democratic Change and the Role of International Democracy Support," March 7–8, 2017 in which the author participated.

6 See for example http://fsi.stanford.edu/docs/215.

7 There are several aid agencies that initiated some new strategies for evaluating the effectiveness of their programs but only in the area of development assistance: USAID's Strategic and Operational Research Agenda (SORA), the Norwegian Agency for Development Cooperation (NORAD), the Canadian International Development Agency (CIDA), the Danish Ministry of Foreign Affairs, German Agency for Technical Cooperation (GTZ), and Development Impact Evaluation (DIME) by the World Bank. For more information see CIDA (2007), Cole *et al.* (2005), Banerjee (2007), NORAD's website www.norad.no/en/evaluation, and GTZ' report "Working for sustainable results Evaluation at GTZ" available at www2.gtz.de/dokumente/bib/06-0796.pdf. However, Bollen *et al.* (2005) examining the evaluation of the US Agency for International Development's (USAID) programs find that the greatest weakness in evaluation studies has been the lack of reference or comparison group to help establish whether other trends and external conditions, rather than USAID's programs, were responsible for the observed outcomes. He concludes that whereas these studies demonstrated some valuable insights, they have not provided compelling evidence of program effects.

1 Theoretical framework

The questions addressed in this book arise largely from ongoing debates in the literature on democracy promotion regarding approaches and effectiveness of strategies used to assist recipient countries in their struggle for democracy. However, this study also engages many other literatures in political science. Some of them lie at the intersection of comparative politics and international relations—specifically research on democratization and democratic consolidation, and the role of external actors in these processes, as well as on regional diffusion of democracy.

Today, democracy promotion is certainly facing unfavorable conditions: a backlash against external democracy promotion (Carothers, 2006; Gershman and Allen, 2006) and emergence of "closing space" policies in authoritarian regimes (Carothers and Brakemaker, 2014; Mendelson, 2015), and weak faith in democracy promotion.[1] As a result, democracy-promoting countries' commitment to aiding democracy overseas has started to wane. Given these circumstances the question is: What would be the solution to rebuild democratic conviction and thus to make democracy promotion more effective?

"Democracy promotion means the process by which an external actor intervenes to install or assist in the institution of democratic government in a target state" (Hobson and Kukri, 2012, p. 3). Whereas democracy promotion has a much broader range of tools and includes various forms of diplomacy, or even democracy imposition by military action, it is sometimes also defined narrowly to describe technical and financial aid and other programs, provided by peaceful means. It is offered for moral and pragmatic reasons because of the belief that democratic states are more secure, and also are better neighbors. This book focuses on democracy assistance as a soft power (Basora, Marczyk and Otarashivili, 2017) that encourages the spread of democratic ideas and institutions. A wide range of states (national governmental agencies' programs), party foundations, international organizations, and NGOs participate in these practices, nevertheless, the research on democracy promotion has primarily been state-oriented, dealing with single actors. In this book, democracy assistance is not understood only as a form of foreign policy, not only as aid provided by the government, embassies or development agencies overseas, but rather as an external force that helps democratize societies in other countries.

In order to rebuild democratic conviction and to make democracy promotion more effective, scholars argue that it is also important to improve the understandings of *what* should be promoted, and *what type of democracy* (Diamond, 2017; Hobson and Kurki, 2012; Jahn, 2012; Youngs, 2012). Democracy remains the only legitimate form of government in the world. However, there is a growing need to understand what democracy is, and how it can work in practice more effectively (Diamond, 2017). Democracy as a system of government, despite all its imperfections, has demonstrated an ability to take root in every single region despite predictions that certain religions or cultures are not compatible with democratic norms and institutions (Basora and Yalowitz, 2017). Nevertheless, today we experience an exhaustion of the "liberal moment" in politics (Krastev, 2007).

Liberal democracy was widely accepted as a panacea, as the answer to all problems after 1989. A liberal democratic consensus model has dominated in the democracy promotion agenda and achieved striking universality (McFaul, 2005). The confidence in liberal democracy prevailed within the democracy promotion community, and NGOs in CEE were also very much influenced by this practice.

However, not all post-communist countries, especially the post-Soviet countries in the Eastern Europe and Central Asia, democratized and followed similar paths in the 1990s. Countries that overcame communist dictatorship, and the various problems and obstacles experienced on their way to democracy, are called post-communist, but in each country this development took a different path. Central Europe and the Baltic states embarked on a (mostly) successful reform course, establishing stable and consolidated democracies and market economies, joining the NATO and the European Union, whereas the post-Soviet countries in the Eastern Europe and Central Asia did not follow a similar path. Their transition to democracy and market economy was fractional, changeable and unstable (e.g., Ukraine). Therefore, one should not equate developments in Slovakia with those in Georgia or Russia.

Although overtly authoritarian regimes have disappeared from many parts of the world, in the post-communist region, they were replaced with hybrid regimes, combining both democratic and authoritarian regimes, and this has been a trend since the end of the Cold War. These regimes adopted the form of electoral democracy but failed to adopt liberal norms (Diamond, 2002; Levitsky and Way, 2002). They were trapped into the gray zone becoming illiberal (Zakaria, 1997), delegative (O'Donnell, 1994) and pseudo-democracies. In the 2000s, given the infrequencies with which stable democracies were emerging despite many years of democracy promotion, the high expectations began to wane (Bermejo, 2009). Often democracy promotion and peace building were going hand in hand (Ottaway, 2003; Paris and Sisk, 2009). A few years later, Fukuyama (2006, p. 67) in order to explain his "the end of the history" said that

> (…) the democratization of Central Europe was a miracle. And, one can react to a miracle either by dramatically raising expectations for a repeat-effect or by being grateful, pocketing one's luck, and reflecting on the

> uniqueness of circumstance. Unfortunately, the democracy promotion community shared the first reaction, and tried to turn the miracle into a natural law.

As a result, many post-communist countries looked like democracies, but were anti-democratic in their nature. Citizens had the right to vote, but counting the votes was not clear and fair. Moreover, in some "transitional countries," although reasonably "regular, genuine elections are held, political participation beyond voting remains shallow and governmental accountability is weak" (Carothers, 2002, 15). Also, disappointment with post-communist democratization: corruption, misled privatization processes, inefficiency, unresponsiveness to society's needs, in addition to electoral fraud, was a reason for the citizens' frustration that had its peak in form of the Color Revolutions (Krastev, 2006; McFaul, 2005), as well as the Euromaidan in Ukraine. These protests in post-communist regions, which were nonviolent, liberal and pro-Western, were not against authoritarianism but democratization from above. People were demanding democracy but at the same time rejecting "democracy" based on what they experienced since the collapse of communism. Even in case of Euromaidan which was dissatisfaction with the President Yanukovich's failure to sign the association agreement with the European Union, and opting for closer ties with Russia, was more about a general discontent with the president and the government (Kuzio, 2015).

As the result of such dissatisfaction, autocracies in post-communist regions preventing the spread of revolutionary spirit in their countries, have tightened their repressive policies. They are pushing back against the advance of democracy, containing democracy by controlling civil society and independent media, imposing limits on political space, clamping down on independent organizations, and thus limiting effectively political and civic space for citizens' activities. Additionally, the initial euphoria of the Arab Spring, which failed to produce any significant gains for democracy, combined with instability spreading in the Middle East (violence in Syria) diminished prospects for the spread of democracy worldwide.

The faith placed in liberal democracy turned out to be too optimistic when democracies in the region also began to experience challenges bigger than at any time since the collapse of the Soviet Union (Basora and Yalowitz, 2017). Hopes of definitive democratic consolidation have been disappointing in the CEE countries, which began to experience backsliding that even the EU is unable to prevent, although they were once considered stable consolidated democracies. With a surge of populism in these countries, as well as the emergence of far-right movements in other liberal democracies in Western Europe (such as Front National in France, Alternative für Deutschland in Germany, Lega Nord in Italy, Sweden Democrats, UKIP in the UK, PiS in Poland, and Jobbik in Hungary), their image as democracy promoters has been undermined. To a greater extent, multiple Middle Eastern crises (with democracy failing to emerge in Afghanistan and in Iraq) and terrorism as well as civil wars that spread to the broader region, mass migration and refugee crises, as well as the 2008–2009 financial crisis that hit Europe and the United States, contributed to the success of right-wing parties and populism which since the late 1990s have been on rise in electoral politics.

The global context is certainly much less favorable than it was in the 1990s; "much of the powerful democratizing momentum (and thus the great optimism) of the 1990s has been lost" (Basora and Yalowitz, 2017, p. xiv), and contrary to Francis Fukuyama's view, history has no intention of ending. Scholars and practitioners agree (Basora and Yalowitz, 2017; Gershman, 2017) that there is a striking contrast between the post-Cold War period and period after 2006. There is a growing debate on whether we are experiencing the reverse wave[2] or global authoritarian resurgence (Diamond, 2015; Fukuyama, 2015; Platter, 2015; Levitsky and Way, 2015), having some scholars also talking in terms of a democratic recession (Burnell and Youngs, 2010).

Jahn (2012) argues from the theory-informed perspective, that unsatisfactory outcomes of democracy promotion policies frequently have their roots in a poor understanding of liberalism and its relation to democracy. Therefore, it is important to remind ourselves *what liberal democracy is* as well as why it is vital to make it central again in democracy promotion. The "freeing of the people" as well as "empowering the people" provides the basis for liberal democracy (Sartori, 1995). Jahn (2012) reminds us that the freedom of the individual is a precondition of democracy, since liberalism was in most cases established before democracy.

Scholars have made an important distinction between "electoral" and "liberal" democracies (Diamond, 1996). Electoral democracy requires universal adult suffrage, free, competitive, fair and recurring elections, multiple political parties and a plurality of sources of information (Dahl, 1971). Diamond and Morlino (2005) identify eight dimensions that constitute a good democracy: the rule of law, participation; competition; electoral accountability; inter-institutional accountability; responsiveness to the needs, interest and expectations of citizens; political and civil freedoms, as well as and socioeconomic rights; equality/solidarity. The former one (liberal democracy) presents the minimalist approach, while the latter is more extensive that since incorporates liberal rights. Both are important but there has been a trend to transform electoral democracies into more robust democratic systems of governments (McFaul, 2002). In fact, today, definitions of democracies vary from the minimal definition that focuses on elections to extensive ones that encompass socioeconomic factors, individual rights, freedoms, and civil society. Moller and Skaaning (2013) combined the classic concepts of Joseph Schumpeter, Larry Diamond and Robert A. Dahl's concepts of democracy and distinguished between minimalist, electoral, polyarchic and liberal democratic regimes. The Varieties of Democracy (V-Dem) project (Coppedge *et al.*, 2011) outlines seven models: electoral/minimalist, liberal majoritarian, consensual, participatory, deliberative, and egalitarian. Similarly Held (2006) also offers a wider range: liberal, direct, elitist, pluralist, socialist, deliberative and cosmopolitan.

Despite all the various concepts of democracy, the most popular distinctions are electoral, liberal, social and participatory forms. The liberal democracy is based on the ingredients in an electoral democracy. However, it also includes additional rights and liberties for example: minority rights, regardless of cultural, ethnic or religious features; multiple of channels for political expression (beyond parties and elections); multiple of sources of information (media pluralism) as well as a wide range of freedoms including freedom of expression (belief, opinion, discussion, speech, publication), assembly, demonstration; as well as the rule of law, securing human rights and protecting citizens from discriminatory judiciary, unjustified detention and terror as well as torture (Diamond, 2015; Lipset, 1995). Liberal democracy can be found in the UK or the US. Social democratic models, like in the Scandinavian countries, put more weight on equality and participatory and deliberative democracy involvement by people in decision-making processes. The most common definition of a democracy has, however, excluded the socioeconomic aspects in a democracy, although these aspects and also other aspects have shed light on democratization as an open-ended process (Diamond, 1999).[3]

The democratization literature generally refers to electoral and liberal democracy (Diamond, 2008; McFaul, 2010). Liberal democracies are characterized by free, fair and competitive elections, protection of civil and political freedoms, and accountability and responsiveness to citizen needs, and the rule of law. Such democracies have been located in Western Europe and North America. However, liberal democracy also spread to the post-communist region with the third wave. The liberal *Zeitgeist* was well captured in Francis Fukuyama's "end of history" thesis, according to which "Western liberal democracy is the final form of human government" (Fukuyama, 1989). Rapid democratization in Central and Eastern European countries with the alignment between advancing democratic values and greater security enhanced by the prospects of EU membership and admission to NATO was a powerful incentive for CEE governments to persevere with the reforms. Moreover, there was support among societies and elites for the general geopolitical reorientation to the West.

The liberal principle identifies democracy with limited government, rule of law, and the preservation of individual liberties. The liberal model assumes a "negative" view of political power as it judges the quality of democracy by the limits placed on government. Principles and procedures must be established so as to ensure that rule by the majority does not result in the loss of individual liberties.

Adherence to liberal democratic identity in democracy promotion also means dismissing democracy promotion as an elite-driven project designed to legitimize the capitalist economy and pursue economic interest, because public disillusionment with capitalism led to liberal democracy facing many obstacles which undermined its importance that need to be rebuilt (Brown, 2015; Gershman, 2017). Neoliberalism was a form of economic liberalism that assumed primacy after the failure of classical economic liberalism. The idea was that increasing economic freedoms tend to raise expectations of political freedoms, eventually leading to democracy. Economic development is not a necessary nor a sufficient condition for stable democracy. In fact, economic development is unnecessary for the development of liberal democracy, as Plattner (2008) said "the philosophy of liberalism contains within itself the seeds of its own liberalization." The emergence of non-democratic but at the same time market-liberal regimes demonstrate that such a general relationship is not maintained. Nevertheless, different actors—states, IGOs, and NGOs—pursued a multitude of different policies ranging from support for economic development through political democratization and institutional support, to the development of civil society. Following the end of communism in CEE, liberal democracy was desired and supported. It was equated with economic prosperity as well, and overall dissatisfaction with the economy and wellbeing translated into dissatisfaction with this type of democracy.

However, scholars also point out that it is not convincing to argue that the problem with democracy promotion is not only lack of adherence to a liberal form of democracy (Youngs, 2012). Some even argue, like Patomaki (2012) that movement towards a global social democratic model is needed today in order to achieve genuine democratization. Therefore, instead, the problem is to defend core liberal norms in a way that would allow local variations and genuine civic empowerment and emancipation to flourish (Youngs, 2012). The dominance of a liberal democratic model also should not blind us to the diversity and varieties that exist today within democracy promotion practice.

Also, in improving democracy promotion, it is important to improve our understanding of the democratization process. Democratic progress will always face difficult and dangerous challenges as neither success nor demise of democracy is guaranteed (Kraemer, 2017). The Western democracies seemed to have higher hopes for the democratization than the CEE countries themselves, because the trajectory of CEE democratization has always been full of twists and turns (Dufek, Holzer and Mares, 2016). Tilly (2007) points out that the story of democracy has been full of uncertainties, and many of the established Western democracies would have trouble satisfying all the criteria of democratic consolidation as well. Long term superiority of liberal values is always "yet to come" (Hobson and Kurki, 2012; O'Donnell, 2007b), and it is important to understand that democracy is an open-ended process and never-ending gap between what it promises and what it delivers. As Havel (1995, p. 7) said an "open system that is best able to respond to people's basic needs—that is as a set of possibilities that continually must be sought, redefined, and brought into being." Just as democratization can never be finished, "democracy may be resending in practice, but it is still ascendant in people's values and aspirations" (Diamond, 2017).

Moreover, scholars point out that it is important to make a distinction between view of democracy and evaluation of democracy (Ferrin and Kriesi, 2016). It does not mean that people do not want democracy—the Revolution of Dignity in Ukraine, the Umbrella Revolution in Hong Kong, and also recent protests and civil opposition in Poland demonstrated that democratic ideas and democratic norms still appeal to people and they demand it. Only public enthusiasm for the functioning of democracy both in the transitional countries as well as those new democracies is waning due to malfunctioning of institutions and wrongdoing of the governing elites. On a positive note, the a number of democracies worldwide still remains higher than in the early 1980s.

Finally, without equating liberal democracy with economic reforms also means distinguishing between purposes of democracy aid and developmental aid. A variety of studies of foreign aid and democratic change have found that aid has an effect, or little effect (Knack, 2004) or even detrimental impact (Licht, 2010). The variation across these findings is a consequence of different approaches that researchers have used to identify the causal mechanisms by which foreign aid may impact democratic change. Some scholars study an indirect effect of foreign aid to promote democratization through economic development (Goldsmith, 2001; Bermeo, 2011; Dunning, 2004). This traditional development aid may indirectly improve democracy performance in the recipient country in the long term, but it also may be used to serve a variety of other foreign policy objectives, and it is difficult to evaluate its impact on democracy. Democracy aid, however, is only intended to support democratization, and thus could be more precisely evaluated and traced.

Literature of democracy promotion shows a growing gap between theory and empirical reality. In most recent studies, the scholars examined a variety of potential relationships by depicting circumstances under which democracy aid promotes democracy (Bermeo, 2016; Kalyvitis and Vlachki, 2012; Luhrmann *et al.*, 2017). As observed by Wright and Winters (2010) as well Dietrich (2013), in evaluating aid effectiveness, the studies tend to assume that governments are the sole recipients of foreign aid (Bermeo, 2016; de Mesquita and Smith, 2007; Morrison, 2007; Svensson, 2000), whereas aid is also delivered through non-state actors. Agreeing with Dietrich (2013), I believe that it is important to move away from oversimplifying the link between democracy aid flows and outcomes and to consider that aid delivered through non-state actors is likely to have a substantially different impact that aid that goes to governments.

Although it is difficult to identify the precise mechanism through which aid is more effective, because direct and indirect mechanisms and conditions are sharply different from those of the 1990s (the period when many current democracy support policies and programs were designed) (Bush, 2015), it does not mean that this is not impossible. In order to establish this, it is important to initiate a deeper reflection on what actors, and what exactly they are doing, what type of democracy they are promoting, how they are promoting it, and what will be the impact of these efforts. Bypass democracy assistance, which is a focus of this book, is a delivery mechanism of democracy promotion that is not only about supporting and networking with NGOs in recipient countries but also about reaching beneficiaries directly—various civil society groups—or by means of domestic NGOs, for example young people. By engaging social networks and actors, bypass democracy assistance helps bridge the gap in understanding of the micro-macro linkage between individuals and structure.

Micro–macro link

Researching external dimensions of democratization, and causal linkages between international agents and domestic actors, must involve the insights of both academics and practitioners (Magen and Morlino, 2009). I understand democratization as an outcome of many factors influencing this process, and democratic consolidation also as process that is influenced by many forces, including the external ones. Until the mid-1990s, the role of the international context was a forgotten dimension in the study of democratization (Pridham, 1991; Burnell and Calvert, 2005). External influences in general include direct democracy promotion, governmental and non-governmental democracy assistance, transnational advocacy networks, and democratic diffusion. Particular attention was given to democracy promotion efforts, which include a wide variety of strategies and actions. It can entail coercive actions, political conditionalities, economic or financial concessions or sanctions, as well as various soft measures such as democracy assistance taken by the democracy promotion community: states, NGOs, IOs, foundations, and the like (Burnell, 2000). Do external factors facilitate or hamper democratic development? Do international actors influence the development of greater civil and political freedoms? Another complex question is to how we should conceptualize and evaluate the impact of international influence. The international dimension of democratization is still a subject of many investigations (Magen and Morlino, 2009b) and with my study I am contributing to this body of research.

Finally, this research contributes to the broader debate in literature of cooperative political and international relations regarding the role of external factors and regional diffusion of democracy. The comparative politics and international relations literatures on democratization and democratic consolidation abound with different explanations about the ways in which a system becomes democratic and solidifies its democratic features, but political scientists are far from consensus on what affects these phenomena (Tilly, 2007). Prior to the 1990s, the studies on democratization and democratic consolidation privileged domestic explanations (Schmitter, 1986). This view began to change particularly in response to transformations in Central and Eastern Europe taking part in the third "wave of democratization" (Huntington, 1991; Pridham, Herring and Sanford, 1997; Whitehead, 1986). The role of external factors in the politics of regime change in post-communist CEE states made scholars realize that domestic factors are not sufficient to explain how countries democratize (Crawford and Lijphart, 1995; Ekiert, 2003; Kopstein and Reilly, 2000; Rose and Haerpfer, 1995). Today, any model exploring the determinants of democratization that does not take account of external factors is underspecified; but the literature devoted to the importance of international forces in democratization is still small.

In addition to influential actors like international organization, an important form of international influence consists of "contagion," "diffusion" or "snowballing," meaning that authoritarian neighbors imitate and learn from emerging new democracies (Bratton and van de Walle, 1997; Huntington, 1991). Diffusion itself can be defined as a process by which an idea, institution, policy, model, or the like, is spread through certain channels to the members of the social system (e.g., within a state or across states) (Brinks and Coppedge, 2006; Bunce and Wolchik, 2006a; Rogers, 1995; Tarrow, 1998, 2005; Tarrow and della Porta, 2005). Today's world map shows that regimes are similar within regions. Scholars find significant effects for regional diffusion (Brinks and Coppedge, 2006; Bratton and Van de Walle, 1997; Gleditsch and Ward, 2006; O'Loughlin *et al.*, 1998; Starr, 1991; Starr and Lindborg, 2003). Also, recently in the literature on post-communism, there have been some efforts explaining observable democracy diffusion in the region (Bunce and Wolchik, 2006b; Jacoby, 2006). Bunce and Wolchik (2006a) address the question of why the electoral revolutions in the post-communist region have begun since 2000.[4] The authors argue that the process of diffusion occurred through complex cross-national collaborations that included not just US democracy promoters but also regional democracy promoters and dedicated local activists willing to take a lot of chances (Bunce and Wolchik, 2006b). Therefore, this research contributes to this literature by taking a disaggregated look at the impact of externally-funded projects to support young people and by evaluating these efforts in a systematic way.

This book is about the interaction between external and domestic factors that may lead to domestic change. Specifically, this study sheds lights on one of the international factors, which is democracy promotion, and the role of actors involved in this activity, channels through which they promote democracy, relations they establish by means of democracy promotion, as well as the impact of their activities. International forces cannot create the emergence of certain values, but can facilitate these norms through various programs. However, it is very difficult to observe the impact at the collective level, and therefore it is worth observing at the individual level. Moreover, aggregate levels can tell us very little about causality of the pathways of connections between external influence and domestic change.

Given the experience and knowledge of non-state actors, bypass democracy assistance can be the conduit through which the diffusion of norms, democracy and transition experience takes place. Actors that promote the democracy norm use specific or different methods of channeling democracy assistance towards domestic actors. This, in turn, may create certain relations and have impact on domestic actors, and in the long-term on democratization. However, I stress that the diffusion of democratic norms depends on the local actors who directly benefit from funding channeled through these projects and their promotion of norms. I argue that a diffusion process is not an automatic and unintended process but rather can be explained by a "public choice theory" (Russell, 2011) or "robust political economy" (Pennington, 2010) according to which recipient non-state actors' motivations and acts are the sum of their individual interests and their interactions with other agents (e.g., politicians or other members of the community). These actors are not passive or reactive, but also actively influence and reshape current attitudes and practices in the society (Acharya, 2004, 2011) and in the context of external influences, they are not only norm diffusers but also norm makers, influencing the donors' perception of what is needed and relevant in the recipient country, given the political, social and economic circumstances.

More empirical knowledge is needed when and how external actors promote democracy and the greater attention to understanding the interactions between external and domestic factors for democratization. However, in reality it is never the case that international factors alone play an independent causal role in the democratization, because it is a mix of independent variables that generate the outcome, which include domestic factors, such actors′ actions and the structure. As scholars point it out, democratization is about the power relationship between the government and other actors, such as soft-liners, opposition groups, civil society actors and the military (O'Donnell and Schmitter, 1986). Thus, a theoretical foundation of my study on bypass democracy aid is rooted in democratization literature on evolutionary models of regime change in which domestic actors play an important role in long-term changes in structure.

This book's contribution to democracy promotion lies in bringing attention to the "micro-macro link," i.e., between the individual actors and macro social processes (Diani, 2003), in other words, between agency and structure, which are two complementary perspectives of how the social world works. Actor-perspective (micro) focuses on individuals and their possibilities of acting, the ability of individuals to make decisions, to exercise free will and make social change. A more extended definition says that agency is a

> temporally embedded process of social engagement informed by the past (in its habitual aspect), but also oriented toward the future (as a capacity to imagine alternative possibilities) and toward the present (as a capacity to contextualize past habits and future projects within the contingencies of the moment).
>
> (Emirbayer and Mische, 1998, p. 984)

On the other side, there is structure (macro): institutions, traditions, stereotypes, cultural norms and ideas that are dominant in certain settings and time. They are putting not only limits on agency but also create opportunities. An interplay between agency and structure make a change. There is no structure without agency. Agents create structure. However, structure also affects agents.

My approach is to propose a conceptual framework that identifies macro-to-micro and micro-to-macro effect. These conceptualizations are not new; it is about the adoption of this accumulated knowledge and findings to understanding better the impact of democracy assistance efforts. Coleman (1990) links activity at the micro level to systemic interdependencies at the macro level, thereby showing that action is always a complex social and interactive phenomenon. He points out that the major problem for explanations of system behavior is that of moving from the lower level to the system level. This has been called the micro-to-macro problem, which is widespread throughout the social sciences, and democracy promotion literature is not free from that, as well.

The character of macro-to-micro and micro-to-macro transitions can be understood by imagining a game between two players: actors and structure. Macro-to-micro transition is the variation in information transmitted from the macro level to individual actors, which can greatly affect the actions they take and thus affect system behavior. In general, the environment, cultural, political, economic, and social contexts, in which a person acts, affects the relative benefits and costs of different actions. The macro-to-micro transition shapes the initial conditions, which provide the context within which actions by the actors are taken; affects the player's interests, given by the goal established by the rules, as well as constrains actions, which are imposed by other rules. In other words, the macro level provides various structural contexts in which agents operate: cultural context (which encompasses symbolic patterns, structure, and formations that constrains and enable action by structuring actors' normative commitment and their understanding of their world and their possibilities within it); social context (encompasses network patterns of social ties that comprise interpersonal, inter-organizational, or transnational settings of action); political; and economic context (Emirbayer and Goodwin, 1994).

Micro-to-macro transition is the situation after the game when the new context emerges which is imposed by actors' actions. This transition is mirrored by the consequences of interference and interaction of actors, thus creating a new context within which the next action will take place. In other words, a human agency is the engagement by actors, be it persons, groups, organizations, things, events linked to others in networks, who are impacted by their different structural environments which through the interplay of habit, imagination, and judgment, both reproduces and transforms those structures in interactive response to the problems posed by changing historical situations (Emirbayer and Goodwin, 1994). If cultural and societal network structures shape actors, then it is true that actors shape these structures in turn. In other words, cultural and social structures do not, by themselves bring about or somehow cause historical change. Thus, concepts of structure and agency can support theory of chance since it focuses on developing relationship between institutions and individuals.

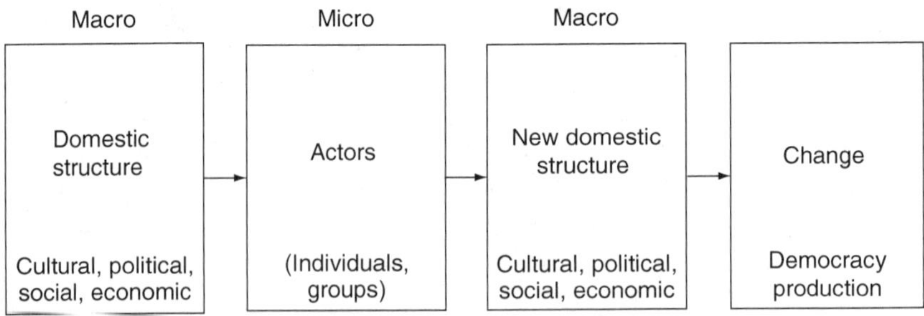

Figure 1.1 Conceptions of the relations between micro and macro levels.

In this view, democracy is a consequence of individuals' actions. If we operate at the micro level in democracy promotion, we should stay at this level and has a good theory that will explain the developments at the micro level and how these micro developments may contribute to macro level. Scholars are more likely to operate at the macro level, and practitioners and donors at the micro. Nevertheless, both do not see the possible connection (positive or negative) between these two phenomena, and how micro can lead to higher FH scores for Ukraine, for example.

For the changes to be ignited by the domestic factors, there must be always motivational forces. My theory that connects micro with macro is through "human empowerment" as the most important driving force behind effective democratization. Micro is young people, as agents of change, who need to be empowered, and macro is a culture, a new domestic structure created by their efforts.

External factors, human empowerment and participant political culture

According to the human empowerment path suggested by Welzel and Inglehart (2008), this is a path that follows a sequence that starts with access to resources that empower people materially by making them more capable of struggling for freedoms. The second next step is mental empowerment—rising emancipative beliefs, empowering mentally by making humans more willing to struggle for freedoms. Although there can be mental and material empowerment provided by democracy aid programs, it is still insufficient if society is not allowed to practice it, which is the final, third step on this path. This is not the only path toward democracy, but it produces "socially embedded and hence sustainable democracy" (Welzel, 2009).

Liberal democracy is a legal component of empowerment. Liberal institutions create legal protections that allow citizens to participate in various associations and in fact to practice the individual freedoms like freedom to associate. Definition of liberal norms includes a broad family of ideas that has evolved over time, such as: individualism, egalitarianism, universalism, belief in human progress, and the ability to make the world better place through human action, which is known as meliorism (Gray, 1995). The process of human development does contain institutional dimensions but liberal democratic institutions would not be in place without people who demand and defend some certain rights, which later become institutionalized in the form of democratic institutions that in turn entitle people to exert these freedoms.

Democracy, greater rights and responsive government are elements of the broader process of human development. But according to a human development sequence, ordinary people need in the first place the resources that make them capable of practicing freedoms, which must be in place before democracy can be effectively practiced. In other words, the socioeconomic dimension precedes the cultural dimension. Resources shape human values and give rise to self-expression values, and these values are favorable to democratic institutions (Inglehart and Welzel, 2005). Just like for a long time post-communist countries were low-income societies, however with greater economic development, greater self-expression and demand for greater rights emerged and affected political institutions.

Democracy assistance creates new opportunities for domestic actors empowering them materially and mentally through various projects that aim to diffuse norms and ideas, and thus these actors through their actions may affect domestic structures. This can take place if the assistance is channeled to the actors bypassing the governments in recipient countries. Bypass democracy assistance also creates the opportunity for forming networks between actors, and there is a great deal of evidence that historical situations are often structured at least in part by cultural and political discourse, as well as by networks of social interaction (Bunce and Wolchik, 2006a; Emirbayer and Goodwin, 1994).

What would it mean to be politically and socially empowered? Although power cannot be directly observed, one can infer that groups possess power to the extent that they: (a) actively participate in in society and in politics (by voting as well as through other forms of non-electoral participation); (b) are involved in civil society organizations or political organizations; (c) secure representation in government, (d) influence decisions regarding their local community or are able to influence political decisions, and set the political agenda; (e) influence the implementation of those decisions.

Democratization literature attaches great importance to participation, which is crucial for: (a) political development; (b) building social skills that are important for political engagement (Brady, Verba and Schlozman, 1995); and for (c) building trust that in turn fosters collective action (Putnam 2000; Putnam *et al.*, 1993). Participation is expected to be one of the most crucial outcomes of political culture (Almond and Verba, 1989; Inglehart, 1990 and 1997; Putnam, 2000). In political culture perspective to democratization, the engagement and participation of civil society play an important role in the process, because the quality and type of political culture depends on their attitudes, behavior, opinion and their level of participation, as well as eagerness to act.

There are two main factors that prevent the proper development of a strong civil society: culture and authoritarianism (Mathews, 1997; Vráblíková, 2017). Political culture in democracies strengthens the role and power of non-state actors vis-à-vis governments. It is an important dimension of democratic systems, and, according to Almond and Verba (1989), it is a systemic-level characteristic capturing prevailing cultural orientations (norms, customs, habits, conventions) that are dispersed across society. Political culture is a characteristic of a political system, but originates from individual citizens, who spread the values and norms through everyday communications and interactions as well as though other mechanisms of social contagion. Those norms that dominate in a society are transmitted to the others (Welzel and Deutsch, 2012).

Political culture perspective implies that democratic institutions can be established in any society provided the mindset of the society—attitudes and behaviors underlying political culture—is favorable for democracy. The causal arrow flows from culture to institutions rather than the other way around. Cultural changes lead to the emergence and flourishing of democratic institutions. According to Almond and Verba (1963), the political culture that is congruent with democracy is the civic culture. This is a political culture that favors pluralism, active citizens, and compromise, which is essential to democratization and a democratic polity.

It is believed that such political culture benefits democracy and explains the stability of a democracy. Of course, as David Rieff (1999) pointed it, people may be "better off with honest and effective governments and legal systems, and with militaries that stay in their barracks, than with denser networks of local associations, which may stand for good values or hideous ones." However, scholars tend to link too much the effectiveness of non-state actors to the relative openness of national political structures (McAdam, 1998), whereas the efforts to change culture can be intensified and it can be achieved through networks with other non-state actors.

However, researchers point out that political culture evolves slowly and it takes generations to form it, but it is also subject to change and evolution (Goldfarb, 2012; Marczyk, 2017) by social actors, and thus offers new opportunities and challenges for democracy. Thus, political culture should not be viewed as an endpoint which is frequently used in most of the literature on norm diffusion, where culture match is used as a determinant for convergence or lack of convergence, in other words whether there is resonance at the local level and without resonance the probability of norm adoption declines. Instead, ideas, norms and practices are seen as the product of processes of construction and also redefinition (Swindler, 1986).

This further indicates that attitudes and societal expectations toward the political process, beliefs regarding the relationship between a state and citizens, as well as behavioral patterns can be transformed both in democratizing countries as well as in fully-fledged democracies that are experiencing crisis. Post-materialist theory also argues that new political values are associated with rising levels of political awareness and new forms of political participation (Inglehart and Welzel, 2005). Citizens may be no less committed to democratic values; they are becoming more critical of democratic government and the way they operate (Norris, 2011). Hence, it is still possible to have a strong belief in democracy while showing dissatisfaction with the political leaders and the ways democracy works in practice.

Participation is also an integral part of liberal democracy. Part of the definition of liberal democracy is that it creates the space for plurality of political and social forms of participation (Dahl, 1989). Democracy is the system that provides the most freedom for people. The minimal definition of democracy proposed by Schumpeter (1952) limits participation in voting and suggests that democracy is not about mass participation. Then, a global measure of polyarchy by Dahl (1989) emphasizes the need for participation and that people should be involved in politics. Overall, the standard definition of what is liberal democracy encompasses not only regular and fair competitive elections, universal suffrage, but also freedom to associate and to assemble, basic freedoms of speech and press.

Political participation is about a citizen becoming an active citizen who takes a role to influence important aspects of life in the broad community, who searches for finding solutions to various social problems (Dwyer, 2000; Delanty, 2000). The recent revolutions in the post-Soviet countries and beyond as well as the recent protests in the new EU member states show it is not sufficient to stand up against the regimes, but to also engage in political action (Gershman, 2017). Protest shows that democracy cannot be reduced to a polling booth once every five years, and something should be done to improve structures that do not deliver. Moreover, much work still needs to be done to make political elites accountable to citizens and greater participation of citizens. Formal and informal political participation is the way to achieve that. Scholarship claims that participation is a key to establishing better governance and ensuring improved quality of democracy in any one country. Citizen engagement with the political process keeps elected political leadership, the government and societal change as a whole under scrutiny (Diamond, 1996; Inglehart and Welzel, 2005; Linz and Stepan, 1996). Civic participation and state-society discussions as mechanisms could correct the failures of democracy.

Although some level of passivity is good for the effectiveness of political institutions, and citizens do not have to be constantly involved in politics (Almond and Verba, 1963), the shallow citizen participation can be something that is threatening, and especially among young people who are the next generation solidifying and passing the norms to other generations. By encouraging greater participation, participant political culture can be built as more people will be willing to be involved in public life and decision-making, and such type of political culture is a proper one for democracies. Scholars tend to link too much of the effectiveness of civil society activity to the relative openness of national political structures (McAdam, 1998; Vráblíková, 2017), whereas the efforts to change culture can be intensified and it can be achieved through networks, whose emergence bypass democracy assistance facilitates.

Post-communist countries are found to have the lowest levels of activism (Howard, 2002; Pop-Eleches and Tucker, 2013); since the relationship between citizenship norms and political participation is usually weaker in newer democracies (Bolzendahl and Coffé, 2013). Therefore, it is important to support civil society towards, as political and civic participation deficit is likely to diminish with generational changes in norms (Pop-Eleches and Tucker, 2013).

Youth as "agents of change"

In mature democracies, there is a vast range of institutionalized arrangements for young people, such as student councils, youth wings of political parties and other organizations that are networked nationally and at the European level. This institutionalization could contribute to emancipating youth as an important social category, but this could be possible once young people themselves have searched for the forums to have their interests and needs heard (Forbrig, 2005a). Young people are expected to determine the evolution of democracy and sustainability of this system. Therefore, in democratizing countries where forms of youth participation are not institutionalized, it is important to activate and encourage young people to be at the forefront of non-institutionalized actions, since these actions can lead to the greater institutionalization of their activities in the future.

Practitioners identify challenges and problems for young people to participate in political arena that originate at the system level: lack of citizenship (civic) education, weak civil society, low political culture, stigmatization of policy, distrust, failing to meet the promises, ineffectiveness of political structures and processes, the suppression of the individual by the system, stigmatization of young people. Political context in which young people live is an important factor affecting political activism but it needs to be coupled with individual factors in order to increase participation. At the individual level, the problem is the lack of knowledge of the system and lack of political socialization, thinking that nothing can be changed by them, cynicism, lack of motivation, negative connotation of politics, and the inability to make a larger contribution to society because of their own interests.[5]

To meet these challenges at the structural and individual levels, many international organizations engage in support to ensure full participation of youth in society, to increase youth participation in the civic life of local communities.[6] However, democracy promoters of various types, believing that habits of political participation or non-participation are acquired early in life, and that they are carried forward into adulthood, chose to direct their programs to support young people, with the belief that, if young people are socialized into the values of freedoms and human empowerment, this will foster the demand for changes.

Young people have already demonstrated their democratizing potential. Well-organized student movements in the former Soviet Union like the Georgian youth movement KMARA (Enough) (Kandelaki and Meladze, 2007) was one of the important forces in bringing about the Rose Revolution that ended President Eduard Shevardnadze's long reign and brought hope that democracy could triumph in Georgia and in the region, thus convincing the Western world that regime change to democracy was indeed possible in the former Soviet Union. KMARA had roots in a group of students at Georgia's largest institution of higher education, Tbilisi State University, who campaigned for radical reform of education in 2000. Several other NGOs joined KMARA along the way namely the Student Movement for Georgia, the Liberty Institute, the Georgian Young Lawyers Association (GYLA) and the Association for Law and Public Education (ALPE). The movement was networked with international NGOs, and had countrywide outreach, including traditionally isolated rural populations, and avoided running for political office, but rather positioned itself as a civic force, and was therefore able to create the conditions for cooperation with opposition parties. The movement received funding through the Election Support Program of the Open Society Foundation in Georgia, but overall many other Western-supported programs in Georgia existed before the emergence of KMARA, similarly to many other post-Soviet countries. Shortly after his resignation, Eduard Shevardnadze was quoted as saying "I did not think I should pay serious attention to these young people running around waving flags and painting graffiti on the streets. I was wrong" (Kandelaki and Meladze, 2007, p. 105).

Another youth movement in the post-communist region was PORA in Ukraine, which was one of the key driving forces behind the Orange Revolution, It was a civic youth campaign (embracing a broad student element: universities, student dormitories, through the network of youth organizations) and its goal was ensuring the democratic election of the Ukrainian president in 2004. It pitched tents on the streets of Kyiv and organized the famous tent city, blockaded administrative buildings, etc.

Youth in these countries was also influenced by a transnational network of outside actors that supported and encouraged as well as, in some cases, even initiated, their activities (Bunce and Wolchik, 2006a). The support provided by transnational networks for democracy promotion was a final factor that influenced these events. Training of activists was supported by small grants provided by the German Marshall Fund of the United States, Freedom House and the Canadian International Development Agency. As mentioned in my earlier research (Pospieszna, 2014), Polish NGOs made a crucial contribution to the organization of the all-Ukrainian student strike that was a key to the Orange Revolution, which mobilized the public about the elections and the election fraud.

As noted by scholars, highly educated young people are often the segment of the population most threatening to the status quo of regimes, regardless of the political system. Behind all important events and new movements such as the Prague Spring in Czechoslovakia in 1968 (Kitschelt, 1994, Forbrig; 2005b), or the new social movements that developed in Western Europe in the 1970s and 1980s, including the Greens, LGBT and anti-nuclear movements, the Color Revolutions (in Croatia and Serbia in 2000, Georgia in 2003 and Ukraine in 2004, as well as Kyrgyzstan in 2005) or the Arab Spring. Young activists also relied on new technologies and new media.

From the perspective of political culture, a typical post-Soviet society was characterized by skepticism, particularly among young people, towards any kind of participation, particularly political participation, which was conditioned by experiences of the Soviet era. In the people's mindset, all elections have been unfair and a change of government through elections not considered as legitimate, making the state look democratic, but were anti-democratic in their nature, because although the citizens had the right to vote, counting the votes was not clear and fair. Therefore, the protests that took place within the Color Revolutions (the Bulldozer Revolution in Serbia, Bieber, 2003; Birch, 2002); the Rose Revolution in Georgia (Karumidze and Wertsch, 2005; Wheatley, 2005); the Orange Revolution in Ukraine (Kuzio, 2005; Way, 2005); and the Tulip Revolution in Kyrgyzstan (Marat, 2006), resulted from disappointment with post-communist democratization (corruption, misled privatization processed, inefficiency, unresponsiveness to society's needs), as well as electoral fraud (Krastev, 2006; McFaul, 2005). These protests, mainly led by young people, were nonviolent, liberal and pro-Western. One could also say that people were demanding democracy but at the same time rejecting what they had experienced since the collapse of communism. Also, the Euromaidan in Ukraine was not against authoritarianism but democratization from above. It was dissatisfaction with President Yanukovich's failure to sign the association agreement with the European Union, and opting for closer ties with Russia, and was mainly general discontent with the president and the government, as well as against Ukraine's closer cooperation with Russia (Kuzio, 2015).

Changes are needed in where and how to promote democracy in these adverse circumstances. I believe, that in times when the conditions for democracy are less favorable, and in countries that are authoritarian, democracy assistance should be reduced to certain types, or should be modified, and adjusted to focus on specific goals, like, for example, youth empowerment. As pointed out by Basora and Yalowitz (2017, p. 179), "selectively targeted policies of democracy support, combined with well-executed assistance programs."

Thus, I am focusing on assistance bypassing governments in recipient countries and delivering aid to young people directly or through youth organizations and other types of NGOs. Youth can be agents of change, but, for that to happen, they need to be empowered. Through participation in the project, and being embraced by the networks, they can become more interested in taking an active role in their societies and in politics.

This book evaluates this bypass democracy assistance of CEE NGOs that is channeled to young people in other post-communist countries. In order to assess its usefulness, it requires answering four questions: (1) Why are youth targeted? (2) How are youth targeted? (3) Is there a need for it? (4) What is the impact of assistance on these beneficiaries?

The argument: bypass democracy assistance and why it matters

It is argued in this book that bypass democracy assistance is the best answer to the current challenges that democracy promoters are facing, as mentioned earlier. It is a chance for the spread as well as sustainability of democratic norms. This book shows the specificity and effectiveness of bypass democracy assistance, by focusing on the non-governmental organizations from Central and Eastern Europe as providers of democracy promotion activities towards young people in other post-communist countries. Four important preconditions need to be fulfilled so that bypass democracy assistance can take place: (1) the NGOs should have been embedded in democracy norms and committed to spread these norms abroad; (2) the NGOs must diversify their funding in order to be independent of the influences of their own governments or foreign donors; (3) democracy-promoting NGOs should be a part of transnational civil society; and finally (4) these NGOs should have close linkages with other non-state actors in target countries.

According to IR literature, there are various international actors in global governance: states, the private sector, and civil society (Keohane and Nye,

1998). Today, instead of only interaction between states, there is interaction between states and non-state actors[7] that results to the emergence of global governance (Cox, 1997). Non-state actors in form of various organizations, civil society networks, corporations, private foundations can be important players in global governance (Acharya, 2016). Non-state actors attempt to extend their influence geographically and functionally. This means that not only international institutions and international law limit state power politics but also cooperation of non-state actors and norms they promote (Sikkink, 2016). Thus, the role of NGOs in international governance cannot be ignored and there are many factors that can legitimize such participation. Civil society groups rely on soft power, and use instruments such as moral authority or the ability to shape views and behavior (Florini, 2000). Their increasing role does not lie in the number of NGOs, but in value and their deep commitment to have their voice heard when relevant decisions are being taken. NGOs are able to exert influence on their governments to pay greater attention to specific topics, and are also able to take an active role in helping the government designing and facilitating agreements, and promoting or restricting public support for various issues, in the end making sure that states and other actors fulfill their commitment.[8]

It is believed here that CEE NGOs which were recipients of liberal democracy assistance in the past, can improve international governance today by drawing on their expertise, grassroots connections with civil society actors in target states. Motivated by liberal norms they are crusaders for a better world both through searching different channels to support civil society. Through their activities and resources, CEE NGOs offer civil society opportunities to be better connected to other like-minded societies, but also to be better connected to local political elites.

I locate my argument within the context of global civil society to which I believe CEE NGOs belong. Global civil society is "the sphere of ideas, values, institutions, organization, networks and individuals located between the family, the state and the market and operating beyond the confines of national societies, polities and economies" (Anheier, Glasius and Kaldor, 2001, p. 17). Globalization facilitates the emergence of global civil society. However, there are challenges in developing a common meaning of globalization as well as reaching the agreement regarding its impact. Some equate globalization with the spread of global capitals or "Americanization" associating it with the negative impact on the environment, with the widening the gap between the rich and the poor, indigenous cultures, and increasing the exploitation of human and natural resources (Rucht, 2003). These negative connotations are due to neoliberalism, which often equates globalization with the effect of modernization. Modernization that took shape in the 1960s-era was marked by impressive economic growth in the Western countries. It was assumed that at the end of the process of decolonization there would be modern, economically developed, and thus stable liberal democracies. Globalization has received increased attention in the post-Cold War era causing the concept of globalization to be replaced with that of modernization. It also was not seen as the process that simply "happens" or as "neutral" or "inevitable" but rather as the deliberate political, economic, and ideological project put forward by those who will profit most from it (Sklair, 1997).

Indeed, globalization became a buzzword of our times. However there are also those who believe that this is an inevitable and desirable process leading to progress and wealth (Smith, 2012). The process of a shrinking of distance and boundary-broadening that frees forces that were so far confined within political, and cultural boundaries, allowing for the free movement of information, capital, goods, services, technology, labor forces but also practices, institutions, and ideas such as democracy and human rights beyond state boundaries (Rosenau, 1997). It is also a process that enables and increases in "networks of interdependence at multi-continental distances" (Keohane and Nye, 2000). Advances of transportation and communication technologies spreading at a breathtaking pace since the late 1980s have fostered an atmosphere in which various non-state actors can increasingly participate more directly in the policymaking process.

In my research, I perceive globalization as a force that has been impacting the cross-border movement of ideas and peoples, leading to the emergence of complex social networks, interconnectedness of societies, interdependency offering mutual support and incorporation into a global society. The growing interconnectedness fosters independence from the government, and challenges the sovereignty of states borders. As Langran and Birk (2016, p. 4) pointed it out, "regardless of how one views globalization, it influences the way that we see ourselves as 'citizens,' how states respond to the challenges it presents, and how non-state actors develop new roles as a result." Thus, the process of globalization progressively changed the notion of citizenship and the "global citizenship" where citizenship is not defined by the states but on a global level. Some see it as a threat to state interests (Ofer and Grove, 2016). Before, it was the role of nation-states to grant the benefits associated with the status of citizenship. Globalization constrained the resources available to states and the role of the states in delivering certain public services and through the inclusion of new actors, non-states actors. These actors are today a crucial factor in the internationalization of liberal norms, and universal (human) rights (Smith, 2012). I argue that CEE NGOs engaged in democracy promotion were influenced by a vision of global democracy and embark on internationalizing liberal norms both domestically and abroad.

Growing interactions among civil society groups in different parts of the world, coupled with increasing international interdependence and advances in information and communication technologies have led to the emergence of transnational civil society. Transnational civil society includes groups that are *not* governments or profit-seeking private entities (Florini, 2000). The rise of international civil society does not mark the fall of the nation-state system, because nations-states although they are weaker, they can never be replaced (Lipschutz, 1992). However, the role of transnational civil society cannot be ignored. It is transnational because involves linkages across national borders. Many connections aim to have a more practical and concrete role, such as those oriented toward environmental issue and this book, however, considers the role of value-driven organizations. Globalization stimulates transnational civil society formation, but true transnational social networks take root where there is a long history of close, interpersonal relations characterized by trust, reciprocity and cultural learning (Tarrow, 1998).

I believe that such conditions are fulfilled in examples of CEE NGO relations with civil society groups in target countries. Just as transnational civil society influences globalization, the CEE NGOs network also can affect democracy promotion at the global levels, conveying credible information to the global community on how to promote democracy. CEE NGOs are interested in transferring values of liberal democracy with focus on participation, activism, and freedoms. They also have knowledge of the region in which they operate. It is not profit-oriented community-based on bonds of solidarity, moral obligation, and mutual respect. Of course, the CEE NGOs engaged in democracy promotion are operational in many cases only because of international funding; however, the way they promote democracy can inspire the whole democracy promotion community and allow for the norms of democracy to be extended in times where democratic values are under threat and something has to be done to strengthen them, and where space for democracy promoters is closing. Also, since democracy promotion also often serves the needs of those groups that are engaged in this enterprise, through spreading networks and diffusing interdependency, the CEE NGOs can remain at the frontline of democracy promotion not only abroad but also in their own countries thus securing their own survival and legitimacy.

The strength and effectiveness of bypass democracy assistance in diffusing democracy norms derives from the following factors on which I am elaborating below. First, bypass democracy assistance means avoiding the governments, thus allowing for the continuation of democracy promotion in difficult times for democracy (authoritarianism staging come back, closing space for civil society and democracy promoters etc.). Second, thanks to cooperation with non-state actors in target countries, and close linkages, it has ability to respond to the cultural specificity of countries and thus facilitating changes that better meet specific needs ("feedback loops with partner countries" are more likely to take place). Third, the strengths of bypass democracy assistance lie in networks,

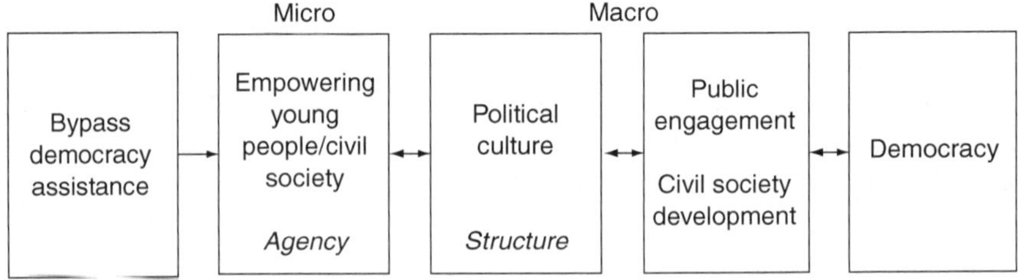

Figure 1.2 Components of the theory.

social ties, long-term cooperation, which are more likely to create social capital and change political culture. Finally, by supporting various beneficiaries (youth, women, teachers, etc.), not only via NGOs, but also directly, it can empower these actors vis-à-vis the state.

Supporting civil society

By arguing that bypass democracy assistance is effective, I also suggest that it is better than other forms of democracy assistance, thus engaging the debate on how to promote democracy, and how support for democracy can be better crafted. The question is not whether there should be democracy assistance efforts, but how democracy promotion countries should do this, and also what delivery mechanisms should be used. Bypass democracy assistance is a specific mechanism to support civil society. In fact, bypass democracy assistance allows for restoring the value of *civil society* as a core component of liberal democracy and as an agent of change.

A well-functioning and sustainable democracy and vibrant public engagement requires a strong civil society, drawing on the classical line of thought of de Tocqueville (2003). The concept of civil society and its role in democratization have become fashionable thanks to the struggles against communist and military dictatorship during the third wave of democratization. However, it also is experiencing a revival due to the Color Revolution in Georgia (2003), Ukraine (2004) and Kyrgyzstan (2005) and the Arab uprisings in 2010/2011, Euromaidan in 2013, and street protests in the new EU member states in 2016–2017.

Civil society is "a sphere of social interaction between economy and state, composed above all of the intimate spheres (especially the family), the sphere of associations (especially voluntary associations), social movements, and forms of public communication" (Cohen and Arato 1992, p. ix). Institutionalization is important for the reproduction of civil society, because, without institutions, civil society is handicapped. Civil society refers to the structures of socialization, association, and organized forms of communication, which are in the process of institutionalization or are already institutionalized. In democratizing countries, this is a process and civil society is institutionalized through laws, but the self-creative and institutionalized dimensions can exist separately.

It is also well-acknowledged that civil society is a broader concept—not only professionalized NGOs, although these are preferred partners of international development agencies (Beichelt and Merkel, 2014). In general, however, the concept of civil society is not homogeneous and includes a broader array of social actors. Civil society refers to

> the arena where people deliberate upon, organize and act around shared purposes and concerns. As an ideal type, it is distinct from government, market and family, though in practice the boundaries between these spheres are blurred and interwoven to varying degrees.
>
> (Howell and Lind, 2009, p. 5)

This embraces various types of groups such as cultural organizations, sports clubs, labor unions, professional associations, chambers of commerce, ethnic associations, religious organizations, student groups, and informal community groups (Carothers, 1999).

Given the fact the organizations are not the monolithic, because there can be GONGOs (governmentally organized non-governmental organizations), MANGOs (manipulated non-governmental organizations) as well as GRINGOs (governmentally regulated and initiated NGOs), civil society is can be mistakenly defined as a complex mixture of good and evil forces advancing not only worthy and altruistic ends but also self-serving and immoral purposes. However, these forces are representatives of uncivil society. In my study, I use a definition of civil society that is oriented by the ideas of basic rights, liberty, democracy, solidarity, justice, and mediation (Cohen and Arato, 1992). It is also a mistake to see civil society as an opposition in liberal democracies. There are antagonistic relations when mediations fail or when democratic institutions are being breached. Fisher (1998) has pointed out that relatively secure governments have a tendency to tolerate different types of NGOs, but less stable regimes are trying to either co-opt or discredit such organizations. Then, NGOs that are watchdogs and are in favor of democracy are falling into the category of government suspicion and repression. One could think that this would apply only to non-democratic countries, However, today Polish NGOs and Hungarian NGOs are facing challenges that so far civil society groups in Russia or Belarus, for example, have been facing.

Many governments still view independent activist groups with great suspicion and therefore afford them no financial incentives at all, and also limit legal protection from state interference. These NGOs play an important role in opposing and challenging government abuses and repression, thus empowering the masses to demand greater responsiveness from the ruling elites. They can use both direct strategies for producing changes, such as policy advocacy, demonstrations, political lobbying, monitoring compliance with agreements and pledges, and promoting new ideas, as well as indirect strategies, such as informing and supporting other grassroots organizations and social movements.

The evidence suggests that NGOs tend to be more effective when the state is relatively healthy (Bebbington and Riddell, 1995). The power and influence depends on organizational factors, such as internal leadership, expertise, size of membership, reliable funding, but also on the degree to which governments and intergovernmental organizations choose to draw on NGOs. Important elements of a healthy civil society sector include freedom from government influence, as well as oppression, the ability to oppose state policies and hold local authorities accountable for their actions, as well as the existence of independence media. These features are unfortunately absent in some regional settings. Therefore, so that civil society could become a part of the global civil society that is able to shape the future, strengthening civil society became a key element in the development policies of Western governments and international organizations that increasingly adopted the aim to promote democracy around the world (Ottaway and Carothers, 2000).

The researchers find that civil society assistance led to some anomalies. Civil society has become mistakenly considered by the donors as a synonym of the non-governmental sector (Carothers, 1999). The dependence of local NGOs involved in democracy promotion on foreign funding created a web of NGOs that have little connection to their populations and exist to take advantage of funding opportunities and provide employment for well-educated, young urbanities in the recipient countries dividing society between those haves and have-nots (Henderson, 2002; Cooley and Ron, 2002, Green and Kohl, 2007). The Western-supported NGO sector has lost its monopoly on "representing" civil society. Outside funding has given rise to a culture of externally supported NGOs. Also, there is a link between increase in support to civil society organizations and anti-NGOs legislation. Most post-Soviet states unaffected by the wave of Color Revolutions recorded a regression on both political rights and civil liberties in 2005, according to the Freedom House Nations in Transit survey. Political conditions worsened in especially in Azerbaijan, Belarus, Kazakhstan, Moldova, Russia, Tajikistan, Turkmenistan and Uzbekistan.[9] Autocrats were worrying about the possibility of democratic contagion spreading to their countries and ousting them from power, but some of the laws were under the guise of anti-terrorism laws. The adoption of a new NGO law in Russia in December 2005 significantly impeded the activity of civil society and restricted its access to funding from abroad. Restrictions on NGO activities were also introduced in Belarus, where the activity of organizations that failed to obtain official registration became punishable by imprisonment (up to three years). These new laws also prohibited receiving money from abroad. New regulations in Kazakhstan, Tajikistan and Uzbekistan restricted the contact of foreign diplomats and media with representatives of the domestic NGO sector. Also, branches of international NGOs were forced to close down in some of these countries (Silitski, 2007).

Despite some mixed results regarding the impact, the opportunities and limitations associated with external funding of civil society activities, today this support is still one of the main areas of democracy aid in particular (Beichelt *et al.*, 2014; Youngs, 2015). There are various ways of channeling democracy assistance through supporting civil society. First, there is the so-called external project method. Carothers (1999) as well as Siegel and Yancey (1992) criticized the external project method used by USAID toward Eastern Europe and parts of the former Soviet Union at the beginning of 1990s because it involved aid for US NGOs' contractors, e.g., consulting groups or trainers. They point out that although the use of this method may be justified in situations when domestic organizations in the recipient countries are poorly institutionalized, they lack reputation and administrative experience and are not also adequately developed to absorb outside assistance effectively. However, there are more costs than benefits associated with this strategy. First, instead of being spent in recipient countries, much of the funding was used by donors or their domestic contactors. Second, such a strategy did not find much approval among civil society activists in recipient countries, who were of the opinion that the "Marriott Brigade" or "fly-in, fly-out" consultants that used to stay at Warsaw's five-star hotels provided training with little knowledge about the CEE reality (Mendelson and Glenn, 2002; Wedel, 1998). Finally, this strategy is characterized by "lack of local ownership" of assistance projects and a lack of flexibility, when, for example, the real local needs and possibilities turned out to be different from what the donor anticipated (Carothers, 1999).

The second method of supporting civil society groups in their struggle for democracy is the direct grant method. This strategy is popular among some of the US NGOs assistance providers, like the Eurasia Foundation and the NED, which provide direct grants to organizations, distributed via a grants competition. This strategy does not involve American intermediary groups in the implementation of the projects and the principle is to provide direct funds for "proposals that originate with indigenous democratic groups." Scholars and practitioners agree that the direct grants method has many advantages—money goes directly into the recipient society, and this method permits greater flexibility in the design and implementation of projects (Carothers, 1999; McFaul, 2005). Although the strategy seems to be more effective in assisting civil society, this approach involves difficulties and limitations as well. In order to avoid any misuse of money, donors might be more likely to finance those more Westernized groups who are familiar with grants proposals and who are well known by the donor (Carothers 1999). It might be difficult to reach local partners, especially in authoritarian countries, and identify whether they are worthy recipients. Finally, donors may be more likely to give bigger direct grants for fewer projects to those organizations that are well known in the region (Aksartova, 2005). Scholars have demonstrated that the side effect of this support is that the donor community weakens those organizations that have veritable ties to society and respond to local societal needs. Donors also create a dislocated civil society, which is business-like in fashion and responds to the goals for the international community rather than of the society (Belloni, 2001; Challand, 2006).

Another approach to assisting civil society groups that is discussed in the literature is a strategy represented by the activity of the Soros Foundation, which can be called a strategy of going local. Unlike many other foundations, the Soros Foundation does involve local people. It established local foundations in each target country, and each of the local organizations has a separate identity with local boards of directors and local staff. However, this method is costly, because of the price inherent in the capitalization of the foundations. The approach also has a problem with allocating money to local groups through the individual national foundations, because funds may be more likely to be distributed to a large extent within a tight circle causing the same effect as mentioned above (Carothers, 1999; Quigley, 1997).

Finally, there is a model that can be called "bypass democracy assistance." A feature that distinguishes this from other democracy assistance strategies is that it involves partnering between civil society actors. If it involves neighbors in geographical sense it is known as "cross-border work" (Pospieszna, 2014). It can be considered as an improvement on external project method, because it involves supporting local NGOs in neighboring democracies so that they in turn assist civil society in recipient countries. Although this is not a new method, there is no research that demonstrates and evaluates this method of democracy assistance. This study aims to fill this gap by exploring initiatives of CEE NGOs in other post-communist countries. Why does it bypass governments? There are several reasons that speak for the usefulness of this model. First, the nature of the bureaucracy makes the development of effective linkages with a government slow. The non-governmental sector is more efficient, more flexible and more cost-effective because it bypasses the bureaucracy and red tape that characterize governments (James, 1989a). Just as NGOs in CEE are more flexible, so is civil society in recipient countries.

I believe that channels that are independent of government funding are more flexible, and allowing for building a network should be prioritized. Western-funded NGOs in post-communist countries in Ukraine, Moldova, Georgia, are disconnected from the public at large. It might seem that loose civil movements use mobilization strategies and social media and are more effective in influencing the state and society than Western-funded NGOs because by doing so they create gaps between well-established groups and active citizens (Lutsevych, 2013). However, research shows that often these rely on NGOs anyway, for their patronage, logistics, etc. Therefore, it is important to invest resources in strengthening civil society through cooperation *with* NGOs to reach direct beneficiaries, instead of only supporting NGOs, and I argue that CEE NGOs democracy assistance efforts serve as an example here.

Flexibility also means more local energy to drive change, bringing democracy support home, neither exporting nor importing democracy, but possibly supporting local efforts and understanding sensitivities involved. Also, ways need to be found to support civil society by taking advantage of the openings that exist. For example, in the case of Belarus where there are severe restrictions on foreign NGOs working in the country, but at the same time the regime permits participation in educational exchanges, and traveling, as well as leaving some space for local initiatives, this could be fertile ground which should be carefully targeted in democracy promotion programs. Again, this would mean supporting civil society, not only NGOs, as it was in practice for many years of democracy promotion.

Second, support to civil society can be a promising response to the spread of closing-up spaces and a tool for (vulnerable) civil society to challenge (powerful and misguided) governments on both sides. There is open resistance to the international promotion of democracy not only in countries like Egypt, Russia, Ethiopia, Venezuela or Zimbabwe but also in the CEE countries. Incumbent governments especially those that feel threated by domestic opposition groups with access to international support—often use restrictions on civil society support in order to weaken those opponents and to retain power. The closing space has received increasing attention by scholars, civil society activists, as well as policymakers. Civil society as senders of aid can adjust their tactics and focus their efforts at a different level, and forge close ties with civil society groups of various types in recipient countries. In these adverse circumstances, when other forms of democracy promotion remain handicapped, bypass assistance can make liberal norms diffusion more likely than through other channels, because it is long-term, based on hard and persistent work, coherent strategic thinking, solidarity and strong democratic convictions, which will "pay solid dividends over the longer term" (Basora and Yalowitz, 2017; Kraemer, 2017).

Third, aid to non-democratic states should be channeled through NGOs to ensure that it does not strengthen the position of authoritarian regimes. It is also difficult for outsiders to impose and change regimes because it requires exerting pressure on the ruling elites, and, if the international community is lacking carrot and stick, it might be not feasible. Moreover, tackling authorities and government directly is not possible in all countries. In authoritarian countries, it is not even recommended, because altering institutions and building new structures mean funding the government that is often corrupt. Also, top-down democratization versus bottom-up driven democratization, both have their merits, since in the end it is up to the elites to introduce changes, but can this be done without pressure from within?

Corrupt and oppressive governments should be avoided in financial flows and impact by NGOs, but it does not mean that the dialogue should not be facilitated. However, the dialogue should come from empowered civil society groups—organizations, but also journalists, lawyers, young people, rights activists, who can further facilitate and spread their engagement to other people and thus progress freedom and democracy. Citizens in Georgia, Moldova and Ukraine have little capacity to influence political developments due to lack of engagement, client list networks and corruption (Lutsevych, 2013). The chance to cooperate with NGOs in CEE is the opportunity to be engaged in networks, from which they can learn how to engage and form a relationship with a government, but also how to pressure the ruling elites.

Fourth, in contrast to civil society assistance "government structures lack the ability or willingness to adopt new ideas" (Madon, 1999). Supporting civil society through organizations and various voluntary associations can be the only option if the idea is to change political culture and to make it more supportive toward the emergence and then sustainability of democracy. The role of cultural dimension and value change cannot be omitted, and these values have increasing emphasis on the civil and political liberties that constitute democracy, which in turn provide opportunity to pursue freedoms and self-realization. As Inglehart and Welzel (2005, p. 12) put it, it is "the naive belief that designing the right institutional arrangement and installing elites who are committed to democracy is all one need to establish democracy." Social capital, political culture, citizenship, and political participation are crucial for the development of democracy, shaping its institutions and legitimizing the system. The cultural perspective sheds light on the importance of pro-democratic orientations, which may contribute to a pluralist civil society that could check and balance the political system.

Diffusion and localization of norms

Both large-*N* studies and qualitative case analyses have shown that democracies cluster together and that democratic ideas, norms, and principles can spread across state borders (Brinks and Coppedge, 2006; Bunce and Wolchik, 2006a; Gleditsch and Ward, 2006; Kopstein and Reilly, 2000). Diffusion is a process whereby past events make future evens more likely (Oliver and Myers, 2003). Although diffusion is considered as one of the external forces that involves a passive spread of democratic ideas and practices (Brinks and Coppedge, 2006; Rogers, 1995), democracy assistance can be one of the causal mechanisms and processes by which democracy diffusion takes place and norms of democracy are being spread. Of course, we have to be also aware of the undemocratic diffusion that comes from the "authoritarian counter-model" (Basora and Yalowitz, 2017), e.g., from Russia and other autocratic regimes in the post-Soviet space that promote strong leadership, appeal to nationalism, constraining free media and civil society, rigging elections, which might also influence individuals.

Diffusion can occur inter alia through direct and interpersonal networks or through networks where a "third actor" connects pro-democracy activists in different countries (McAdam and Paulsen, 1993; Tarrow, 2010). In fact, the transmission of "innovations" between people, are impossible without some kind of interaction and contact or network tie between individuals (Centola, 2010). Nadelmann (1990), Risse, Ropp and Sikkink (1999), and Keck and Sikkink, (1998) mention that the key actors who spread "universal" norms are transnational agents, whether they are individuals or social movements. Norms are understood as "regulated modes of behavior that are based on inter-subjective validity" (Finnemore, 1996; Klotz, 1995; Zimmermann, 2017). They are "prescribed patterns of behavior that give expectations as to what ought to be done" (Hurrell, 2002). Norms regulate interpersonal relationships by solving problems of collective action; they are like a benchmark. Norms are important because they influence the creation of identities and preferences by providing standards as to what is right or what is not; shape also the possibility of action (Hurrell, 2002).

Acharya (2011) noted that little attention is paid to explaining the link between global and regional norms. Zimmermann (2017) in an attempt to better understand that process classifies interaction modes between norm promoter and norm-taker according to the following four types: incentives and sanctions, praising and shaming, teaching, arguing. Norm promoters can opt for one of more conditionality-oriented alternatives—incentives/sanctions or praising/shaming or for one of the more persuasion-oriented approaches, such as teaching and arguing. It is unlikely that any of the activities will occur in pure and isolated form; combination is most likely. She finds that the effect of external rule-of-law promotion is not unidirectional. It is a dynamic model and interaction between domestic context and international actors occurs. Moreover, she finds that where norm promoters adopt a conditionality-oriented approach in order to influence full norm adoption this had in fact an opposite effect, thus actors shift towards a more persuasion-oriented mode of interaction but at the same time seeking to retain control over the direction of domestic translations.

Levitsky and Way reduce these modes to two main forces influencing democratization in other countries: linkages and leverages. Leverage is understood as a bargaining power of the external actor vis-à-vis recipient country, whereas linkages "encompass the myriad networks of interdependence that connect individual polities, economies, and societies" (Levitsky and Way, 2010). Linkages include: economic, intergovernmental, social, informational, and civil society ties. Similarly, they found that linkages are more powerful predictors of democratization than leverage.

Following Acharya (2004, 2011), my research also stresses the need to view norm creation and diffusion as a bottom-up process. In order to explain the role of norms in creating political change, Finnemore and Sikkink (1998) observed that a "norm-cycle" consists of three stages: *norm emergences*, a *norm cascade* and *norm internationalization*. They also point out that "international norms must always work their influence through the filter of domestic structures and domestic norms, which can produce important variations in compliance and interpretation of these norms" (Finnermore and Sikkink, 1998, p. 89). Zimmermann (2017, p. 207) also added that senders of norms and recipients should not be considered from a unidirectional perspective, since "a norm is something that has to be brought to life in its new context by a process of "discursive interaction, negotiation and contestation." In other words, norm diffusion is a process that is an interactive process between norm promotion and norm translation, something that has not been considered in research exploring global governance during the 1990s and 2000s. Today, adapting global norms to the local context is viewed as the best strategy to improve the effectiveness of democracy promotion.

As mantra has been repeated by the donor community and scholars, the need to avoid templates and tailoring democracy to the local context, however localization of democratic norms, has not been studied extensively yet. The process of how beneficiaries become norm-takers is what Acharya refers to as "norm localization." Specifically, localization is a process of norm transmission in which the local agents borrow foreign ideas and fit them into indigenous traditions and practices, in other words create a fit between those norms and local norms (Acharya, 2004). Zimmermann (2017) in her book raises the question to what extent global norms are localized, and who decides whether global standards or local particularities prevail, and how external rule-of-law promotion affects norm translation in post-conflict states. She points out that there is a distinction between norm-socialization and norm localization. The former focuses on questions of compliance and asymmetric interactions, while the latter focuses on how local actors adapt global norms (Zimmermann, 2017). Socialization is strongly focused on the notion of full norm adoption while localization is focused on the contestation and localization of norms.

This book deals with the question of what are the conditions that may affect the likelihood of norm diffusion and localization by means of CEE NGOs' activities. It is argued here that what is unusual about CEE NGOs democracy assistance is that they do this in the form of partnership, within the networks, bypassing the government, making peer-to-peer learning possible. By doing so, they allow for interaction and "back and forth process" helping reinterpret and reshape norms to local context (Zimmermann, 2017). The way the CEE NGOs promote democracy through partnership resembles how social networks and their impact should be analyzed and understood. It is believed here that by having established closed linkages with partner organizations, CEE NGOs are able to learn about the situation on the ground, and this knowledge form the field, allows them to link their experience to local needs. As argued by Madon (1999), networking strategies with intermediate NGOs and beneficiaries are crucial to gaining learning experiences from the field. Important and influential information for learning takes place through informal and individual contacts. Also, it can be believed that learning from the field is something that makes the CEE NGOs credible and trustful amongst recipients and those NGOs accountable to beneficiaries of their projects.

Today's civil society landscape in CEE countries is quite diverse. There are various forms of civil society organizations (CSOs) that do not necessarily resemble non-governmental organizations, some professional organizations and trade unions. There are those that are co-financed by the state in order to provide services in the local community (serving as an extension of government structures) (Hartay, 2017; Krajewska and Makowski, 2017; Ronovska and Vitoul, 2017). There are also partly organized, local community-based initiatives and self-help groups based on informal mechanisms and organizations operating at the grassroots which pursue member-oriented objectives, for example, youth organizations, family associations and religious communities. However, this book focuses on a large number of liberal non-governmental organizations that were established in the region in the 1990s through foreign donor programs (Domber, 2008; Pospieszna, 2014; Wedel, 1998; Quigley, 1997), which also played an important role in the overturning of communist regimes and in the post-1989 democratization processes (Bernhard, 1996; Keane, 1997), and, as the results of Western funding faded away in the 2000s, decreased in number leaving only those rooted in the society and well-networked. I call them norm entrepreneurs (Badelt, 1997), who through being a part of the larger transnational networks promote norms of liberal democracy. This book deals with the question why CEE NGOs as transnational agents want to diffuse these norms.

These CEE NGOs are today subject to criticism, and their activities are constrained by the populist governments since they perform lobbying and advocacy functions, and engage in monitoring vis-à-vis the state. They have done a great deal of work to engage in cross-border civil society initiatives, and are in larger movements and networks. However, they support other community-driven, grassroots organizations in their countries and abroad including them in the global civil society network where they have been for quite some time. Those liberal organizations together with their networks are the focus of this book. Today, they not only play an important role in encouraging the growth of democracy in neighboring countries but also engage in democracy promotion efforts also at home. In fact, effective democracy promotion needs to have two dimensions, external and internal, as noted by Kořan (2017). There is "a tradition of idealism and courage" that is present in the region which has valued individual freedoms and humanism and which in times when democracies in the region show little resemblance to their idealist dreams, there are some hopes that these values "can serve as a source of possible democratic renewal" (Kořan, 2017). Regional norms are an important factor in making transnational networks better tools for reforming governments (Kumar, 2000).

NGOs promote norms among civil society in recipient countries believing that emergence of norms is a process that does not appear out of the blue. Recipients/beneficiaries adopt new norms and become agents that have the intention to make some changes in their community and eventually to create some domestic pressure for change. *I argue that because of the CEE NGOs' presence in the region, and because they have close linkages with civil society in recipient countries, their democracy assistance efforts and norm diffusion are consistent with a local context (beliefs, practices). They are an intervening variable between global norms, which they view as worthy of selection and then localizing.*

An analysis in this book is based on norm adoption at the micro level. Adoption and implementation of a norm may be measured at the collective level, for example legal adoption of certain norms promoted by the international organizations (Schimmelfennig *et al.*, 2006). However, it can also be measured at the individual level, although this is more difficult than the adoption and implementation of certain norms by the states (Zürn and Checkel, 2005), because the question arises of whose habits and patterns of behavior to measure. In my research, I chose to focus on young people and their norm adoption and implementation.

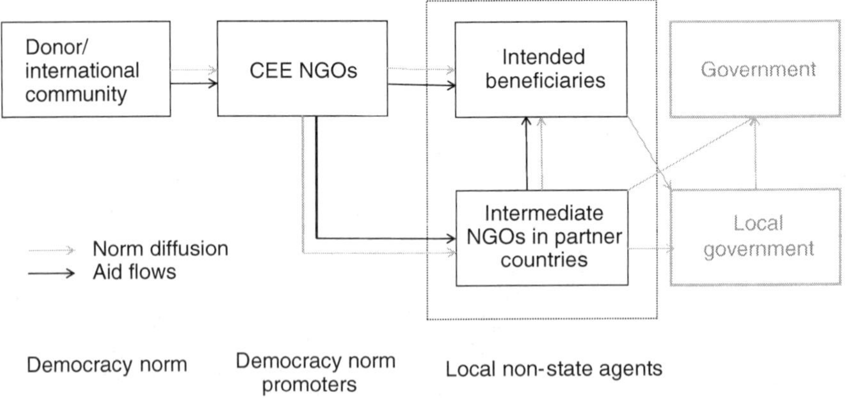

Figure 1.3 Bypass democracy assistance delivery mechanism including pro-democratic NGOs from Central and Eastern Europe.

This study does not consider norms to be adopted into law, but focuses on norms of liberal democracy. Some scholars point out that the more precise the norm, the greater its chance of being adopted (Finnermore and Sikkink, 1998; Legro, 1997).

The question is what liberal norms are being promoted and how they can be measured. In my study, I focus on so-called "norms of engaged citizenship" which include (1) social and political responsibility in local and national affairs; (2) actual participation in political and civic life; (3) being active in social and political associations and keeping a watch on government to prevent any abuses of power; (4) respecting rights of minorities and helping those worse off in order to prevent polarization of the country (Bolzendahl and Coffé, 2009, 2013; Dalton, 2006, 2008).

Citizenship norms are a shared set of expectations about the role of citizen participation in politics and government prescribing engagement in a democratic system (Dalton, 2008). Dalton (2006, 2008), in his work examining citizenship norms in the United States and other old Western democracies, finds that there are two dimensions of citizenship: one based on duty, involving allegiance to law and order, the duty to vote, the duty to report crime, etc., and the other an engaged-type of citizenship, which "spans several elements that are typically described as liberal or communitarian norms of citizenship" (Dalton, 2008, p. 77). The second perspective perceives citizens as "engaged citizens"—citizens that form opinions, are active in watching government, choosing environment friendly products, help those less privileged, and active in associations (Dalton 2008). The norms of engaged citizens are close to post-materialist or self-expressive values. Dalton (2008) finds that "duty-based" citizens are more likely to vote than citizens with a lower sense of duty, but "engaged" citizens are more likely to participate in a variety of political activities, both electoral and non-electoral (e.g., signing petitions, protesting). Similarly, Hooghe, Oser and Marien (2016) and Vráblíková (2017) find that norms of engaged citizenship increase activism, while norms of citizen duty have an opposite effect.

I believe that pro-democratic CEE NGOs promote participation and engagement in civic and political affairs, and thus democratic citizenship. One might ask how norms of engaged citizenship apply to liberal norms. A liberal democracy consists of high level of competition (among individuals and organized groups, especially political parties), participation (through regular and fair elections and other forms of participation) and civil and political liberties (Lipset, 1995). Norms of engaged citizenship are based on the concept of the importance of the individual rights and its participation in society, which lies at the heart of liberal democracy.

Democracy cannot be reduced to a polling booth once every five years. Protesters disapproved of structures which did not deliver. Political activism involves participation in a variety of activities, including voting, contacting politicians, joining demonstrations, attending political rallies or meetings, and so on. Norris (2002) points out that political participation has undergone a transformation from conventional or institutional participation unconventional or protest politics. Youth is the age group that is more likely to choose unconventional political participation (Dalton, 1988). Young people's participation is also influenced by the historic events that take place and when they became politically aware. Hooghe and Dejaeghre (2007) also argue that there must be interest in politics before citizens engage in politics. "Monitoring citizens" or "standby citizens" control the people in power, and are interested in politics, because monitoring is connected with distrust of politicians, and for this reason they stay informed (Rosanvallon, 2008). According to Amnå and Ekman (2013), "bystanders" do not have hostile feelings about politics. They simply stay alert, keep themselves informed and occasionally are willing to participate. Then, in order to transform from non-participants to active citizens, they have to be empowered.

Researchers agree that citizenship norms theoretically and empirically predict participation in various political and civic activities. Therefore, the assessment of citizenship norms is a useful way to analyze the impact of programs on citizens' expectations about their role in the political system, because views about their own responsibilities guide actual behavior. Bypass democracy assistance as a delivery mechanism facilitates diffusion of democratic norms and practices, and thus is an opportunity for political culture change. Shared cultural values, in turn shape citizens' views of their responsibilities, which in turn have important consequences for democratic participation.

Social networks, social capital and empowerment

The effectiveness in diffusing liberal democracy norms and helping them to be localized in recipient societies increases with bypass democracy assistance because of social networks. Bypass democracy assistance is not only a support for civil society or the presence or absence of civil society or its strength (weak/strong), but it is also about networks of civil society. Zimmermann (2017) points out that linear perspective according to which norms diffusion ranges from rejection to full adoption is problematic, thus frequent interactions between civil society groups allows for reconstructing norms to create a fit between those norms and local norms. Also, once norms are diffused, the process does not end; it should be sustained, because norms are in a constant process of negotiating and renegotiating (Acharya, 2004, 2011; Panke and Petersohn, 2012; Zwingel, 2012). Thus, networks allow diffusing and sustaining norms and also altering existing political culture.

The impact of networks on civil society actors also includes: (1) an access to critical or alternative resources, such as social capital; (2) empowerment; (3) an opportunity to exert pressure through TANs in order to compel governments. In network approach, one focuses on network structure as an explanatory variable. A social network is a social microstructure defined by four elements: positions, authority, rules, and agents (Emirbayer and Goodwin, 1994). Social networks represent a less formal social structure, since there is fluidity of occupants, rules, procedure, resources, and they may evolve naturally or may be constructed for a particular shared focus or interest (Lin, 2001). Osa (2003) has found that the mere presence of opposition organization is not sufficient to make some changes. States can use coercive measures to prevent coalition formation, but supporting structures—such as networks or external allies must be in place prior to large-scale collective action (like before the Orange Revolution).

IR scholars have done much to help identify the role of transnational NGO networks in the global diffusion of norms. They have developed models to describe the ways in which states were socialized into international communities. These models are "norm-life-cycle" (Finnemore and Sikkink, 1998), boomerang (Keck and Sikkink, 1998), and norm-diffusion spiral (Risse *et al.*, 1999). Later, researchers also enlarged the scope to include the socialization of states into democracy (Schimmelfennig *et al.*, 2006).

The role of NGOs has been strengthened in transnational advocacy networks (TANs) encompassing networks of international and domestic NGOs, international organizations, foundations and other bodies, so-called "norm entrepreneurs," because NGOs became equipped with "blaming and shaming" tools to exert impact on the target governments (Clark, 1991). In other words, transnational advocacy networks bypass the governments and direct their activities only toward the beneficiaries, letting them engage in discussion of their rights with the governments. NGOs mobilized international public support and form networks with other NGOs both domestically and internationally to bring pressure from above and from below in order to compel governments, and this process is known as the boomerang effect (Keck and Sikkink, 1998). Domestic and international NGOs are not the only groups involved. A network can include local social movements, foundations, experts, churches, members from media, and other civil society groups (Keck and Sikkink, 1998). Research shows that human rights NGOs, international NGOs, churches, trade union and political foundation have united to establish human rights standards in international law, and to create monitoring institutions, and also to link up with groups in the domestic civil society of many norm-violating states to help them bring about change in human rights (Keck and Sikkink, 1998; Risse, 2000). International advocacy networks are most likely to emerge around issues when channels of communication between government and peoples are blocked, because activists believe that networking will help them get better results thanks to international contact (Keck and Sikkink, 1998).

Stiles (2000) makes an argument that international NGOs make it possible to challenge the governments from outside and inside. Networks that are formed as the result of bypass democracy assistance can perform a similar function for civil society groups in recipient countries who can search out international allies to bring pressure on their states from outside. Organizations that are in touch with CEE NGOs can also use these networks, and also articulate a variety of positions tactics for confronting the state. When political opportunities are not plentiful, and where cultural contributions are weak, then one can rely on networks. Under democracy, because of press freedom and civil associations, the illiberal, or anti-democratic governments, are challenged. Non-democratic states are not subject to oversight by journalists and the civil society is curtailed. The methods of repression of dissent are diverse ranging from press censorship, secret police surveillance of citizens, restrictions on travel. The absence of collective actions is the norm, but as the social movements emerge, they begin via networks which are built and then expanded, and which challenge state power. This was the case of CEE NGOs. They lived through this, and they owe their growth and sustainability to these networks established before and during the transformation (Osa, 2003; Pospieszna, 2014), and expand this network further.

The network perspective is exciting because it proposes ways in which we can delineate this micro-to-macro process (Coleman, 1990). Social networks exist not only in organizations, but also in the interrelations among individual actors (Lin, 1982), so that transactions and exchanges take place not only within organization and between organizations, but also among actors. I argue that networks in which CEE NGOs operate as a force that might influence the interactions between actors and structures in target countries via impacting actor's perceptions and behaviors. Unless we identify and describe how their efforts to influence young people, we will not be able to understand how agency of recipients and their structure may interact.

Networks can strengthen local groups vis-à-vis their government through civil society empowerment projects. Bypass democracy assistance through well-crafted programs can inform and educate society and thus legitimate their claims, allowing them to feel their independence and physical integrity with other people who think and behave alike, and then letting domestic civil society mobilize itself to directly approach national governments. Certain individuals may have better access to embedded resources than others, thus the nature of social networks and social ties becomes the focus of this analysis. *Democracy assistance that diffuses material resources through networks gives the opportunity empower individuals materially since they are able to practice freedoms which they would not be able to do while being dependent on the state.*

Echoing Edwards (1994), I argue that any international NGOs, including CEE NGOs, are not well positioned to directly challenge foreign governments, and that they do not have legitimacy in representing grassroots views. Instead, CEE NGOs even though they have good knowledge and expertise, should support local civil society (financially, technically, and logistically), facilitating dialogue without taking into account the local context, appreciate differing conditions and avoid applying a standardized approach to all cases.

Resources embedded in social networks are crucial for the success of such networks—their emergence, growth and impact. Resources in such a social structure are distinguished from resources possessed by individual actors. The theory of social capital focuses on the resources embedded in social networks and how access to and use of such resources benefit individuals' actions (Lin, 2001). Social capital is rooted in social networks and social relations and is conceived as a resource embedded in a social structure that is accessed/mobilized in purposive actions (Lin, 2001). In social networks, directly or indirectly interacting actors carry varying types of resources—some of these resources are in their personal possession, but most of the resources are embedded in others with whom each actor is in contact, directly or indirectly (Lin, 2001). These socially embedded resources are social capital for the actors in the network. Human capital, however, consists of resources possessed by the individual, who can use and dispose of them, and when invested for expected returns in the marketplace, they become social capital.

There is a controversy generated from macro perspectives whether social capital is collective or individual goods (Lin, 2001). Most scholars agree that it is both collective and individual goods that can benefit both. At the group level, social capital is discussed as collective or even public goods. It is some aggregation of resources (social, culture, political connections) of members interacting as a network or networks.

Social capital is a capital captured through social relations. Social networks need social capital and it is a necessary condition for the network to preserve, but can be built on experience of solidarity and trust. It often defined as an investment in social relations with expected returns in the marketplace (Lin, 2001). The market can be economic, political, labor, or community. Lin (1982) argues that there are two types of resources to which an individual can gain access to it and use: personal resources and social resource. Personal resources are possessed by an individual, and social resources are accessed through individual social connections. However, social resources outweigh personal resources in their potential usefulness to individuals (Lin, 2001). Individuals engage in interactions and networking in order to produce profits.

What the networks offer must be different to organizations and individuals from to the world that surrounds them. Also, in case of bypass democracy assistance projects, organizations as well as participants or candidates in recipient countries should be able to see the benefits. Networks provide channels through which information circulates, so diffusion of information happens. Networks also allow for the use of social contacts for raising money, locating, and sharing the material resources which is what the CEE NGOs are doing through their networks. The CEE NGOs have to rely on foreign donors, and civil society in democratizing countries on networks with civil society that are already well established in global, transnational networks. Through the access to social capital embedded in bypass democracy assistance, organizations and beneficiaries can hope to maintain and promote self-interest for survival and preservation (wealth, reputation, and power) and also to reinforce their identity and recognition. In other words, they can be empowered to become agents of change in their countries. Some societies do not have access to resources and this is why democracy promotion matters.

Notes

1 Although some scholars object (Wolff and Poppe, 2015).

2 Samuel Huntington captured the up and downs of democratization in "waves" and "reverse waves."

3 Munck and Verkuilen (2002, p. 9) argue that the fully expanded definition of a democracy, including the socioeconomic aspects of a society, often referred to as the social

democracy, may be too broad because it may lead to a concept that has no empirical referents, and even if a concept is defined in such a way that empirical instances can be found, maximalist definitions tend to be so overburdened as to be of little analytical use.

4 Since 2000, there have been four mass mobilizations that have occurred in the post-communist region, such as the "Bulldozer Revolution" in the Federal Republic of Yugoslavia in 2000, the "Rose Revolution" in Georgia in 2003, the "Orange Revolution" in Ukraine in 2004, the "Tulip Revolution" in Kyrgyzstan in 2005. The common usage for these events is "Color Revolutions" which were characterized by the massive street protests following disputed elections and led to the resignation or overthrow of political authorities considered to be authoritarian and bringing into power elites in favor of democracy. For more about revolutions in the post-communist region see Fairbanks (2004), Karatnycky (2005), Thompson and Kuntz (2004), and special journal issues on the Orange Revolution such *as Problems of Post-communism* 52 (2), March–April 2005 and the *Journal of Democracy* 16 (2) April 2005. Outside Europe there was a so-called "Cedar Revolution" in Lebanon.

5 www.civict.eu/index.php?e_id=29&pid=&lang=eng.

6 The League of Young Voters and the European Youth Forum are leading a Europe-wide reflection on how politics can include young people (#youthup initiative). The European Commission fosters youth participation and has involved young people in policymaking since 1988 (Cammaerts *et al.*, 2016). The 2001 white paper on "A New Impetus for European Youth" contains the objective of the European Commission to ensure full participation of youth in society, by increasing youth participation in the civic life of local communities and in representative democracy, by supporting youth organizations as well as various forms of "learning to practice," by encouraging the participation of non-organized young people and by providing quality information services (European Commission, 2009, p. 8). The Lisbon Treaty (2009), Article 10.3 TEU, as well as Article 165 states that the EU should encourage the development of youth exchanges and encourage the participation of young people in democratic life in Europe. Examples of initiative are ERASMUS andYouth in Action. There is also the UN Program on Youth, which falls within the Division for Social Policy and Development (DSPD) of the United Nations Department of Economic and Social Affairs.

7 The study considers non-profit civil society organizations and excludes other types of non-state actors in global governance, such as private sector corporate actors, named transnational corporations (TNCs) or multinational corporations (MNCs).

8 Marta Schweitz's speech in Proceedings of the 89th Annual Meeting of the American Society of International Law in New York, April 5–8, 1995 "NGO Participation in International Governance: The Question of Legitimacy."

9 Nations in Transit surveys for 2005 and 2006 are available online at www.freedomhouse.hu/nit2005.html and www.freedomhouse.hu/nit2006.html).

2 Democracy assistance bypassing governments

The goal of this chapter is to present how CEE NGOs were embedded into the liberal thinking and how they became non-state actors involved in democracy promotion in the post-communist region. There are two arguments that are tested in this chapter. The first refers the type of democracy: I argue that CEE NGOs that were established in the 1990s were embedded by the liberal concept of democracy that shaped their understanding of the type of democracy that should be promoted in other post-communist countries. I demonstrate the beginning of civil society organizations in the region based on the Polish example, because civil society in Poland received Western democracy assistance already in the 1980s as a means to support democratization in the region. Second, given their close linkages and knowledge on the ground, they developed the ability to respond to the needs of recipients. The arguments are supported by the interviews,[1] collected materials and a database of youth projects.

The involvement of the CEE countries in supporting democracy and sharing experience in the process of transformation raises research questions that need to be answered: Who are these CEE NGOs engaged in democracy assistance? How did they emerge? When did they begin their involvement in democracy assistance? Did the fact that these countries were the recipients themselves help influence their approach to promoting democracy? What are some of the key CEE NGOs' know-how and unique niche? Is there a way to promote democracy in development aid that distinguishes these countries? Do all CEE countries consider supporting democracy as an important area of development cooperation? What similarities can be observed, and what differences are there between CEE democracy promoters?

CEE NGOs' engagement in democracy assistance

After the fall of communism in CEE, civil society associations flourished under conditions of democracy, and previously suppressed groups, such as religious associations, were free to pursue their activities, both at national and regional levels. New legislation facilitated the upsurge in civic activity in these post-communist countries. By the mid-1990s, CEE countries, especially Poland, the Czech Republic and Slovakia had witnessed the emergence of almost every form of non-profit organization known in consolidated democracies (Bútora, 2007). Today, there are different NGOs in CEE which following a common typology can be divided into (1) service delivery—relief, welfare, basic skills; (2) educational provision; (3) public policy advocacy, lobbying monitoring and promoting state policies (Stromquist, 2002).

This third category of organizations is the focus of this book. These are the NGOs as well as the think tanks that emerged in the 1990s and which were active abroad and survived mostly because of the financial support coming from abroad. They were established assisting the third sector with various services channeling funding, providing training and information, as well as providing policy analyses. They have acted as watchdogs of democratic governance and worked on improving the quality of democracy. Many NGOs were involved in activities related to democracy both at home and abroad. Those active during the transformation used their experience to support democratic efforts elsewhere in Eastern Europe, lending assistance to activists in other post-communist countries. Today, their engagement makes them vulnerable vis-à-vis the authorities in Central and Eastern European countries, and because of the policies adopted by the governments today, including the legislation that makes financial flows to NGOs more difficult, some of them gaining status as opposition or even foreign agents which undermine the state.

Another feature that defines them, is they were impacted by liberal thinking in the field of civil society, which was due to the circumstances conditioning their emergence, as discussed later, as well as the support they were given from abroad, and the important role that these organizations played in the post-1989 democratization processes (Bernhard, 1996; Keane, 1997). Moreover, these are the CEE NGOs that today are involved in transnational networks of non-state actors who are the promoters of rules and norms in international relations and who help define the category of "liberal states" (Risse, 2000). CEE NGOs are advocates of universal democratic values, who strive to pass along to others democratic norms and practices, are able to reach pro-democratic opposition movements abroad, educate their neighbors to embrace these norms, and to strengthen pro-democratic forces abroad. These internationally-oriented NGOs in CEE are the focus of this book, but in order to understand their engagement in democracy promotion, it is important to briefly recall the origins of the civil society organizations in CEE.

Beginning of civil society organizations in the region

The communist regimes of Central and Eastern Europe collapsed one after another beginning in 1989. CEE has a relatively rich history of political opposition and dissent. However the 1989 "Velvet Revolutions" were unexpected, especially the speed and ease by which they were able to dissolve the regime and establish new institutions. The fall of the Soviet satellite state system and then democratization of the CEE countries was the triumph of liberal democracy. Francis Fukuyama (1989) argues that the fall of communist regimes provided proof that liberal democracy is "the end of history." The events of 1989 made scholars argue that civil society played a key role in overthrowing communist regimes in CEE countries (Gellner, 1991).

Although freedom of assembly and association and the freedom to express opinions were rarely, if even, guaranteed in the former regimes of Central and Eastern Europe and it was hard for the opposition groups in communist CEE to emerge in civil society that was slowly creating a fertile environment for the establishment of post-communist liberal democracies. Though there was no political society (Ekiert, 1996), opportunity structures in communist CEE opened. Hungary was at the vanguard of the anti-Soviet movement and the fight for freedom among Eastern European nations—the 1956 Hungarian Revolution was a symbol of Hungary's determination to build a democracy as well as a market economy since the Hungarians tried to blend some free-market economics into their non-market economy. Then, opportunities emerged during the Prague Spring. However, a breakthrough was the signing of the Helsinki Accords in 1975, which had an important impact on dissidents in Eastern Europe. The clause in the Accords which was of most interest to opposition was Article VII (Respect for human rights and fundamental freedoms, including the freedom of thought conscience, religion or belief) that obliged signatories to promote and encourage "the effective exercise of civil, political, economic, social, cultural and other rights and freedoms all of which derive from the inherent dignity of the human person and are essential for his free and full development."[2] This legal basis led to the emergence of Charter 77 which was "a loose, informal and open association of people of various shades of opinion, faiths and professions united by the will to strive individually and collectively for the respecting of civic and human rights" in their own countries and throughout the world.[3] It did not form the basis for any oppositional political activity, but rather aimed to conduct a constructive dialogue with the state authorities, acting as a mediator in conflict situations, and drawing attention to cases where human and civil right were violated. Nevertheless, this treaty was important for dissident movements because it ensured that communist governments guaranteed certain rights and freedoms and the resistance movement to be legal. Moreover, Charter 77 criticized the system and although the communist party did not interpret their activities as oppositional political activity, there was harassment and persecutions against Charter 77 (Skilling, 1981).

During the Cold War, society in the Central and East European countries experienced population control, coercive measures used by the socialist government to defend their power; it was arena of dramatic political struggles, and political repression. However, despite these domestic and international challenges and pressures, the Solidarity movement emerged. Later events of 1980–1981 in Poland (Arato, 1981; Rupnik, 1979) brought some attention to the new opposition in Poland characterized by the activities of KOR (*Komitet Obrony Robotników*/The Committee for the Defense of Workers). The goal was to create a pluralist social movement that would challenge the communist government, and thus mobilizing behind the cause of workers who responded to the proposed increases in food prices by striking in 1976. The goal of KOR, which was established by the intellectuals was to provide legal and material assistance to the families of workers imprisoned or unemployed as the result of protests (Bernhard, 1993b). The communist governments declared this organization as illegal and detention, interrogation and imprisonment of prominent KOR members like Michnik, Kuroń and Lipski took place. The Polish government did not recognize KOR's existence. Nevertheless, this was the first sign of emerging civil society that the communist government could not ignore. Poland's economic situation was not helping the communist government since price increases provoked strikes again in 1980, and one of the most influential strikes broke out at the Lenin shipyards in Gdańsk in July with Lech Wałęsa emerging as the spokesperson for the strikers (Garton, 1999; Kubik, 1994). As the result of these activities a formal agreement was reached and signed in Gdańsk, which led to the creation of Solidarity as a trade union, which became a new political force in society, although denying at the beginning its political aspirations.

Solidarity was a well-organized and large-scale dissident movement, that began reaching and appealing to the Polish people as a whole causing the Soviet Union to be concerned about Solidarity's actions, and as the result General Jaruzelski declared Martial Law on December 13, 1981. Civil liberties and freedoms were suspended, as were the activities of the legally registered associations and organizations, Solidarity was dissolved and the arrests of the Solidarity leadership and restrictions forced it underground. Martial Law restrictions also affected freedom of media, and therefore books and periodicals were sold via underground distribution networks, failing to eliminate oppositional movement. The regime was unable to solve the current economic crisis, new waves of strikes, which led to the roundtable negotiations and relegalization of Solidarity in 1989. The succession of Mikhail Gorbachev and policies of glasnost and perestroika changed the relationship between Eastern Europe and the Soviet Union, leading to withdrawal of the Soviet military threat in Eastern Europe through the so-called Sinatra Doctrine, and allowing in October 1989 the formation of the Mazowiecki government (Bernhard, 1993b; Havel, 1985).

The activities of Solidarity's predecessor's KOR can be treated as the rebirth of civil society in Poland (Rupnik, 1979), which provided a solid foundation for successful transition in Poland, the collapse of the Berlin Wall and served as a good example of a path away from totalitarianism and toward a more open economy and society. Cohen and Arato (1992) argued that the early Solidary movement became a key element in their formulation of the idea of civil society. It was a participatory, non-violent, movement for social change in society where opposition was against the law. Activities were taking place within civil society, by people for people, drawn together by a desire to freely engage in activities of their own choosing, and they acted as if political life was democratic. There was an increase in the number of dissident groups in Czechoslovakia that were political like the Movement for Civic Freedoms in 1988 or Movement for Civil Liberties and Democratic Initiative, that formed themselves under the umbrella organization Civic Forum. However, most of their leaders were members of the Charter 77 dissident movement. The aims of Civic Forum were clearly to alter the status quo, and their actions led later to the Velvet Revolution.

Democratization literature and theories of civil society, and social capital that were emerging in 1990s owe much to the East European experience. Democracy was premised on an engaged citizenry. Solidarity was the key promoter of participation. The union served as the facilitator of a vast array of civil activities—cultural, student clubs, etc. Even after union was officially disbanded during the martial law period and its leaders were arrested, civic activity continued in the 1980s, laying the basis for the roundtable negotiations of 1989 that ended the communist system. Civil society structures were able to develop freely only after 1989, and since communist regimes in the region did not permit voluntary organizations, these were communist societies which were active in citizen groups contesting the communist dominance (Bahry and Silver, 1990). This means, however, as Osa (2003) pointed out, that even in the absence of collective action and civic associations in an authoritarian state, the barriers to autonomous social action can sometimes be surmounted. Protests can be organized, and occasionally social movements can emerge, and under difficult, risky conditions, people do form organizations which challenge the state's power.

Opposition organizations in former regimes of CEE formed around individuals who shared either some social characteristics or ideological commitments. However, it was possible by means of material empowerment that was coming to these dissident movements from abroad, mainly from the US. Additionally, the perspective of "the return to Europe" was an enticing motive for a large part of the society and a sufficient reason to suppress any conflicts.

Later during the transformation period, many grant-making programs provided resources to organization that were not available locally for activities in social, cultural, and educational fields, as well as in fields of human and minority rights, monitoring of government agencies and political actors, the fight against corruption. The major donors providing funding were the Open Society Foundation, the Civil Society Development Foundation financed by the European Union's PHARE Program, the United States Agency for International Development (USAID), Charles Stewart Mott Foundation, the German Marshall Fund of the United States, the Jan Hus Educational Foundation, the British Know How Fund, the Fund of Canada, the United States Information Service (USIS) and others. In other words, a rebirth of civil society in CEE in the 1990s was possible thanks to the support of foreign donors and was facilitated by the prospect of EU membership (Domber, 2008; Quigley, 1997; Wedel, 2001). Almost all democracy assistance programs were targeted at civil society and many NGOs in the regions were encouraged or even formed by Western philanthropic organizations and aid agencies (Carothers, 1999; Youngs, 2006). A pattern was repeated through Central and Eastern Europe, the former USSR, the Middle East and Latin America.

Networking with West and East and becoming a global civil society

Under the newly won conditions of freedom of expression and assembly following the collapse of communism, civic associations, foundations and other forms of non-governmental organization proliferated. They maintained linkages with the donors that supported their project financially both domestically and abroad during the transition period. CEE NGOs engaged in the transition were often created by former opposition activists who obtained foreign funding for this purpose. With many donors, contacts have survived since the 1990s when organizations received help from them for activities related to adapting the societies to changing conditions as a result of systemic transformation and for their greater participation in public and social life.[4] Although some may question the role of civil society organizations in the enlargement process (Börzel, 2010), organizations interviewed for this study from Poland, the Czech Republic and Slovakia did provide their governments with important support—educating societies, channeling information and expertise, promoting European integration and European values through various programs. Some even assumed the role of watchdog for the EU Commission monitoring the implementation of EU policies at the national level and putting pressure on domestic government (see also Pleines and Bušková, 2007).

CEE NGOs also began cooperation with counterparts in the democratic world. These civil society organizations started to create coalitions, as well as umbrella organizations and networks within and across borders (Demeš and Forbrig, 2007). These umbrella organizations were, for example, Czech Forum for Development Cooperation (FoRS), Hungarian Association of NGOs for Development and Humanitarian Aid (HAND), Grupa Zagranica from Poland, and Platforma MVRO from Slovakia. Membership of these federations allowed member organizations to be part of the AidWatch initiative, in which members commit themselves to monitoring national development policies. These movements' umbrella organizations also affiliated themselves with the Confederation for Cooperation of Relief and Development NGOs (CONCORD), an organization that is a pan-European platform associating national federations of non-governmental organizations that operate in the area of development support and humanitarian aid. With the membership of the EU, these non-governmental organizations gained the opportunity to apply for grants from the European Commission as well as the possibility of lobbying through CONCORD. CEE think tanks, however, were engaged in PASOS, an umbrella organization, in order to promote and protect democracy, human rights and open society values—including the rule of law, good governance, and economic and social development—by supporting civil society organizations in the wider neighborhood of Europe and Central Asia.

Democratic communities in these countries had maintained communication with their counterparts and experts in other CEE or Western democracies. Non-governmental organizations from Poland, the Czech Republic and Slovakia that have been associated in national federations belonging to CONCORD identify themselves as global civil society. They undertake actions aimed at exerting influence on the government's foreign assistance policy, lobbying for a change in the field of financial assistance or countries that need it. These non-governmental organizations in the CEE countries are also involved in spreading awareness of global development through various types of campaigns and informal development education. They have had partners not only from national umbrella organizations, but also maintain relationships with international organizations and independent media, and academia.

The NGO sector in Central and Eastern European countries not only lobbied for more emphasis on supporting democracy as part of emerging aid programs, but also called for the EU to become more involved beyond its eastern border. Thanks to the determination of the leaders of civil society in the CEE countries, non-governmental organizations managed to provoke public debate at the highest levels of EU decision-making and cause greater interest of the EU in programs supporting democracy in the EU neighborhood. The International Visegrád Fund—founded by the governments of the CEE countries is another example of effective and well-focused activities aimed at supporting democracy. In particular, programs such as Visegrád 4 Eastern Partnership Program and Visegrád+ have been created to finance projects contributing to the democratization and transformation of processes in selected countries and regions, especially non-EU countries in Eastern Europe, the Western Balkans and the Caucasus.

CEE NGOs that emerged in the 1990s in order to influence democratic changes in their countries and then to share their experience with democracy elsewhere in the post-communist region, are civil society groups that took an active role in influencing the government's decision-making process and reforms during the democratization period. Some standards, as well as norms that they were spreading as well as ideas regarding how the states should be governed were incorporated. It is difficult to trace similar examples of human rights transnational advocacy networks, however each country has examples of active NGOs that played an important role in drafting or creating a law like FRDL in Poland's administrative reform. Some may not become laws but are still shared standards of behavior as is the case for emerging norms about how governments should treat people.

Observations and analysis of twenty organizations working in the area of democracy and human rights in Poland show that while being engaged in the transition to democracy in their countries in 1990s, they were also engaged in cooperating with societies in other post-communist countries. While bilateral and diplomatic contacts have been used to put pressure on governments also in neighboring countries to the former communist bloc to support democracy, civil society organizations from Central and Eastern Europe supported grassroots initiatives by implementing joint projects so that the experience of Polish transformation could reach beyond boundaries.

CEE countries were undergoing transformation and were asking for support from foreign partners. At the time, these initiatives were not financed by governmental programs in Central and Eastern Europe or by the EU, but mainly by instruments and assistance mechanisms offered by the United States (e.g., Ford Foundation, the C. S. Mott Foundation, the Rockefeller Brothers Fund), Canada as well as some Western European countries to implement these joint projects. In Poland, for example, the Foundation for the Development of Local

Democracy (FRDL), which made a significant contribution to the establishment of Polish local government reform, from the very beginning of its activities, was also carrying out assistance programs in Ukraine and Belarus related with this theme. Similarly, the Education for Democracy Foundation which was founded by the activists of the Polish democratic opposition and the American Federation of Teachers in 1989, in the period of transformation, supported Polish educational environments, simultaneously enlarged its activities to support pro-democratic and pro-civic initiatives in former Soviet republics. Some foundations, such as the Polish-American Freedom Foundation (PAFF), established in 1990 to support the market economy by the Polish-American Enterprise Fund from the very beginning, had a goal to develop local communities and support democracy but also to share Polish experience with the others in the neighborhood. The flagship project funded by PAFF can be considered a nine-month scholarship Lane Kirkland program, implemented since 2000, which has been focusing on supporting democracy and free-market transformation in the post-communist countries. In addition, PAFF has also been financing the Transformation Program in the Region (RITA) since 2000, whose task is to share the Polish experience in the field of democratic changes, as well as shaping, among others, the elite in society and new leaders (Janiszewska and Michałowski, 2010). The program has also been dealing since 2004 with the implementation of study visits in Poland (Study Tours to Poland-STP) for professionals and young people from Eastern Europe, aimed at educating about democracy and increasing civic awareness.

While organizations engaged in democracy promotion both inside and outside the countries have benefited from an enormous amount of voluntary work, from contributions of local business and private donors, the support provided by the European and US donors, mentioned above coming from both the private and public sectors, was of critical importance. Those linkages with these donors built a trust and in certain situations the donors were able to provide flexible funding with simplified application procedures like in case of the OK'98 campaign in Slovakia (Bútora and Bútorová, 1999). Many Slovak NGOs representing organizations active in the field of civil society and democracy building created the Civic Campaign OK '98 (Občianska kampaň '98, in English Civic Campaign '98), such as the Institute for Public Affairs, Partners for Democratic Change Slovakia, Association for the Support of Local Democracy, The Foundation for a Civil Society [NOS]), Gemma'93, SAIA-Service Center for the Third Sector, Sandor Marai Foundation, Foundation Citizen and Democracy. The campaign was strongly critical of the government, and expressed dissatisfaction with the legislation regulating the electoral process and how it was prepared and presented to the public. The 1998 elections were an important moment for Slovakia—a choice between two alternatives: the continuation of a non-democratic, semi-authoritarian trend under Prime Minister Mečiar, or the return to the original ideals of 1989, towards democracy and an open society, and the rule of law and a market economy and OK '98 campaign contributed to the latter.

Scholars studied the situation of civil society in post-communist countries and argued that there were the obstacles to the emergence of strong civil society due to the legacies of communism, and that civil society was weak because of low membership of organizations, apathy of CEE citizens, and lack of institutional and interpersonal trust (Howard, 2003; Petrova and Tarrow, 2007; Pop-Eleches and Tucker, 2013; Raiser, 2001; Rose, 2001; Rose-Ackerman, 2001). However, I find that given the differences across the CEE region (Ekiert and Foa, 2012), as well as various organizations and their engagement in CEE and in other post-communist countries these were "simplistic generalizations" that should be abandoned (see also Ekiert, 2012; Jacobsson and Korolczuk, 2017). First, the end of socialist system led to a considerable change in the operation of civil society organizations. There were organizations that represented interests that had not been organized before. Second, the problems were not legacies of communism but the post-communism period (see also Ost, 2011). Like other civil society organizations in emerging democracies, they lacked financial sustainability—lacking the funding to pay full-time employees, which was also exacerbated by a decreasing number of donors, a small portion of support coming from private sponsors, membership fees and state funding (see also Kopecky and Mudde, 2003; Mudde, 2007; Zimmer and Priller, 2004). Third, the former oppositionists who had promoted the concept and practice during the communist era, began to marginalize it when they came to power. Nevertheless, although financial viability was the weaknesses of organizations, they benefited from EU funding for the NGOs as well as from their collaborative networks with the US. Although some scholars criticize the dependence on Western funding, I argue that because this funding was diversified (Pospieszna, 2014), it prevented NGOs' dependence on domestic funding or on one of the foreign donors or agencies. Otherwise, it would have fostered recklessness or organizational deterioration.

Moreover, representatives of civil society organizations engaged in democracy assistance in other post-communist countries are of the opinion that what would make them strong is the network in which they are embedded. Representatives of organizations in Poland, the Czech Republic, and Slovakia are convinced that they have taken part in the internationalization of civil society initiatives in CEE, and that their transnational activity brought benefits to the growth of civil society in their countries (see also Chimiak, 2016; Stanowski, 2002). Hungarian organizations, however, although active domestically and abroad, are more skeptical about the strength of their networks, and impact of domestic civil society.[5] Nevertheless, in times of anti-democratic offensives and the alarming democratic deterioration in Hungary, they rely on the networks and turn to them for support.[6] Internationally-oriented NGOs in CEE consider themselves Western liberal, pro-democratic and pro-capitalist.

They used to be targets of democracy promotion, and having an interest in "belonging to the club" they were later incorporated into the cohort of democracy promoters. For them, the support they give to other post-communist countries is recognition of the critical role they have played in bringing about democratic change. All the CEE countries focus on their immediate neighborhood—especially in the countries of Eastern Europe and the Western Balkans—which are either in the process of consolidation of democratic efforts or have not yet begun the path to democracy. According interviews, support is needed for societies in other post-communist countries because: (1) there is a political culture that is conservative and patriarchal whereas the culture of active participation is weak often because of co-optation, forceful connection between the ruling elites and population (national government are other actors, who regard civil society as an object of their policies and political action); (2) resources available within the country for the support are inadequate. The activists quote the example of Georgia, where the opportunities for civil society organizations emerged after 1995, when Eduard Shevardnadze's ruling Citizens' Union of Georgia offered NGOs the possibility of participation in its "reformist" political agenda (see also Kandelaki and Meladze, 2007). This led to a wave of development in the civil sector. Numbers of emerging NGOs were skyrocketing but membership of NGOs was not widespread and many organizations consisted of little more than their founding member or members. Also NGO activity was largely concentrated in the capital, Tbilisi, and did not develop countrywide outreach, so did not have genuine grass roots. The government's decision to allow limited liberal freedoms did not anticipate that challenges coming from the opposition or the civic sector.

Slovak NGOs, however, often refer to the situation in the Western Balkans where the first stage of development assistance focused on reconciliation and reconstruction, building bridges in Serbia. Then, later, Slovak NGOs changed their assistance and moved towards offering technical assistance and transfer of preparation for EU membership, or in Macedonia moving from infrastructure and capacity building to the transfer of experience, civil society capacity building, and rule of law. Ukraine, however, is at a pivotal point in its history since the revolution and annexation of the Crimean Peninsula, and it is struggling with bad governance and weak institutions, but has many non-state actors that are very active—journalists, civil society organizations, which should be supported. All activists admit that in other post-communist countries there is still a lot to be done in the area for building political culture, fighting against corruption, building democratic institutions and reforming public administration, and ensuring greater social inclusion in partner countries.

CEE countries chose these countries as democracy promotion priorities but it is also true vice-versa. Most of the Hungarian NGOs active in democracy promotion are engaged in the Western Balkan States. Slovakian NGOs, however, are active in the Western Balkans but also in Georgia, and Ukraine. Traditionally, the NGOs from Czech Republic and Poland pay more attention and devote more resources to the countries of Eastern Europe—Belarus, Ukraine and Georgia, who are also foreign policy priority partners. After the Arab Spring, the CEE countries recognized that transformation experience can be useful not only in the immediate neighborhood, but also in the Middle East and North Africa (MENA).

Table 2.1 Main recipients of democracy assistance of CEE NGOs

Czech Republic	*Poland*
• Albania • Belarus • Bosnia-Herzegovina • Georgia • Kosovo • Ukraine	• Belarus • Georgia • Moldova • Ukraine
Slovakia • Bosnia-Herzegovina • Georgia • Kosovo • Moldova • Ukraine	*Hungary* • Bosnia-Herzegovina • Kosovo • Macedonia • Moldova • Montenegro • Serbia

Many of NGOs in CEE countries that are involved in democracy assistance projects in other countries, were very active during the democratization processes and contributed to important changes in their countries. They also were recipients of aid themselves. These two important experiences as well as the cooperation of partner countries are used by them to explain their involvement in supporting society in post-communist countries.

Among the NGOs in Central and Eastern Europe there are still strong memories related to supporting dissident movements, such as Charter 77 in Czechoslovakia and Solidarity in Poland by the United States, when Europe's involvement in the communist countries was small. In particular, help came from the US government (mainly from the National Endowment for Democracy) and from private donors, such as George Soros's Open Society Institute. US support was also important at an early stage of transformation, when many non-governmental organizations were formed thanks to support coming from the US. At the same time, the prospect of EU membership for Central and Eastern European countries meant that these countries, fulfilling the Copenhagen criteria, made progress in the development of democracy, the rule of law, protection of minorities and an effective market economy.

Geographical proximity as well as the relevance of the assistance, and the demand for so-called CEE transition experience, which is perceived as adequate to social and political realities in other post-communist are the important reasons for the involvement of the CEE non-governmental organizations in projects in other post-communist countries. As expressed by one of the NGO activists:

> It is our added value as compared to France, for example, that we have this experience [with transition toward democracy], we have some "lesson learned" about what was good, what was less successful, and this is one of the reasons why some countries are more willing to cooperate with the

> Czech Republic than with other countries that are far away not only from a geographical but also from a mental point of view.[7]

The need to share transition experience has also become the main reason for the CEE NGOs to lobby their governments to make democracy assistance one of the major pillars of development cooperation from the beginning of the 2000s.

CEE NGOs as main actors sharing transition experience

Young democracies in Central and Eastern Europe, that were recipients of aid until recently, such as Poland, the Czech Republic, Slovakia and Hungary joined the group of countries supporting development in other countries. These countries' membership of international organizations, mainly the Organization for Economic Cooperation and Development (OECD), which brings together rich and developed countries, and then in the European Union (EU) where the main indicators associated with the pressure of making an effort to help poorer countries and change their status. The Czech Republic became a member in 1995, followed by Hungary and Poland in 1996 and Slovakia in 2000, although becoming a member of OECD did not automatically guarantee membership of the Development Assistance Committee (DAC). The countries have been active providers of development co-operation since 2004 when they joined the European Union and were later accepted as full members of the OECD Development Assistance Committee (DAC), except Hungary which joined I 1016 2016). This was perceived as a symbolic accomplishment for ten years of integration into the international donor community.

The European Union clearly stated that member states that joined the EU after 2002 should strive to increase their percentage of official development assistance (ODA) to GDP to 0.33 percent.[8] Although achieving this goal is not treated as a requirement, these guidelines have become a point of reference for new members, policymakers and non-governmental organizations involved in activities that often refer to this threshold. Although the countries have not been able to reach the ODA/GNI target set for new EU members, mainly because of economic crises, they have tripled the volume of ODA since 2004. The countries are also committing to multilateral development assistance, providing contributions to the EU development budget, the European Development Fund, the World Bank, the IMF Multilateral Debt Relief Initiative, the IMF Poverty Reduction and the Growth Trust Fund, European Bank for Reconstruction and the Development, Council of Europe Development Bank.

The EU does not specify for what purpose and to which countries bilateral aid should be allocated, which is disbursed through government assistance programs in ministries of foreign affairs. Therefore, all new donors have chosen to spend a significant chunk of their bilateral aid to neighboring countries, specifically other post-communist countries. This was expressed by Miroslav Lajčák, Deputy Minister of Foreign and European Affairs:

> In 2003 when development aid was only beginning, Western Balkan countries were only at the beginning of their European integration efforts. Slovakia was a great inspiration and motivation for them and it was natural that this country was to become the main priority of SlovakAid.[9]

In his opinion, the authorities of Slovakia have had a unique experience to share, because there was an awareness that what the country has achieved was not only due to valuable help of the developed countries and they should repay this debt, but also because of membership of OECD and sharing with other post-communist countries similar historical experiences, close economic ties, similarity of languages and culture, and common interest in spreading stability and prosperity within the region. The Western Balkans has not only been the main tourist destination for Slovaks, but Pavol Demeš from German Marhsall Fund stated, "we are emotionally feel attached to these countries and we feel that this is the region where we can develop these connections." Most Hungarian ODA is also channeled to the neighboring countries, with particular emphasis on the Balkan States. In Slovakia, a lion's share of the aid goes to Serbia and Montenegro. In the Czech Republic and Poland, most of the aid is destined for Belarus, Ukraine and Georgia, who are foreign policy priority partners guaranteeing regional stability and economic cooperation.

Scholars and practitioners looked into how the new EU donors—countries that joined the EU in or after 2004—support the development agenda of the transition in the post-communist countries and found that democracy assistance became one of the main pillars of developmental aid to these countries; (Mariyasin, 2013; Petrova, 2014; Pospieszna, 2010, 2014; Szent-Iványi and Végh, 2018). They chose to use their experience gained in the transformation to democracy, with market economies and open societies as an important added value in international development cooperation. This means that, in addition to traditional development goals, such as reducing poverty, improving health care and education, which the CEE states have declared to support, sharing transition experience has become a key element of their development priorities.

There are four main reasons why the CEE countries are committed to supporting democracy. First of all, support for democratization processes in other countries, and in particular neighbors, can be treated as an instrument of foreign policy and implementation of strategic goals related to security and the creation of good political relations. Second, the countries of the CEE are committed to supporting democracy with a desire to "pay off debt," because they have been recipients of this type of aid. Third, for new EU member states the areas, such as democratization, market liberalization and integration with EU structures, as well as the transition from a centralized planned economy to a market economy is the "transition experience" that these countries have been facing so recently. The CEE countries not only devote part of their bilateral assistance to democracy assistance but also participate very actively in democratic transformations by sharing their transformation experience. For example, there has been a belief among Slovak experts interviewed that the Slovak know-how can help them in their integration process, institution building or developing a market economy. The transition experience covers a whole range of political, legal, social and economic reforms of the state as well as social and cultural undertakings. The term is mainly used in connection with the reform processes achieved by the Central and East European countries on the way to their membership of the EU, which entailed good governance of public affairs based on the principle of subsidiarity, transparent and comprehensive rules, judicial independence, respect for human rights and civil liberties, market economy management as well as a strong and responsible civil society

The fourth reason why these countries are committed to supporting democracy, which is treated as a "competitive advantage" of the new EU member states, is that they have repeatedly lobbyied the structures of the EU and other member states for greater involvement in supporting democracy. For example, the Hungarian presidency of the Council of the European Union led to the successful conclusion of accession negotiations with Croatia, and the Polish presidency also contributed to a more precise EU response to the deteriorating situation in Belarus after the presidential election in 2010. Nevertheless, a very important manifestation of the impact of the Polish presidency on strengthening the EU's presence in building democracy abroad was the creation of the Eastern Partnership—a special EU instrument aimed at the direct eastern neighbors of the European Union. The Czech presidency then led to the finalization and adoption of the Eastern Partnership concept by organizing the first Eastern Partnership Summit in May 2009 in Prague. During the second summit of the Eastern Partnership in Warsaw, meetings between the Eastern Partnership Business Forum and the Civil Society Forum were held, as well as during the first regular session of the Eastern Partnership Parliamentary Assembly (EURONEST) where regional cooperation was started (CORLEAP).

However, the question remains whether, in fact, all the CEE countries consider supporting democracy as an important area of development cooperation. The documents regarding development cooperation in these countries have certainly been helpful in answering this question (see Table 2.2.). In Czech and Slovak documents, one can observe a strong reference to the Millennium Development Goals (MDGs) and the new Sustainable Development Goals (SDGs), that have been replacing them since 2016 or with the EU Agenda for Change[10] and EU documents. It is hard not to notice that the MDGs and the more detailed SDGs, adopted after their expiry as a result of the post-2015 process, have had a huge impact on setting the goals of development assistance. Reference to these documents is included in every official document related to the development assistance of the CEE countries. Poverty reduction and sustainable development appear to be the main goals in both countries, but there are also other objectives related above all to the promotion of human rights and democracy. Czech and Slovak cooperation strategies underline the countries' readiness to promote human rights, good governance, civil society and democracy, sharing the experience of transformation.[11]

Support for democracy is listed among the priorities of most CEE countries' official development assistance in addition to their structures focusing on development and humanitarian assistance. Poland and the Czech Republic have created organizational structures. In the Czech Republic, a separate department responsible for transition promotion and human rights was established at the MFA to run the country's Transition Promotion Program (TPP), housed at the Ministry of Foreign Affairs, and aimed at supporting democratic transition in partner countries. According to Jan Látal

> The fact that as a special program named Transition Program under MFA was created in 2004, with the first budget allocated in 2005, shows the importance of sharing Czech experience with political and economic transition.[12]

The "Act on Development Cooperation and Humanitarian Aid and Amending Related Laws" lists the promotion of democracy, human rights and good governance among the priorities of Czech development assistance, and the development cooperation strategy for 2010–2017 lists democracy promotion and human rights as a sectorial priority.

Poland's Solidarity Fund that is both an NGO and a governmental institution occupies a special place in the system of Polish development cooperation. The Solidarity Fund is a State Treasury foundation established in 2001 at the initiative of the president of the Republic of Poland and reactivated in 2011, in accordance with the Development Cooperation Act, entrusted with projects supporting democratization processes (free media, citizen empowerment, development of civil society organizations) and activities of Polish civic organizations in other countries, in particular in the Eastern Partnership area. Polish documents differ from the others because poverty reduction is mentioned in them as an intermediate goal only. According to the Polish law on cooperation, the main goal of Polish development assistance is to promote democracy, and the secondary goal is a long-term social and economic development, which leads to the poverty reduction.[13] The development cooperation program for 2016–2020 emphasizes that Poland's development cooperation focuses primarily on eight thematic priorities: supporting good governance, democracy, human rights, human capital, entrepreneurship, the private sector, sustainable agriculture and environmental protection.[14]

For a very long time, Hungary was the only CEE country that did not have a law on development cooperation. The necessity of enacting such a law was repeatedly raised by non-governmental organizations. Despite creating many works and projects, the government did not approve the law. It was adopted only in 2014 and entered into force on 1 July 2015. The Act explicitly refers to the definition of development aid understood as financial aid for recipient countries classified as developing countries by the OECD DAC, whose aims are primarily combating poverty, promoting minority rights, supporting sustainable development and international security.[15] The Hungarian government also quite late in the day created the strategic framework for development assistance. Hungary regards development aid primarily as a benefit for the country and sees opportunities for growth in its economy through increased exports and improved cooperation between the public and private sectors. The strategy, which was approved by the government at the beginning of 2014, emphasizes that the goal of Hungary's development cooperation is to support the achievement of the Millennium Development Goals.[16] In addition, the strategy says directly that the goal is to obtain markets for Hungarian companies and to support certain areas of the public sector, such as education and health. The strategy also refers to a number of the EU documents.

The OECD data related to development assistance, confirm the involvement of the governments of the CEE countries in supporting democracy. Undoubtedly, Poland and then the Czech Republic allocate most resources to support good governance and civil society. According to OECD data, Hungary does not allocate funds for development assistance under the government program for this purpose, which confirms information contained in the law and development strategy. Nevertheless, in Hungary there was a non-profit organization financed by the state budget, the International Center for Democratic Transition, whose aim is to share the experience of recent democratic changes among those countries that want to follow this path. This organization has been also very active in supporting the development of civil society in Serbia and Bosnia. There are also other organizations, such as Demnet, which has been active in the field of democracy assistance in the Western Balkans and countries of the Eastern Partnership for more than a decade.

CEE NGOs have become active in development assistance, once the programs were established at the ministries of foreign affairs through providing democracy assistance in post-communist countries and humanitarian missions in

Table 2.2 Legal documents and development cooperation strategies of the CEE countries

Country	*Law basis*	*Development strategies*	*Democracy promotion*
Czech Republic	The Act on Development Cooperation and Humanitarian Aid, and Amending Related Laws	Czech International Development Cooperation Policy Paper 2010–2017 Human Rights and Transition Policy	Yes
Poland	The Development Cooperation Act of September 16, 2011 (updated October 2013)	A long-term development cooperation program for the years 2016–2020	Yes
Slovakia	The Act 617/2007 Coll. on Official Development Assistance)	Medium-Term Strategy for Development Cooperation) for 2014–2018	Yes
Hungary	The Act XC of 2014 on International Development Cooperation and International Humanitarian Assistance)[a]	Hungary's International Development Cooperation Strategy 2014–2020)	No

Note

a Hungary's International Development and International Humanitarian Assistance Activities in 2015 http://nefe.kormany.hu/download/a/16/a1000/NEFE_beszamolo_2015.pdf.

more distant countries in Africa or even in Asia. However, it should be noted that the CEE countries started development cooperation and democracy in the 1990s and the years following 2000. Once the new EU donors from CEE became active in official development aid, they searched for the domestic partners to help them disburse the money (ministries, government agencies, local government authorities, private companies, research centers and individual experts, but most of all civil society organizations). Mainly owing to legal provisions which prohibit governments from sending money directly to other actors, the NGOs became the main domestic partners. They were also engaged before governmental development assistance programs were created. Bilateral aid is disbursed through annual grant schemes to NGOs to incorporate projects with partner countries. Calls for proposals are broadly defined and refer to capacity building, local NGOs, strengthening civil society, promoting civic participation. In fact, 90 per cent of aid that goes for democracy assistance purposes via bilateral aid goes through Czech NGOs,[17] and very similarly via Polish NGOs.

CEE NGOs are heavily involved in sharing transition experience as contractors of the governments, and thus are a very important partner for the CEE governments, without which development aid could not take place. Because of the projects implemented by these organizations with partner organizations or other civil society entities in the recipient countries, the governments of the CEE countries can pursue development cooperation goals. NGOs in CEEs have also played an important role in shaping national aid programs.[18] They were raising awareness about the need to be involved in democracy assistance. Whereas the goal to promote democracy by the CEE governments is deeply embedded in their foreign policy goals and the belief that democratic states are more peaceful, have stronger domestic economies, and provide better welfare benefits for people, the CEE NGOs, although they support foreign policy goals embedded in aid provision, use strategies that are more independent. Over the last decade, the CEE countries have not only built support programs and instruments but have also expanded the network of contacts in partner countries, and this was mainly due to the activities of non-governmental organizations in these countries.

CEE NGOs receive government funding for their work and programs abroad, but they have been using it for other purposes, which are not dictated by the government. NGOs were shaped by set of internal and external factors. They received an impulse from Western donors to conduct activities in other post-communist countries (they were also trained to develop experience with partners in countries struggling with democracy) and to share their experience, but also an initiative came from within civil society. CEE NGOs engage in development assistance because they treat it as investment into their own future.[19] Many Polish activists belonging organizations located in south-eastern Poland, are of Belarusian or Ukrainian descent, and they engage in democracy promotion because they would like their relatives to have the same civil liberties. Owing to the historical past and shared culture with their neighbors, CEE NGOs find it easier to cooperate in other post-communist countries because they feel confident traveling to other post-communist countries and that there are no language barriers.

CEE NGOs implement norms and principles of development cooperation while also monitoring whether governments abide by these principles. NGOs' viewpoints, as well as those of the academic sector or think tanks serve an important input for increasing the efficiency and effectiveness of ODA system, although they sometimes differ from the perceptions of the official authorities. These divergences should enrich discussions and help find better solutions to the common goal, but, sometimes NGOs' opinions are not taken into account. For example, CEE NGOs argue that supporting democracy and sharing transition experience should continue to be directed toward countries where this experience could be useful and which have a similar past as well as historical and social determinants. However, the transition experience can be considered an asset and added value only if it is adapted to the requirements of partner countries. Therefore, the areas in which NGOs wish to cooperate with civil society counterparts are not supported by the governmental program. These areas covered by NGO projects are differentiated from activities oriented towards the political process, such as: promoting among societies regular, free and fair elections; supporting and developing democratic institutions through bottom-up processes at the national and local level; and control and balance of civil liberties, political rights and the rule of law and for activities aimed at supporting civil society development, such as: support for social groups and individual entities that perform important functions in the civic community, including media.

It is not only the areas and themes of the projects that matter, but also the philosophy of support. The principles that distinguish the promotion of democracy by the CEE NGOs speak also for the effectiveness of democracy assistance. First of all, in supporting democracy through development aid is the principle of partnership, which consists of the fact that non-governmental organizations from CEE countries cooperate with civil society in the recipient countries in the framework of jointly implemented projects. The last principle of cooperation are actions aimed at consolidating changes in the partner country by creating long-term cooperation with organizations and other entities of civil society. Unlike local government units, embassies or private enterprises, non-governmental organizations are more flexible, willing to take risks and be active in uncertain and difficult environments that prevail in countries and develop such cooperation despite difficulties. For CEE NGOs, democracy assistance is mainly about working with people, helping to improve their quality of life. Peer-to-peer learning can be a very effective mechanism and bypass democracy assistance is this type of mechanism.

Bypass democracy assistance as *spécialité de la maison* of CEE NGOs

The NGOs' experiences undoubtedly shaped their view on how other countries should be assisted in their struggle to democracy. They also had a chance to learn from the mistakes of their donors, which also helped them develop a unique form of passing on their experience and a good example to other

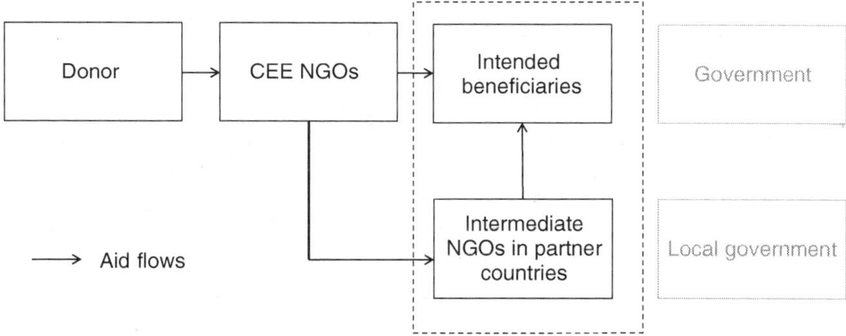

Figure 2.1 CEE NGOs' democracy assistance: delivery mechanism and design.

countries, which also claimed to be more effective by many interviewees for this project. CEE NGOs has developed a specific model of cooperation with civil society and channeling aid through non-state actors in partner countries—named by scholars as "bypass aid" delivery mechanism (Dietrich, 2013), or "East-East cooperation in the European context, "peer-to-peer learning" and by CEE NGOs as "cross-border work" or "the principle of partnership."

In this model, CEE NGOs are members of the transnational network and they link up with domestic groups bypassing the governments in partner countries. As communicated to me by the activists, the idea is to pressure governments by empowered civil society groups, which are equipped with information, and often money by transnationally operating CEE NGOs. In other words, the purpose of this network is not to put direct pressure on governments in recipient countries, but rather to empower domestic opposition groups by legitimating their claims, informing and educating as well as by allowing them to feel their independence and physical integrity with other people who think and behave alike. CEE NGOs engaged in democracy assistance disagree that there is a need to cooperate with states and national governments, although sometimes, if there is a need coming from the partner, such cooperation can be facilitated by letting domestic civil society mobilize itself, and to directly approach national governments. The graph below summarizes this model of democracy assistance discussed in this section.

Bypassing governments in recipient countries

This form of assistance in practice means that Czech and Georgian NGOs, for example, share responsibility and tasks over implementation, and that the Czech organization assists, rather than imposes upon, the Georgian partner what and how it should be done. The partnership also means greater ownership of the project. The partner in the target country communicates the needs and then the project outline is agreed before applying for the grant to donors. The principle of partnership is related to the fact that responsibilities related to the implementation of the project are divided according to the competences of the partners—for example, the Polish NGO provides substantive support, and the Ukrainian organization deals with the organization and reaching direct beneficiaries. Such a solution is also a guarantee of effective operation and provides the opportunity to achieve the intended goal. At the same time, it shows that the Polish NGOs do not use ready-made solutions in transferring their knowledge. This kind of project is also promoted by the donors of the programs, which often require the NGOs to demonstrate such partnership while applying for funding. Also, many Western donors of Polish NGO projects stress the importance of partnership. The National Endowment for Democracy, which is still one of the major US donors funding CEE countries' projects in the Eastern Europe, recognizes the importance of such cooperation and finances such projects, as well.

By promoting this type of model, the CEE NGOs position themselves beyond the traditional donor-recipient of the North–South divide, and that the way they cooperate with the neighboring countries can make a difference for achieving goals related to democracy assistance. They believe that, through such a cooperation, other post-communist countries can learn from the practical experiences of their peers. If the direct participation of the partner in the implementation phase is not required, the partner can be engaged in the preparation phase, and could, for example, engage in searching for possible targets or simply serving as so-called "local points," offering assistance or advice if needed as well as disseminating information about the project. CEE NGOs underline the need to support community-based organizations, believing that the local community needs to be bottom-up, but CEE NGOs are selective of the type of organizations they choose to work with, particularly those types of civil society that are liberal in outlook. CEE NGOs argue that they are more likely to advance their cause and to be more effective if they act through local partners, since in this way accommodating local sensitivity is more likely to succeed. Although such partners are mainly organizations in recipient countries, sometimes, especially in authoritarian states, beneficiaries are reached directly, and these are schools, teachers, young people, women, etc.

It is of high importance to them to assist their neighbors during their democratic and economic transition and to help them create lasting stability and prosperity. The CEE NGOs consider their own experience, and are convinced that they have all the possibilities to become a driving force in this process through a continued knowledge exchange, discussion and deepened relations between them and members of civil society in partner countries, possibly the future decision makers, and thus decisively contribute to the achievement of these goals.

CEE NGOs do not find themselves to be well positioned to directly challenge foreign governments, and that they have no legitimacy in representing grassroots views. Instead, CEE NGOs even though they have good knowledge and expertise, find it important to support (financially, technically and logistically) local civil society, which in turn can advise and pressure their own governments. They prefer not to engage in assisting foreign governments, especially in authoritarian states which often prove to be inefficient and often corrupt, and facilitate dialogue without taking into account the local context, differing conditions and avoid applying a standardized approach to all cases. However, it does not mean that at times some non-state actors on both sides choose to incorporate local governments in the projects. The reason for doing so is to facilitate dialogue to improve state-NGO relationships. However, whereas it has been possible in Ukraine, in Belarus and Russia it is unlikely to happen elsewhere (Pospieszna, 2014).

Bypassing governments not only in recipient countries but also in sender countries

Despite many similarities, there are some differences and new challenges related to the promotion of democracy within the development aid programs by the CEE countries, which may have long-lasting effects. CEE NGOs, who consider themselves liberal and pro-democratic actors, find themselves nowadays to be in opposition to the governments in these countries. The fact that they continue implementing programs in post-communist countries adds the credibility to democracy assistance coming from this region. Nevertheless, it requires them to be creative in securing funding for their projects. To some extent, CEE NGOs can be also be perceived as intermediary institutions through which funding goes to NGOs and civil society groups to protect them from excessive donor influence.

Bypassing governments means being independent of government sources. It does not, however, mean relying on foreign funding only. There has been some criticism regarding the funding coming from abroad. Scholars point out that accepting foreign funds may diminish the legitimacy of NGOs and thus instead, NGOs should try to get a larger portion of their funds locally and increase their organizational transparency (Edwards and Hulme, 1996). However, although such prescription could be valid in democracies, where civil rights are protected by constitutions, the mass media is uncensored and opposition is tolerated, however, recent developments in CEE show something contrary to that. Given the current efforts to limit local funds, and centralize the system of grant disbursement it is questionable whether local public institutions can ever be independent of influence. The current efforts in Poland to create a center through which all foreign funds will be disbursed may jeopardize the independent position of Polish NGOs, which I elaborate in the last chapter of this book.

Moreover, regarding the criticism of external funding and the risk that the goals of the NGOs may change to better accommodate the agenda of the donor organization, CEE NGOs are of the opinion that this possible negative impact depends on the NGOs' goal. If a goal is non-market, NGOs can avoid all pitfalls because they build their influence and power based on knowledge.[20] NGOs can maintain their autonomy if minimize their financial dependence on foreign donors and they can to this by diversifying their sources of funding and attracting local participation to reduce costs. CEE NGOs strive to protect their reputation and integrity by seeking financial and political independence. This is not to deny that some organizations are often driven by commercialism and the availability of donor funds. However, those who lack the competence and the capacity to generate positive results in the long-term will vanish.[21]

CEE NGOs are aware of the fact that overreliance on foreign funds may undermine NGOs' autonomy and flexibility of action and in the end NGOs' comparative advantage may suffer, because donors may dictate performance standards staff members could lose contact with their beneficiaries and become poorly informed and less committed to solve domestic problems. But NGOs can limit donor influence by diversifying their sources of income, developing political leverage over donor governments, and acquiring unique and specialized expertise in their fields.[22] The activities of non-governmental organizations in supporting democracy go beyond projects financed from development aid (Polish Aid program operated by the Ministry of Foreign Affairs of the Republic of Poland, Hungarian Ministry of Foreign Affairs and Trade, Ministry of Foreign Affairs of the Czech Republic, and Slovak Aid at the Ministry of Foreign and European Affairs of the Slovak Republic). Many non-governmental organizations continue to receive funds from foreign sources. For their programs implemented in post-communist countries, CEE NGOs receive funds from various sources, including other countries, international governmental or quasi-governmental organizations, international non-governmental organizations, US and US-based private donors quasi-governmental and non-governmental organizations, foundations, such as the National Endowment for Democracy (NED), the Open Society Institute in New York, the Ford Foundation, Charles Stewart Mott Foundation, international organizations such as the World Bank, and the Organization for Security and Co-operation in Europe (OSCE). They also receive funding from European governmental programs, civil society organizations, and foundations like Germany's Foundations (Friedrich Ebert Stiftung, Robert Bosch Stiftung and Konrad Adenauer Stiftung), the Swedish Agency for International Development Co-operation (Sida), Norwegian Funds, as well as the European Commission initiatives, such as the European Initiative for Democracy and Human Rights (EIDHR), the International Visegrád Fund, the European Endowment for Democracy (EED). CEE NGOs can be seen as intermediary institutions for these donors, who enables them to assist civil society in partner countries directly.

Projects of non-governmental organizations not only involve the benefits of partnering and networking among civil society groups, but also the experience that neighboring partners can share. This experience and knowledge seems to be more important on the other side of the border than in geographically distant countries, often because of the historical past and culture shared by neighbors (Carothers, 1999). Activists in Polish NGOs believe that their own experience of democratic and free-market reforms is more useful in neighboring countries than elsewhere. For example, FRDL was involved in the preparation of Polish administrative reforms, which were considered among the most successful reforms in the post-communist region (Regulska, 1999). With this experience of engagement, FSLD has made efforts to transfer its experience to countries where local government reform is under discussion or is in the public interest. The contribution of the

FRDL, and the Institute of Public Affairs, for the development of local self-governance in the post-communist region consisted of training of public sector employees of the of beneficiary states and political parties as well as translating and publishing the Polish Act on Administrative Reform in the languages of the post-Soviet region, including Belarusian and Azeri. Similarly, because Polish NGOs were active in preparing Poland's membership of the European Union and disseminating information about the EU, today they share their experiences with Ukrainian partners, as presented earlier in the chapter.

Some may question whether any experience can be seen as a comparative advantage in democracy promotion, and point out that it is difficult to draw any clear conclusions (Horký-Hluchán, 2012; Szent-Iványi and Lightfoot, 2016). It is argued that there should be improved impact of knowledge sharing through better definitions of what constitutes the transition experience, establishing clear "feedback loops with partner countries," involving non-state actors more systematically, and coordinating their assistance with other donor countries (Mariyasin, 2013). Szent-Iványi and Végh (2018) show that democracy aid has added value in the eastern neighborhood based on Polish and Czech engagement in Georgia; however, more conscious efforts are needed to improve effectiveness on the donor side. They argue that neither country has systems in place to ensure that they actually support Georgian priorities; evaluations are ad hoc and feedback loops missing and there is significant scope to improve coordination with other donors. Therefore, to improve this assistance, it is more feasible to allow democracy assistance to be conducted by non-state actors.

Bypass democracy assistance is about networking

Although there is some skepticism regarding benevolent impact on civil society in CEE, it is well-established in the literature that this support contributed to the development of a specific type of what some literature calls "transactional activism," which is characterized by the connections between organized non-state actors (Petrova and Tarrow, 2007). However, this network is important for diffusion of the programs, like those youth programs that were possible. Moreover, CEE NGOs are intermediary institutions through which funding goes to NGOs and civil society groups to protect them from excessive donor influence.

Whereas aid flows go in one direction, it should be noted that in this model also, civil society groups in recipient countries (opposition groups, NGOs, and social movements) bypass their government and directly search out allies/support/information/knowledge in order to bring pressure on their states from outside. CEE NGOs become for them the natural choice given geographical proximity, lack of cultural and language barriers.

CEE NGOs consider themselves members of the transnational network that links with groups bypassing the governments both in their countries as well as in recipient countries. However, the purpose of this network is not to put pressure on governments (often inefficient and often corrupt) in recipient countries directly, but rather to pressurize governments indirectly through empowered civil society groups themselves, which are equipped with information, and often money from transnationally operating CEE NGOs. They find that helping citizens in the post-Soviet space to understand and then to cherish freedoms and take responsibility in a democratic system of governance is crucial, and they also express the opinion that perhaps they might soon be helped in order to survive, sustain liberal-democratic norms in CEE countries and even to use networks such as TANs to pressure governments. CEE NGOs were utilizing the boomerang effect themselves during the transition period.

CEE NGOs that were incorporated into the network of organizations advocating and promoting liberal values and norms, are spreading these connections across national borders. The emergence and growing strength of transnationally allied civil society organizations was visible especially in international adoption of norms on human rights, and the environment. There are examples from human rights and environmentalist advocacy groups that NGOs have typically influenced governmental decisions by participating in intergovernmental forums and joining transnational issue networks (Clark, 1995). CEE NGOs do not engage directly in a decision-making process like organizations that work in the area of international security, human rights, or the environment. However, although this is not about shaming strategies that were used to highlight human rights violations, NGOs through their embeddedness in networks, use their authority and information to convince in particular domestic organizations, instead of governments and international organizations.

Relatively few analysts have looked at the efforts of these networks/transnational civil society. Osa (2003) collected network data for the year 1966–1970 and 1976–1981 in order to analyze the social structure that developed during the protest waves in Poland with the goal of identifying and analyzing the oppositional networks that developed and to search for the relationship between oppositional network developments and protests in Poland. Bunce and Wolchik (2006b) find that some pro-democracy activists in Ukraine, because of these linkages, learned about strategies and tactics to challenge electoral fraud from direct relationships with activists in Slovakia who were engaged in the OK'98 movement, and through NGOs networked to CEE regional actors or international, like the US.

CEE NGOs consider themselves as a segment of transnational civil society that solves problems of global governance, and believe that they are needed in order to preserve and spread democratic norms that are severely weakened and ignored by the governments both in CEE countries as well as those where democracy has never been established. Through their networks, they can be an effective instrument of democracy promotion across territorial boundaries, linking civil society organizations and individuals. Thus, CEE NGOs act as norm entrepreneurs at the domestic and international level, advocating particular polices, and influencing the agenda-setting process. The CEE NGO network also affects democracy promotion at global levels, conveying credible information to the global community, especially in current unfavorable and illiberal directions taken by governments in CEE countries.

CEE NGOs are forming a vast number of connections across national borders. There is the cultural work behind the emergence of social network ties, and failure to acknowledge the cultural construction of social networks means we see only half of the real picture. Homans (1950) postulated the reciprocal and positive relationship between interaction, sentiment and activity. The more individuals interact, the more likely they are to share sentiments. The more individual share sentiments the more likely they are to interact and engage in collective activities.

Scholars believe that supporting links between citizens and other groups in civil society is of fundamental importance both for building and strengthening civil society (Henderson, 2002; McMahon, 2000; Richter, 2002; Wilde, 2002). Nonetheless, one of the important criticisms of the assistance provided by states and organizations in the Western world was the lack of networking between social groups. Foreign aid meant that these organizations in recipient countries that received funding for projects were also the main beneficiaries. This resulted in disproportions between those organizations that had easy and permanent access to foreign funds and those who did not receive such help ("the haves and the have-nots") because they were powerful enough or could not write requests for help in English (Narozhna, 2004). The lack of a network of connections may lead to the disappearance of developing cooperation, solidarity and trust among citizens, as well as the marginalization of groups within civil society (Henderson, 2002).

Taking into account this criticism, it can be said that cooperation on the principles of partnership, which Polish NGOs apply, seems to be a better strategy, because it facilitates the formation of internal links between groups of civil society in the recipient's country. By encouraging permanent partner organizations to search for partners from other areas of Ukraine and introducing projects to new groups within civil society from other locations, they contribute to the expansion of the non-governmental sector and the creation of new ties and thus the building of social capital. Such projects are the projects mentioned in the earlier parts of the chapter that connect western and eastern Ukraine.

CEE NGOs are of the opinion that too much of the effectiveness of domestic non-state actors is attributed to the relative openness of national political structures, because the efforts of making a change in society and changing culture can be achieved through networks with CEE NGOs.[23] CEE NGOs adjust their tactics and focus their efforts on a different level, and forge close ties with civil society groups of various types in recipient countries.

Finally, in supporting democracy, researchers recognize that building a sustainable civil society requires continuity in financing and maintaining long-term cooperation.[24] One of the main benefits resulting from the partnership of non-governmental organizations with civil society is the long-term and lasting nature of cooperation. The relations of CEE non-governmental organizations with NGOs or civil society groups in other post-communist countries have been ongoing for many years and thus in their opinion can contribute to the development of civil society and bring about the intended results.

Bypass democracy assistance contra traditional civil society assistance

There are different forms of supporting civil society. Some donors, like NED, are grant-making organizations and provide grants directly to domestic organizations, whereas the Open Society Institute through its offices and presence on the ground provides assistance that is difficult to provide through external cooperation. However, such a field-based model can also be inefficient and cannot operate in authoritarian countries, but in countries where democracy is feasible and have potential for reforms. The direct grant method might be suitable in authoritarian countries but also has its downsides, because domestic NGOs can be less professional and do not have access to human and technical support. In case of bypass democracy assistance projects, civil society can learn by cooperating with their counterparts or can receive support and access to mental and material resources.

Scholars and practitioners (Gräwingholt, Leininger and Schlumberge, 2009; Green and Kohl, 2007; Grimm and Leininger, 2012; Gulrajani, 2014) developed an important criterion to assess to what degree the aid is effective: whether the donor takes into account the local context, including how it addresses the needs of non-state actors and engages them in bottom-up initiatives, and simply whether the activities are locally driven. In order to fulfill this criterion, it is important for the donor to be able to analyze the local context and tailor its assistance accordingly. In the opinion of the interviewed representatives, bypass democracy assistance does that.

In the interviews, many NGOs, especially in Poland, were referring to one of the most frequent criticisms that appears also in research[25] on the support of civil society by the Western donors in other post-communist countries. When promoting civil society, they overlooked the fact that civil society was an aggregate of local needs and interests as well as of local culture and politics. They argue that programs jointly implemented with organizations in partner countries contrast with the model often used in CEE countries in the early 1990s, known as the "Marriott Brigade," namely training about democratic change and building a free-market economy offered by Western consultants in the Marriott hotel, without understanding and not knowing realities.[26]

NGOs seem to be better aware of the challenges of such cooperation. By resigning from "imposing democracy" and exporting "ready-made solutions" to countries at various stages of the democratic process, to share their own experiences and assist in project implementation, they revealed great potential for civil society partner cooperation in diffusion of democratic ideas and attitudes. Owing to the better knowledge of neighboring partners and understanding of internal conditions, norms and the political situation, the projects of CEE NGOs have a chance to be more effective than other strategies in the field of democracy assistance "since democratization is a different experience in different countries and regions, democratization assistance should be adapted to the recipient's country." As a result of the partnership, the so-called "local ownership"[27] of the assistance projects is the knowledge and tools provided by aid donors in the hands of the local community, not only during their implementation, but also after implementation.

The bypass democracy assistance allows for feedback loops because it engages non-state actors on both sides, and if projects are implemented in cooperation,

> it must be locally driven change, otherwise will be useless and our efforts will be go in vain; our projects realized through partnership are local initiative and on local demand so that they could become more inclusive and sustainable in the long term.[28]

Bypass democracy assistance programs increase the probability that democracy assistance is tailored to individual needs, so it should be more effective. Organizations, due to cooperation with other organizations in partner countries, have an insightful knowledge of the needs of the society and insight into the possibility of carrying out certain projects, due to which foreign assistance can be better adapted to local conditions. In contrast to the way of promoting democracy by Western countries, which focused on the duplication of the same pattern and, above all, building institutions, thanks to non-governmental organizations, the CEE countries take into account the separate needs and conditions of partner countries.

All representatives of governmental and non-governmental entities engaged in democracy assistance interviewed for this study share an opinion that partnership is the added value of democracy assistance offered by CEE NGOs. Because the partners know better how to promote the project to the local community, as well as better knowledge of the needs of the local community, the project has a greater chance to be better tailored to the needs of its beneficiaries, which in turn may contribute to its overall success. Second, more importantly, such a relationship with partners that lasts for years may contribute to an overall better way of diffusing democratic ideas and values. In case of one of the Czech organizations, People in Need, such lasting cooperation led to the creation of local offices in partner countries that employ local people working closely with other organizations, often allowing them after some time to fully to take over the projects. Civic activists in CEE countries also point out that being part of the opposition and having experience of the underground during the authoritarian regime, believe that they are prepared to work with civil society groups that operate in oppressive regimes, like in Russia or Belarus, and to cope with obstacles coming from these regimes.

In order to support this argument, I bring the arguments developed during my interviews with non-governmental organizations belonging to the Zagranica Group. It is a federation of Polish non-governmental organizations involved in international development cooperation, supporting democracy, humanitarian aid and global education. Nevertheless, supporting democracy is the most popular direction for the involvement of Polish organizations associated with the federation (Matus, 2011). Interviewees referred to the projects implemented by the organizations in two neighboring countries, Belarus and Ukraine. They were

Table 2.3 Democracy assistance tailored to the situation in Belarus and Ukraine

Belarus	*Ukraine*
Cooperation with outlawed pro-democratic organizations and/or directly with young people, teachers, parents and local leaders	Cooperation with non-governmental organizations, local authorities, the media, independent journalists, research institutes, think tanks
Projects having indirect democratizing character-actions in the areas of education, culture, tourism and local initiatives	Projects supporting system changes increasing the capacity of the state and its institutions
Development of social and human capital	Increasing the legitimacy and transparency of the administrative public sector through projects between the public and the authorities
Actions aimed at increasing the sense of belonging and social solidarity	Actions aimed at unification of Ukrainian society in which the historical, linguistic, cultural and political diversity is strongly marked (West-East projects)
Local development and increasing participation in social life	Raising public awareness of the desirability of decentralizing Political system
Promoting Belarusian national identity	Raising awareness and knowledge about the European Union, and thus increasing the support of society and the ruling elites for European integration.
Creating new electronic media as sources of information and communication	Strengthening independent TV stations, press and journalists

asked to refer to the programs that have been cyclical and have been ongoing for almost two decades. Of course, it should be noted that in comparison with the diversity and multiplicity of other projects that have been implemented by organizations since the 1990s, they are only a small part of the activity of Polish NGOs. Table 2.3 demonstrates some differences in projects targeting Ukraine and Belarus, taking into account their different political conditions.

Summing up, in-depth analysis of the collected documentation about interviews and years of cooperation with non-governmental organizations concludes that Polish NGOs actively share their experience of systemic transformation and cooperation which takes into account the historical, political, social and cultural background of the countries that are beneficiaries of support. The current challenges posed by the Euromaidan revolution, such as the Crimea crisis and pro-Russian sentiment in eastern and southern Ukraine, which endangers the sovereignty of Ukraine, are reflected in the activities of Polish NGOs in Ukraine. Projects aimed at the local communities in eastern and southern Ukraine to support Ukrainian pro-democracy circles have become popular. Actions are not only informative, but they are also intended to develop local civic initiatives, strengthen dialogue between the public and authorities to develop specific pro-democracy strategies, and prepare an action plan necessary to implement reforms. This trend can be noticed not only among projects financed by the International Solidarity Foundation from development assistance within the area of democracy support, but also among projects financed by the Polish–American Freedom Foundation.

Despite the fact that the CEE NGOs are relatively young democracy promoters, they constitute a new generation of democratic promoters who, sharing their best experience, avoid some of the mistakes for which Western countries have been criticized. By supporting projects of Polish NGOs addressed to Belarus and Ukraine, donors seem to appreciate the value and potential of this cooperation. Representatives of NED, a quasi-governmental organization from the United States, which continues to support these bypass democracy assistance projects of Polish NGOs in Belarus and Ukraine, for example, gave a few reasons why the organization decided to cooperate with Polish NGOs. First of all, they treated Polish NGOs as reliable partners because they had been cooperating with them since the period of transformation when they were recipients of aid. Second, Polish NGOs are more active in supporting civil society, which results from the fact that they have some experience first acting in the underground and then as legal organizations. Third, due to long-term cooperation with Belarusian and Ukrainian partners, Polish NGOs are not only able to reach these groups easily, but also have better information about the situation of civil society in Belarus and Ukraine, which translates into better-aligned projects. According to representatives of NED, Poland has had a much more effective experience of systemic transformation most other countries, and its successes include: reforms in civic education, local government reforms and the creation of a local independent press. What is more, Poland is the only country in Central and Eastern Europe where there are many NGOs operating abroad and which are not only located in the capital, but also in other regions of Poland, which in turn translates into their experience of activating the local community.

It should also be emphasized that there are democracy support projects that do not take into account the specifics of the partner country. Such projects include study visits, internships, scholarships and other educational projects that take place in Poland and are addressed to many participants of the Eastern Partnership countries. Of course, the organizers took into account the specificity of the country at the time of recruitment and reaching potential participants, but the content conveyed and substantive knowledge are universal for all recipients.

CEE NGOs recognize formally constituted organizations as an important element of civil society, because they help citizens solve social problems, lobby the government on behalf of citizens, promote awareness and exert pressure on transparency in government and business. Nevertheless, they are aware of the fact that they cannot and should not be an end in themselves, and in countries where repression is used against independent organizations, as a result of which they cease to exist. Putting an equals sign between supporting civil society and non-governmental organizations is inadequate.[29] Therefore, CEE non-governmental organizations try to reach different social groups, especially in the case of Belarus where the freedom of independent organizations is limited. Also, in the case of Ukraine, the majority of representatives of Polish NGOs are convinced that their cooperation with students, teachers and other social institutions had some influence on what happened in 2004 in Ukraine. The Orange Revolution was supported by people who, during the ten-year period preceding the event, had an opportunity to contact Polish civil society (Pospieszna, 2014).

In summary, peer-to-peer learning through bypass democracy assistance has a chance to be effective for the following reasons: (1) programs activities adapted to the political situation, context and situation of the partner; (2) a cooperation which respects for the cultural specificity of countries, due to which implemented changes better meet specific needs; (3) a cooperation not only with NGO but with various social groups; (4) a cooperation aimed at long-term cooperation. Geographical proximity is another important factor that cannot be omitted in the analysis of projects of CEE NGOs, because it facilitates the diffusion of norms, attitudes and democratic values. The table below summarizes the characteristics of bypass democracy assistance vis-à-vis traditional forms of civil society assistance and critique that it received in the literature.

Bypass democracy assistance allows for targeting direct beneficiaries, which in times of backlash against democracy promotion is important and allows for the continuation of democracy assistance efforts. Their engagement in supporting the development of a strong, independent civil society in the post-Soviet space, but especially youth in the region through youth organizations in order to empower them vis-à-vis the state and encourage to be active citizens as well as to be supportive of liberal norms, deserves attention.

Table 2.4 Bypass democracy assistance versus traditional civil society assistance

Traditional civil society promotion and contradictions	*Bypass democracy assistance*
Impersonal donor-recipient relationships	Partner relations in the implementation of projects
Knowledge and tools in the hands of donors or commissioned organizations	Creating "local ownership"
A template approach without considering the specificity of the recipient's country (one-size-fits-all template)	Inclusion of historical, political, social and cultural background
A universal approach to democratic development (transition paradigm)	Taking into account the national and local context in the process of democracy
No models to follow; inadequacy of the donor's country experience	Usefulness of the transition experience to democracy and free-market reforms
Only supporting NGOs	Support for various social groups, not only for non-governmental organizations
Creating a division of civil society between "the haves and the have-nots"	Creating a network of connections between social groups
Leading to activism induced by financial reasons (creating "grant-eaters" and "grantoids")	Leading to value-oriented activism
short-term financing	Long-term project financing and lasting nature of cooperation

Source: Based on own analysis and criticism of supporting democracy and civil society in literature.

Supporting youth through bypass democracy assistance

Why do CEE NGOs find it important to support youth in other post-communist countries? First, they perceive young people as an important component of civil society, the generation that is the future of these countries. Therefore, it is crucial to work with young people especially those aged between fifteen and twenty-five, because at this age their opinions and attitudes are being formed and thus can be influenced. Moreover, the young people in these countries have demonstrated some interest in being active citizens in contrast to their parents who lived through communism and do not think they can change or improve anything.

Second, representatives of CEE NGOs are of the opinion that youth in both democratizing and authoritarian countries are not regarded as "serious citizens" and the reason could be twofold. In mature democracies, a vast range of institutionalized arrangements have emerged for youth to take part in, such as students' councils, youth wings of political parties and other organizations that are networked nationally and at the European level. This institutionalization could contribute to emancipating youth as an important social category. However, this could be possible since young people themselves have searched for the forums to have their interests and needs heard. Therefore, given that young people are expected to determine the evolution of democracy and creation of such mechanisms, it is important, according to CEE activists, to stimulate them, increase the quality of their competencies through rising awareness and empowering them so that they can be included in public life, especially decision-making processes at the local level.

Youth in electoral authoritarian countries and democratizing countries are not aware that their role does not have to be reduced to a polling booth, and that that can escape formal political structures in favor of more direct action, such as campaigning for causes that matter to them, volunteering and social movements, online and offline, simply searching for better ideas, better relationships with local community, and simply looking beyond parties and elections. Young people can take advantage of such opportunities in different countries and contexts. There is a belief that young people become mobilizing agents in their communities and that NGO programs can create opportunities for such groups to flourish. Moreover, social capital can be boosted if people become active, because they lose fear, and distrust.

Third, there is also the other side of the coin to support youth activism, especially in Belarus, Georgia, Moldova, Ukraine, as well as in some Western Balkan countries. The support for youth is also justified for more practical reasons—to create more secure, stable and friendly neighborhoods that in turn may lead to mutually fruitful political and economic cooperation between the countries. Also, by connecting with civil society abroad, and by aiding youth in democratizing countries, the CEE are also safeguarding the future of their own societies and countries.

It has become clear that CEE NGOs aim to support young people along liberal-democratic lines. As it was mentioned during the interviews, CEE NGO projects aim to educate young people about democracy in a direct way through training and workshops, or indirectly through study visits and exchange programs when young people can see how democratic norms and principles are practiced by other young people, organizations, and local authorities. The main message of education projects conveyed to young people is that citizens have their rights and that activity of citizens is crucial. Political participation allows the citizens to communicate their views, needs, and thus the ruling elites can make decisions that are better-informed, and that in fact without citizens' involvement, any decisions that are made by the officials may lack democratic legitimacy.

CEE NGOs rely on education for participation hoping to make a difference in young people's minds and behaviors through the mechanism of knowledge, but organizations also acknowledge that this might not be sufficient. Therefore, the goal of some projects is to create a real opportunity for the young people to boost their activity. Therefore, many projects are about increasing young people's skills, helping them to organize and mobilize themselves, financing their activities, and thus increasing their independence. They teach them leadership skills, and to be more responsible for their community. People in Need, for example within one of its cyclical projects in Georgia aimed for inclusion and better engagement of young people in decision-making at the local level in different target districts of Georgia, and assisted in developing the concrete mechanism, such as municipal advisory committees. Such committees include representatives from local government, NGOs, youth, the private sector, and the media, and are responsible for creating, implementing and monitoring the municipal action plans. Owing to such solutions, youth are perceived as an important player in society. The role of the young generation in municipal decision-making process is strengthened, and they become more empowered to tackle issues facing their communities jointly with the local government. Also, witnessing their ideas turn into action makes young people even more eager to actively participate in addressing local issues.

More tangible results also bring capacity building of youth, which is about providing training on proposal writing, project management and reporting, but more importantly provide small grants. Small grants, like these offered by People in Need, are provided on the basis of open competition to young people for the realization of their projects. Other small grants, like those provided by the Pontis Foundation in cooperation with a Belarusian partner, were aimed at making possible the work of independent young researchers, scholars and outstanding students in Belarus. What is less tangible but might bring long-term results is that such programs from civil society organizations in CEE create opportunities to be a part of the international network and thus increase the resources at the disposal of civil society organizations.

It was quite often emphasized by the organizations that it is not about exporting the CEE model to other countries. CEE NGOs seem to understand that adoption of democracy should be preceded with commitment to democratic values, and knowledge regarding the advantages and disadvantages of democracy. This was never the template applied in democracy assistance, especially since other post-communist countries, despite having similarities, are different in many ways. Some have experienced a bloody conflict (like the Western Balkans), and others, like Ukraine are currently at war. Some have a functioning government which ensures economic wellbeing, while others are experiencing economic problems.

In order to test whether bypass democracy assistance delivery mechanism is used in youth projects, a dataset of youth projects in democracy assistance was created. The database contains youth projects of NGOs from CEE that were conducted between 2000 and 2017. Non-governmental organizations have been

Table 2.5 Organizations from CEE engaged in youth assistance 2000–2017

Country	*Organization*
Czech Republic	ADRA
	A person in need
	Diakonie CCE
	The Multicultural Center Prague
	Palacky University in Olomouc
Hungary	Artemisszio Foundation
	Foundation for Development of Democratic Rights (DemNet)
Grupa Zagranica	Ari Ari Foundation
	Center of International Relations
	Civil Society Development Foundation FERSO
	College of Eastern Europe
	Democratic Society EAST Foundation
	East European Democratic Center
	Education for Democracy Foundation
	European Institute for Democracy
	European Meeting Centre—Nowy Staw Foundation
	Foundation Center for Citizenship Education
	Helsinki Foundation for Human Rights
	Information Society Development Foundation
	Institute for Eastern Initiatives
	Institute of Public Affairs
	International Initiatives Bureau
	Krzyżowa Foundation for Mutual Understanding in Europe
	Management Initiatives Foundation
	One World Association
	Partners Poland Foundation
	Polish Forum of Young Diplomats
	Polish Robert Schuman Foundation
	Polish-American Freedom Foundation
	Polish-Czech-Slovak Solidarity Foundation
	Polish-Ukrainian Cooperation Foundation PAUCI
	St. Maximilian M. Kolbe's House for Reconciliation and Meeting
	Stefan Batory Foundation
Slovakia	ADRA—Adventistická agentúra pre pomoc a rozvoj
	Človek v ohrození
	Nadácia Pontis

selected which are dealing with youth assistance within democracy assistance through the following two-step procedure. First, I selected the umbrella organizations from four CEE countries affiliated with the Confederation for Cooperation of Relief and Development NGOs (CONCORD).[30] These umbrella organizations were: the Czech Forum for Development Cooperation (FoRS), the Hungarian Association of NGOs for Development and Humanitarian Aid (HAND), Grupa Zagranica from Poland, and Platforma MVRO from Slovakia. In the second step, only those NGOs which were members of the above-mentioned umbrella organizations and work in the field of youth assistance were chosen. As the result of such selection, the sample of NGOs dealing with youth assistance in Belarus, Bosnia and Hercegovina, Georgia, Moldova, Russia and Ukraine included: six NGOs from Czech FoRS, only two out of fourteen from HAND, twenty-six from Polish Grupa Zagranica, and three out of twenty-four organizations from Platforma MVRO. See the list on p. 90 of selected NGOs.

The youth projects implemented by the organizations were identified based on the materials obtained during the interviews as well as information published on the websites of the selected organizations. The choice of the time frame 2000–2017 was motivated by the fact that either considerable amounts of data of the projects were missing or many organizations did not have their websites, which today are important sources of information. The unavailability of some data has reduced the database to 305 projects, the majority of which have been implemented by the Polish NGOs (63 percent of all projects), eighty-one implemented by Czech NGOs, twenty-five by Slovakian organizations, and six by Hungarian NGOs. Most projects (203) were directed exclusively to one of the recipient countries: Belarus (forty-one projects), Bosnia-Herzegovina (twelve

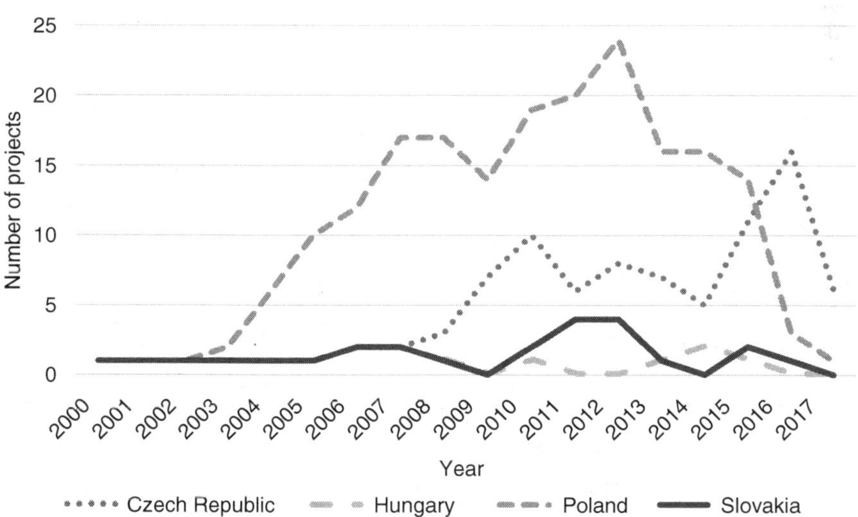

Figure 2.2 Number of youth projects implemented by CEE NGOs, 2000–2017.

projects), Georgia (thirty-three projects), Moldova (thirty-three projects), Russia (nineteen projects), and Ukraine (sixty-five). More than 10 percent of projects were directed toward two countries, and almost 25 percent of the projects were directed toward young people from three or even four countries. Czech NGOs implemented their youth projects mainly in Georgia, Moldova and Ukraine; Hungarian NGOs in Bosnia-Herzegovina, as well as in Moldova; Polish NGOs, however, in Belarus and in Ukraine; and Slovak NGOs in Belarus, Bosnia-Herzegovina, and in Moldova.

One-third of projects implemented in the recipient countries, as predicated, were implemented in partnership with other non-state actors bypassing the governmental institutions both at the central and local levels, political parties as well as trade unions. The major partners in all countries were NGOs and other civil society organizations (45 percent), excluding GONGOs. Other partners identified were universities (12 percent), secondary schools (15 percent), and other public or private educational institutions such as libraries, museums and theaters (11 percent). The partnership with organizations was the most popular in Ukraine, and universities were the second choice of partner in Ukraine as well, whereas secondary schools and public or private educational institutions dominated as partners in projects with Moldova. Interestingly, 36 percent of all projects implemented in partnerships had two or three partners, and these types of projects.

The youth assistance database contains information on funding sources, and Table 2.6 shows the most popular donor agencies in youth assistance. These are governmental and quasi-government agencies domestic and foreign, international NGOs, foundations, international organizations, domestic and foreign private donors. Most Polish NGOs' youth projects are funded by the Polish-American Freedom Foundation (Poland/US) (33 percent of all Polish projects),

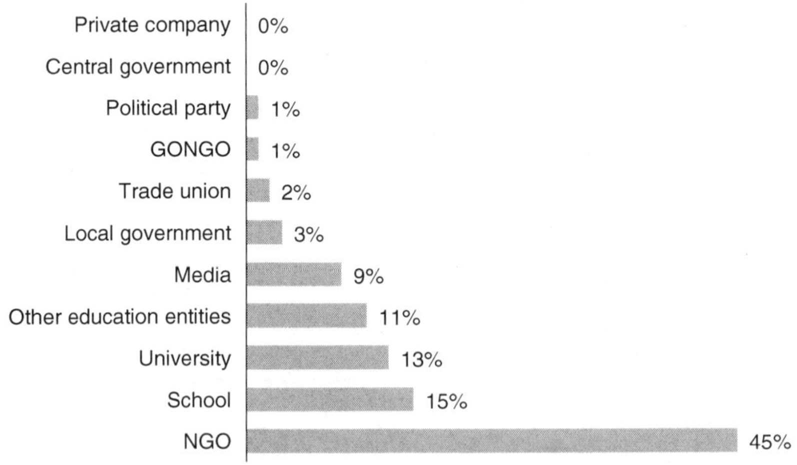

Figure 2.3 Partners of CEE NGO projects in recipient countries, 2000–2017.

next is the Polish Aid program operated by the Ministry of Foreign Affairs of the Republic of Poland, in tandem with the International Solidarity Foundation. Almost half of Hungarian youth projects surveyed are funded by Visegrád Fund, 33 percent by Hungarian Ministry of Foreign Affairs, and 16 percent by the European Endowment for Democracy (EED). Almost all Czech youth projects as well as Slovak projects were funded through the Ministry of Foreign Affairs of the Czech Republic (Czech Development Agency—Transition), and Ministry of Foreign and European Affairs of the Slovak Republic (Slovak Aid), respectively. There are twenty-six cases when funding was coming from mixed financial sources. More than half of such cases included the projects implemented by Czech NGOs and funded by the Ministry of Foreign Affairs of the Czech Republic and the European Union. In four cases, it was Municipality of Wrocław and Ministry of Science and Higher Education of the Republic of Poland financing Polish NGOs projects. Other examples included matching funds between Stefan Batory Foundation in Poland and the German foundation Robert Bosch Stiftung, the Polish Ministry of Foreign Affairs and NED, or The International Solidarity Foundation and USAID.

Table 2.6 The most active donors of CEE NGOs youth projects abroad 2000–2017 (percentage of total number projects)

Donor	*%*	*CEE NGOs*
Ministry of Foreign Affairs of the Czech Republic (CZ)	35.7	CZ
Polish-American Freedom Foundation (PL/US)	18.1	PL
Ministry of Foreign Affairs of the Republic of Poland (PL)	11.9	PL
European Union (EU)	10.1	PL
Ministry of Foreign and European Affairs of the Slovak Republic (SK)	7.0	SK
United Parcel Service-UPS (US)	3.1	PL
Municipality of Wrocław (PL)	1.8	PL
Visegrád Fund	1.8	H, PL
National Endowment for Democracy-NED (US)	1.3	PL
European Endowment for Democracy-EED	0.9	H
German-French Youth Office DFJW (PL/D)	0.9	PL
Ministry of Science and Higher Education of the Republic of Poland (PL)	0.9	PL
Polish-German Youth Cooperation (PL/D)	0.9	PL
Stefan Batory Foundation (PL)	0.9	PL
The International Solidarity Foundation (PL)	0.9	PL
Charles Stewart Mott Foundation (US)	0.4	PL
Education for Democracy Foundation (PL)	0.4	PL
Hungarian Ministry of Foreign Affairs (H)	0.4	H
Ministry of National Education (PL)	0.4	PL
Mykolaiv Oblast (Ukraine)	0.4	PL
National Centre for Culture (PL)	0.4	PL
Robert Bosch Stiftung (D)	0.4	PL
The Centre for Polish-Russian Dialogue and Understanding (PL)	0.4	PL
The Educational Society for Malopolska (PL)	0.4	PL

Although the intended beneficiaries of the youth projects were young people—university students, or school students—there were also other recipients identified as second or third beneficiaries of the projects, such as: youth-led organizations and other NGOs and grassroots organizations (20 percent of all projects), headteachers, teachers, lecturers and other educators (13 percent), as well as parents (2 percent).

Given the above statistics, it can be confirmed that youth assistance driven by CEE NGOs shows a bypass delivery mechanism pattern, which means that it takes place without the presence of government in recipient countries. Bypass democracy assistance allows for a better adjustment of aid, and feedback loops are in fact one of the main benefits of this mechanism of assistance. Moreover, I believe that since there have been few methodologically sound impact assessments, this could blur the picture.

In interviews, representatives of CEE NGOs when asked about the results of their activities indicated the measurable impact of projects, but they are convinced that the results of democratization projects can also be measured not only by seeking influence on institutions or in society as a whole, but also by seeking changes in people's lives, i.e., beneficiaries of these projects.[31] Activists of CEE NGOs give numerous examples of changes in attitudes and activation of CSO partners and project participants that can be attributed to the impact of the organization's activities. In this book, I intend to evaluate this impact on youth in more rigorous terms, but before it can be done, it is important to see whether there is a need to support young people, and the latter part of the project undertook this endeavor.

Conclusion

The goal of this chapter has been to identify CEE NGOs that are engaged in democracy promotion and to demonstrate the circumstances in which these organizations became proponents of liberal-democratic norms. As the recipients of similar assistance in the past, they developed their own ways of sharing their experience but also to pass to civil society organizations the best practices developed in their countries. These organizations are bypassing the governments in recipient countries and often in their own countries as well in order to form linkages and networks with civil society organizations in target countries or to directly reach beneficiaries. Bringing together the representatives' opinions regarding bypass democracy assistance, this chapter shows how this model is different from well-known ways of supporting civil society. It has been supported by the collection of youth projects of NGOs from CEE that were conducted between 2000 and 2017.

CEE NGOs were created and sustained mainly through foreign sources and were able, thanks to porous international borders, to continue their work beyond national frontiers and to advance the agendas and values of the West ensuring the spread of democracy and globalization. Internationally-oriented NGOs are transnational actors, which emerged at times when liberal thinking shaped the roles of the states and the market and impacted on civil society. CEE NGOs engaged in supporting civil society in target countries perceive themselves as norm entrepreneurs and norm promoters and diffusers.[32]

They engage in supporting civil society in other countries due to the following reasons: (1) the obligation of assistance resulting from the fact that CEE NGOs were themselves recipients of aid in the past; (2) an impulse from Western donors to conduct activities in other post-communist countries and to share their experience; (3) geographical proximity and a higher probability that the help will be well used; (4) demand for CEE transition experience, which is perceived as adequate for social and political realities in other post-communist countries; (5) complementarity with diplomatic actions within the framework of foreign policy in which the post-communist countries have always been perceived as priority countries; (6) personal reasons.

As regards the question of *how* CEE NGOs are delivering aid, bypass democracy assistance became their powerful device. Youth assistance from CEE NGOs takes place without the presence of government through bypass delivery mechanism and design. When using this form of support, CEE NGOs are motivated by the key principle: that in order to be useful one must be relevant, meaning that the support to civil society in recipient countries should be locally owned and where possible based on the long-term strategies of partner countries. The NGOs from the Czech Republic, Slovakia and Poland have been identified as the most active and consistent promoters of democracy from the CEE region. Polish NGOs are active in Ukraine and Belarus, and for Hungarian NGOs the Western Balkans are among the top priorities for development cooperation. Organizations in the Czech Republic are also systematically supporting the reform and transformation agenda in the Western Balkans. When supporting democracy, they are trying to implement participatory projects, which include all of project partners who, before the project is implemented, discuss what the actual needs are, how to address them, what is the best methodology to ensure the best possible outcomes within limited time. Therefore, they are more likely to cooperate with partners in target countries. These partners, as demonstrated are mainly organizations in other recipient countries, although the second biggest groups are also formal educational institutions. In Ukraine, local governmental authorities are also engaged in the projects but not as a major partner but rather as a secondary one.

Scholars point out that universal approaches to youth programs fail to recognize the importance of the context in which they are applied (Vráblíková, 2017). As demonstrated, CEE NGO programs are tailored to the country's context. However, the question is how far context sensitivity can go and who should decide which is context sensitive and which is not (Zimmermann, 2017). Context sensitivity entails external actors deciding what form adapted versions of liberal-democratic institutions should take (Hobson and Kurki, 2012).

In the next chapter, I analyze how non-state actors involved in democracy promotion actually understand democracy, and whether CEE NGO projects supporting youth abroad are aimed at promoting liberal-democratic norms and practices, and what CEE NGOs are actually delivering to the partner organizations and young people in recipient countries.

Notes

1 To ensure confidentiality, some respondents remain anonymous.
2 www.osce.org/helsinki-final-act?download=true.
3 Charter 77, "Declaration of Charter 77," Making the History of 1989, Item #628, http://chnm.gmu.edu/1989/archive/files/declaration-of-charter-77_4346bae392.pdf [accessed December 10, 2017].
4 In Poland for example the Stefan Batory Foundation is one of the non-governmental organizations that aimed to support the development of democracy. It is noteworthy that it was the first registered private foundation in Poland after the transformation of 1989. Its main founder was George Soros, an American entrepreneur and social activist.
5 Interview with representative of Hungarian organization, Foundation for Democratic Youth, July 14, 2015, Budapest, Hungary.
6 Interview with representatives of the Hungarian Association of NGOs for Development and Humanitarian Aid (HAND), July 16, 2015, Budapest, Hungary.
7 Interview with Radomir Spok, Executive director of the EUROPEUM Institute for European Policy, Prague, February 17, 2015.
8 European Consensus "Joint declaration by the Council and the representatives of the governments of the member states meeting within the Council, the European Parliament and the Commission on the development policy of the European Union entitled The European Consensus," Official Journal, C 46 of February 24, 2006.
9 Miroslav Lajčák expressed this opinion during the international conference entitled "10 years under the logo of SlovakAid" which took place at the Ministry of Foreign and European Affairs, under the aegis of the Deputy Prime Minister and Minister of Foreign and European Affairs, October 16–17, 2013. See also www.nadaciapontis.sk/data/files/Pontis%20Digest%202013-01%2010.pdf.
10 The full text of the Agenda can be found at: https://ec.europa.eu/europeaid/policies/european-development-policy/agenda-change_en.
11 Czech International Development Cooperation Policy Paper 2010–2017, www.mzv.cz/file/762314/FINAL__Development_Cooperation_Strategy_2010_2017.pdf; Slovak Medium-Term Strategy for Development Cooperation for 2014–2018: http://pdc.ceu.hu/archive/00007077/01/MFEASR_Development-cooperation-strategy_2014-2018.pdf.
12 Interview with Jan Látal, Human Rights and Transition Policy Department, Ministry of Foreign Affairs of the Czech Republic, February 17, 2015, Prague, Czech Republic.
13 The Development Cooperation Act, September 16, 2011, www.polskapomoc.gov.pl/Ustawa,o,wspolpracy,rozwojowej,1128.html.
14 The long-term development cooperation program for the years 2016–2020, www.polskapomoc.gov.pl/Wieloletni,program,wspolpracy,rozwojowej,na,lata,2016-2020,2080.html.
15 Act XC of 2014 on International Development Cooperation and International Humanitarian Assistance http://nefe.kormany.hu/act-xc-of-2014-on-international-development-cooperation-and-international-humanitarian-assistance.
16 Interview with Ilona Toth, Deputy Head of Department, Ministry of Foreign Affairs and Trade of Hungary, Department of International Development, July 16, 2015, Budapest, Hungary.
17 Interview with Jan Látal, Human Rights and Transition Policy Department, Ministry of Foreign Affairs of the Czech Republic, February 17, 2015, Prague, Czech Republic.
18 Chimiak (2016) and Ociepka (2014), Zalas-Kaminska Dudkiewicz (2016) write about the growth of NGDOs in Poland and their role in the evolution of the Polish aid system.
19 Lenka Surotchak Director of the Pontis Foundation, expressing her opinion on the occasion of the tenth anniversary of Slovak Aid, available at www.nadaciapontis.sk/data/files/Pontis%20Digest%202013-01%2010.pdf.
20 Similar argument made by Ilon (1998).

21 Interview with the representative of People in Need, February 17, 2015, Prague, Czech Republic.

22 Already, at the end of 1980s, mentioned by James (1989a and 1989b).

23 A similar view regarding the strength of networks was expressed by McAdam (1998).

24 Short-term foreign funding can help in the development of NGOs, but it is not enough to ensure the widespread democratic values of the community and the rapid development of civil society. A similar point is made by Siegel and Yancey (1992), Ottaway and Chung (1999), Quigley (2000), Henderson (2003, p. 153), Jarábik (2006, p. 86), Tudoroiu (2007, p. 340).

25 There is a vast literature that discusses this topic, see Aksartova (2005), Carothers (1999, 2004), Grugel (1999), Hadenius and Uggla (1998), Henderson (2000, 2003); McMahon (2002, 2004), Narozhna (2004), Mendelson and Glenn (2002, p. 4), Ottaway (2003), Ottaway and Chung (1999), Quigley (2000, p. 192), Siegel and Yancey (1992, pp. 57–58), Sundstrom (2006).

26 Wedel (2001) as well as Kieżun (2011) talk about this extensively.

27 Carothers (1999), Quigley (2000).

28 Interview with representatives of the Pillar Foundation, July 13, 2015, Budapest, Hungary.

29 When Western donors assured that they could provide aid to support civil society, they usually referred to support for non-governmental organizations (Carothers, 1999, p. 210; Hadenius and Uggla, 1996; Mitilin, 1998; Raik, 2006, p. 175; USAID Mission to Poland Europe and Eurasia, 1999).

30 CONCORD is a member-led organization which includes twenty-eight national associations, twenty international networks and thre associate members that represent over 2,600 NGOs. https://concordeurope.org.

31 Some scholars also expressed such opinion see for example Quigley (1997) and Richter (2002, p. 56).

32 About the relationship between social ties and activism, see McAdam and Paulsen (1993); diffusion of innovations Rogers (1962); and the spread of behavior, see Centola (2010).

3 Identifying bypass democracy assistance programs targeting youth

The goal of this chapter is to provide an answer to the question of what kind of youth assistance is given to young people in recipient countries and what kind of attitudes, behaviors, and norms are being promoted for young people through the programs implemented by CEE NGOs. It answers these questions by providing some examples of youth support. By investigating these programs, we can also learn how non-state actors involved in democracy promotion actually understand democracy.

Researchers point out that habits of political participation or non-participation are acquired early in life, and they are carried forward later into adulthood. Also, there is a belief (Hadenius and Uggla, 1996; Mitilin, 1990) that the strength of civil society depends on youth engagement and that youth empowerment also important for political culture. Given their democratizing potential, young people have become a common civil society group targeted by international and non-governmental organizations, and donors, as well as by researchers. Despite an overall agreement on the necessity of youth empowerment, there is no consensus in the literature on how exactly this political and social potential of young people should be boosted effectively. Also, the domestic empowerment mechanisms in authoritarian states that only recently began the democratization process are usually insufficient to create such opportunities for young people, or they simply do not exist. Thus, a youth empowerment mechanism might not be created from within, but rather from outside the country.

The purpose of this chapter is to analyze externally-driven youth empowerment efforts within democracy assistance of CEE NGOs in other post-communist countries. Specifically, the chapter demonstrates the attempts of CEE NGOs to build and increase the activism of young people in authoritarian and democratizing countries. The discussion about the democratization process as well as democratic consolidation in the post-communist region is linked to the importance of participation since the vitality of democracy is determined by citizens' involvement in different forms of participation in political and public life (Norris, 2002; Teorell, 2003). Relying on the interviews conducted with representatives of NGOs who worked on these democracy-assistance programs directed toward young people in Eastern Europe, as well as the database of youth projects compiled for this project, I attempt to show some of the projects and the effects of particular types of youth assistance projects.

Before I present the examples of youth assistance projects, it is important to introduce concepts, as well as some theoretical and empirical accounts of the link between democracy and youth involvement. Thus, the development of categories of youth assistance programs is guided by the scholarly literature on youth, student activism and political engagement of youth (Diuk, 2012; Flanagan, 2013; Hensby, 2017; Roberts, 2009), also by what kind of features of civil society are important for democracy and what kind of democracy, and by the role of young people in democratization processes, as well as a broad literature that explains political participation (Dalton, 2014; Norris, 2002; Vráblíková, 2017; Barret and Zani, 2015). Moreover, various documents and initiatives of the European Union and United Nations directed toward young people were helpful in grouping youth assistance programs into the classification of schemes already used by practitioners.

Civic education

Active youth and vibrant civil society is a crucial precondition for sustainability of democracy (Almond and Verba, 1963; Putnam, 1993; Galston, 2001). Political knowledge is believed to enable citizens to better understand the democratic process and to feel empowered to participate actively in this process, thus civic education seems to be interrelated with building active citizenship and strong civil society. The process of encouraging young people to become active starts with civic education (Campbell, 2009; Campbell and Niemi, 2016; Maroshek-Klarman, 1996; Putnam, 2000; Torney-Purta *et al.*, 2001; Zukin *et al.*, 2006). Research shows that greater awareness and knowledge may inform young people's choices and enhance their commitment in political and social spheres, as well as to democratic identity. Although developing youth attitudes towards democracy has been usually the role of formal schooling, the role of informal civic education programs implemented by NGOs is increasing. Finkel and Smith (2011) for example found that through large-scale assessment of individuals who attended civic education workshops organized informally prior to elections in Kenya, were then more likely to understand constitutional reform provisions.

Civic education (also referred to as "citizenship education," or "education for democracy") has been associated with a school subject that aims to provide knowledge about political concepts, political processes and institutions at various governmental levels, as well as to make young people aware of possible forms of citizen engagement and citizenship skills (Solhaug, 2013). In fully-fledged democracies, the importance of building and strengthening democratic attitudes as well as political and social engagement has been a part of curricula (Eurydice, 2012). Also, in some new democracies schools have offered citizenship and democratic education since the early 1990s. In new democracies, developing a sense of civic responsibility and the acceptance of the democratic way of life is even more important (Malak-Minkiewicz, 2007).

Research on the effect of citizenship education shows that formal education can influence youth attitudes toward democracy. However, at the same time scholars have also found that civic education at school can be irrelevant because it often focuses too much on formal institutions and democratic procedures (Solhaug, 2013; Torney, Oppenheim and Farnen, 1975; Torney-Purta *et al.*, 2001). Torney-Purta (2007) points out that frequently young people are taught civic education without relevance their own lives. She and other researchers (e.g., Banks, 2004; Osler, 2012; Solhaug, 2013) suggest that civic education should help students become more engaged and interested in local issues, and to understand better the relationship between local, state and global levels. Thus, there is also room for informal civic education performed by domestic but also international non-governmental organizations (Himmelmann, 2013; Schulz *et al.*, 2008; UNESCO, 2014). However, still little is known of whether and how citizens can be educated about the idea of responsible citizenship and participation outside the educational system, especially in countries where citizens' freedoms are limited. We also have insufficient knowledge of what role NGOs can play in this process, especially from neighboring countries. Since NGOs of CEE countries engage in this type of activity at home and abroad, I fill the gap by demonstrating NGO-level civic education programs below.

Representatives of NGOs when asked about their organizations' involvement in civic education programs said that schools especially in post-communist countries that are going through democratization either are not well prepared to teach civic education or the educational reforms do not reach certain types of schools (e.g., vocational) or regions (e.g., distant rural areas). Various organizations take on the educational efforts in order to strengthen democracy and to qualify citizens for participation. Moreover, fragile political arenas that change drastically from election to election introduce chaos and confusion among young people about whether democracy is indeed a good system. Therefore, local organizations as well as other non-state actors can play an important role by providing informal civic education and diffusing positive democratic experiences in relation to specific local problems.

Moreover, civic education in schools is often considered by young people as a boring subject, because the instructors merely teach about rights and constitutions.[1] NGOs' representatives, however, are of the opinion that if they put the young people in and environment that is very different from that at school, young people through their participation can see that their activities matter, that they can take initiative and make changes, which further encourages young people to think about the social dilemmas which really affect their own lives. It is believed by the representatives of NGOs that more practical civic knowledge may be also a strong predictor for further engagement in civic and political life, and that can strengthen civil society skills.

However, at the same time CEE NGOs seem to understand well that schools are communities where young people should be able to experience democracy and learn about democracy and thus to support civic and democratic values, and that schools' influence on the young people does not only have a direct effect through teaching political issues but also and indirect effect through socialization processes and being confronted with the others' preferences, and values (Torney-Purta *et al.*, 2001). Therefore, various civic education programs, as presented below, aim to improve the role of schools as a place where democratic attitudes and values, as well as belief in democracy and motivation to protect democratic attitudes is built, because without knowledge and commitment, a capacity for action cannot be nurtured (see also Norris, 2002).

Educating for democracy

All NGO projects that aim to transfer knowledge about democracy by means of this informal form of civic education fall within this category of projects. Moreover, interactive training sessions and discussions of the concepts related to democracy bring democratic values (values as justice, respect and trust) into the learning environment, and thus equip young people with knowledge and skills of how to participate in a democracy. These projects are directed toward students and skip other beneficiaries although sometimes local partners are involved.

Some projects are on specific topics, such as human rights or the role of civil society in the society like the project of one of the Polish NGOs entitled "Youth builds democracy" which was implemented with the Ukrainian organization with the aim of making young people realize that in order to build democracy it is important to strengthen civil society in Ukraine. Students were recruited from the pedagogical departments of five Ukrainian universities and were trained about modern teaching methods and rules of working with children and young people in the field of building active civil society. The Polish organization was responsible for developing training techniques and for providing experienced trainers. Additionally, this type of project has been often organized as summer schools in Ukraine where both CEE and Ukrainian students come together. The aim of such schools has been to facilitate the exchange of CEE–Ukrainian experience in building civil society and working with school students.

Projects aimed to directly educate about democracy especially in the recipient country are rare in Belarus and Russia, as well as in Bosnia-Herzegovina. It is more likely for students to be invited to undertake such training in CEE country. An example, which a provides long-term cyclical program is Study Tours to Poland, which is financed by the Polish American Freedom Foundation and implemented by various Polish NGOs. Within this program, twice a year, more than 100 young people aged between eighteen and twenty-one from four post-communist countries, Belarus, Moldova, Russia, and Ukraine come to Poland for twelve days. They are divided into smaller groups and are hosted by various Polish NGOs. With the example of Polish experience, presented from the perspective of local government, NGOs and local entrepreneurs and Polish academic centers which young people visit during their stay in Poland, these young people can learn about democratic change and the development of civil society. The NGOs interviewed for this study as well as the main coordinator of the program believethat this program helps young people learn about Poland and exchange experiences in democratic and free-market transformations, building the rule of law, strengthening local communities and civic initiatives.

The Łódź city representative of one of the hosting NGOs, when asked about the impact of the program, thought this comprehensive civic education program familiarized young participants with the essence and action of the NGO sector in Poland and inspired them to be active and conscious citizens. During the two-week visit, students got to know the realities of social activity in Łódź through events organized for them (e.g., they took part in a city game through which they learned about Łódź and its history as well as visiting various museums) and what they learned from the representatives of local NGOs, business, the media, and local government authorities gave them a better idea of how various actors cooperate with each other at the local level.

The bulk of the civic education programs teaching about democracy are implemented outside the partner country. These could be for various reasons. First, more practically, events scheduled in Visegrád countries engage many experts and include activities that would be realized in partner countries. Second, especially in case of authoritarian countries like Belarus where students have been subjected to unusually strong indoctrination in schools and universities, bringing a group of young people to one of the Visegrád countries can be more promising because such visits expose young people to life in democratic countries, and may encourage them to act as advocates of pro-democratic changes. Third, simply the idea of some educational projects does not allow for a different form, and such projects are scholarships, internships, summer schools, exchange programs, and study missions programs which require young people to come to Poland.

Teaching about Europe

Projects related to European integration and which aim to teach young people about the European Union are distinguished here as a separate subcategory of civic education projects. These projects are directed toward young people via schools and teachers, like in the example of a series of projects under the title "Europe at school" organized by Ukrainian schools. The idea of the projects has been to train regional school authorities and secondary-school teachers in some regions of Ukraine on how to teach about European integration. Participants in this educational program became authors themselves of teaching materials to be used also in secondary schools in other parts of Ukraine. Similar series of projects on the implementation of European integration themes into secondary-school curricula have been organized in Bosnia-Herzegovina. Under the project "EU at school," regional school authorities and teachers of secondary schools in canton Tuzla developed teaching materials on European integration to be used also in other schools countrywide.

Whereas projects on curricula development regarding the topics of EU integration have been possible in Ukraine and BiH, in the example of Belarus, the direct beneficiaries of Teaching about Europe projects are young people who come to one of the CEE countries. One example is the Slovak NGOs' "Research and education in the field of international relations and European affairs for Belarus," whose primary goal was to improve the skill and knowledge of Belarusian students in the field of European integration and institution building and good governance in connection with the agenda of the European Union. This goal was achieved through attendance at lectures focusing on European affairs, which were implemented by Slovak experts as well as invited lecturers.

Teaching about Europe projects are also realized in the form a series of information meetings about the European Union. Within the framework of the project "Europe in a suitcase," meetings on European issues have been organized for groups of young professionals between the ages of twenty and thirty from Western Europe, CEE as well as from in Ukraine, Belarus and Moldova, who together visit universities, youth clubs and NGOs and take part in meetings during which they can learn about the European Union, the challenges facing accession countries in terms of political and economic adjustments, how, for example, Polish citizens reacted to the changes and challenges during the transformation process, also about the role of the media and the importance of self-government with respect to European integration. Participants can also learn about the issues such as CEE countries' road to the European Union, the Eastern Partnership and also the EU policies toward other countries in the neighborhood.

Sometimes the projects on EU integration do not focus on political or economic topics but rather touch upon cultural aspects. For example, the "European Youth Week" project aimed to present the culture of European countries, with an emphasis on their elements which are fundamental to understanding the traditions of each EU member country. Exhibitions and more than 100 workshops on the European Union and its individual members (Spain, France, Germany, the Netherlands, Belgium, Austria) and non-member European countries (Moldova, Georgia) were prepared by European volunteers from the above-mentioned countries, which were working under the aegis Polish NGOs organizations. A cyclical project "Together for Europe—school exchanges between Poland and Ukraine" in which 600 pupils and teachers from both countries participate annually has had a similar focus. During the exchange program which lasts for few months, pupils and teachers participate in the activities prepared by the pupils and teachers of the host school which include taking part in joint lessons, workshops on European integration, cultural differences, cultural events, and integration meetings, as well as visits that allow them to learn about the history and culture of both countries.

Some civic education programs implemented in the partner country may take a form of the knowledge contest. The Czech organization and think tank EUROPEUM which is part of PASOS, an association that promotes and protects open society values, including democracy, the rule of law, and respect and protection for human rights by supporting the entities promoting integration within the EU, has organized such contests. The program, sponsored since 2003 by the Czech Ministry of Foreign Affairs and International Visegrád Fund, involved participants from all over the world with strong representation from southern and eastern European non-EU member countries. The contest motivated students to learn about European integration, as well as political, social, and security issues, and their knowledge was tested in two rounds: an online test, and an analytical essay on a topic that the organizer provided. The third round was at the same time a prize, because the second-round winners were invited to come to Prague for a week, during which they participated in workshops and seminars. The same organization organizes annual civic education summer schools to teach university students from non-EU countries about the European Union, political and economic integration, European values, and benefits for citizens, from the perception of Central and Eastern European new member states.

Enhancing citizenship knowledge and skills

I would regard these projects as separate category of civic education projects that aim to educate about the role and obligations of citizens in a democratic country, and have them value universally accepted certain norms. After analyzing these projects, my understanding is that they aim to create global citizens who through their identification with a world community would contribute to building this community's values and practices also in their countries. What would be the features of global citizens shaped through these projects?

First, with respect to cultural diversity, such projects aim to make young people develop skills to facilitate the integration process in a multicultural environment, for example through voluntary work or through training organized by mentors from the European Voluntary Service from the following countries: Portugal, Romania, Poland, Spain, Georgia, Armenia, France, Austria, Slovenia, Ukraine, Moldova. Training focused on issues that are important in intercultural integration such as cultural shock issues, intercultural differences in everyday life and work. Similarly, there was a "Pan-European youth meeting" attended by young people from various countries of the Council of Europe, which was meant to promote intercultural dialogue, multiculturalism and tolerance (as the European Commission announced 2008 as a Year of Intercultural Dialogue). The organizers were various NGOs from European countries and the meeting took place in Warsaw. More than thirty participants from Bosnia-Herzegovina, Germany, Italy, France, Turkey, Poland, Belarus, Armenia, Ukraine, Belgium and Slovenia discussed topics such as multiculturalism, intercultural dialogue and tolerance. Also, the participants could learn from the practitioners who in their daily life deal with topics on multiculturalism, like for example those involved in work with children from the refugee centers. The youth also had an opportunity to learn about the instruments of cooperation and reconciliation offered by the Council of Europe and the Youth in Action Program.

CEE NGOs seem to understand well that knowledge of and respect for cultural diversity leads to peace and tolerance. Thus some projects teaching different cultures have the word "peace" in the title. For example, a project "Forest of Peace" has been directed toward schoolchildren with the aim of supporting dialogue between young people from Germany, Poland and Belarus to overcome cultural stereotypes and to learn about each other's traditions and cultures. The first meeting took place in Poland, while the second meeting took place in Brest, Belarus. Participants participated in drumming workshops, as well as, in theatrical workshops, assisted by tutors and animators. The end of the project was to prepare for the joint performance in Brest. Also, a project "Citizens of Europe-European Peace Summer School" was promote through this informal type of civic education to equip young people with the knowledge and skills necessary to understand better various cultures and to find similarities between cultures. Students from combatant countries in World War I and its successor states come together to discuss the effects of World War I on their countries. Similarly, the project "Cultures of Remembering" directed towards young people from Germany, Poland and Ukraine aimed to create a shared memory by analyzing different perspectives and exploring individual memories about places and history.

Second, in promoting and protecting minority rights, CEE NGOs project organizers feel that it is important in their civic education projects to convey the message that tolerance is a crucial foundation of liberal democracy, and as well as that, leads to its sustainability. Therefore, in ethnically diverse countries, like Bosnia-Herzegovina, there are educational projects which aim to increase teachers' awareness in ethnically divided schools and provide them with resources for inclusive education so that they are able to avert ethnocentrism, as well as activating young people to prevent xenophobia. However, in addition to the rights of ethnic and racial minorities, there are various projects which boost tolerance of various religious and LGBT minorities. "The color behind the rainbow" was a project created to increase tolerance and social acceptance of LGBT people. Within the project, young people met and discussed tolerance and acceptance, and the situation of LGBT people in Poland as well as in other countries, and how to prevent discrimination in its various forms. The visible result of the project was street action, which included local communities, and was considered by the organizers as a positive impact of the project because these activities were welcomed with great openness and enthusiasm by the inhabitants. Projects aimed promoting equality between people, regardless of their sexual orientation, can take a form of exchange programs between young participants, like the program in which young people from Poland, Spain, Turkey, Belarus, Armenia could learn how to increase their self-esteem and self-acceptance of LGBT youth. CEE NGOs when asked about the impact of such programs mentioned that it is important to use specific methodical tools in intercultural learning, such as working in mixed groups, involving young people in joint theatrical exercises, stimulating creative thinking, inspiring participants, and overall providing them with an encouraging environment.

Third, there needs to be a willingness to learn other countries' history and politics. When asked why civic education programs are devoted to the topics of history, economic and political relations, I was told that studying another country's history can make young people more willing to adapt and learn from other countries, as well as make them more flexible, creative, and tolerant towards their neighbors. The idea of the "Solidarity Academy" cyclical international project is to nurture and develop the tradition of Solidarity by conveying to young people the different dimensions of social-historical, economic, socio-political, and above all moral solidarity. The purpose of the meetings is to reflect on the heritage of the Solidarity movement—its history and significance—and how the idea of solidarity in certain areas of civic life such as economics, the third sector, and local government are realized. Apart from obvious connotation with the Polish experience of August 1980, the organizers of the project stress also the reference to John Paul II's belief that solidarity is the basic principle of social behavior. The organizers started this project believing in the need to implement the idea of solidarity in the transnational sphere, because the challenges of the present day require cooperation going beyond the borders of states, and that is particularly true for the countries of the former Eastern bloc that have a common history and experience of communism.

Learning about neighbors' history and politics is a way to overcome prejudice, and such as goal is realized within a cyclical project "The Polish–Russian School: History—Politics—Culture" which targets the young elites of Poland and Russia, is an educational undertaking aimed at promoting democratic values, shaping the skills of critical thinking and deepening reflections on the history and current political relations between Poland and Russia. The young elites, who are the beneficiaries of the projects include doctoral students, teachers, young researchers, inventors, journalists, publicists and social activists of both countries, who within the project take part in lectures, roundtables, seminars, workshops, as well as study visits. A similar forum has another annually organized project "East Winter School" which by including young people from a larger number of post-communist countries (Ukraine, Russia, Belarus, Kyrgyzstan, Armenia, Macedonia, and Tajikistan) provides lectures, seminars, book promotion, film screenings, as well as presentations by institutions in order to teach social, historical, political and cultural issues in the context of Central and Eastern Europe. The activities are led by international groups of specialists in the area of Central and Eastern Europe from Germany, the Czech Republic, Hungary, Lithuania, Slovakia, Latvia and Poland.

Representatives of CEE NGOs, who are in charge of projects spreading the knowledge of history and politics of other countries, stress that only regular and long-term work in this field can produce tangible results. When asked about the impact of the program, they provided the number of journalistic and scientific publications produced by the participants of the program that are distributed among opinion-making circles in countries covered by the program. Also, students who participate in such programs collect materials and knowledge which they incorporate into their Master's theses. Other impacts reported as successful included "the opportunity to learn" and the "deepening of knowledge of history," as well as "familiarity with cooperation between countries" like the example of a project oriented towards groups of children and youth from Belarus who came to Kłodzko Land which is called the land of three cultures, because it is part of the history and culture of three countries.

Fourth, environmental awareness is another principle that is being promoted through enhancing citizenship knowledge and skills projects. A good example is a project directed toward young journalists on raising awareness of ecology in Ukraine. It is aimed at increasing the involvement of young Ukrainian journalists in shaping ecological awareness among Ukrainian society through exchanging knowledge between Polish and Ukrainian environmental journalists. A second goal was the development of independent and new media, and in general the improvement of the role of modern media (newspapers, radio, television and Internet platforms) in environmental education and the raising of ecological knowledge and activating society in this field. Oftentimes, environmental topics are promoted by volunteers who devote their activities and time to raising the awareness of different age groups in the field of culture and ecology with partner organizations from many countries in different regions of Europe, as in the example of the European Voluntary Service project. Finally, some CEE NGOs share their experience of increasing youth awareness about the natural resources through establishing school centers for environmental education.

The fifth and final principle, is a willingness to learn about the local community's needs and readiness to take an action. As one of the representatives interviewed mentioned "Young active social and political activists are the greatest potential and longevity of any organization regardless of the country of origin." Having this idea in mind, CEE NGOs approach young people who are beginning to be involved in social and political activities in order to help them acquire knowledge and skills in political marketing and organizational structures, for example, or to establish contacts with Polish counterparts. Sometimes, a specific group of young people is targeted, such as future lawyers from Belarus, who were approached through a project organized by a Czech NGOs, which aimed to increase young people's awareness of local problems via meetings with regional organizations in Belarus. Volunteers are another important group. Recognizing the potential of volunteering in diffusing good practices, norms and behaviors, many projects are oriented towards this group of young people. For example, through the study visit "Modern methods of volunteering" organized by one of the CEE NGOs, young people are able to widen their perspective about new ways of volunteering, deepening their skills of diagnosing local needs and involving others in the community to solve them. The study tour was designed for youth workers and volunteer project coordinators from the following countries: Poland, Portugal, Romania, Spain, Georgia, Armenia, France, Austria, Slovenia, Azerbaijan, Moldova and Ukraine. The organizers confidently maintained that through meetings with youth policymakers and youth organizations, these young participants learned good volunteering practices to create a bridge between EU countries and the partner organizations. Specifically, they raised their awareness of new ways of involving volunteers, such as creating alternative parks, street art, paintings, murals, organizing peaceful demonstrations on bicycles. The NGO coordinators were of the opinion that it was very important for young people to visit local organizations, through which sharing information about how they were going about local and international volunteering projects, depended on their knowledge of activities, structures and management methods.

Establishing links between formal and informal civic education

The idea behind these projects is to enhance civic competences of young people through the combination of formal and informal educational efforts. Since civic education is not only the domain of schools and national educational systems, but also of other actors who engage in this field, such as non-governmental organizations both domestic and international, these two domains can complement each other in order to educate young people to be more active citizens and thus build a well-functioning and strong civil society. CEE NGOs find it important to help schools in recipient countries cooperate with them on joint projects. For example, the Czech NGO, People in Need through its local office in Georgia, organizes a cyclical project "Education through documentary films," which focuses on cooperation with schools on the delivering attractive methods of teaching human rights issues. As the result of such cooperation, the "One World in Schools" educational program was created, which had originally started in the Czech Republic in 2001, and combines documentary films, other audio-visual aids and follow-up activities and helps teachers to teach more effectively about complex social topics, such as human rights, and democratic values, as well as conflict prevention or mediation. As communicated by the organization, the project's success lay in the fact that more than 250 Georgian schools received educational toolkits consisting of documentary films and didactic materials used to teach students to be active and responsible citizens, and that this methodology has been used by more than 300 teachers, and contributed to increased awareness of human rights among the Georgian youth and to more active involvement in social debate on human rights and their promotion.[2] The films, which were watched by over 27,000 students aimed to raise awareness, educating and thus activating these young people. People in Need proudly reports that these initiatives led to the creation of various organizations, such as the Children's Rights Club by young people, and also motivated them to participate in civic initiatives and to proactively solve concrete problems in their local community.

Civic education projects beyond teaching institutional political settings aim to shape dimensions of active citizenship, such as knowledge, skills, attitudes, values, and intended behavior/disposition (see Print, 2013). Projects embrace not only young people but also teachers, educators and NGOs. For example, the "European experiences in education for Ukraine" project was a joint venture of the Polish Robert Schuman Foundation, the Ukrainian School Headmasters' Association, with the support of the Central Teacher Training Center. Within these projects, participants had the opportunity to establish contacts and partnership between schools, to develop common concepts based on the experiences of the three countries. Teachers and experts from Poland, Germany and Ukraine met to share their experiences in the field of civic and European education, youth activation and to work on international cooperation projects. The activities included theoretical and practical classes and visits. The guests were able to verify how interactive the pupil's work is in practice, and how much initiative can be demonstrated by the pupils when properly guided.

CEE NGOs seem to understand well that informal civic education can provide knowledge about political concepts, political processes and institutions, as well as to increase understanding of citizens' engagement in the decision-making process. Given different knowledge and understanding of the role of the state as well as the citizen, organizations run workshops during which young people can share their experience and knowledge. For example, within the project "History that unites," in which participants from Armenia, Georgia, Moldova, Russia, Ukraine and Poland took part, the organizers used the common and unifying point in shared history, which was the experience of post-communism, so that the young people could understand and compare the situation in different countries and diagnose current socio-political problems. Projects that aim to shape knowledge do so in the form of offering debates, small group discussions and workshops on stimulating topics and issues since they allow confrontation of diverse knowledge and experiences, and also build a lasting bond not only between young people but also between teachers. In other words, such projects allow the practice of real democracy within informal civic education projects and to spread this within a formal school learning environment.

In addition to shaping knowledge, the civic education programs run by NGOs also shape values of young people directly or indirectly through teachers who take part in these projects. For example, one of the Slovak NGOs often organized study visits for Belarusian educators and representatives of the non-governmental sector, whose goal is to show how formal and non-formal education in Slovakia takes place. During such visits, teachers from Belarus met with experts on education reform, learn about modern teaching methods, media education or e-learning, but more importantly they learn how non-governmental organizations work with schools in teaching civil rights, human rights and value building. Other values that have been shaped and shared within the projects included the importance of civil society in democratic society. One example is project called "Educational Institute for Democracy and Civil Society in Eastern Ukraine" implemented by one of the Czech NGOs. The aim of this project was to establish an educational center that would provide informal civic education on issues related to democracy, civil society and EU integration, but which would also engage teachers and educators from schools.

Such projects establishing links between formal and informal civic education efforts shape values as well as behaviors. For example, a project called "Through civic education to civil society in Ukraine," consisted not only of series of workshops and training but also included research that participants themselves undertook in Ukraine, which aimed at learning about the values and aspirations of Ukrainian society, especially the changes that took place in this area after the 2004 presidential elections. A comparison of the results obtained with the results of earlier studies on similar problems allowed the impact that the Orange Revolution has had on society to be analyzed and help determine the possible direction of further transformation in Ukraine. Within another project, young participants in cooperation with the State University in Chisinau and a local non-governmental organization took action to provide a nationwide response to the phenomenon of the children left behind which was incorporated into a broader reform of the social care system in Moldova. The project mapped the needs and current services for children left behind, followed by a communication campaign aimed at parents and social workers, building a database of children left behind, as well as a strategy document for social care for these children.

Improving civic education programs at schools

This last type of civic education programs is directed toward developing and enriching curricula development, in other words: how school-based civic education aiming to develop democratic knowledge and skills can be improved. In this kind of project young people are secondary beneficiaries, although sometimes they would have some input how the process can be enhanced. Nevertheless projects are mainly directed toward teachers, headteachers, and NGOs. For example, "School open to the world" implemented by one of the Polish NGOs together with two Ukrainian counterparts was intended for teachers and psychologists to teach them and also help them develop practices in the fields of preventing bullying and developing crisis response at schools. Within this project, Polish and Ukrainian experts jointly developed educational materials to assist teachers and psychologists in dealing with aggressive behavior among students. These materials were shared with other schools in order help them solve other problems related to aggression. Similarly, a project carried out with the Georgian Association of Local Democracy in Georgia, aimed to increase the competence of Georgian school psychologists in the field of effective coping with school and individual school institutions and to raise awareness among Georgian school psychologists about the possibility of creating institutional psychological support for schools. Workshops for forty-eight teachers and school psychologists from Gori and Tbilisi took place within the framework of the project, while didactic materials have been developed which will enable effective integration and therapeutic activities in schools.

Overall, the tangible impacts of such projects include didactic materials, as in some of the projects mentioned earlier, preparation of interactive teaching methods and development of new methods of teaching some specific subjects, or integration of new topics into curricula, such as corporate social responsibility at the School of Business and Management of Technology at Belarus State University. This was assisted by Belarusian academics who conducted CSR-related research and who have published on the incentives and obstacles to cooperation between private companies and non-profit organizations in Belarus. Also, there were other projects with more measureable results, such as the project on increasing Belarusian teachers' access to modern science teaching methods, or the project to increase the competence of Georgian psychologists through establishing psychological and pedagogical support centers at secondary schools. The activities within such European Schools Clubs would include debates on European integration, workshops, collection and dissemination of information about the European Union, as well as meetings with people involved in social activities and with experts on European and civic education. Polish NGOs given their positive experience with the 3,000 plus European School Clubs in Poland, also promote this idea in other countries, believing that self-governing clubs through the involvement of teachers and students and raising awareness among society in recipient countries about the principles of democracy and civil society, training and stimulating local communities to take public actions can promote democracy, civil society and the idea of a united Europe in schools and in local communities, as well as eventually contributing to increasing the number of social initiatives.

Czech NGOs also aim to share their know-how from the transformation of the Czech higher education system. Within the project "Assistance in increasing quality of higher education in Ukraine," Czech organizations aimed to improve the quality of Ukrainian agricultural universities according to the Bologna principles of European Higher Education, through intensification of relations between Czech and Ukrainian agricultural universities and by direct collaboration of Czech and Ukrainian teachers of courses related to agricultural economics and agricultural technologies. The project was implemented in several rounds at various Ukrainian universities, and according to the organizers, it assisted Ukrainian universities with the transformation of study programs and creation of study plans and new methodological materials in line with the reforms in the education sector in Ukraine. It supported both development of university self-government and democratic principles, and furthermore improved international exchange for Ukrainian students, participation in academic mobility programs such Erasmus or in Horizon 2020. Similar projects are also organized in Georgia. CEE NGOs seem to also promote the benefits of improved civic education programs in schools for local development. For example, one of the projects was tasked with the development potential of Shida Kartli Province by improving the quality of science education and increasing student interest in further education in engineering.

Projects aimed at improving formal civic education that produce less tangible impacts, include an array of various projects that aim to train teachers, some of which have the greater goal to reform the teaching of civic education. For example, some projects at schools in Bosnia-Herzegovina, Moldova and Ukraine, implemented in cooperation with local organizations, included a number of activities aimed at: training teachers about civic education, offering e-learning courses with the aim of contributing to the modernization of learning and enhancement of IT skills, organizing courses offered to the teachers in order to increase their knowledge of the EU; training and workshops that would increase teachers', headteachers' and local key stakeholders' knowledge of the benefits of inclusive education, and the like. One of the Czech NGOs, for example, implemented a project entitled "Improving the quality of university education in Bosnia-Herzegovina, Moldova and Serbia," which aimed at improving the quality and the number of courses taught at partner universities in these countries as well as establishing new cooperation. Faculty members and administrative staff of the partner universities had internships at educational institutions in the Czech Republic and because of the training received, they were able to include new topics in their courses and in study plans.

Although the above-mentioned projects have been introduced in Bosnia-Herzegovina, Moldova, Georgia, and Ukraine, they have been rare in Belarus. Given the current political climate in which Lukashenko regime is hostile to any foreign intervention, it is unlikely that the civic education programs of this type could be introduced with cooperation of the organizations from abroad. Nevertheless, projects on euro clubs and reforming civic education in Belarus used to be available during the 1990s (for more on changes in democracy promotion projects see discussion in Pospieszna, 2014). Currently, apart from a few curricula development projects that do not concern topics of civil society development, democracy, citizens' rights and obligations, there are civic education projects within which teachers are invited to come to CEE countries on study visits. The purpose of these study visits is to share the experiences of active civic education, to introduce active teaching methods, provide Internet training, and help improve school work.

In sum, the aim of this type of civic education project has been to improve formal civic education programs in schools, share good practices to improve teaching techniques, provide educational materials, develop new courses and textbooks in order to shape the attitudes, values, knowledge of young people that are in favor of the democracy process both in schools and beyond, ready to engage in dialogues. Education for democratic citizenship programs, civic education programs or education for active participation, are designed to also enhance participation through the mechanism of knowledge. Conducting educational activity aimed at propagating the idea of democracy and preparing people to work for the benefit of democracy—improving young people's understanding about their role and ability to solve problems in their local community, region or even country—is an important element of youth empowerment. However, it is not sufficient, because young people should be given opportunities to participate.

Political participation

If democracy is rule by people, then political participation is important, and is a necessary condition for the survival of democracy, because through participation citizens can exert their rule. Participatory channels are various and are not related primarily to elections (Dalton, 2000, 2014; Norris, 2002; van Deth, 2014; Vráblíková, 2017). In the minimal definition of democracy, Schumpeter (1952) proposes to limit participation in voting and suggests that democracy is not about mass participation. Then, Pateman's (1970) participatory democracy emphasizes the need for participation and that people should be involved in politics; participation is also incorporated in a measure of polyarchy by Dahl (1989). In other words, citizens can and should be involved in politics between elections and participate more directly.

Participation matters for a vibrant democracy (Almond and Verba, 1963; Hart, 2009; Pateman, 1970; van der Eijk and Franklin, 1996). This political science literature argues that participation has the potential to foster a sense of citizenship, because participation makes citizens identify better with their political system and feel responsible for others and even more interested in taking initiatives in their personal lives as well as collectively. However, there are large differences in participation across countries (Dalton, 2014; Norris, 2002; Vráblíková, 2017). In democracies, there can be crises of participation which can be a consequence of a lack of interest, apathy, cynicism and alienation, and young people do not care about politics, see it as irrelevant (Buckingham, 2000; O'Toole, 2004) or are not satisfied with existing political outcomes. Nevertheless, despite a sense of powerlessness or inefficacy, there is an opportunity to participate and young people, if they wish, can be represented and their voice can be heard. The situation is different in democratizing countries.

In countries where democracy has not yet taken root as a political system, it is important to support and promote activism because there is no participatory need for representation and the desire to participate is not sufficiently boosted. Moreover the culture of active participation is weak often, because of co-optation, forceful connections between the ruling elites and the population, and also because available resources within the country for support are inadequate. By encouraging greater participation, participant political culture can be built as more people would be willing to be involved in public life and decision-making, and put pressure on the system to offer opportunities to participate. CEE NGO projects concerning political participation and youth assistance are presented below. They support dialogue and help youth to build or improve spaces for young people to discuss key political decisions, as well as strengthen their leadership skills. The representatives of organizations share the opinion that it is important to target powerful local actors, so-called local leaders who through their participation in their programs might spread their civic training within their social networks in the community.

Improving various forms of youth political participation

Political participation includes actions, such as demonstrations, petitions, meetings, joining a political party, etc., of citizens intended to influence the decisions of other actors, mainly decision-making actors, aimed at solving collective/community problems, or to express political aims (see for example definition in Vráblíková, 2017). Such a definition emphasizes activity as well as readiness to take actions and positive attitudes related to participation. The projects organized by CEE NGOs aim to facilitate political participation of young people in public affairs and politics more generally. For example, the cyclical project "Visegrád School of Political Studies" aims to create opportunities for young professionals, future journalists, experts, researchers, and policymakers, aged between twenty and thirty-five from both from the Visegrád (V4) and Eastern Partnership countries to share and enrich their knowledge and their ideas and delve into discussions with V4 experts from different fields regarding regional cooperation, political decision-making and lobbying, the role of social media campaigns, fighting corruption and political transparency, as well as on civil society and youth wings of political parties.

Some CEE NGOs initiatives reach emerging politicians, like for example the "Training of Young Moldovan Politicians" projects aimed at improving the functioning and organization of democratic political parties Moldova, which is a transition country. With regard to Moldova's 2009 elections, the objective of the project was to share knowledge of how elections can be conducted and how a democratic institutional system can function properly. Participants who represented political parties with at least 3 percent public support took part in a training course in Budapest, where they learned how to build, run, and use a political party in practice. During the training sessions, general techniques of political management were illustrated, and brainstorming sessions held. The Moldovan party representatives met with the representatives of Hungarian political parties, political analysts, campaign groups, and well-known experts in the field of political management. The young Moldovan politicians could also learn how parties work in local government. The experts, many of whom were involved in the first democratic elections in the region 20 years ago, shared their experience and gave advice on how to choose the best model for Moldova to follow. The representatives of ICDT organization believed that introducing the experience of Hungarian political parties is an effective means of preparing political party activists in Moldova for significant participation in the political life of their country, especially in combination with experiences of political parties from "older" democracies.

Political participation projects aim to strengthen skills of all young people to take action relating to political activity, for example through helping them find more opportunities and mechanisms for participatory policymaking across different fields, teaching them about election campaigns that address young people directly, or provide training on governance assessment tools to examine how adequately national policies respond to youth concerns. The project funded by the National Endowment for Democracy and implemented by one of the Polish think tanks, the Institute of Public Affairs (IPA), matches this type of political participation project since within this project young future leaders in the recipient countries were offered training focused on the development of analytical skills and the transfer of know-how in various public policy areas. Each of the participants under the supervision of IPA experts conducted her/his own research project in his/her chosen field that referred to a specific public policy. This project was intended for young Russian analysts and researchers and was implemented with the cooperation of the Moscow Levada Center. However, for political reasons, this project has been redirected to other post-communist countries.

Moreover, the political participation projects aim to build connections between young regional professionals, hoping, that in the long run, these projects also serve as important tools to improve relations and foster cooperation between the post-communist countries. For example, the cyclical project entitled "The National Schools" emerged as a result of a response to the need to educate elites, future leaders in social change in target countries, significant people in science, culture, politics, the media and civil society. The project is aimed at the intellectual formation of young people from Armenia, Azerbaijan, Belarus, Georgia, Moldova, Russia, and Ukraine, who have adopted of democratic values, human rights, and are engaged in the construction of civic society in their countries. Activities planned within each wave of the project include debates on the history and current political events conducted during seminars and roundtables by one of the Polish NGOs, the College of Eastern Europe. Lectures by prominent people are also organized with the cooperation of the University of Warsaw, as well as cultural events and meetings. The formula of each school is long term with the goal of improving cooperation between participants and giving them the opportunity to play a key role in shaping the future image of their own countries.

Leadership assistance

These are the democracy promotion projects that foster political participation among emerging young leaders who have a potential to be political leaders. What is unique in this project is that they all have "leader" in their titles, for example "Young Leaders in Politics and Diplomacy," "Young Leaders of the Western Balkans" or "Leaders for Democracy." Projects have been popular in Ukraine, Georgia, and the Western Balkans (Albania, Bosnia-Herzegovina, Kosovo) but are rare in Russia and Belarus. The organizers invite young leaders pursing political and diplomatic careers to seminars devoted to specific themes to widen their intellectual horizons, improve the capacity of these young leaders, and empower them to effectively address challenges within the field of their professional career. For example, the ICDT has already implemented various projects in the Western Balkans directed toward young leaders on EU integration recognizing that although all countries of the region have expressed their desire to join the EU and considerable efforts have been made towards this goal, the developments of internal and external affairs are volatile and a lot of work is still needed in these countries to achieve sufficient progress in the political, economic and societal fields to become EU members. An important aspect that could also support this endeavor is cooperation among the countries of the Western Balkans. The intention of such summer courses is to empower young leaders in the Western Balkans by using the example and experience of the Visegrád Group within the European Union. Young political leaders learn the significance of European integration and regional cooperation initiatives, and their possible contribution to the development of the Western Balkans. At the same time, the participants from the V4 countries will also have the chance to become acquainted with the situation and the future prospects of the Western Balkans.

CEE NGOs find it important to target the so-called young leaders because they are future political elites who will introduce changes in their countries and have been already involved in political transformation or will be responsible for bringing democracy, like in the example of Belarus, as well as for maintaining and consolidating democratic institutions, norms, and practices. Recognizing the fact that political leaders in the first place should become local social leaders, many projects aim at improving leadership skills by teaching technical and organizational skills, helping young people find the way and resources to be proactive in their communities, and enhancing communication and creating a network of support to mobilize the community to address concerns. One example is a project directed toward young social leaders from Moldova who come for training in order to gain knowledge and skills in the field of youth activation, and learn techniques of self-presentation. Another example is a project aimed at young leaders from Ukraine and Belarus who have demonstrated their potential by building organizations or by involving young people in civic engagement. The project aims to integrate and encourage collaboration between Ukrainian and Belarusian leaders both at the organizational and personal level. It also aims to raise awareness of strengthening the youth wings of non-governmental organizations in Belarus. However, given the current unfavorable climate for organizations to operate in Belarus, those young people and local youth organizations, who are invited to participate in the project, work in the fields of culture and environment.

The representatives of NGOs who are involved in the implementation of the project that strengthens linkages between young social leaders, believe that such projects serve as a base for democratic forces and citizen transformation, the development of youth organizations in these two countries, and for establishing cooperation between youth organizations from both countries. Such a social platform for Ukraine and Belarus is important, according the view of activists, because they facilitate exchange of experience between young leaders in Belarus and Ukraine and various joint activities, and prepare Belarusian youth to be ready to scale up their activities in the future. As expressed by another activist that implements projects toward the future elites:

> We wanted to convey the knowledge that would allow them to act effectively, "take the crowds" and become leaders (…). An important element of our program was the study visits in which the guests from Belarus had the opportunity to familiarize themselves with the practical side of functioning of NGOs in our country. The visits also made it possible to exchange experiences and establish new contacts. The project was also designed to prepare active leaders to promote Belarus' participation in European structures and to continue the democratic transition in that country.

Therefore, contrary to unfavorable conditions in Belarus, CEE NGOs observe the involvement of various communities in Belarus for civic activism. Young leaders, deeply involved in making changes in their immediate surroundings, identified by a Polish NGO, came to observe regional elections and to experience how to activate people and organize them around some local problem. Such activities, according to the organizers, allowed for the creation of "new faces" of pro-democratic change in the future. The goal of the cyclical project is to strengthen and activate local elites in Belarus. It is primarily aimed at promoting activities involving larger groups of citizens and their daily social problems. The project aims to create people in the local community who will become local authorities. Also, as part of the project, Belarusians attend quarterly meetings of the group of leaders, attend workshops in Ukraine, and are given micro grants to implement projects in their small communities.

The principal objective of the selection process to such leadership assistance projects is that leaders, and/or organizations they are affiliated with, do not belong to the ideological structures of the state. Also, some organizations narrow down the group of leaders to demonstrate their leadership potential and activity during election campaigns or immediately after, as well as during specific political events, such as in Ukraine. Sometimes, the organizations choose the leaders from a specific occupational group. For example, in countries like Russia or Belarus, the selected leaders may be social workers already active in civil society and who are potential pro-democracy leaders in local communities. Journalists are another profession frequently targeted. For example, "The Forum of Young Journalists" is a project aimed at exchanging experiences among emerging young journalists in Ukraine who work for student magazines or local newspapers. Within this project, young journalists are trained how to write about political events, and they have to produce various articles, such as a brief analysis of the media market in their country, for example, or on the perception and coverage of European integration issues. Usually, a group of participants consists of fifteen leaders.

The young leaders are also selected for projects based on the carefully prepared recruitment procedure in which either they have to write an essay on a specific topic in addition to documenting their past activities, or are tasked with describing how they envisage the further development of youth organizations and the direction of their work. The recruitment procedure also involves at times testing the knowledge and skills of the leaders. During the project, their knowledge and skills in leadership are meant to be expanded. Sometimes young people are allocated to projects organized in form of camps and educational workshops for youth leaders where, for example they became acquainted with project management and are required to practice it. They are being exposed to practical knowledge from various areas of NGO activity and provide technical knowledge about how the NGO, dealt with issues such as: defining what social activity (definition of the third sector) is, building coalitions and networks of NGOs, defining the mission of the organization, the program of action, and working methods. Young trainees participate in workshops, meetings and study visits with non-governmental organizations, but they also meet other important stakeholders, such as politicians, civic leaders, and people from the business sector. Some leadership programs take a form of scholarships, and it is worth mentioning the Lane Kirkland Scholarship offered to young leaders from Eastern European countries, the Western Balkans, and some Central Asian countries. Kirkland scholars are young leaders from public administration, academia, business, media or politics. The aim of this initiative is to allow the participants learn about Polish experiences with economic, social and political transformation either directly through the education they receive when studying at Polish universities, or indirectly through holding student status and living in Poland. Participants in the program take courses and undertake research in areas of interest, such as economics, management, public administration, business administration, law, and social sciences. The condition of this agreement is that when these young leaders return to their countries after completing the program they must share their experience.

Civic participation

It is believed that in analyzing youth activism we should broaden the scope to include civic engagement as well (Flanagan, 2013). Civic engagement involves joining community groups, volunteering to help others, addressing local problems or leading grassroots efforts and important for the health of democracy and for personal growth and identity during the transition to adulthood (Barrett and Zani, 2015; Flanagan and Levine, 2010). It is believed that youth are more likely to be civically active in their adulthood if they had opportunities to engage in collaborative work and to discuss issues with peers, teachers and parents. The young generation becomes a member of the democratic community through participation, sharing activities and undertaking collective work. Thus, activism is a process that results from the accumulation of knowledge, capital, self-confidence and access to networks and areas where participation is valued and encouraged (Hensby, 2017).

Representatives of CEE NGOs interviewed for this study, see the importance of projects that foster civic participation. These include activities which are focused on helping others within a community, solving a community problem, participation in the life of a community, membership of other non-political organizations, undertaking organized voluntary work, etc. It is believed that participation in projects foster networks of colleagues, creating bonds, norms and thus encourage broader engagement in community affairs as well as leadership skills, political awareness and identity. In other words, rather than focusing on trying to get “better politicians,” these projects focus on producing “better citizens.”

Strengthening youth participation in community

As an example of projects within this category may serve projects which already indicate in their titles that their aim is to support active citizenship and involvement of youth in public life. Czech NGO Agora Central Europe together with People in Need and Transition Online implemented such a project in eight municipalities in the Western Georgia (Ambrolauri, Samtredia, Terjola, Tkibuli, Kutaisi, Chokhatauri, Ozurgeti a Lanchkhuti) between 2011 and 2012. The target groups of the project included secondary-school students, journalism students, secondary-school teachers and local government representatives. The goal of this project was to increase the quality of citizen competencies of Georgian youth and to enable a gradual increase of its influence on public life in Georgia. The main activities included: a democracy summer school, a study visit of Georgian teachers to the Czech Republic and seminars in schools. When asked about the tangible results that allow its impact to be measured, the organization mentioned that students were making evident progress in their democratic skills and teachers and schools were keen on implementing new methods of teaching. Therefore, the organization regarded this project as successful.

Improving civic engagement can also take place through equipping young beneficiaries of the project with practical skills on how to search for local needs, initiate a project that will address the local problems and implement the solutions by means of local resources and support. One example is the Moldovan Youth Civic Engagement Initiative implemented by Polish NGOs, its goal being to ensure wider civic engagement of young activists through their participation in youth volunteer networks that searched for the ways to combat corruption and promote greater transparency at the local level. The young activists were trained to use advocacy strategies and methods as well as working through online activism. A similar project aimed at involving young people in public affairs at the local level was implemented in Bosnia-Hercegovina by the same Czech NGOs in collaboration with partner organizations AEOBiH in BiH, with the support of the Ministry of Foreign Affairs of the Czech Republic between 2012 and 2016. The primary target group of our project is secondary-school students in BiH. It should be said that since the project was aimed at activating young people at the local level. It had an initial phase before its launch which consisted of a youth debating project in order to increase validity and effectiveness of the project. The project also began with an education phase so that the young people could learn the basic functions of municipal policy and its position in the political system of the country. Young people could meet local councilors and members of the city government and engage in a simulated council meeting as well as debates on important local public issues with their peers. The organization measured the effectiveness of the program by checking how well young people could work as a team and think strategically about solving local problems, their knowledge of local politics, and how they could be involved in solving problems.

Encouraging youth engagement in voluntary services

A project of this type is a cyclical European Voluntary Service (EVS) project co-financed by the Youth in Action Program and coordinated in Poland by the Robert Schuman Foundation. As part of the project, Polish volunteers are sent to EU countries and partner countries for six to twelve months, as well as various Polish non-governmental, social and educational organizations in different regions of Poland which accept young people from other countries to do voluntary work. Another project of this type was implemented for the development of the voluntary movement in the eastern part of the Kaliningrad Oblast by one of the Polish NGOs. So, what is the goal of such projects? Volunteering is being perceived as an opportunity for a young person to get to know another EU country, its language, traditions and culture. Additionally, volunteering means the actual participation of young people since within their voluntary work they are often responsible for designing and implementing projects. Organizations with which I spoke about the effectiveness of such programs, gave me many examples of projects implemented by young volunteers in the sphere of activating children and youth, ecology, or media education within which they organized thematic workshops, seminars, multicultural events, and intercultural exchanges. Moreover, during the projects they had a chance to work with various local entities, educational institutions, schools and youth clubs, representatives of religious communities in Poznań and the like. The DMK organization, which often acts as a host for volunteers, believes that voluntary work also helps young people learn team work. The FERSO organization, however, as a result of evaluation of EVS concludes that the project contributes greatly to the development of intercultural dialogue, better mutual understanding between Europeans, and the recognition of common values and tolerance for cultural diversity.

Facilitating linkages between youth groups

The goal of such projects is either to improve the networks between the youth organizations of various types within a given country or to help them be included in cross-border initiatives. An example of the first type of project is "Integration of non-governmental youth organizations in the southern regions of the European part of Russia," implemented by the Polish NGOs. The aim of the implemented projects was the mobilization and integration of young people active in non-governmental organizations in selected districts of the southern part of the Russian Federation and the participants in the project were broadly defined: young activists in non-governmental organizations, informal groups, student organizations, and volunteers. Oftentimes the activities planned went beyond organizing the meetings or seminars on various topics (such as leadership issues, decision-making, teamwork, or strategic planning) but also, in the example of the program on enhancing integration of non-governmental youth organizations in Ukraine, it was a grant contest that allowed the implementation of mini-projects by the mixed groups.

Most projects in this category, however, are about forming linkages between youth organizations in recipients' countries and similar groups in CEE countries or with broadly similar organizations in EU countries. I could name two of the most typical example of these types of integration projects: (1) exchange programs; or (2) implementation of joint programs initiated by the youth organizations. With respect to the exchange programs these are often similar to the exchange program initiated by one of the Polish NGOs. A series of meetings between Polish and Russian youth, joint workshops and tours in Poland and Russia were organized, giving an opportunity to build contacts and knowledge about young people from these two countries, about culture, history and current Polish-Russian relations, but also confront the similarities and differences in the lives of young people in both countries. Examples of such projects can be also be found between Polish or Slovakian and Ukrainian youth as well as young people from Belarus. Slovak NGOs organized study tours to exchange knowledge and experience between young people from Slovakia and Belarusian regional and youth organizations. They met with experts from various NGOs and action groups either in Bratislava or in regional cities in Slovakia with the aim of discussing participation of citizens and civil society in Slovakia, cooperation between the non-governmental sector and state administration as well as regional projects of youth groups. In addition to organizations from CEE and Eastern Europe, youth organizations from Germany or other Western EU countries are also invited, just like the "Moving borders" project where a group of young people from Germany, Poland and Ukraine traveled by train via Berlin, Warsaw, and Lviv and organized a series of meetings and exchange of views for young people along the route.

A series of meetings like this can be devoted to specific topic like the youth exchange program in Georgia financed by the Youth in Action Program, which brings me to the second type of integration project. Within this program a group of young people from Poland, volunteers from the Polish NGO, and from Georgia met in order to tackle a specific topic which was international dialogue through art. Each of the groups involved in engaged in a form of art. For example, a group from Poland specialized in so-called street art. Other groups organized mini photo exhibitions, theatre performances and folk-dance shows. As I understand from the NGOs, the project was successful because these art undertakings and provocative discussions on the role of art in the integration of young people from Europe and the Caucasus proved to be extremely productive and resulted in new ideas and the establishment of many new friendships. Also, in a similar way, the project "Youth can make a difference" matched the youth organizations from Western and Eastern Europe with the goal of helping them prepare and implement common projects on specific topics.

Additionally, forming linkages between youth organizations in recipients' countries with similar groups in CEE countries or with broadly defined groups in the EU countries, may also take a more creative form, such as Eurobus, which has become an annual event following the celebration of Europe Days in Ukraine. Since 2007, the PAUCI Foundation became a partner of the project and supported the project's implementation in Poland and Ukraine. The idea is that a team of young people from the EU and Ukraine travel across Ukraine for over two weeks during which they visit towns or villages to celebrate Europe Days, integrate, and conduct training sessions for other young people. Young people involved in this initiative not only disseminate information about the EU but also about youth programs as well as help launch initiatives proposed by young people, with the support of the local community. Given the success of the program, in the opinion of the organization, the program was extended to Moldova with similar types of action reaching activists, young leaders, and in general young people there.

On a larger scale than the others is the RAZOM project, implemented by the PAUCI organization, which is an exchange program with Ukrainian young people. Every year young people from both countries get together and work on common projects. Within this initiative, young people from Ukrainian and Polish partner schools are engaged in joint activities of different kinds, from soccer games to protecting the common cultural heritage. As a representative of PAUCI organization said, "these are maybe not ambitious projects; but they mobilize young people to do something together and learn about each other and get teachers interested in some initiatives, as well."[3]

Capacity building of youth organizations

Civic participation is about the engagement young people in solving a community problem, and participation in the life of local community, it is also about membership of organizations, forming social networks, which in turn contributes to building social capital (Norris, 2002; Putnam, 2000). The role of organizations and their potential to influence young people is well documented by the researchers. Organizations, community groups, voluntary association, and various groups that consist of neighbors, friends, workers are believed to be capable of encouraging political engagement, provide social network and through cooperative actions generate more social trust, and social trust in turn generates more cooperation and social capital, which is defined as "connection among individuals—social networks and the norms of reciprocity and trustworthiness that arise from them" (Putnam, 2000). Norris (2002) points out that this is a structural as well as a cultural phenomenon. It is cultural because it is about social norms.

In other words, involvement or membership of NGOs and various associations is a variable which assesses young people's commitment to democratic life (Newton, 1999). Nevertheless, one must also consider criticism of the role of NGOs. In the 1980s and 1990s, there was the NGO-ization of civil society (Howell and Pearce, 2001; Lewis, 2010) and the criticism that NGOs have gone too far in accommodation with states and funders. The NGOs have come to embrace the material logics because of resource dependence on foreign donors. Other NGOs co-opted by the state and also dependent on funding from national governments (Alcock and Kendall, 2011; Lewis, 2005). The emergence of various protest rallies which took place on Maidan Nezalezhnosti Square drew attention to informal movements, as phenomena detached from NGOs. However, Glasius and Ishkanian (2015) found that activists rely on NGOs for technical support—meeting space, offices, printing—as well for expertise, information, legal aid, and their links with government. Thus, activists taking part in street protests and loose informal civic groups relate to NGOs and treat them "like a resource center that always exists" (Glasius and Ishkanian, 2015). They find that the boundaries between the formal NGOs and informal groups of activists are blurred since there is much cross-over and collaboration.

These scholarly findings also strengthen the role of organizations and question whether it is possible to become an activist without being involved in an NGO. For young people, associational life is an important experience of democratic decision-making outside school. These NGOs help students reflect on their role as citizens, and can help them develop democratic attitudes even if their schools do not create opportunities for democratic experience and developing democratic attitudes.

Given the above, I have found that a lot of projects target youth organizations to strengthen their organizational governance; strategic planning; the management of finances, people, and projects; and to improve publicity and fundraising, in other words: everything what youth organizations need to survive, adapt, grow, and simply serve their beneficiaries. For example, representatives of Ukrainian youth organizations were trained by Slovak experts as part of the project "Support for Non-Governmental Organizations in Eastern Ukraine" in the area of project management donor organizations, international cooperation of NGOs, as well as the transformation process and the establishment and functioning of the non-governmental sector in Slovakia. Moreover, the project was not only to provide knowledge but also to create opportunities for mutual cooperation of NGOs from the eastern regions of Ukraine.

This type of project was also popular in Ukraine in the mid-2000s among Polish NGOs under the banner "Support for third sector in Southern Ukraine" which was aimed at strengthening the capacity building of local NGOs in southern Ukraine and the exchange of experiences between Polish and Ukrainian NGOs. Participants of the project were representatives of local NGOs and initiative groups from selected regions of Ukraine, who participated in the exchange of experiences during study visits to Poland and Ukraine. A study visit was held in Lublin, Poland, where ten people participated. As part of the visit, the participants took part in a series of meetings with NGOs, local officials, and schools. The courses in which Ukrainian participants representing youth organizations took part ranged from "How to Teach Your Target Group" or "Leadership and Teamwork" to "Promoting the Educational Success of Children and Youth."

Polish NGOs also put a strong emphasis in their projects directed toward youth organizations in Ukraine on the development of NGO cooperation with the media (including the presence of NGOs on the Internet), local authority (what is successful cooperation with the government, evaluation of advisory and consultative bodies, cooperation in solving important social problems), as well as volunteering. Ukrainian youth organizations that were embraced by the projects received visits from CEE NGOs who were monitoring the changes and local actions. As part of the visit, the visiting experts had a chance to get acquainted with activities of supported Ukrainian NGOs, and their cooperation with local stakeholders.

Representatives of Polish NGOs believe that Ukrainian youth organizations have grown and become more self-sustained and well-linked regionally and nationally as well as with Western donors and organizations. However, there is still a lot to be done to improve conditions of youth organizations in Moldova. The Czech NGOs with Moldovan partners took a lead in implementing projects that aimed at supporting the transformation of Moldovan society. Within one of the projects, the People in Need (PIN) organization, aimed to build the capacity of small civic initiatives in selected districts of Moldova. In the framework of the project, the participants, mainly representative of youth organizations, took part in training focusing on civic participation in public affairs, project management and work with the media. Additionally, youth organizations presented their ideas of projects, and a few small projects of local civic initiatives were selected and supported based on a call for proposals open to all civic initiatives. The projects implemented by youth organizations focused on local issues such as strengthening women's participation in community, support for disabled children or renovation and improvement of educational infrastructure. The youth organizations that were awarded these small grants were required to engage the public and local public authorities in the projects in various ways ranging from public meetings to financial participation. Representatives of the PIN organization felt that the project was a success because all planned activities were successfully implemented and the expected results and objectives of the project were reached. More importantly, all supported youth organizations from Moldova that participated in this project also received a long-term technical support from PIN after the end of the project.

Support for youth organizations in Moldova and Georgia is also driven mainly by Czech and Slovak NGOs. In general, while promoting development of civil society within their programs they mostly pay attention to the promotion of youth initiatives and emerging youth non-governmental organizations in Georgia and Moldova. From 2008 to 2017, Czech and Slovak NGOs has financially supported over eighty youth civic initiatives and NGOs in Georgia, which have undertaken more than 100 projects to promote human rights, protect the environment and integrate people with disabilities into society. Slovak NGOs, especially the Pontis Foundation, have also been active in Belarus since 2000 when it provided support to youth organizations prior to and during the election campaigns of 2001. Later on, the Pontis Foundation was engaged in fostering public debate on socioeconomic issues, with strong involvement of the Belarusian expert community, in order to reinforce their research capacity which would positively influence public policymaking processes in the country. Since 2006, we mostly focused on the topic of public policy development in Belarus rather than supporting youth organizations. Similarly, support for youth organizations as such is rare in Russia today.

Over the past twenty years, youth organizations from Poland, Russia and Ukraine have gathered a lot of interesting experiences and have worked out many interesting working methods in their fields of activity (especially in youth work, social initiatives and ecology). There are also new standards of NGO activity (openness, transparency and broad involvement in the local community). The aim of the projects has been to promote cross-border cooperation and exchanges of experience between youth organizations from Russia, Poland and Ukraine, and to provide a platform for exchanging experiences and best practices of non-governmental organizations. The activities' planned writing projects included: a study visit to get to know the leaders of Russian and Ukrainian youth organizations in order to induce cooperation between them; seminars on various topics important for the youth organizations in three countries, as well as meetings for a larger number of NGOs' representatives in order to get acquainted with the activities of organizations working in the fields of volunteering, social assistance and rehabilitation, civic education, environmental protection, legal protection, monitoring and election observation, as well as in the areas of support and regional development of the media. The activities in the last two years were very limited. Unfortunately, non-governmental organizations from Poland, Russia and Ukraine do not share a lot of common activities and projects to share experience or initiate new cross-border projects.

Social and economic equality

Welzel (2013) equates human development with the empowerment of people to exert their freedoms. But, in the first place, ordinary people need the resources that make them capable to practice freedoms. They must be in place before democracy can effectively practiced. These resources are knowledge, time and skills, but also money. Very early studies of political participation have reported that people with higher socioeconomic status tend to be more active in politics (Barnes *et al.*, 1979; Verba *et al.*, 1978; Verba and Nie, 1972). Economic status seems to be an important predictor of participation. Growing material resources empower ordinary people (give rise to emancipative values), and make them more capable of launching any activity (Welzel and Inglehart, 2008) and thus more capable of struggling for freedom. Economic development means also better access to higher levels of education, which in turn leads to individual autonomy, and a greater critical attitude toward institutions (Inglehart, 1999). Knack and Keefer (1997) also find that civic engagement is linked to economic development as well as subjective-well-being. The transition process is accompanied often by worsening macroeconomic conditions, declining social trust, which weakens civil society development, therefore economic empowerment of young people in these countries is important for democracy to grow.

Although projects that are aimed at empowering youth especially in poor local communities are relatively small as compared to all the types mentioned above, it is worth acknowledging them. The rationale behind their implementation is a belief among CEE NGOs that economic empowerment can enhance the action of young people. The goal of a project like the Kharkov incubator for entrepreneurship is to teach young people entrepreneurship, and promote social and economic inclusion as examples of the projects below show.

Improving social inclusion and participation of youth with special needs

This type of youth projects is directed toward organizations, parents, and schools that either deal with such people or need to facilitate the integration of children with special needs school environments and local society. These projects were often organized as seminars, as was the case in several project organized by Slovak NGOs in Bosnia-Herzegovina or Polish NGOs in Georgia, on facilitating the learning process of youth with special needs, but also to help young people to become independent by developing a special infrastructure, therapy and rehabilitation system. The themes of such seminars and training were mainly focused on the elimination of prejudices, intolerance, discrimination and the description of the needs of socially or otherwise disadvantaged children. There also projects directed toward young people with a specific kind of disability. Polish NGOs carried out several projects to improve the quality of assistance for visually impaired young people in Georgia. The activities planned within these projects included a series of lectures introducing knowledge of assistance given to the blind, as well as typhoid therapeutic training in Poland to improve the knowledge of Georgian typhoid instructors and other specialists. The projects also involve people and organizations in recipient countries dealing with the visually impaired, so that they could improve educational campaigns for children, adolescents and adults, and present the problems of to raise awareness of the problems of the blind and visually impaired. In addition to training and workshops designed for activists from non-governmental organizations and institutions, activities planned within the projects directed toward young people with disabilities included the exchange of knowledge and experience through visits to CEE local governmental institutions, NGOs, social welfare homes, schools, treatment centers, health care institutions, and meetings with social activists, experts, teachers, people with disabilities, socially excluded people, workers, students, therapists, and educators.

A better inclusion of young people, in the opinion of CEE NGOs, starts with providing a better access to education in childhood, regardless of social and economic status and health. For example, the project entitled "Expanding the successful model of inclusive early childhood education in Moldova," which was undertaken in cooperation with an elementary school in Moldova established mechanisms, which facilitated the access of children to education. The outputs of such project were documents such as an internal manual for inclusive kindergarten, educational curricula and standards of inclusive preschool education. Moreover, thanks to the Czech NGOs and their partners, the kindergarten provided the transportation and professional care (physiotherapy, speech therapy, etc.) for children with special needs. The project also included training, focusing on both the kindergarten staff and the parents of children with disabilities. The project aims to fulfill the obligatory obligations of Moldova to provide compulsory education for inclusive education. Additionally, the reconstruction and supply of equipment for kindergartens took place.

Projects supporting vulnerable youth from families with many children or incomplete families in poor communities or those in difficult life situations belong to this category, such as projects organized by a Czech NGO in selected regions of Western Georgia. How did the NGOs measure the impact of such programs? I was told that organizations through their local partners traced the level of integration of youth in society. Another important consquence of the project for them was the increased capacities of local authorities, which provide social services to vulnerable groups, and realize that the program aiming at economic development of this region is important as well; furthermore, measuring the increase of awareness among those who were embraced by the project, as well as the general public, about the problems of vulnerable groups, and tangible solutions that they implemented.

Strengthening the resources of communities

Some projects in this category also include material support for youth in poor rural communities and bridging the gap in order to ensure a fairer distribution of the benefits of economic growth. When asked about the reasons for such a project I was told that by providing resources they want people to focus on other aspects of their lives and utilize these resources in order to be capable of doing other things. Moreover, resources improve their status and empower them materially. For example, since 2006, the PAUCI Foundation has implemented "Support for Rural Schools in Western Ukraine" which aims to upgrade facilities in rural schools located close to the border between Poland and Ukraine. Concerning one of the schools in Western Ukraine, the organization reports that the following achievements of the project were possible with the support of business partners, as well as involvement of the local community. These included a new gym and a set of sports and tourist equipment, computer labs, better adaptation of classrooms to provide art, as well as dance and music courses, the purchase of school bus, and new set of furniture. Within this program, the best students in the supported schools were also entitled to grants in order to continue their education in the junior high school in the regional capital.

Other projects in this youth assistance category of are those of Slovak and Czech NGOs which are aimed at supporting access to safe water and sanitation in kindergartens in southern Moldova. This project was a reaction to the challenges of insufficient access to drinking water and to safe sanitary infrastructure of the rural population in Moldova. The project's goal was to increase the quality of living conditions in two rural districts by achieving the following objectives: increasing access to safe drinking water and sanitation in kindergartens, raising communities' awareness in hygiene and the environment and promoting inclusive education in eight kindergartens in the same districts. The representatives of the NGOs believe that the objective has been met, because the project has addressed the need to enhance personal hygiene standards among the local population and the lack of preschool education opportunities for children with special educational needs through various activities. During these project activities, water purification systems and waste water treatment systems were installed in eight kindergartens. In addition, a campaign was conducted as well as awareness workshops on hygiene and the environment for staff and children in kindergartens and for their parents. Moreover, the success of the project was due to the fact that the impact of these activities was scaled up from individual to national level thanks to the wide range of project activities.

Other examples include a series of projects under the title "Modernization of the Public Education System in Ukraine" which consist of series of reconstruction activities such as reconstruction of the kindergarten, school building and the student dormitory, and supplying IT equipment for universities and schools. Resolution 167 of the Czech government on April 12, 2014 focused on providing Ukraine with help and support during the democratic transformation between 2014 and 2016. The main focus of development aid has been on the education sector. By following the standards of European Union the education system in Ukraine went through a period of many reforms and new legislative adjustments. Apart from legislative and system reforms the Ukrainian education system lacks funds for the operation of educational institutions evacuated from the war zone such as, Donetsk National University (now in Vinnytsia) and Slavyansk (originally in Donetsk).

Finally, this type of assistance considers young people who have experienced war. CEE NGOs seem to understand that the country context and current political climate matter for young people to be active. Thus, some projects directed toward young people in Ukraine take into consideration the ongoing military conflict taking place in eastern Ukraine. One example of such a project is one implemented by Polish NGOs intended for young Ukrainians who had to flee because of the conflict to other parts of Ukraine and reintegrate themselves in a new community. Additionally, as a result of war in eastern Ukraine, the Ukrainian education system lacks funds for the operation of evacuated education institutions located in areas controlled by pro-Russian separatists which were moved to areas under Ukrainian administration. Much of the equipment of those institutions was confiscated by separatists. According to the Ukrainian Ministry of Education and Science, seventeen state universities have been evacuated.

Based on the discussion presented above as well as examples of projects, I have allocated the youth assistance projects to the following categories: (1) Civic Participation; (2) Political Participation; (3) Civic Education; (4) Economic Empowerment; (6??5??) Capacity Building of Youth Organizations. Figure 3.1

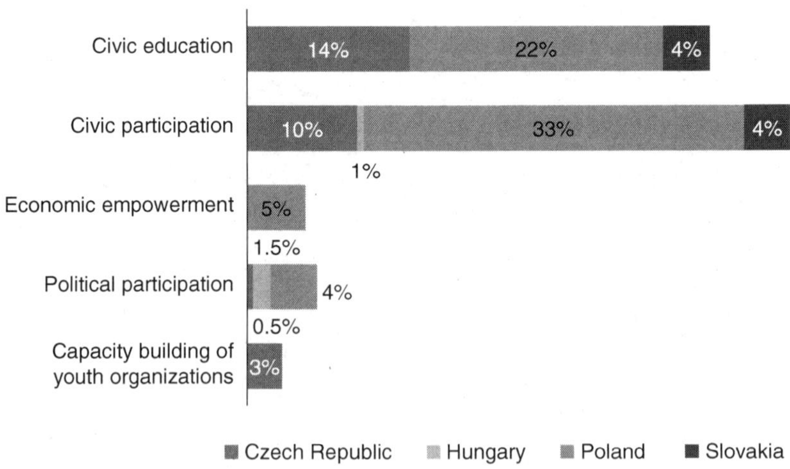

Figure 3.1 Types of CEE NGO youth projects in recipient countries 2000–2017.

shows almost half of all types of youth projects were aimed at strengthening civic participation of young people, and 40 percent consisted of civic education. Whereas Hungarian, Polish and Slovak NGOs prefer to focus on enhancing young people's civic activism in local communities in the first place, Czech NGOs focus mainly on civic education. Civic education projects, as compared to other types of youth projects in given recipient countries, predominate in Moldova and Ukraine. Civic participation, however, predominates in Belarus, in partnership with schools.

Conclusion

In this chapter, by exploring the projects, I have embarked on demonstrating the way CEE NGOs support youth and whether youth political and civic participation, as well as attitudes toward democracy, are intended to be facilitated and increased within the NGOs projects. It also shows whether CEE NGOs take into account the context of the recipient country, especially in countries struggling with democracy.

Youth projects in the post-communist region focus on democratization in a political cultural perspective according to which what makes democracy, and its institutions succeed and flourish, are the social foundations of democracy.[4] Specifically, it is social capital, engaged citizenship, and participation that are crucial for democratic political culture, for the development of democracy, and for shaping its institutions and legitimizing the system. It seems that a driving factor considered by CEE NGOs is civic engagement and the role of such projects is to build a sense of responsibility towards others and overall individual empowerment by making them feel that they can influence changes in their lives as well as the community to which they belong. CEE NGOs bypass democracy-assistance projects and aim to build social capital by making people more tolerant towards others, and thus hoping to enrich and empower the lives of citizens.

Active young people are important for democracy, and their activity building starts with civic education. Civic education, i.e., activities aimed to teach citizens of recipient countries basic values, knowledge, and skills relating to democracy, has become a popular form of promoting democracy by Poland, the Czech Republic, and Slovakia in countries that are currently struggling with democracy. Active, aware, informed and determined citizens are important for building and maintaining democracy. In this study we have explored how citizen's participation can be ignited among the "functionaries of democracy" (Ekiert, Kubik and Vachudova, 2007): the young people. Since authoritarian and democratizing countries often lack sufficient sources, programs and overall youth empowerment mechanisms, we have taken a closer look at the efforts of external forces, especially young democratic countries that engage in supporting democratic values and behaviors and sharing their democratization experience. Civic education activities included: training programs for teachers, headteachers and other educators with the goal of teaching young people citizenship values and to bring democracy to schools; education for democracy; forming partnerships between formal and non-formal education providers (creating opportunities within the program for schools to partner with youth organizations to run joint citizenship education programs on various issues, such as human rights, immigration, the environment); and supporting education reforms.

However, promoting youth participation is not only about raising awareness and knowledge but also about promoting the cooperation of young people with local authorities, the creation of real mechanisms of engagement and capacity building. CEE NGOs seem to understand that as well. Projects concerned with political participation included supporting dialogue and helping youth to build or improve spaces for young people to discuss key political decisions with local/city/town youth councils; strengthening public opinion-making skills of young people to take action relating to political activity (elections campaigns that address young people directly, finding more opportunities and mechanisms for participatory policymaking across different fields, such as introducing quotas or training in public speaking); improving monitoring, i.e., training in governance assessments, assessment tools to examine how adequately national policies respond to youth concerns. Youth assistance efforts within economic empowerment included projects aimed at empowering youth especially in poor local communities, teaching young people entrepreneurship skills, and promoting inclusion, as well as material aid to support school renovations and all types of infrastructure projects. Finally, capacity building included projects aimed at developing and strengthening the skills, processes and resources of youth organizations so that they can better serve the needs of young people.

I find that NGOs from Central and Eastern European countries, which are at the forefront of democracy assistance, attach great importance to the development of local and participatory community life in which young people should play an important role. It seems that a driving factor considered by CEE NGOs is civic engagement and the role of such projects is to build a sense of responsibility towards others and to overall individual empowerment by making them feel that they can influence changes in their lives as well as in the community to which they belong. CEE NGOs emphasize in their program the need to educate and activate young people to be more socially responsible for their local community, region and country. Civic participation youth assistance included teaching how to create an organization, activities focusing on youth-led media and organizations, youth rights and social inclusion, as well as general activities focusing on youth activism.

It comes as no surprise that CEE NGOs convey in their projects directed toward young people in other post-communist countries these types of norms and values since, as discussed in the previous chapter, CEE NGOs were embedded in liberal thinking. These norms are norms of engaged citizenship (participation in political and civic life); meliorism—a belief in human progress and the ability to make the world better place through actions; social and political responsibility in local and national affairs; participation in political and civic life; keeping a watch on government to prevent any abuses of power; respecting rights of minorities and helping those worse off in order to prevent polarization of the country.[5]

The overview of the projects also shows that CEE NGOs operate in a local context knowing that the universal approach to youth programs fails to recognize the importance of the context in which they are applied, and those projects implemented are in the form of partnership with organizations in target countries to help reinterpret social, and even political and economic contexts and reshape them.

Notes

1 An interview with Victoria Takacs from the Foundation for Democratic Youth (July 14, 2015).
2 The source of this information is "People in Need. Annual Report 2013" obtained during a meeting with Pavla Štefanová, Regional coordinator for Southern Caucasus, Eastern Europe, Western Balkans, and Mongolia.
3 Interview with Jan Piekło, Director of Poland-Ukrainian Cooperation Foundation (PAUCI), June 30, 2008, Warsaw, Poland.
4 For more on cultural foundations of democracy see Inglehart and Welzel (2003), and the linkage between social capital and tolerance see Morgan and Streb (2001).
5 I find it very similar to the definition of liberal values in Bolzendahl and Coffé (2009, 2013); Dalton (2006, 2008) and Gray (1995).

4 The need to provide democracy assistance to youth in target countries

Many of the new democracies in the post-communist region have not yet been consolidated, and some countries have regressed to their previous unstable democratic system. Although the older generation in post-communist countries has not experienced a long tradition of stable democracy, the younger generation is growing without ever having experienced communism and takes democracy or some type of hybrid regime as the only system in which they are growing up, with the exception of Belarusian youth who live in an authoritarian system. Through extensive interviews with representatives of the youth organizations and young people, I have learned that different types of participation in social and political life are simply not equally available to all young people, and there are discrepancies not only across countries but also within countries. I am fully aware of the fact that in order to understand youth activism one must take into account the context of the country and trends shaping political participation in these countries and opportunities and spaces created for the citizens. Given unfavorable political and socioeconomic circumstances for young people to be active citizens in Bosnia-Herzegovina, Georgia and Ukraine, one could say that young people need to be supported via democracy assistance programs.

Nevertheless, the effectiveness of any strategy of societal actors in transnational network depends not only on the political structure of the target state, but also on its social and cultural norms and beliefs. Moreover, a democratizing state is more than democratic institutions and laws. It cannot be sustained without certain human and social values (beliefs and principles). If young people are politically active there is a greater chance that they will be in favor of democracy. Also, any kind of social participation in form of membership of civic organizations leads to a better opinion of democracy and its features in general. The argument also goes the other way around—the more people support democracy, the more likely they will be willing to participate both at the civic and political level.

Therefore, in this chapter I explore concepts, beliefs and values of young people, potential beneficiaries of youth programs who are most likely to be targeted by the NGOs in recipient countries that implement youth projects and compare them with young people from Central and Eastern European countries. I focus on how young people think about political phenomena, about what democracy means to them, whether the younger generation is knowledgeable about politics and the democratic processes in general, and whether it is motivated to participate. This chapter examines these questions drawing on my own survey to measure youth attitudes and political and civic engagement, that was based on research on youth participation as well as inspired by existing surveys, such as the International Social Survey Program and the World Values Survey.

Despite differences in the detail, democracy has become a universal value (Ferrin and Kriesi, 2016; Norris, 2011). Therefore, in line with these findings in the literature that most people have strong preferences for living in democracy and consider democracy to be important (having a broad and far-reaching understanding of democracy), I expect to find that there is no difference between youth conceptions of democracy in CEE and EE countries. I believe that these conceptions are unrelated to the country in which young people live and do not depend on contextual factors, because of the diffusion of democratic ideas and concepts through various channels. However, as researchers point out, it is important to distinguish between views and evaluations of democracy, in other words between democratic values—support for democracy—and confidence in democratic institutions (Klingemann, 1999). Although democracy seems to be generally demanded, this universal consensus seems to hold only for the abstract idea of democracy and ordinary citizens disagree on the specific democratic arrangements and their individual political attitudes vary, which affects the political culture (Welzel, 2013). Therefore, I expect to find differences in citizens' evaluations of democracy between young people in post-communist countries, also in the levels of social trust, which is a cultural dimension (Norris, 2011), and also differences in the level of political and civic engagement.

Individual political attitudes, social and political trust, political efficacy norms of citizenship, as well as interest in politics and overall engagement make up a political culture. Democratic political culture includes three measures: interest in politics, confidence in political institutions, and satisfaction with democracy (Horowitz *et al.*, 2003). Features of social life, networks, norms, and trust, allow participants to act together and pursue shared objectives. Norris (2011) points out that this is a structural as well as a cultural phenomenon. It is cultural because it is about social norms. What people think and feel has implications for social capital, which in turn is important for democracy, according to Putnam's theory of social capital. Decline in social trust and civic engagement, cannot be considered a failure in regime performances only, but can be explained in cultural terms. For example, it has been suggested that today's youth are not interested in politics any more, and mistrust increases further, excluding them from decision-making processes, which further undermines the legitimacy of democracy. Faced with a political system that does not respond to or reflect them, young people are trapped in a vicious circle of disengagement. How can this circle be broken? It can be broken by searching for better ideas, a better relationship with democratic life, and for young people to be engaged through campaigning for causes that matter to them, volunteering and social movements, online and offline, beyond parties and elections, through membership of youth organization, protests, petitions, or advocating for specific changes, etc. There is an impressive body of research documenting that engagement of youth is positively related to their civic involvement in adulthood. However, it can be problematic not only in countries where the democratic process is relatively new and still unstable but also in many developed democracies. Therefore, it is important to support individuals and empower them, and thus create a culture of democracy, where citizens want to take responsibility, participate in the life of the community and have a voice that is listened to.

To empower youth, it is necessary to understand properly how young people participate in political life nowadays, what participation and activism means to them, and on the basis of this knowledge, which might be useful for practitioners to learn how to educate and activate youth effectively through democracy assistance programs. Thus, the goal of this chapter is to provide insights about young people's views, opinions and participation.

Collecting data, sampling participants and survey administration

The surveys were conducted by means of an established NGO collaborative network. There were two main reasons for administering the surveys especially in Bosnia-Herzegovina, Georgia and Ukraine through NGOs. First, the purpose of this study was to understand better the need for youth support in recipient countries. NGOs which were partners in this project are youth organizations obtained funding for their projects from abroad, inter alia from CEE countries, and are directing their activities towards young people. Thus, by surveying young people, who were sampled by the NGOs, not only the potential project beneficiaries were reached but also recipients of funding from CEE. Second, given the fact that big cities became attractive places for young people, mainly capital cities, and large cities close to borders, and also that different local and national contexts across countries mattered, the surveys conducted by NGOs from various regions ensured greater representativeness. By contacting NGOs from different regions of Bosnia-Herzegovina, Georgia, or Ukraine, variation among young people was obtained within these three democratizing countries.

The NGOs that were selected to conduct surveys are organizations which were recommended by the Czech, Slovak, Hungarian and Polish organizations engaged in democracy assistance programs, as presented in the previous chapter. NGOs in Bosnia-Herzegovina, Georgia and Ukraine were mentioned by the CEE organizations because they have either similar program orientations or have worked together on the implementation of joint projects directed toward young people sharing experience, technical and personal participation in the fulfillment of joint projects, and provision of logistics and transportation. One of the organizations in Ukraine, was even created by a former participant in one of the Polish long-term youth projects.

For the sake of this study, it was important to find organizations in recipient countries that are engaged in non-formal education about democracy, and in activities aimed at promoting participation and active citizenship among young people. Learning about the importance of democracy does not occur solely in organized settings (Flanagan, 2013; Nieuwelink *et al.*, 2016). Civic organizations provide more possibilities to take the initiative and to gain democratic experiences than formal schooling (Biesta *et al.*, 2009). As Putnam (2000) claimed, civil society organizations are "free schools for democracy" and other researchers following him demonstrated that those who participate in civil society tend to have more positive attitudes towards democratic values (Fung, 2003). Young people in Ukraine, Georgia and Bosnia-Herzegovina are exposed to, and are often recruited by, such NGOs. However, we do not know who these people are, what their views and evaluations of democracy are and how how they perceive social and political systems as well as the role of the citizens, and whether and how they engage in politics. However, before I present potential youth beneficiaries of democracy assistance programs, it is worth introducing these twelve organizations (four from each country) that conducted surveys.

The CEE NGOs that were selected work in the field of youth assistance and are members of umbrella organizations affiliated with the Confederation for Cooperation of Relief and Development NGOs (CONCORD), such as the Czech FoRS, the Hungarian HAND, Grupa Zagranica from Poland, and Platforma MVRO from Slovakia. The survey conducted by these NGOs was named Youth Participation Study (YPS) and was conducted between January and April 2017 (see Appendix). Four NGOs from each country were asked to conduct fifty surveys in their regions. The original version of the survey was produced in English and then it was translated into three languages by one of the partner organizations in a given country. The questionnaires were distributed via NGO staff asked to give the young people the paper version of the survey, and then to enter all records into the online survey created at the website of this research project Demoaid (http://demoaid.amu.edu.pl). Given the nature of this distribution process, it was difficult to calculate response rates. In the end, the study drew on the sample of 1,247 respondents. In the final part of the survey, the respondents were asked about their gender, age, education, the education of their parents, place of residence and about their perception of their financial situation. Although this is not a random sample, this does not limit our ability to determine the relationships between the variables of interest with confidence. Generalization of statistics referring to the general population, however, should be done with some caution especially since that the sample consists of young people who are potential beneficiaries of democracy assistance projects since they were reached by NGOs who implement such programs. This means that they should have common characteristics that are typical for this group of young people, but which arc different from the characteristics of the broader population of young people. Nevertheless, the organizations were asked to ensure that the sample is representative—that these young people either already participated in the programs led by this organization with cooperation with counterparts from CEE, or are more likely to be selected once the program is implemented.

Table 4.1 Profile of NGOs from Bosnia-Herzegovina, Georgia, and Ukraine and the CEE countries implementing youth projects

Vision and goals	• Motivating youth to develop their personal potential as individuals and responsible citizens. • Fostering active participation of young citizens in civil society through promoting volunteering • Promoting human rights, tolerance, cultural diversity, social inclusion, anti-racism, gender equality, equal conditions for people with disabilities • Promoting non-formal methods of education • Contributing to the strengthening of civil society through the support to young people and youth organizations • Supporting collective actions of youth groups and NGOs (mutual cooperation and networking) • Building friendly environment for the development of young people through establishing a framework for effective relations with the governmental and profit sector • Empowering youth to actively participate in the transformation of the society • Empowering youth to take an equal and active role in the public and private spheres • Raising awareness of entrepreneurship among young people in order to combat poverty and unemployment • Providing a platform for exchanging opinions and experiences of the topics young people find difficult to discuss or have difficulties exploring
Main activities	Organizing festivals, training courses, seminars, youth exchanges, conferences, local activities, debates
Target	Young people aged 16–30 Schoolchildren Students Vulnerable young people and young people with social disabilities
Partners	Various types of non-governmental NGOs in country and abroad Schools, universities Educators working in primary and secondary education Local authorities Other organizations and institutions working with children and young people (e.g., orphanages, centers for disabled children)

Table 4.2 Youth survey demographics: balance statistics (country and gender)

	Female	*Male*	*Total*
Target countries			
Bosnia-Herzegovina	107	45	152
Georgia	111	87	198
Ukraine	128	72	200
Total	**346**	**204**	**550**
CEE countries			
Czech Republic	94	123	217
Poland	131	100	231
Slovakia	61	39	100
Hungary	71	78	149
Total	**357**	**340**	**697**
TOTAL	**703**	**544**	**1,247**

Beginning with balance across country, we see that respondents were not evenly distributed by country across the treatment categories, but the differences were not vast. In general, more respondents came from the CEE countries than the three target countries. Also, there were more females responding to the survey in the target countries than males, whereas in case of respondents from the CEE countries we can observe a rough balance on gender. Additionally, young people were asked about their parents' education, financial situation, and residence. We can observe a balance on parents' education since respondents from all countries are children of adults with secondary education or higher, with an average financial situation, although young people from the CEE countries were significantly more likely to come homes which were better off financially (or at least perceived that they did) and from less densely populated.

It is important to introduce the Youth Participation Survey in more detail (see also Appendix). The survey sought to measure young people's views on political systems, especially democracy (Part I), opinion and feelings about political and social life as well as interest in public affairs in their countries (Part II), and then, in the final part, to measure young people's current political and social participation as well as potential participation (Part III). In Part III, young people were asked about their current and intended participation with the aim of explaining not only *how* people participate and also *why* they participate or do not participate. Young people were asked about voting and the reasons why they vote or do not vote. They were also asked about other forms of political participation (demonstrations, petitions, meetings, being members of political parties etc.) as well as about social participation by asking them to indicate their engagement or lack of engagement in the activities of civic organizations. Finally, knowing that often young peoples' participation is the derivative of the political situation and opportunities and spaces for young people to participate, two hypothetical questions were asked to understand better what would they do and how would they behave towards the government and officials in certain situations.

Table 4.3 Youth survey demographics: balance statistics (social status)

	Mother's education (mean)	*Father's education (mean)*	*Financial situation (mean)*	*Residence (mean)*
Target countries	**4.10**	**4.50**	**3.33**	**4.49**
Bosnia and Herzegovina	3.60	4.23	3.30	3.95
Georgia	4.43	4.65	3.25	5.28
Ukraine	4.25	4.67	3.43	4.23
CEE countries	**4.30**	**4.44**	**3.65**	**3.90**
Czech Republic	4.08	4.24	3.48	3.45
Poland	3.47	3.64	3.91	3.15
Slovakia	4.13	4.37	3.45	3.46
Hungary	5.51	5.52	3.73	5.59
Diff. Means	**0.20**	**0.06**	**0.32*****	**0.59*****

Notes
Entries are mean scores of parents' education on 1–8 (1 Incomplete secondary education; 2 Secondary education; 3 Secondary vocational/Technical; 4 Incomplete higher education; 5 Higher education; 6 Technical higher education; 7 Academic degree; 8 I do not know/hard to say); Financial situation on 1–6; (1 We live very frugally we do not have enough money even for basic needs; 2 We live modestly—we manage our budget very carefully to provide what we need on a daily basis; 3 We live averagely—we have enough money for day-to-day expenses, but we need to save for major purchases; 4 We live well—we have enough to live on without special savings; 5 We live very well —we can afford luxuries; 6 No answer), and Residence on 1–8 (1 Village; 2 Town of up to 20,000 inhabitants; 3 Urban area of 20,000–50,000 inhabitants; 4 Urban area of 50,000–200,000 inhabitants; 5 Urban area of 200,000–500,000 inhabitants; 6 Urban area of 500,000–1 million inhabitants; 7 Urban area of 1–5 million inhabitants; 8 Urban area with more than 5 million inhabitants). Mean differences were calculated with additional t-test for equality of means, ***p=<0.001.

There were twenty questions in the survey with eight questions concerning respondents' demographics and social status for statistical purposes only. All respondents were ensured about confidentiality. In Part I of the survey respondents were asked to specify the importance on a Likert scale ranging from 1 (Very important) to 4 (Not important), as well as to indicate the agreement with the statements also on a Likert scale ranging from 1 (Fully agree) to 4 (Fully disagree). In another part of the questionnaire, young people were asked to answer if they are proud to be a citizen of their country and in a multiple-choice question to choose the things which they were most proud of. There was also a multiple-choice question asking their opinion on what is the most important for a young person in their country to enter politics successfully. Young people indicated what should be the citizens' obligations and activities by choosing a number from a 4-point Likert scale from Fully agree (1) to Fully disagree (4). They were also asked to specify how they update themselves about the public affairs and how often by choosing frequencies (Nearly every day, About once a week, From time to time, Never) that was most relevant for them.

Youth understanding and evaluation of democracy

In this section, I am taking a closer look at the responses of young people from three target countries in order to analyze views and opinions and perceptions of these young people regarding the political system they have, democracy and trust toward political institutions. Although I am mainly interested in looking for similar patters across three nations and for analyzing the individual-level correlates of views and evaluations, such as socioeconomic factors and political attitudes, I am also comparing the results with responses of young people from the CEE countries.

Following the recent distinction in comparative politics literature between *views* and *evaluations*, I have analyzed in the first place views of young people on democracy that refer to their normative ideal of democracy, and evaluations of democracy, meaning their assessment of the way the democratic principles have been implemented in their countries (Ferrin and Kriesi, 2016). The survey questions regarding the views of democracy (support for the ideas about what democracy should be) and evaluations (satisfaction with democracy) are grounded in political theory and democratization literatures, and were consulted with various public opinion polls, such as Eurobarometer, Latinobaromenter, Asianbarometer, World Values Survey, and European Social Surveys, and with the measures of democracy, such as Freedom House, Varieties of Democracy (V-dem).

The literature names various dimensions of democracy. Dahl (1971, 1989, 2000a) expanded Schumpter's (1976) minimalist definition of democracy, and provided the most influential definition of democracy: all members of the polity are included in the electoral process, can participate effectively, equal voting rights, and an equal share in controlling the public agenda. Additionally, this election-centered definition also implies the existence of civil liberties, which is the core liberal element of liberal democracy. Dahl lists several civil liberties, such as: freedom of expression, freedom of association, and access to information (freedom of the press). Thus, electoral democracy and civil liberties is what Dahl named "polyarchy." Liberal democracy is defined as polyarchy that also includes the rule of law (Ferrin and Kriesi, 2016).

Since liberal democracy dominates political theory, and is a model for European democracies (Ferrin and Kriesi, 2016), most of the attributes of democratic systems are based on this vision of democracy, and these principles are taken into account this study. Another vision of democracy, which provides elements against which I compare the citizens' evaluations of democracies, is social democracy. In the social democratic vision, poverty reduction and pursuit of social equality are considered to be a part of this model (Bratton *et al.*, 2005; Dalton *et al.*, 2007; Wedel, 2011).

Although majority of people have strong preferences to live in democratically-governed countries (Norris, 2011), an evaluation of democracy varies across countries. A satisfaction with democracy, which is a difficult concept to be tested, as discussed below, remains controversial. To a greater extent, it depends on the political and economic context, as well as the quality of democracy in a given country, however individual factors play an important role as well. In my analysis, I focus on individual-level factors that have impact on the way young people, the beneficiaries of democracy assistance programs, evaluate democracy: resources (class, education and income), individual political attitudes (political and social trust, interest in politics), and socialization, expecting to find cross-country variation.

Democratic awareness and importance of different principles of democracy

The survey sought to capture opinions and attitudes of young people toward the principles of democracy. The list of attributes included items covering essential aspects: elections, the rule of law, civil rights, and various freedoms, as well as social justice elements. Free and fair elections, rule of law, and basic civil rights are considered as indispensable in liberal democratic template. Young people were asked to express their awareness regarding the importance of these specific attributes.

Electoral elements in addition to *free and fair elections*: the questionnaire also included questions regarding young people's views on whether elections link citizen and state by giving them the opportunity to punish a bad government and to remove it from power (*vertical accountability*), as well as an ability to choose between parties representing different political options that might offer alternative frames (*alternative offers*). Moreover, since elections allow the government to be held to account for their decisions, and ensure that citizens can protect themselves against dishonest and corrupt governments and choose to vote against them in the next elections, young people were asked whether there should be fixed-term elections and an limited number of terms for people occupying high offices of state (*fixed-term elections*).

As Table 4.4. below shows, free and fair elections were considered the most essential for a good functioning of the state by young people in target countries, as compared to other functions of elections. There is only a small variation between states. Almost 91 percent of Georgian young people find free and fair elections as very important, whereas young people from Bosnia-Herzegovina attached 70 percent and Ukraine 83 percent importance to this principle.

Scholars argue that rule of law out of all elements of liberal democracy is the most important because the abuse of power by the states endangers most democratic principles (Diamond and Morlino 2005, p. xv). Thus, support for the principle of rule of law measured by questions on the importance attached by young people to: (1) equal protection by the law, equal access to the judicial system, and equal treatment by the judicial system and institutions (*equality before the law*); (2) freedom of courts to decide impartially without any restriction or improper influence (*independence of the judiciary*); (3) separation of judiciary, executive and legislative branches, and thus checks on governments by the courts (*horizontal accountability*).

Table 4.4 Support for democracy among youth beneficiaries from Bosnia-Herzegovina, Georgia and Ukraine

Elements of democracy	*Very important (%)*	*Rather important (%)*	*Rather not important (%)*	*Not important (%)*
Electoral elements				
Free and fair elections	82.2	15.5	1.6	0.7
Vertical accountability	45.1	39.8	12.6	2.5
Fix-term elections	43.3	42.0	12.9	1.8
Alternative offers	49.1	36.9	10.9	3.1
Liberal elements				
Rule of law				
Equality before the law	82.7	13.3	2.6	1.5
Independence of the judiciary	69.5	21.1	6.9	2.4
Horizontal accountability	54.0	32.6	10.2	3.1
Civil liberties				
Freedom of expression	62.4	29.6	5.5	2.6
Little state intervention	40.4	35.1	17.3	7.3
Freedom of association	44.9	36.6	15.8	2.7
Minority protection	58.4	30.9	7.5	3.3
Media freedom	73.6	19.6	5.5	1.3
Media pluralism	53.8	37.5	6.6	2.2
Freedom of movement	55.1	36.9	6.6	1.5
Economic freedoms				
Protection of property rights	69.8	24.7	4.0	1.5
Freedom to run a business	56.2	32.9	7.8	3.1
Social justice elements				
Protection of workers' rights	84.2	14.0	1.1	0.7
Equal access to education	82.4	15.8	0.9	0.9
Fulfillment of basic needs	79.8	16.4	2.0	1.8
Protection against poverty	74.2	21.8	2.4	1.6
Redistribution income differences	66.2	26.0	5.8	2.0

Notes

N=550, Note: Percentages by row.

Question: "Which of the following descriptions of the state you consider as important, and which not, for creating a good standard of living? Instruction: Please answer all questions by choosing the answers that best describe your attitude."

In addition to the two conditions that constitute the cornerstone of liberal democracy, equality before the law and free and fair elections, liberal elements comprise also other principles, such as guaranteeing citizens' basic civil rights, the independence of social organizations/NGOs from the state (*freedom of association*), media pluralism, freedom of expression, and protection of minority rights, freedom to choose residence in the country or abroad, as well as *economic freedoms*, such as protection of property rights by the state, freedom to run a business free from state interference.

Some find that people may perceive democracy in terms of the fulfillment of basic needs (better job opportunities), access to education, income equality or elimination of poverty, rather in terms of liberal democratic rights (Bratton *et al.*, 2005; Ferrin and Kriesi, 2016; Welzel, 2011); therefore young people were asked about the importance of these elements. Namely, whether in a democracy it is important for the state to ensure equal access to education; provide funding for health care, science, culture; ensure fair living conditions for the poorest; and to have an active state policy in the fight against social inequalities.

The findings demonstrate, that in addition to free and fair elections and the rule of law (83 percent of all respondents considered equality before the law to be very important), there are other elements that youth in target states tend to consider as highly important in democracy: media independence and economic freedom. Civil rights such as freedom of expression, independence of NGOs form the state were considered by most respondents as important, but not as important as social rights. It is worth mentioning that young people expect the state to ensure equal access to education, to finance health care, science, culture; protect workers' rights; and to guarantee fair living conditions for the poorest. These social justice principles seem to be more important than limited state intervention into the lives of citizens. A good argument for social justice elements as well as economic freedoms might be associated with portraying Western democracy as the political system that provides better standards of living, and will bring economic prosperity and other social benefits (Dalton *et al.*, 2007).

Table 4.5 below presents the mean scores for young people from the target countries as well as from CEE countries to see whether there are major differences between countries regarding individuals' attitudes to democracy. What we can conclude from this overview is that although some small differences exist between countries, there is a broad understanding of democracy by all, meaning that young people from democratizing countries have a good knowledge of what democracy is just as young people from democratized countries. These findings are similar to earlier studies (Norris, 2011; Ferrin and Kriesi, 2016) that people share a common understanding of democracy. According to polls conducted in Europe, 90 percent of Europeans agree that democracy is better than other forms of government, despite problems (European Value Study, 2009). These findings show that young beneficiaries of the democracy assistance programs value free and fair elections, the rule of law, but also basic civil rights are considered as indispensable in most models of democracy. Liberal democracy is unthinkable without these specific elements of democracy. However, they also attribute great importance to features like social equality, although since they are not essential for democracy in general they should attribute less importance to them.

There is indeed some homogeneity on how young people understand democracy, but the extent to which youth support each of the attributes of democracy varies across countries. The question is, whether in promoting democracy, we should attach importance to the abstract commitment to democracy. I believe that we should attach importance to the abstract commitment to democracy (view of democracy), because it is also a good indicator showing that democratic

Table 4.5 Support for democracy: cross-country means for the different principles of democracy

Elements of democracy	*BiH*	*GE*	*UA*	*CZ*	*HU*	*PL*	*SK*
Electoral elements							
Free and fair elections	1.37	1.10	1.20	1.37	1.09	1.17	1.24
Vertical accountability	1.53	1.70	1.88	1.92	1.33	1.58	2.00
Fixed-term elections	1.64	1.72	1.81	2.21	1.92	1.92	2.11
Alternative offers	2.08	1.43	1.62	1.71	1.52	1.54	1.31
Liberal elements							
Rule of law							
Equality before the law	1.23	1.23	1.16	1.21	1.23	1.28	1.26
Independence of the judiciary	1.68	1.15	1.46	1.31	1.21	1.32	1.22
Horizontal accountability	1.75	1.47	1.66	1.45	1.33	1.43	1.36
Civil liberties							
Freedom of expression	1.39	1.42	1.50	1.26	1.36	1.38	1.28
Little state intervention	2.08	1.85	1.75	1.69	1.60	1.55	2.10
Freedom of association	1.88	1.74	1.75	1.69	1.64	1.64	1.74
Minority protection	1.45	1.42	1.73	2.06	1.94	2.13	2.11
Media freedom	1.58	1.19	1.28	1.45	1.25	1.25	1.34
Media pluralism	1.92	1.28	1.57	1.55	1.55	1.54	1.73
Freedom of movement	1.62	1.53	1.50	1.52	1.30	1.38	1.53
Economic freedoms							
Protection of property rights	1.45	1.23	1.42	1.52	1.25	1.41	1.56
Freedom to run a business	1.74	1.35	1.62	1.57	1.54	1.58	1.55
Social justice elements							
Protection of workers' rights	1.12	1.13	1.22	1.52	1.25	1.40	1.31
Equal access to education	1.13	1.17	1.27	1.49	1.23	1.39	1.37
Fulfillment of basic needs	1.18	1.27	1.23	1.27	1.52	1.48	1.27
Protection against poverty	1.26	1.17	1.41	1.88	1.64	1.74	1.69
Redistribution of income differences	1.35	1.42	1.45	1.98	1.97	1.86	1.71

principles and norms do spread across countries, and that democracy diffusion takes place, which could have been a result of democracy assistance programs directed toward young people. However, in order to answer the question if there is need to provide such support and provide it at all to democratizing countries, we need to look at the evaluation of democracy and various individual-level factors that affect both conceptions and evaluations of democracy.

Evaluation of democracy and assessment of the quality of democracy

Support for democracy does not automatically translate into a support for the democratic regimes in a given country (Canache, 2006; Inglehart, 2003). Views refer to the citizens' normative ideal of democracy, what democracy should be. Evaluations however, refer to the citizens' assessment of the way the specific principles of democracy work in their countries (Ferrin and Kriesi, 2016). Nevertheless, young people when asked about the importance of these principles, could have incorporated their assessment regarding what political systems should look like, the role of authorities, and overall attitudes toward some aspects of social and political life, so their answers could have been influenced by their current experience with democracy. Young people's greater expectations beyond the fundamental aspects, that a democratic regime should produce socioeconomic equality, in the example of young people from Central and Eastern Europe, may indicate lesser satisfaction with the liberal democratic model in their countries. Also, since electoral processes are institutionalized in different ways (Lijphart, 1999), this might shape young people's opinion regarding the ability to choose between parties representing different political options (*alternative offers*).

The conclusions depend on the type of items which have been used to measure citizens' satisfaction with democracy. In searching for more straightforward indicators of evaluations of democracy, scholars came up with so-called Satisfaction with How Democracy Works (SWD) when people have been asked in various polls to express their level of satisfaction with the way democracy works in their country. The question, "On the whole, are you very satisfied, fairly satisfied, not very satisfied, or not at all satisfied with the way democracy works in [country]?" is the most frequently used in various surveys, such as Eurobarometer, Latinobaromenter, Asianbarometer, World Values Survey, and European Social Surveys (Ferrin and Kriesi, 2016). However, there is no agreement on what it measures exactly (Canache, Mondak and Seligson, 2001). This an abstract measurement which means something for some people or something else for others (Alonso, 2016; Canache, 2012). It is, perhaps, interpreted very differently by individuals within and across countries and time (Canache, 2006; Canache *et al.*, 2001). However, some researchers argue that SWD is not a bad indicator because citizens' understanding of democracy does not vary dramatically among individuals (Fuchs and Roller, 2006). Linde and Ekman (2003) argue that satisfaction with a democracy indicator is influenced by factors which have nothing to do with the functioning of democracy.

Informed by the literature and the surveys mentioned above, I have asked young people to express their opinions on a set of statements regarding democracy—whether democracy has an advantage over all other forms of governments; influences the quality of life of its citizens; and has a positive impact on the economic development of the state. They were also asked to measure their inclination toward authoritarian standards, and they were asked whether sometimes non-democratic government can be preferable to a democratic one, and whether governments based on strong leadership are better than democratic ones. Also, I have included a question on whether development of democracy is desirable in all countries of the world, regardless of their political tradition and culture ("Democracy works everywhere"). These questions may indicate reluctance, lack of satisfaction on how democracy works in their countries. Finally, the question that could be treated as single measure of satisfaction with democracy is "Democracy is a good regime for my country."

When asked about democracy, they favorably perceived democratic systems. They were convinced that democracy leads to prosperity of citizens and growth as well as it can be adopted in any countries regardless of their political tradition and culture. The majority considered a democratic system to be a good regime for their countries (almost 80 percent "fully agreed" and "rather agreed"), and that it has advantage over other forms of governments. However, quite worrying, at the same time, is the fact that 57 percent agreed with the statement that sometimes undemocratic governments might be more desirable than democratic ones, and that governments based on strong leadership can be better than democratic ones (52 percent), because a strong leader can do more for the country than the law, discussions and consultations with society. Interestingly, these results seem to be driven by Georgian and Bosnian youth, although more than 83 percent and 60 percent respectively agreed on welcoming democracy in their countries. The Ukrainians were least happy about authoritarian features. More than 50 percent disagreed with the statement that non-democratic governments can be preferable and the strong leadership is better than democratic ones, although the majority agreed that this type of government can be more effective.

At first glance it appeared that young people from target countries shared a common understanding of democracy, and they somewhat positively evaluated the democratic system in their countries, although some differences in satisfaction can be observed. The question is whether there is a relationship between strong commitment to democracy as indicated earlier, and the measure of satisfaction. Thus, I am looking at the relationship between the answer to "Democracy is a good regime for my country" and the questions related to the attributes/principles of democracy for all countries in the sample, differentiating between youth program beneficiaries in target countries and CEE countries. It allows us to see whether a positive evaluation of democracy is, or is not, linked to liberal or social justice elements of democracy, and also whether it varies across countries (Alonso, 2016).

Table 4.6 Perception of democracy by youth beneficiaries in the target countries (percentage of respondents in each country that responded "fully agree")

	Bosnia-Herzegovina	*Georgia*	*Ukraine*
Democracy is the best form of government	34.21	50.51	31.50
Democracy leads to the wellbeing of citizens	21.71	41.92	24.00
Democracy leads to economic growth	21.71	42.42	23.50
Democracy works everywhere	33.55	40.91	19.00
Democracy is a good regime for my country	22.37	51.52	39.00
Sometimes non-democratic government is preferable	25.00	32.83	14.50
Strong leadership is better than democratic leadership	24.34	30.30	12.50

Notes

N=550.

Question: "How much do you agree or disagree with following statements? Instruction: Please answer all questions by choosing the answers that best describe your attitude."

Young people from CEE countries link satisfaction with democracy measured by "Democracy is a good regime for my country" question with both the liberal and social democracy scale. However, young beneficiaries of programs from the target countries, who report a strong commitment to democracy, do not link democracy to social equality but rather to liberal components. Rule of law and civil liberties seem to be appreciated by young people especially from Ukraine. The results for young people from Bosnia-Herzegovina, as well as from Georgia, are intriguing since the correlations are not statistically significant between all components and satisfaction with democracy, but only one which is *freedom of expression* in case of Georgian youth beneficiaries. This may even though these young people have a good understanding of specific ideal democratic principles they do not link their satisfaction or lack of satisfaction with any specific components. It could be because these elements of democracy are not fully provided in these countries, and young people have not had a chance to practice them yet.

However, satisfaction with democracy and overall support for democracy have also impact other individual-level factors, such as individual political attitudes: trust in political actors, trust in legal institutions, trust in liberal institutions, party identification, interpersonal trust, interest in politics (watching politics on TV) as well as level of socialization and socioeconomic status.

Factors affecting views and evaluations of democracy

Although there seems to be a lack of difference between EE and CEE regarding views of democracy, it is important to explore factors affecting views and satisfaction, such as political and social trust, interest and participation (civic and political), as well as perceived economic status. If these factors are low—they might have a detrimental impact on youth support of democracy. In consolidated democracies, a decline of trust in government and less satisfaction with the way democracy works, does not mean that the citizens will cease to prefer democracy over other forms of government. However, in fragile democracies, dissatisfaction with the way democratic institutions work may lessen participation and preference for other forms of government. Therefore, questions in the next part of the survey concerned individual political attitudes, such as ideology, trust, and interest in politics, which affect democratic demands.

Overall, it is important to keep in mind that contextual factors, such as (1) Strength of democratic institutions and communist legacies; (2) General political conditions and the quality of democracy; (3) Cultural context conditions (however, as Inglehart and Norris (2003b) put it: democracy has become the only political model with global appeal no matter the culture); (4) Social capital which plays key roles in accounting for what citizens think democracy should be like. Scholars find that when evaluating the political system, citizens take into account the part that governments, to which they are accustomed, have played in their lives. For example, the findings by Torney-Purta, Wilkenfeld, and Barber (2008) show that young people in the US expect the government to protect human rights but fewer than peers in other nations for the government to take a proactive role in controlling the economy. In other words, it might be expected that youth tend to approve those arrangements are familiar to them. They are more likely to accept them as fair and just. However, according to their perception other factors also matter since young people experience the state and the principles of the system in their everyday interactions with not only authorities, but also peers, teachers and parents. Other factors such as the media also exert important influence on youth perceptions.

This means that although citizens' attitudes to democracy cannot be studied independently of the country in which they live, as well as without historical lenses, these factors are also intertwined with individual-level factors. For example, if social capital is a driver of support for democracy, the dense social networks of people strengthen it through interpersonal trust (social trust). Social links, relations with other people form social capital, which in turn leads to greater engagement in public affairs. Various voluntary associations and organizations, even if not directly targeting political elites, facilitate the fulfillment of shared goals and the solution of common problems, and create, as Putnam (2000, p. 19) put it, "social networks, norms of reciprocity, and trustworthiness," which is known as social capital. Thus, social capital is built where trust is, both interpersonal and political, as well as the linkages between people and mutual exchange. Also, the economic situation, an interest in politics, as well as one's own experiences with democracy are key sources of democratic attitudes.

Given the fact that individual-level factors influence the way citizens view and evaluate democracy, and that it matters if young people are socialized into the values of freedoms for human empowerment, which in turn will foster the demand for liberal democracy, I am exploring these factors. Specifically, the young people were asked about their (1) Individual political attitudes: political efficacy, political trust, social trust, norms of citizenship that they value; (2) Interest in politics; (3) Socioeconomic status. In the latter part of this section, I am modeling empirically the question how and to what extent young people make use of their democracy ideal (view of democracy) when assessing satisfaction with democracy, and vice versa, while controlling for individual-level factors.

Individual political attitudes

Political efficacy and trust: political efficacy is a subjective evaluation of political competence. There can be internal and external types of political efficacy (Hayes and Bean, 1993). Internal political efficacy evaluates individuals' confidence that people are able to understand and participate in politics—the higher the better and increase participation (Armingeon, 2007; Dalton, 2014; Vráblíková, 2017). External political efficacy evaluates the feeling that people have an impact on politics and that politicians are responsive to them. Internal efficacy relates to the perception of inclusion of a citizen within the political system, ability to intervene in political affairs. It is important because if low they will feel inadequate and irrelevant. External efficacy is the perception that the system will react to one's democratic impetus as well as the perception of a citizen's own democratic power, the power and influence on democratic outcomes (Cammaerts *et al.*, 2016; Craig and Maggiotto, 1982). Since the perception of democracy depends on these factors, the young people were asked about political efficacy regarding national and local governments in target countries.

The respondents were asked whether the laws passed affect them, and whether the governments improve conditions in their countries. There seemed to be no differences between the perception of respondents regarding the impact of national government. The majority of respondents recognized that legislation originates at national (almost 80 percent of all respondents) and local levels (76 percent) and affects day-to-day life. However, whereas, overall, they believed that local governments in their countries could improve their conditions, this cannot be said about the national governments (63 percent disagree). It is worth noticing that those least favorable toward national government seem to be Ukrainian youth, because more than 60 percent of them disagree with the statement that their living conditions can be improved through actions taken by the national government, and seem to trust local government. Young people were also asked whether they feel respected by citizens and by government, and whether there would be equal treatment and serious consideration if they had had some questions or tried to explain their views to the governmental officials. The respondents from these three countries agreed that whereas it is possible that their voice is likely to be heard, and there would be an opportunity to ask questions, the demands would *not* be considered (57 percent of all respondents). When asked to express their opinion on the statement regarding the impact of citizens on politics, almost 60 percent said that they fully agree or rather agree that people like them do not have any influence what the government and politicians are doing in their countries, as Table 4.7 shows.

Scholars have noted that trust is an important foundation of democratic governance, and it is expected to increase political activism (Bernhagen and Marsh, 2007; Vráblíková, 2017). Newton (2001, p. 211) finds that there is the relationship between social trust and social capital, as well as political trust and political capital, although this is not straightforward. Social capital and civil society is a collective property of the social system, whereas social and political trust are individual features. However, the more society demonstrates social trust the greater are the chances that social capital will be stronger, which in turn, will strengthen civil society. A vast majority (57 percent "Fully agree") answered this survey are think that most politicians, regardless of what they say, care only about their career. Such an opinion about the officials as well as conviction that key political decisions are taken in secret situations (83 percent "Fully agree" and "Rather agree") shows a very low trust and disbelief that the government serves the needs of citizens in their countries. In an interview with a young Ukrainian participant in the youth project, I was told that if someone joins a party it means that they motivated by material self-interest and willingness to enrich themselves and, because of this perception, many people did get involved in politics. According to her, young people voted for Poroshenko, because he is already an oligarch who would not scoop up state money.

The survey generally found apathy and low levels of trust among young people in politicians, political institutions and politics in general in these three countries. However, on the other hand when young people were asked how they perceive their situation and opportunities to enter politics, many believed that this depends on their personal characteristics and skills—education, leadership skills, as well as charisma—rather than informal connections or financial support. However, young people do not regard experience in politics or experience in various civil society organizations to be crucial for them to become politicians.

Norms of citizenship: scholars also attach an importance to norms of citizenship, because they capture what people think a good citizen should do or should not do (Dalton, 2008; Vráblíková, 2017). These norms are related to people's belief regarding citizens' role in the society, regardless of the political situation. There are two types of norms, "norms of citizen duty" and "engaged citizenship." The first one is a limited participatory role for citizens—allegiance to law and

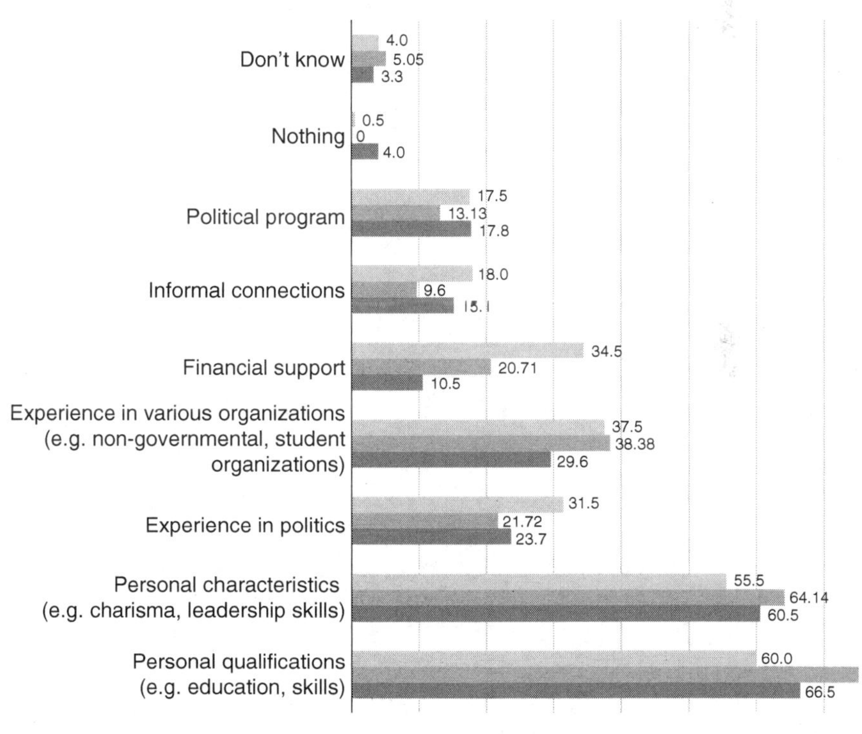

Figure 4.1 Young people's perceptions (%) regarding opportunities to enter politics in target countries.

Table 4.7 Relationship between conceptions and evaluations of democracy[a] by youth program beneficiaries

Elements of democracy[b]	*BiH*	*GE*	*UA*	*CZ*	*HU*	*PL*	*SK*
Electoral elements							
Free and fair elections	0.01	0.01	**0.20**	**0.29**	**0.23**	**0.16**	**0.27**
	(0.903)	(0.893)	(0.005)	(0.000)	(0.006)	(0.017)	(0.007)
Vertical accountability	0.13	0.07	0.09	**0.14**	**0.19**	–0.06	0.06
	(0.121)	(0.320)	(0.216)	(0.045)	(0.020)	(0.3846)	(0.523)
Fixed-term elections	0.10	0.11	0.12	–0.03	**0.19**	0.08	0.18
	(0.197)	(0.106)	(0.108)	(0.663)	(0.019)	(0.194)	(0.067)
Alternative offers	0.13	–0.02	**0.30**	**0.21**	0.085	**0.16**	**0.21**
	(0.117)	(0.789)	(0.000)	(0.002)	(0.304)	(0.016)	(0.032)
Liberal elements							
Rule of law							
Equality before the law	0.04	–0.01	**0.20**	**0.24**	**0.18***	**0.15**	**0.29**
	(0.654)	(0.868)	(0.004)	(0.000)	(0.026)	(0.020)	(0.004)
Independence of the judiciary	0.01	0.03	0.04	**0.32**	**0.23**	**0.13**	**0.26**
	(0.931)	(0.710)	(0.594)	(0.000)	(0.005)	(0.050)	(0.009)
Horizontal accountability	0.050	0.07	**0.23**	**0.19**	**0.29**	**0.13**	**0.17**
	(0.543)	(0.294)	(0.001)	(0.005)	(0.000)	(0.047)	(0.080)
Civil liberties							
Freedom of expression	0.10	**0.12**	**0.16**	**0.25**	0.12	**0.13**	**0.24**
	(0.204	0.096)	(0.020)	(0.000)	(0.152)	(0.046)	(0.014)
Little state intervention	0.06	0.02	0.10	0.09	0.15	0.01	**0.20**
	(0.472)	(0.750)	(0.156)	(0.148)	(0.062)	(0.864)	(0.050)
Freedom of association	0.08	0.09	**0.24**	**0.28**	**0.19**	0.10	0.15
	(0.334)	(0.202)	(0.000)	(0.000)	(0.020)	(0.114)	(0.139)
Minority protection	0.03	0.05	**0.13**	**0.18**	**0.19**	–0.03	**0.32**
	(0.663)	(0.458)	(0.050)	(0.009)	(0.020)	(0.680)	(0.001)

Media freedom	0.08	0.11	**0.18**	**0.37**	**0.30**	0.08	**0.21**
	(0.321)	(0.128)	(0.012)	(0.000)	(0.000)	(0.242)	(0.037)
Media pluralism	0.10	0.01	**0.10**	**0.20**	**0.24**	**0.15**	0.09
	(0.238)	(0.916)	(0.015)	(0.003)	(0.003)	(0.022)	(0.363)
Freedom of movement	0.098	0.098	0.13	**0.18**	**0.28**	**0.13**	0.06
	(0.230)	(0.171)	(0.070)	(0.007)	(0.000)	(0.046)	(0.525)
Economic freedoms							
Protection of property rights	0.12	0.03	**0.20**	**0.20**	0.04	0.01	0.11
	(0.133)	(0.696)	(0.004)	(0.003)	(0.579)	(0.846)	(0.289)
Freedom to run a business	0.02	0.06	0.06	**0.14**	0.11	0.02	0.02
	(0.759)	(0.371)	(0.414)	(0.036)	(0.166)	(0.803)	(0.834)
Social justice elements							
Protection of workers' rights	–0.01	0.03	0.08	**0.13**	0.12	**0.20**	**0.23**
	(0.866)	(0.708)	(0.285)	(0.050)	(0.172)	(0.000)	(0.020)
Equal access to education	–0.05	–0.03	**0.21**	**0.17**	**0.14**	**0.13**	**0.28**
	(0.560)	(0.689)	(0.003)	(0.011)	(0.078)	(0.044)	(0.005)
Fulfillment of basic needs	–0.08	–0.02	0.00	0.00	**0.19**	**0.20**	0.08
	(0.321)	(0.783)	(0.939)	(0.969)	(0.020)	(0.003)	(0.427)
Protection against poverty	0.02	–0.06	–0.06	–0.05	0.13	**0.14**	0.20
	(0.779)	(0.368)	(0.380)	(0.473)	(0.097)	(0.027)	(0.363)
Redistribution of income differences	0.80	0.20	0.11	0.05	**0.21**	**0.13**	0.13
	(0.335)	(0.176)	(0.117)	(0.461)	(0.011)	(0.042)	(0.182)

Notes

a Evaluation of democracy variable: responses for the statement "Democracy is a good regime for my country" answers "Fully agree" were coded as 1 and otherwise as 0, $N=498$.

b Elements of democracy: answers marked as "Very important" were coded as 1 and otherwise as 0. Statistical significant correlations in bold, p values in parentheses.

Table 4.8 External and internal political efficacy: young peoples' opinions on national and local governments

	% "fully agree" and "rather agree"
The activities and the laws passed by the *national* government have a great effect on your day-to-day life in your country	78.9
The activities and the laws passed by the *local* government have a great effect on your day-to-day life in your country	75.6
On the whole, the activities of the *national* government improve conditions in your country	46.5
On the whole, the activities of the *local* governments improve conditions in your country	50.5
Suppose you had some questions for a *government official*—for example, a tax question or housing regulation questions—you would be given an equal treatment	55.6
Suppose you explained your point of view to the *governmental official*, you would be given serious consideration	42.9
People like me do not have any influence on what the government and politicians are doing	58.6
Most politicians, regardless of what they say, care only about their career	93.3
Key political decisions are taken in secret situations	82.7

Notes
N=550.
Question: "What is your opinion about the role of the national and local government?
Instruction: Please answer all questions by choosing the answers that best describe your attitude."

order, duty to vote, duty to report crime, etc. The second one, however, perceives citizens as "engaged citizens," citizens who form opinions, are active in following government, choose environment-friendly products, help those less privileged, and are active in associations (Dalton, 2008). The norms of engaged citizens are close to postmaterialist or self-expressive values. Vráblíková (2017) finds that norms of engaged citizenship increase activism, while norms of citizen duty have an opposite effect. When people think that participation is their duty they tend to participate more.

A properly functioning democracy needs the support and activity of citizens in order to work. All three countries are on their road to become consolidated democracies; therefore, they were asked in a survey (similar to *Citizenship Norms items from 2014 ISSP module on citizenship*) about their perception of their roles as citizens. The respondents said that there was an important obligation to follow the law (71 percent "fully agree"), to pay attention to the natural environment (74 percent), to loyal and respectful to the country (60 percent), and to vote (65 percent). Also, a vast majority thinks that working honestly (66 percent), and paying taxes (60 percent) are citizens' obligations. However, not many respondents stated that "engaged citizenship" matters, and that taking part in activities of political parties or non-governmental organizations is crucial for them as citizens.

When asked about the things in their countries that they are the proudest of (Figure 4.2), they mentioned the characteristics of people in the first place, and then the physical attributes of the country (Georgian youth were also proud of spiritual virtues and religion as well as contribution to arts), whereas governmental and political institutions together with economic systems were the least favored answers.

Interest in politics and socialization through media

The last variable in the section on political attitudes and values that might affect support for democracy as well as satisfaction with democracy is an interest in

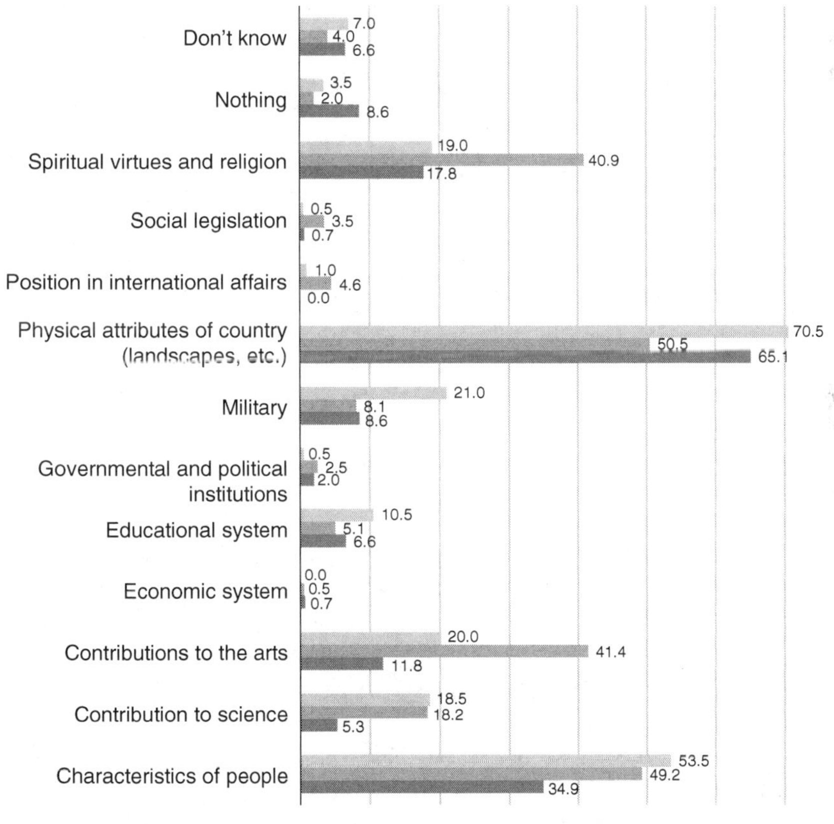

Figure 4.2 Components of patriotism (%) by youth in the target countries.

Table 4.9 Roles and duties of a citizen (percentage of respondents in each country that responded "Fully agree")

	Bosnia-Herzegovina	*Georgia*	*Ukraine*
Displaying the flag during national days	29.0	30.8	38.5
Following current affairs	22.4	38.4	22.5
Following the law	55.9	74.8	79.5
Homeland defense (military)	42.1	66.7	39.5
Knowing the history of your country	52.6	65.7	50.5
Loyalty and respect for you country	52.6	80.8	43.5
Paying attention to the natural environment	65.1	89.4	66.0
Paying taxes	40.8	76.8	51.0
Taking part in the activities of local government	32.9	47.0	27.5
Taking part in the activities of political parties	18.4	30.3	42.0
Taking part in non-governmental activities	30.9	34.9	31.0
Volunteering	50.0	49.5	41.5
Voting	63.2	61.6	69.0
Working honestly	59.9	63.6	74.0

Notes
N=550.
Question: "What should be the citizens' obligations and activities? Instruction: Please answer all questions by choosing the answers that best describe your attitude."

politics. Political interest can be understood as the attention that people pay to politics and strongly and positively affects all kinds of activities (Bernhagen and Marsh, 2007; Vráblíková, 2017). By following the media, youth can also stay informed of current events and acquire knowledge (McLeod, 2000). Mass media is an important determinant of political education. Watching television news or reading the newspaper help young people acquire political knowledge, form political attitudes and orient themselves to the political world around them. Hooghe and Boonen (2016) found in their research conducted among young people in Belgium that following political news is not a priority for young age groups. Also, many young people seem to be more inclined to express their opinions in social media than in the polling booth (Hooghe and Boonen, 2016).

For democracy to deliver, citizens need information on governments' undertakings, whereas only 30 percent of those surveyed found it important to follow current political affairs. The question is how citizens stay informed, and further in to the survey there are questions about the use of traditional and modern media. Online consumption exceeds the consumption of traditional media—TV, radio, newspapers. The respondents only read newspapers from time to time, hardly ever listened to the radio to follow the news, and only 38 percent watched TV almost every day in order get information on current affairs. Online media and Internet websites (other than online media—e.g., political parties' websites, government websites, international organizations' websites, etc.) as well as social media (e.g., Facebook, Twitter, blogs, etc.) are used abundantly by young people for information about the current affairs (above 52 percent of young

Table 4.10 Young people's news consumption in target countries

	Nearly every day	*About once a week*	*From time to time*	*Never*
Newspapers and magazines (printed)	16.0	14.7	36.4	32.4
Radio (traditional—not online)	13.1	16.2	29.5	41.3
TV (traditional—not online)	38.0	25.1	23.5	12.6
Online media (press/radio/TV)	52.7	24.6	14.6	8.2
Internet websites	51.5	19.8	15.1	13.6
Social media	72.6	14.4	7.5	5.6
Talking to other people (e.g., friends, family)	44.0	28.2	21.1	6.7

Notes
N=550.
Question: "How do you update yourself about the public affairs and how often? Instruction: Please answer all questions by choosing the answers that best apply to you."

people nearly every day). This might be due to the concern that there is high degree of distrust among young people regarding the news they receive through traditional media in their countries, even though there are other broadcasters besides public ones. The young generation distrusts the traditional media as much as the general population does and this might also be in line with distrust of political institutions and politics detailed earlier. Another reason is the overall tendency among young people to use the Internet to stay informed (Bruter *et al.*, 2016). However, it is worth noticing that there are some differences between respondents in target countries. Almost 50 percent of young respondents from Bosnia-Herzegovina as well as from Georgia are still watching traditional TV nearly every day. As compared to Georgia and Ukraine, almost twice as many respondents from Bosnia-Herzegovina said that that they still read newspapers (33 percent) and listened to the radio (26 percent) nearly every day in order to update themselves on current public.

An ability to talk about political affairs with others is also an indicator of *social trust* (Newton, 2001). On average 42 percent of young people have discussed politics or political news with someone else nearly every day, with some differences between countries which are worth highlighting. It seems that Georgian young people the most interested in discussing the public affairs with the others (65 percent every day) as compared to their contemporaries from Bosnia-Herzegovina (39 percent), as well as from Ukraine (26.5 percent). Talking to other people seems to be the second most important source of information, after social media, for Georgian young people.

Socioeconomic factors

Social class background is often given as an important factor explaining young peoples' views, values, satisfaction with democracy and overall engagement in participation. Specifically, socioeconomic factors such as education, parents' education, financial status, and place of residence (urban vs. rural areas) also contribute. They are commonly referred to as *resources.* Social class also plays an important role in young people's opportunities for learning. Education and high socioeconomic status emerge as correlates of liberal democratic views, and frequently have a positive impact on trust in government, authorities and on overall satisfaction with political system (Newton and Norris, 2000). According to Inglehart and Welzel (2005), and modernization theory focusing on the role of material and cognitive resources in shaping conceptions of democracy, the demands for political self-expression arise in response to rising socioeconomic resources that make people economically and socially dependent.

Families are the earliest context and also the most enduring in which young people' attitudes and expectations are formulated. Youth views reflect the educational background of their parents. Youth from families with low levels of education are more favorable towards government support. Families provide the space for the discussion of current events about politics in general which leads to forming views, opinions, and knowledge about democracy. Discussions are important since they increase the likelihood that a young person will understand some political phenomena better, like, for example, what democracy means. Participating in such discussions might make young people more open having different perspectives, and such discussion of current events is more common in families with higher levels of parental education (Flanagan, 2013). Also, the family is an important factor in encouraging civic participation in direct and indirect ways.

The impact of social status variables on views and attitudes toward democracy measured by income, education, or education of parents, find support in the literature. However, scholars point out that it depends on the type of regime in which a respondent is living. In liberal democracies, people who enjoy privileged positions in society are more likely to support democracy than individuals with lower social status. Low status individuals living in liberal democracies are less likely to see a liberal democracy as sufficient (Ceka and Magalhães, 2016). Studying Hungarian youth, Toth (2001) found that young, working-class people felt insecure about their futures and were ambivalent about the current political system.

In order to conclude the understanding and evaluation by young beneficiaries of democracy assistance projects in target countries it is important to test the impact of various individual-level factors mentioned above on perception and satisfactions. Therefore, Table 4.11. shows the regression analysis of the liberal and social attributes of democracy as well as of political attitudes, and socioeconomic factors on satisfaction with democracy (Models 1 and 2). It also includes the regression analysis of the explanatory variables on support for liberal democracy (Models 3 and 4).

In order to create a "Satisfaction with Democracy" variable, I have added up the answers to the following variables: (1) "Democracy is the best form of government"; (2) "Democracy leads to the well-being of citizens"; (3) "Democracy leads to economic growth," (4) "Democracy works everywhere"; (5) "Democracy is a good regime for my country." There were four possible responses to these statements "Fully agree," "Rather agree," "Rather disagree," "Fully disagree." These five variables were added up to create a new one, an index variable: "Satisfaction with democracy." Each component has the same weight. Since larger values of new variables meant more responses to "Fully disagree" whereas the smaller values of "Fully agree" were recoded in order to indicate that the higher the number of the variable the greater agreement among the respondents that democracy works well and is desirable.

The "Support for liberal democracy" variable represents the liberal democracy index composed of electoral liberties, civil liberties, economic freedoms and rule of law elements mentioned earlier. Specifically, the following principles were taken into account: (1) Free and fair elections; (2) Vertical accountability; (3) Fixed-term elections; (4) Alternative offers; (5) Rule of law; (6) Equality before the law; (7) Independence of the judiciary; (8) Horizontal accountability; (9) Freedom of expression; (10) Little state intervention; (11) Freedom of association; (12) Minority protection; (13) Media freedom; (14) Media pluralism; (15) Freedom of movement; (16) Protection of property rights; (17) Freedom to run businesses. These seventeen variables were added and, as above, the variable was recoded so that the higher values indicate higher support for liberal components, and thus overall support for liberal democracy. Additionally, I have included the "Social democracy components" variable which includes only those elements that refer to the social dimension, which were excluded from the liberal democracy variable: (1) Protection of workers' rights; (2) Equal access to education; (3) Fulfillment of basic necessitates; (4) Protection against poverty; (5) Redistribution of income differences. The variable is an index created from the responses to these statements and recoded as mentioned above.

Political views and attitudes variables included: (1) Political efficacy; (2) Political trust; (3) Social trust; (4) Norms of citizenship; and (5) Interest in politics. The internal political efficacy variable was measured by the "People like me do not have any influence on what the government and politicians are doing" statement. Respondents had four options to address this statement with 1 coded as "Fully agree," and 4 "Fully disagree," meaning that the more respondents disagree with this statement the more confident he or she is that their role as citizens does matter. The variable for external efficacy, however, was recoded since the higher response to the statement "If you explained your point of view to the governmental officials, you would be given serious consideration" indicated lower confidence in officials responding to citizens' needs. The political trust variable was measured by the statement "Most politicians, regardless of what they say, care only about their career." Reponses "Fully disagree" to this statement meant that young people have trust in politicians. Social trust, however was indicated by willingness to talk to other people about politics and political affairs (e.g., friends, family) and the frequency of doing so. Respondents had four options to address this issue with "Never" (recoded as 1), "From time to time," "About once a week," "Nearly every day" (recoded as 4).

Table 4.11 Determinants of satisfaction with democracy and support for liberal democracy among young beneficiaries of democracy assistance programs

	Satisfaction with democracy		*Support for liberal democracy*	
	(1) Target countries	*(2) CEE countries*	*(3) Target countries*	*(4) CEE countries*
Satisfaction with democracy			0.240**	0.610***
			(0.074)	(0.063)
Support for liberal democracy	0.087**	0.137***		
	(0.027)	(0.022)		
Social democracy components	–0.040	0.286***		
	(0.589)	(0.043)		
Political efficacy				
External efficacy	0.506***	0.371**	–0.344	–2.58
	(0.137)	(0.123)	(0.240)	(0.223)
Internal efficacy	0.297*	0.368**	–0.814***	–0.918***
	(0.134)	(0.114)	(0.231)	(0.204)
Political trust	0.574**	0.550***	–1.094**	–0.792**
	(0.212)	(0.138)	(0.361)	(0.249)
Social trust	–0.116	–0.177	0.564*	0.668**
	(0.133)	(0.115)	(0.229)	(0.001)

Norms of citizenship				
Norms of citizen duty	0.164***	0.025	0.106	–0.001
	(0.045)	(0.037)	(0.079)	(0.979)
Engaged citizenship	0.078	0.103*	0.483***	0.259**
	(0.191)	(0.041)	(0.100)	(0.206)
Interest in politics	0.585**	–0.213	–0.758**	0.705*
	(0.168)	(0.155)	(0.293)	(0.277)
Student	–0.698	–0.093	–0.360	0.172
	(0.128)	(0.503)	(0.793)	(0.906)
Parents' education	0.048	0.023	0.233**	0.107
	(0.044)	(0.037)	(0.075)	(0.066)
Financial status	0.131	–0.020	0.133	0.043
	(0.121)	(0.115)	(0.208)	(0.206)
Urban vs. rural areas	0.117	0.078	0.557***	0.182*
	(0.061)	(0.051)	(0.104)	(0.091)
Gender	0.549*	0.475*	–0.486	–0.055
	(0.278)	(0.213)	(0.481)	(0.384)
Constant	–0.484	0.147	19.82***	18.4***
	(1.501)	(1.116)	(2.130)	(1.84)
Number of observations	544	687	544	688
Adj R-squared	0.2134	0.2484	0.2265	0.2338

Notes
Statistical significance *** $p<0.001$; ** $p<0.01$; * $p<0.05$. Std. Err. in parenthesis.

As discussed earlier, norms of citizenship are divided into "norms of citizen duty," indicating a limited participatory and somewhat conventional role for citizens, and the second "norms of engaged citizen" which are recognized the participatory role of the citizen. In order to create the first measure, I have created an index, which is composed of the following elements: (1) Flying the flag on national days; (2) Voting; (3) Following the law; (4) Military duty; (5) Loyalty and respect for the country; (6) Paying taxes; (7) Knowing the history of your country; (8) Working honestly. There were four possible responses to the question "What should be the citizens' obligations and activities?": "Fully agree," "Rather agree," "Rather disagree," "Fully disagree." These seven variables were added up to create a new one, and an index variable: "norms of citizen duty." Each component has the same weight. Since larger values of new variables meant more "Fully disagree" responses, whereas the smaller values of "Fully Agree" resulted in fewer responses, the variable was recoded accordingly in order to indicate that the higher the number of the variable the greater was the agreement among the respondents with the elements belonging to "norms of citizen duty." In order to create the "norms of engaged citizen" variable, I have also created an index composed of the following elements: (1) Paying attention to the natural environment; (2) Taking part in local government activities ; (3) Taking part in activities of political parties; (4) Taking part in non-governmental activities; (5) Volunteering. The same procedure of creating the variable and recoding it was created.

The interest in politics variable is measured by agreement with the statement whether following the current political affairs is important and was recoded so that the higher response to the statement indicates the higher agreement and greater interest in politics.

According to Inglehart (1999), socioeconomic factors are important predictors, since economic development and access to higher levels of education lead to individual autonomy, and greater critical stance toward institutions. Socioeconomic factors include variables measuring the education of young respondents and whether was a student (coded as 1) or not (coded as 0). In order to create a parents' education variable, I have created an index, which is composed of the following elements: (1) Mother's education; (2) Father's education. There were eight possible option responses: 1 Incomplete secondary education; 2 Secondary school, 3 Secondary vocational/technical; 4 Incomplete higher education; 5 Higher education, 6 Technical higher education, 7 Academic degree; 8 I do not know/hard to say. Education of mother and father variables were added up to create a new variable, an index: "parents' education." The larger values of new variables meant higher education of both parents, whereas the smaller values indicated lower levels of parents' education, whereas responses "I do not know/hard to say" were recoded to 0. The financial situation variable ranges from 1 ("We live very frugally—we do not have enough money even for basic needs") to 5 ("We live very well—we can afford a luxury"); 6 (No answer). The higher the number the greater financial well-being was perceived by the respondent. Respondents were also asked to state their where they lived ranging from 1 ("Village") to 8 "Above 5 million inhabitants").

The higher scores indicate the higher density of population and urbanization of the place where respondents live.

Individual political attitudes, such as political efficacy, political trust, and interest in politics, affect democratic demands and satisfaction with democracy in target countries as well as in CEE. However, in target countries and in CEE different norms of citizenship are playing the role. In target countries, norms of engaged citizenship are not affecting satisfaction with democracy, but they do have an impact on support for democracy, whereas, in CEE, norms of engaged citizenship are important for positive assessment of democracy and for the support. In CEE countries, support for social components of democracy also seem to have positive impact on satisfaction with democracy. Interestingly, the more people trust each other in target countries and in CEE countries the more they are in favor of democracy.

Socioeconomic factors are not important predictors of the support and satisfaction with democracy as indicated in the results table. Nevertheless, if parental education is above average, this is positively related to support of democracy, which means that parental education is an important predictor of support for liberal democracy in target countries. Also, young people from urban areas both in target and CEE countries seem to be more in favor of democracy. Neither education nor place of living seem play an important part satisfaction with democracy. However, the results of the survey show that young females are more satisfied with democracy in CEE countries.

Patterns of youth engagement and action

While the views on democracy and citizenship are important, this perception might not automatically imply participation or willingness to participate. After learning opinions and feelings about political and social life as well as interest in public affairs in their countries, it is important to take a look at young people's participation. In this section, I am taking a closer look at the responses of 550 young people from three target countries in order to analyze the political and social participation of young generation in these countries.

The political scientists used the European and World Values surveys (see for example Inglehart and Baker, 2000; Kirbis, 2013) or the General Social Survey (GSS) in order to determine the level of participation among citizens. One of the most common findings from political participation surveys is that young people as compared to other age groups are not generally active in public affairs and politics. In this chapter, following Thijssen *et al.*'s (2016) advice, I am testing the arguments that younger generations are either not committed or engaging in alternative political forms. However, fairly convincing is Zukin *et al.* (2006) arguing that in order to understand the current nature of citizen engagement, it is critical to separate political from civic engagement. Also, we need to extend our understanding to what youth participation looks like outside the Western context. It could be that young people are disengaged from politics because of the way the politics is done in this country. Therefore, in order to have a better understanding, in the survey conducted for this study, young people, potential beneficiaries of democracy assistance programs, were asked about their different forms of political and civic participation they were involved in, as well as being given vignettes to test their future participation.

This section also assesses the relationship between political and civic participation and the impact of various factors affecting youth participation such as satisfaction with democracy, support for liberal democracy, and individual-level factors, such as political attitudes, interest in politics and socioeconomic status.

Youth political participation: being and becoming participant

I adopt the following definition of political participation that "a voluntary action by ordinary citizens intended to influence the decisions of other actors that is related to the State, aimed at solving collective/community problems, or meant to express political aims" (Vráblíková, 2017). Such definition emphasizes activity not just attitudes related to participation like the intention to participate. People can be involved in political activities in very diverse ways and through these ways influence politicians (Bennett and Segerberg, 2013; Norris, 2002; van Deth, 2001). Political engagement beyond elections includes activities such as contacting politicians, participation in protests, demonstrations, and petitioning, activities conduced on the Internet using social media, also considered as political activities. These modes of non-electoral participation are believed to contribute to improving the quality of democracy.

Following a popular typology, I have investigated institutionalized (voting, being a member of political party, being a candidate) and non-institutionalized (collecting signatures for a petition, participating in a protest or demonstration) form of political participation among young people from target countries. Older people participate more in institutionalized forms, in other words, conventional activities. Youth are more likely to choose unconventional political participation (Dalton, 1988). However, we should keep in mind that these divisions are not mutually exclusive, since some non-electoral forms are used by large numbers of people today and thus cannot be treated as unconventional any more, or some of them, like petitions and demonstrations, are legally institutionalized channels which can be organized by political parties, etc. Therefore, it can be problematic to regard non-electoral participation as "unconventional" or "non-institutional" (Vráblíková, 2017).

Here, when dichotomizing political actions, I am presenting trends among three target countries regarding different types of political involvement, as well as differences between three countries. As it was observed earlier, free and fair elections are important feature of democracy for young people and they consider voting as an important form of civic activity. Voting is considered in the literature as the conventional form of participation along with being a member of a political party, or organizing or participating in meetings, or contacting governmental officials. It seems that what they believe translates into action. More than 60 percent of respondents had voted in local or national elections in the past, and

Table 4.12 Youth participation in elections in target countries

	Why will you vote?			*Why will you NOT vote?*		
	Bosnia and Herzegovina	*Georgia*	*Ukraine*	*Bosnia and Herzegovina*	*Georgia*	*Ukraine*
I do/don't believe that my voice could change something	50.46	55.26	37.50	36.00	51.85	12.00
I do/don't consider voting as my civic duty	65.14	67.97	53.50	0.00	11.11	4.50
I do/don't feel responsible for my country and/or region	30.28	37.25	24.50	4.17	11.11	19.20
I want to express my dissatisfaction with a party or a candidate/I sometimes find campaigns silly or ridiculous	19.27	11.76	7.50	37.50	18.52	11.50
I do/don't want to express my support for a party or candidate	10.09	12.50	7.50	16.67	3.70	0.50
I am/I am not interested in politics	10.09	2.61	1.00	12.50	11.11	12.50
I always vote/don't always vote	10.09	3.92	5.50	4.17	18.52	11.00

Notes
Number of respondents that will vote = 480, Number of respondents that will not vote = 70.
Questions: "1) Will you vote in any upcoming political election at the local or national level? 2) Why will you vote/why will you not vote? Instruction: This is a multiple-choice question—you can choose up to three answers."

71 percent of young people from Bosnia-Herzegovina, 76 percent from Georgia, and 79.5 percent from Ukraine declare that they would vote in any upcoming political election. When asked why they would vote, 61 percent of respondent considered voting as their civic duty and 46 percent felt that their voice could change something in their countries. A third option chosen from the list of motivators was "I feel responsible for my country and/or region" (30 percent). The least important reason for voting was to express dissatisfaction with of support for a party or candidate. Those young people who responded that they would not vote in upcoming elections (13 percent) admitted that their voice would not change anything as their main reason.

In my study, I also asked, last year, if young people also participated in other non-conventional forms of political actions, such as collecting signatures for petition, participating in a protest or demonstration (Hooghe and Boonen, 2016).

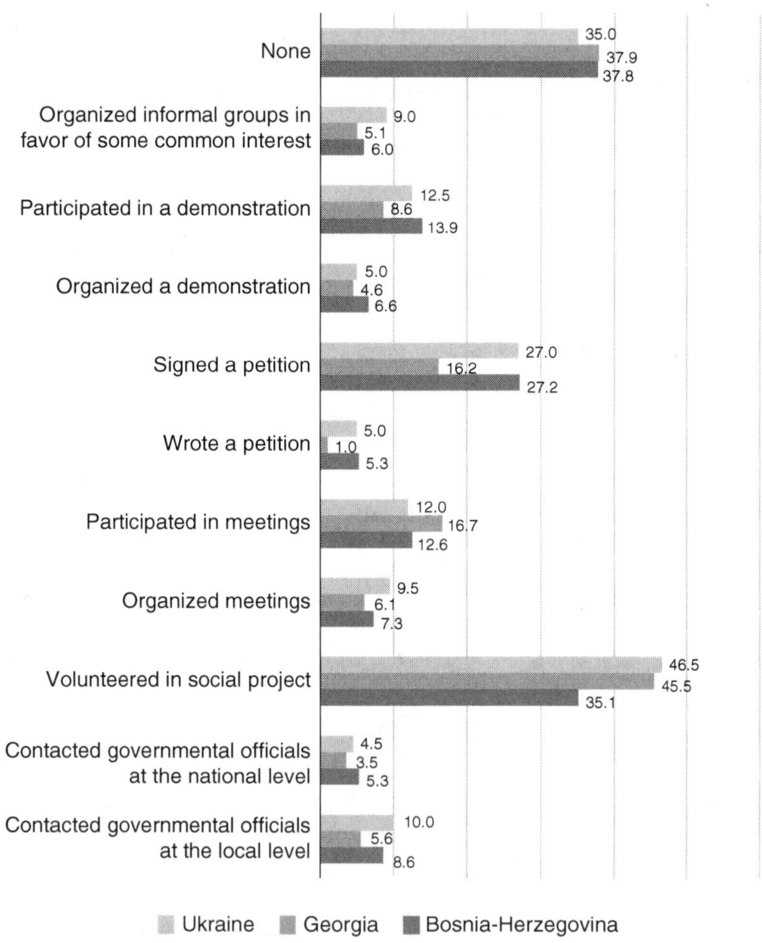

Figure 4.3 Forms of youth political engagement (%) in target countries.

Similar to the *ISSP module on Citizenship (Political Participation)*, the respondents were asked to choose several answers from the list. It should be noted that 37 percent of young people did not engage in any of the activities. Those who did, chose volunteering in social projects as a form of activity (43 percent), followed by signing petitions (23 percent), although writing the petition was the least liked form of participation. Some young people chose participation in meetings focused on the matters of local community (14 percent), although being less interested in organizing one. People expressed some interest in participating in demonstrations (11.5 percent), but also were less interested in organizing collective actions of this type or even organizing neighbors, co-workers or other groups in favor of some common interest.

If having interest or the need to contact governmental officials or politicians, young people are more likely to communicate with those at the local level than the national level. Additionally, young people were asked about whether they know who the major politicians and government ministers are in their countries. They were asked to say how quickly they would be able to provide the surnames of the political figures, if they were asked about this. More than 70 percent would give the name of the resident in one second, whereas only 46 percent could name the Prime Minister in such a short time, and 23 percent needs a short time to think (up to ten seconds). Young people needed a longer period of thinking or even checking on the Internet be able to name the minister of foreign affairs, the minister of internal affairs, the leader of the ruling party, and the leader of the biggest opposition party. More than 50 percent of young people would have to search in order to verify the name of a well-known human rights defender.

The results above show the engagement of youth in political affairs in the past. Additionally, the students were tested what these young people would do *vis-à-vis* their government in order to convert their grievances into action. In other words, youth's readiness to engage in different forms of activity was tested. Young people were asked to respond to the hypothetical vignettes "If you had a chance to influence the national government, what would you do to try to influence the national government about an unjust regulation or action?" They were asked to choose up to three from the list provided. The same vignette was given regarding local government. The most popular form of influencing the national government seemed to be consulting a lawyer or appealing through the courts (32.5 percent of respondents). Next, the second most popular option was directly contacting political leaders. This could be writing them a letter or visiting them (31 percent), and, the third, protesting (almost 30 percent). The other ways to express their disapproval would be voting against the offending politicians in the next election (27 percent) or organizing an informal group to write letters of protest or signing a petition (24.5 percent). As far as attempts to influence local government were concerned, the respondents would choose the same strategies. However, there are interesting differences in the order of preferences between the three countries. Young people from Bosnia-Herzegovina would choose in the first instance voting in the next election against politicians who

Table 4.13 Youths' readiness to engage in potential activities

	Towards national government			*Towards local government*		
	Bosnia and Herzegovina	*Georgia*	*Ukraine*	*Bosnia and Herzegovina*	*Georgia*	*Ukraine*
Consult a lawyer or appeal through the courts	24.3	46.0	25.5	23.8	41.9	23.5
Directly contact administrative (nonelected) officials	15.8	18.7	33.5	19.7	19.2	40.0
Directly contact political leaders (elected officials)	32.2	29.3	32.0	29.6	27.8	29.0
Protest	30.3	24.8	30.5	26.3	23.7	30.5
Organize an informal group	19.7	33.3	19.5	21.1	27.3	22.5
Work through a formal group	12.5	19.7	12.0	15.8	21.7	14.5
Work through a political party	11.8	11.1	4.5	10.5	8.1	4.0
Take some violent action	11.2	5.6	5.5	8.6	3.5	3.0
Vote against offending officials at the next election	42.1	13.6	28.5	44.1	18.7	21.0
I would not try at all	4.0	7.6	8.5	3.3	7.1	12.5
Don't know	7.2	10.1	15.0	10.5	11.6	18.5

Notes

N=550, % of respondents, percentages do not add up because the respondent had three options to choose.

introduced unjust regulation or policy (42 percent in case of the violation at the national level, and 44 percent at the local), Georgian young people, however, would appeal through the courts (46 percent and 42 percent). In Ukraine, however, direct contacts with both administrative officials or with elected officials were the favorable options to put pressure on national and local governments to change their offending actions.

Findings in the previous section on youth perception and opinion demonstrate that young citizens in these three countries do not have that much influence on their governments and on what the politicians are doing, therefore vignettes were introduced to test what these young people would do *vis-à-vis* their government if the circumstances and opportunities in their countries were different.

In sum, the results show that voting seems to be a dominant form of political engagement of young people from the three target countries. Voting is crucial, because it is the elemental form of participation. If there is too few votes, the elected government does not have sufficient popular support and may lack a mandate. Moreover, voting allows the government to be held to account for their decisions and ensures that citizens can protect themselves against dishonest and corrupt governments and choose to vote against them in the next elections. Thus, elections have a monitoring function, provided citizens do vote, and young people, as Table 4.7 shows recognize this opportunity. Nevertheless, although young people demonstrate some interest in non-conventional forms of political participation, such as signing petitions, there is variation in the amount and type of non-electoral participation among young people from the target countries.

Civic participation

Scholars have argued that institutions alone are weak underpinning for democracy. What ensures democracy, according to them, is a large number of people who participate in civic affairs who are tolerant of peers who disagree with them (Sullivan and Transue, 1999). Democratic dispositions develop because young people engage in certain kinds of practices as well as relationships. Certain settings and institutions, particularly schools and community-based organizations shape and nurture civic dispositions, and skills for actions. Young people are more likely to be active in their adulthood if they have and opportunities to engage in collective work and to discuss matters with peers, parents, teachers, and the like. Youth who have been engaged in community-based youth groups are more likely than their peers who have not been involved in such groups to be interested in current events (Flanagan, 2013). Relationships and interactions with other people, membership of organizations also enhance the likelihood of getting recruited into some form of public life. On the other hand, there are some concerns that younger generations may see this type of activity as an alternative rather than a motivator of political mobilization (Galston, 2001). Participation and doing collective good bring about social rewards and personal satisfaction. Politics is done in relationships and collaborations with others, as Flanagan (2013) pointed out: such organizations are "mini-polities" or "free spaces" because spaces are provided where younger generations work out what it means to be a citizen of the larger polity. Cooperative behavior is contagious and may have spillover effects on other interactions with individuals who were not engaged.

Scholars have presented different empirical investigations regarding the ways in which associations contribute to democracy finding multiple mechanisms through which association improves democracy and sustains it. In authoritarian regimes or where democratic institutions and practices are young and also fragile, the verifying function of civil society is even more important; the principal contribution of organizations to democracy is to provide resistance to political authority. Associations offer resistance to power, hold government to account (Fung, 2003), improve the quality and equality of representation. Their role depends on contextual features of particular societies, under authoritarian rule their role of resisting government authority might more important than the same role in democracy. Even in current times where many informal groups of activists have emerged, NGOs still matter. Sullivan and Transue (1999) found that the boundaries between the formal NGOs and informal groups of activists are blurred since there is much cross-over and collaboration. Their findings show that although at first glance NGOs may seem disconnected from street activism, the situation is more complicated, because in practice this is not correct. Sullivan and Transue call this phenomenon "surreptitious symbiosis" (1999, p. 2622). In democracies however, there is less conflict and more cooperation between state and organizations.

Above all organizations are aggregators of citizens' interests and are intermediaries between citizens and the elites and have various ways to put pressure on ruling elites (van Deth, Montero and Westholm, 2007). Many scholars have found that participation in associations positively affects political participation and recognize the need for decentralization of power in the country, in other words, the issue of transferring state responsibilities to the local government (Verba, Schlozman and Brady, 1995; Welzel, Inglehart and Deutsch, 2005) or the role of NGOs as a consultant and partner of the public sector. Not only do associations represent interests of civil society *vis-à-vis* government; they transmit the needs and preferences to the policymakers which can be translated into law or policy. Given this role, young people were asked about the importance of organizations, and they believe that the role of non-governmental organizations cannot be neglected as Table 4.14 demonstrates.

There are also other functions of associations, which are less tangible but are well-documented in the literature. Associations have been considered "schools of democracy" or "free schools" where people can learn the "general theory of association" (Tocqueville, 2000). This claim, which was very popular especially in the 1990s (Tocqueville, 2000 [1835–1840]) notes that associations stimulate political actions, and people are socialized to be politically active. Some kinds of organizations create avenues for direct participation in the field of social welfare for example. Moreover, participation in shared activities induces people to think and also to take care of others, and through, cooperating with others within jointly organized events, and meetings, their civic skills (such as critical thinking) and political efficacy are stimulated. Van Der Meer and Van Ingen (2009)

Table 4.14 Importance of civic organizations perceived by young people from the target countries

	Very important (%)	*Rather important (%)*	*Rather not important (%)*	*Rather not important (%)*
The delegation by the state widest possible competence of the social organizations/NGOs	32.7	42.7	20.9	3.6
Consultation with the interest groups on important state decisions	60.7	32.2	4.9	2.2

Notes
N=550, Note: Percentages by row.
Question: "Which of the following descriptions of the state do you consider as important, and which not, for creating a good standard of living? Instruction: Please answer all questions by choosing the answers that best describe your attitude."

find that instead of "schools of democracy" they are "pools of democracy" (p. 281). Through associations, people join social networks which are important for participation in a democracy.

Since the role of organizations and the membership impact on young people is very important, young people were also asked, similarly to the Civic Engagement (organizational involvement) measures taken from World Values Survey W6, whether they have participated in any activities of organization and if yes, in what kind of organization. It has turned out that 67 percent of them did participate. Young people were participating in cultural organizations (according to 32 percent of respondents)—as well as in leisure time/sport organizations, the second most favored type of organization. Young people did not look for participation in activities of faith-based organizations as well as in political organizations. Country variations demonstrate some interesting findings. Among the less interested in participation in any type of organizations were Ukrainian young people (42 percent). As compared to other nations, young people from Bosnia-Herzegovina were active in organizations promoting human rights, whereas Georgian young people participated in organizations promoting environmental issues, and Ukrainians in trade unions.

There are many ways to take part in a democracy. Democracy contributes to associations. Liberal democracies respect a broad range of individual rights, and associations result naturally from these rights because they pursue private and collective goals. Since the collective work of youth groups is important for building democracy in fledgling democracies, young people, when asked about their overall civic participation, as presented in Figure 4.4, chose volunteering in social projects as a form of activity. Overall, young people's commitment to participate in the civic affairs is higher among young people who engage in voluntary work, which confirms Roberts' (2009) and Flanagan's (2013) findings that that majority of young people in Eastern Europe have any experience of

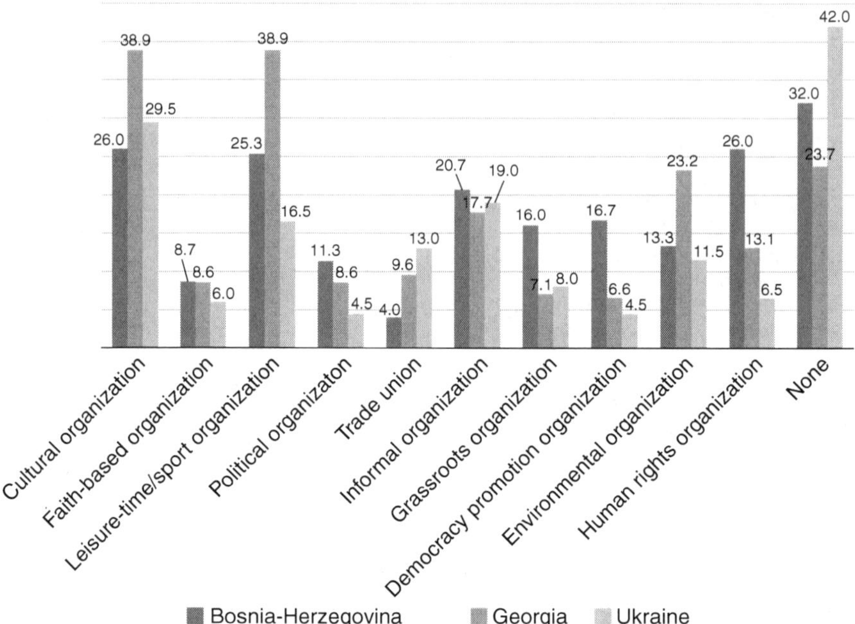

Figure 4.4 Youth participation in civic organizations (%) in target countries.

Note
N=550.

Question: "Have you participated in any activities of listed organizations? Instruction: This is a multiple choice question—you can choose several answers."

voluntary associations. The comparison with young people from CEE countries shows they seem to be less likely to be interested in participating in informal organizations. Although youth in the three nations in transition are only slightly less involved in organization when compared to their peers in CEE countries, they are much less involved in non-conventional forms of political participation.

It should be noted that the survey was conducted among young people who have a high potential to be selected by NGOs in recipient countries to participate in the democracy assistance projects. Given the fact that organizations are more likely to choose young people who are already active (Pospieszna and Galus, 2018), one could expect that these young people would more engaged in organizations. Without participation, without activism, organization may cease to function and they are essential for beginning and strengthening the democratization process and for sustainability of democracy.

A lack of associational behavior in post-communist societies can be explained by many factors, and one of the most important could be the sense of insecurity and distrust. Scholars have noted that trust is an important foundation for democratic governance. Social trust is related to tolerance and civic engagement. People who believe that other human being are fair and trustworthy tend to vote

Table 4.15 Political and civic engagement of young people: target vs. CEE countries

	Target countries	*CEE countries*
Political participation		
Conventional		
Voting	62.36	66.33
Participation in political organization	7.85	13.07
Organizing or participating in meetings	18.03	16.93
Contacting the governmental officials	10.40	7.89
Non-conventional		
Organizing or participating in protests/ demonstrations	14.94	18.97
Signing or writing petitions	24.23	38.36
Organizing informal groups	6.74	9.05
No political participation	36.79	30.27
Civic participation		
Cultural organization	31.93	30.75
Faith-based organization	7.66	12.64
Leisure-time/sport organization	27.01	36.49
Trade union	9.31	2.87
Informal organization	18.98	27.16
Grassroots organization	9.85	11.37
Democracy promotion organization	8.58	10.06
Environmental organization	16.24	12.07
Human rights organization	14.23	10.92
No participation in civic organizations	32.66	30.89
N	548	620

Note
% of respondents, percentages do not add up because the respondent had three answers to choose.

and join organizations (Flanagan, 2013). Putnam (2000) argued that the detachment of Americans from politics and public life was due to decreasing engagement in associations and smaller social trust which led to decreasing social capital. Putnam (2000) implied that social capital is the main bases for political participation, and that social capital emerges in civil society, where social networks can be created. Therefore, organizations, namely, voluntary associations of various types, are venues where social capital can be built since they connect those with similar interests, attitudes as well have the potential to bond various groups. Through participation in organizations various civic virtues can develop, such as empathy, tolerance, trust, and reciprocity, as well as civic behaviors such as solving problems cooperatively, which in turn contributes to building social capital and democracy.

Participation and its correlates

Studies have shown that membership of voluntary organization and associations increases activism (Eliasoph, 2013; Vráblíková, 2017). Overall, people who are more involved in social groups tend to participate more. There are two factors explaining this correlation. First, associations are places where individual civic skills are produced (Verba, Schlozman and Brady, 1995); social capital theory expects that social networks among individuals that are created by means of organizations they belong to, produce trust and reciprocity, and thus social capital, which leads to higher participation in politics (Putnam, 1995 and 2000). Social networks are stable links connecting individuals to a wider political environment and people who are in those networks are more likely to get political information or receive requests to participate. Second, due to group membership, there is higher recruitment probability. Organizations are those environments in which individuals can be mobilized (Teorell, 2003).

In other words, associations are mobilizing actors, and serve as a bridge linking the political structure and individual behavior (Walgrave and Rucht, 2010). They make judgments, inform, persuade and recruit ordinary citizens to take part in political actions. We can observe in recent years, that political participation in various non-electoral events is coordinated and organized by associations, activists, and various social groups (Boulding, 2014; Rosenstone and Hansen, 2003). The mobilizing actors that organized and coordinate political involvement beyond voting and appeal to ordinary citizens to get involved are such actors as social movements, interest groups, trade unions, community groups, various political or civic associations, social networks and media (Norris, 2002; van Deth, 1997). Given these findings, I investigate the correlation between membership in civic organizations and political participation and the results are reported below in Table 4.16.

A strong positive correlation can be observed between membership of civic organizations of any type and both conventional and non-conventional forms of political participation among young people in target countries. The only associations that do not seem to have any impact on political participation are faith-based organizations, whereas engagement in informal or grassroots, as well as those promoting democracy drive this positive relationship. However, van Der Meer and Van Ingen (2009) examining seventeen European countries find no evidence for a direct causal relation between associational involvement and political action, but rather an indirect one. Meer and Van Ingen find that a bivariate association between civic participation and political actions might be explained by selection effects: "people with socioeconomic resources and pro-social dispositions might be civic participants and politically active at the same time, without direct relations between the two forms of involvement" (2009). In other words, one may expect that a relationship between civic participation and political actions is more likely through socialization. Civic skills and virtues explain much of the correlation between involvement in associations and political activism. People join organizations for the same reasons that they become politically active, namely reach specific political goals or get involved in political discourse (Van der Meer and Van Inken, 2009).

Since pattern of participation or non-participation cannot be analyzed within the broader context and all possible factors affecting these patterns, following

Hooghe and Boonen (2016), I develop an analytical model in which I examine the influence of other individual-level factors, such as education, age, gender, family education, nationality on the probability to engage in traditional (i.e., institutionalized) forms of participation and non-institutionalized as well as in civic participation. Moreover, I also include the way citizens view and evaluate democracy, and other factors affecting civic engagement and political participation as indicated by the literature. Table 4.17 reports the results.

The earlier literature treated political dissatisfaction as a factor that decreased participation and instead somewhat motivated illegal, violent or even radical activities (Almond and Verba, 1963). However, postmaterialist interpretation is different, because dissatisfaction is regarded as a trigger for more participation (Dalton, 2008; Armingeon, 2007; Vráblíková, 2017). I expect that in the case of democracies dissatisfaction indeed might facilitate greater engagement, but in the case of democratizing countries it might have an opposite effect. A dissatisfied democrat who is critical of the actions taken by the government, will engage and take political action in Poland, the Czech Republic, Slovakia, whereas in weak democratizing countries he or she will be less likely to take action and engage. It can be expected the main difference between CEE fully-fledged democracies and those developing post-communist democracies, such as Bosnia-Herzegovina, Ukraine and Georgia. In other words, young people from Bosnia-Herzegovina, Georgia, and Ukraine may engage in civic and political activities if they are satisfied with democracy, and will not if they are dissatisfied with democracy, whereas young people from CEE will also engage if are dissatisfied. Nevertheless, I did not find support of these claims. Satisfaction with democracy is not an important predictor. Instead, support for democracy plays an important role in young people's political participation. In CEE countries, however, support for social democracy components, rather than liberal ones, induces eagerness to engage in politics.

Individual political attitudes do not have an impact on whether young people get involved in politics in target countries, but rather on membership of associations (civic engagement), mass media use, and level of parental education (the higher level of parental education, the greater the probability of such engagement). In the case of young people from CEE countries, various political perceptions, beliefs, feelings, and motivations regarding the role of citizens and the role of government matter. Particularly important are political attitudes and values that refer to subjective evaluation of political competence, so-called political efficacy, especially the internal type of political efficacy where efficacy evaluates individuals' confidence that people are able to understand and participate in politics. External efficacy, however is the feeling that people have an impact on politics and that politicians are responsive to them. Similar to other scholars (Armingeon, 2007; Cammerts *et al.*, 2016; Craig and Maggiotto, 1982; Dalton, 2014; Vráblíková, 2017), I find that the higher perception of efficacy the better since this increases participation. Rosenstone and Hansen (1993) point out that people would not participate in politics if they believed that activity is hopeless, because they have no influence on what the government does and when the

Table 4.16 Membership of civic organizations and political participation of youth program potential beneficiaries in target countries

Civic organizations	*Conventional political participation*			*Non-conventional political participation*			
	Voting	*Participation in political organization*	*Organizing or participating in meetings*	*Contacting the governmental officials*	*Organizing or participating in protests/demonstrations*	*Signing or writing petition*	*Organizing informal groups*
Participation in any organization	**0.117** (0.006)	**0.156** (0.000)	**0.254** (0.000)	**0.187** (0.000)	**0.251** (0.000)	**0.197** (0.000)	**0.166** (0.000)
Cultural	0.057 (0.180)	0.048 (0.266)	0.187 (0.000)	0.127 (0.003)	0.156 (0.000)	0.118 (0.006)	0.112 (0.009)
Faith-based	–0.030 (0.480)	0.043 (0.311)	0.061 (0.155)	0.062 (0.147)	0.015 (0.721)	–0.01 (0.676)	0.0045 (0.916)
Leisure-time/sport	–0.030 (0.480)	0.052 (0.226)	**0.099** (0.020)	0.021 (0.620)	0.013 (0.761)	0.071 (0.098)	**0.115** (0.007)
Trade union	0.068 (0.111)	0.047 (0.275)	**0.160** (0.000)	–0.006 (0.880)	**0.150** (0.000)	**0.143** (0.001)	**0.239** (0.000)
Informal	0.031 (0.461)	**0.118** (0.005)	**0.184** (0.000)	**0.185** (0.000)	**0.244** (0.000)	**0.217** (0.000)	**0.185** (0.000)

Grassroots	0.005 (0.907)	**0.131** (0.002)	**0.179** (0.000)	**0.168** (0.000)	**0.156** (0.000)	**0.086** (0.045)	**0.155** (0.000)
Democracy promotion	**0.091** (0.034)	0.153 (0.000)	**0.144** (0.001)	**0.280** (0.000)	**0.203** (0.000)	**0.178** (0.000)	**0.151** (0.000)
Environmental	0.006 (0.883)	0.037 (0.386)	**0.192** (0.000)	**0.190** (0.000)	**0.235** (0.000)	0.087 (0.041)	**0.158** (0.000)
Human rights	0.037 (0.383)	**0.114** (0.007)	0.189 (0.000)	0.203 (0.000)	**0.230** (0.000)	**0.198** (0.000)	**0.182** (0.000)
No participation	**–0.131** (0.002)	**–0.174** (0.000)	**–0.236** (0.000)	**–0.174** (0.000)	**–0.224** (0.000)	**–0.201** (0.000)	**–0.156** (0.000)

Notes

Pearson's *r* in the first row, *p* value in parenthesis.

Non-conventional political participation: "What kind of actions did you take during the last year? Instruction: This is a multiple-choice question–you can choose several answers." Questions regarding voting: "Did you vote in any political election at the local or national level? Instruction: Please choose one answer that best describes your experience: Yes; No, I didn't; No, because I was too young to vote Don't know. Participation in political organization: "Have you participated in any activities of listed organizations?" Statistical significant correlations in bold, p values in parentheses.

Table 4.17 Factors affecting civic participation and political participation

	Political participation		*Civic participation*	
	(1) Target countries	*(2) CEE countries*	*(3) Target countries*	*(4) CEE countries*
Satisfaction with democracy	0.026	–0.002	0.016	0.033
	(0.021)	(0.018)	(0.020)	(0.021)
Support for liberal democracy	**0.035***	0.019	**0.027****	**0.035***
	(0.013)	(0.011)	(0.012)	(0.012)
Social democracy components	–0.053	**–0.072*****	–0.052	**–0.068****
	(0.036)	(0.021)	(0.034)	(0.023)
Political efficacy				
External efficacy	–0.043	–0.003	0.040	–0.044
	(0.067)	(0.059)	(0.065)	(0.066)
Internal efficacy	0.069	**0.144****	0.070	**0.193****
	(0.065)	(0.055)	(0.063)	(0.061)
Political trust	–0.047	**0.192****	–0.041	**0.281*****
	(0.103)	(0.067)	(0.100)	(0.075)
Social trust	–0.043	0.089	0.038	**0.234*****
	(0.068)	(0.128)	(0.066)	(0.065)
Norms of citizenship				
Norms of citizen duty	–0.002	0.011	–0.034	–0.026
	(0.022)	(0.015)	(0.022)	(0.017)
Engaged citizenship	0.008	**0.048***	0.052	**0.092*****
	(0.029)	(0.020)	(0.028)	(0.022)
Interest in politics	–0.067	**0.152***	0.005	–0.014
	(0.082)	(0.074)	(0.080)	(0.083)

Membership in associations	**0.918*****	**0.717*****	—	—
	(0.133)	(0.111)		
Mass media use	**0.043****	**0.056*****	**0.041****	0.017
	(0.016)	(0.016)	(0.016)	(0.018)
Student	0.356	0.103	–0.276	–0.397
	(0.222)	(0.241)	(0.215)	(0.270)
Parents' education	**0.052***	–0.015	**0.061****	0.033
	(0.021)	(0.018)	(0.020)	(0.020)
Financial status	–0.071	–0.054	–0.078	–0.090
	(0.058)	(0.055)	(0.168)	(0.161)
Urban vs. rural areas	–0.003	0.007	0.026	–0.046
	(0.030)	(0.024)	(0.029)	(0.027)
Gender (female)	–0.182	–0.195	0.004	–0.213
	(0.136)	(0.103)	(0.130)	(0.114)
Constant	–0.353	–1.077	0.511	–0.451
	(0.739)	(0.53)	(0.713)	(0.597)
Number of observations	542	680	543	685
Adj R-squared	0.1480	0.2093	0.0578	0.1464

Notes

Statistical significance *** $p<0.001$; ** $p<0.01$; * $p<0.05$. Political participation variable was created as an index encompassing the following variables indicating both conventional and non-conventional forms of political participation: (1) Voting; (2) Participation in political organization; (3) Organizing or participating in meetings; (4) Contacting governmental officials; (5) Organizing or participating in protests/demonstrations; (6) Signing or writing petition; (7) Organizing informal groups. The index is a sum of these dummy variables. The higher the values of the new variable the greater participation in various forms of political participation. *Civic participation* variable is also an index. The respondents were asked to choose from the list of various organizations whether they have ever participated in any activities of these organizations, and they could choose several answers. The answers to were added up so that the new variable indicates the level of civic engagement, the higher the variable, the more organizations the respondents have been involved in. Statistical significance in bold, p values in parentheses.

government does not care what they think. On the contrary, people who believe more strongly that politicians are responsive to them tend to participate more. Vráblíková (2017) also finds similar support. Whereas I do find support in case of young people in CEE countries, I do not find that efficacy seems to play an important role in inducing political engagement among young people in the three target countries.

Social and political trust is expected to increase political activism. However, findings are diverse in the literature. They are either positive, negative, or have no effect on political activism (Bernhagen and Marsh, 2007; Hooghe and Marien, 2012). Vráblíková (2017) finds that, in the case of democracies, people who trust politicians less tend to participate more in non-electoral politics. But the question is whether this is the case in democratizing countries as well. It seems that young people in target countries do not participate in politics because of social or political trust. However, in the case of young people in CEE it is a strong predictor of both political participation as well as civic engagement.

Scholars tend to agree that the assessment of citizenship norms is a useful way to analyze citizen's expectations about the citizen's role in the political system. As already mentioned, earlier norms of citizenship play an important role in measuring the impact on satisfaction with democracy as well as support for democratic principles. There is a belief that these norms explain individuals' views about their own responsibilities, which, in turn may guide actual behavior (Bolzendahl and Coffé, 2013; Dalton, 2006, 2008; Hooghe, Oser and Marien, 2016). They should predict participation in political and civic activities. "Citizen duty" norms refer to the limited participatory role for citizens, mainly meaning allegiance to law and order, duty to vote, duty to report crime, etc. However, "engaged citizen" norms of citizenship refer to a more active role of the citizen, who is watching the government, helping those less privileged, participating in associations (Dalton, 2008). Dalton (2006) finds that "duty-based" citizens are more likely to vote than citizens with a lower sense of duty, but "engaged" citizens, meaning those who value "norms of engaged citizenship" are more likely to participate in a variety of political activities—both electoral and non-electoral (e.g., signing petitions, participating in demonstrations). Similarly, in their analysis of twenty-five countries, Bolzendahl and Coffe (2013) find that norms related to the duty of paying taxes and obeying the law ("norms of citizen duty") negatively predict party membership, voting, and political activism. Conversely, norms such as those regarding the importance of being active in civic and political associations, keeping a watch on the government, and helping those worse off in your country and the world were associated with a higher propensity to vote and to be engaged in political activism. Vráblíková (2017) finds that norms of engaged citizenship increase activism, while norms of citizen duty have an opposite effect. My results conform to the findings in the literature, however, with respect only to young people from CEE countries. In the case of young people from Bosnia-Herzegovina, Georgia and Ukraine norms of citizenship do not play an important role in predicting young people's engagement in politics and associations.

When people are interested in politics, and when they think that participation is their duty they tend to participate more. Political interest can be understood as the attention that people pay to politics and strongly and positively affects all kinds of activities (Bernhagen and Marsh, 2007; Vráblíková, 2017). Active citizens are those who are either involved in political participation or simply have declared readiness and interest in political activities, Amnå and Ekman (2013) called them "standby citizens"—in other words readiness is not passivity, it rather represents a postmodern form of citizenship (Gvozdanovic, 2016). The findings show that indeed in the case of young people from the CEE countries, interest in politics is an important predictor of participation, but not in target countries.

Political socialization is a process by which a person acquires skills to function in the political world. It is an ongoing and changing process that occurs over a lifetime. Young people learn about politics from parents, at school, from the media. These are considered transitional agents of political socialization. If young people are socialized into the values of freedoms, and human empowerment this will foster the demand for liberal democracy, social capital and networks. Parents and the family are considered as the primary agent of political socialization—young people model the behavior and attitudes of their parents, although researchers also find that while parents have a high influence young people in adolescence, over time parents and children tend to disagree over some political issues. Nevertheless, if emulation is not the mechanism, economic and socio-cultural factors may have a considerable influence on the role of parents and the family in a direct way (how parents affected for example negatively by unemployment can relate their political attitudes to their children) and in an indirect way (social status, education, etc.). Moreover, it can also be discussion and independent thinking about political issues that is encouraged by parents, and can have an important influence on political attitudes, and knowledge.

Besides the impact of families and schools, individuals participate more in politics when they are: (1) recruited by various agents—politicians, organizations, (2) are involved in social networks or are members of associations; (3) discuss politics with others. Various civic organizations play an important role in these processes. As mentioned earlier, some authors argue that there is a socializing explanation for why membership of organizations increases participation through increasing civic skills and social trust. Others emphasize that membership of organizations, regardless of the specific focus of the organization, increases the probability of being recruited for participation (Dian and McAdam, 2003; Teorell, 2003). Vráblíková (2017) finds a direct effect of group membership on the political activism of individuals in developed democracies, as well as indirectly through recruitment.

Organizations are the socialization agent in shaping civic knowledge and also engaging the younger generation in extracurricular activities, participating in debates, stimulating interaction with fellow citizens to accomplish common goals. They are simply structures for creating opportunities for activism (McAdam, 1986). A useful tool for understanding the new forms of political participation is theory of civil society development and social capital. Social links, relations with other people form social capital, which in turn leads to greater engagement in public affairs. Various voluntary associations and organizations, even of not directly targeting political elites, facilitate the fulfillment of shared goals and the solution of common problems, and create, as Putnam (2000) put it, "social networks, norms of reciprocity, and trustworthiness," which are known as social capital. Thus, social capital is built where there is trust, both interpersonal and political, linkages between people, and mutual exchange. Also, by means of organization, greater communication is possible and communication plays an essential role in the process of political socialization. Discussion of politics via communication with friends, and political discussion should facilitate participation mainly because it conveys political information (Leighley, 1990; McClurg, 2003). The results in Table 4.17 show that membership of associations positively affects political participation only in CEE countries.

In addition to the discussion of politics and civic engagement, participation in organizations, mass media use[1] is expected to be related to participation. Questions regarding the source of information that young people use in order to update themselves about public affairs demonstrate that traditional sources are not considered to be important. Interestingly, traditional media does matter for the support of democracy, whereas there no significant relationship between new media and support for democracy. Political participation of young people in both target and CEE countries is positively via media usage. Those young people who read printed newspapers, listen to the radio, and watch TV also vote, join political parties, and take part in meetings. However, those who update themselves about current affairs by using social media, also chose voting as means of political participation. It is no surprise that new media is positively correlated with organizing protests or demonstrations, singing or writing petitions, or forming informal groups.

In order to participate, people need resources such as time, money and skills and very first studies of political participation have reported that people with higher socioeconomic status tend to be more active in politics (Barnes and Kaase, 1979; Verba *et al.*, 1978). More educated, wealthier and middle aged people are more like to participate (Stolle and Hooghe, 2011; Teorell, Torcal and Montero, 2007). People of higher socioeconomic status are more likely to participate in politics because it costs them less than poor people (Brady, Verba and Scholzman, 1995). The political activity of youth is closely entwined with education which is related to family origins and social class. More educated people know more about politics, understand it better and are able to process political information. They also have better knowledge of how to search through information (Dalton, 2014). Social status is determined by parents' education. There are many other determinants including gender. Gender difference has also been identified with males being more interested in politics. Men and women often differ in their level of political interest, participation in organizations or even in voter turnout (Inglehart and Norris, 2003a).

According to Inglehart (1997), social developments in post-industrial societies replace the materialist values, which were associated with security and authority, with postmaterialist values associated with a greater concern for people, for individual autonomy, self-expression, human rights, and the environment, etc. However, he implies this postmaterialist values come into play with greater subjective wellbeing, higher quality of life, which also lead to newer and non-traditional forms of expression and challenging elites.

What is the role of socioeconomic factors in this study? Young people, mainly males, from Bosnia-Herzegovina as well as from Georgia are more likely than Ukrainian youth to choose voting as a form of participation. Ukrainian youth in turn are in favor of party membership or participating in meetings and contacting governmental officials. They also like all three forms of non-institutionalized forms of participation: petitions, protests and informal groups. Females in general prefer protests or demonstrations as well as organizing informal groups around some common interest. In general, young people who are students in all disciplines engage in both conventional (voting, party membership) and non-conventional forms of participation (signing or writing petitions, organizing informal groups). However, there are some interesting variations among academic majors as well.

Youth, because of increased socioeconomic insecurities tend to withdraw from public engagement, and in order to make up for lack of funding, support or any personal connection that can be adopted, thus take up the beliefs and values that are transmitted to them by the older generation that support and offer its patronage to young people (see Diuk, 2012, p.140). As regards, the impact of education, we have to keep in mind that education has been modernized with countries opting for European school system, aligning their educational system with the Bologna Declaration. According to this declaration of 1999: states agreed that by 2010 they would have established comparable degrees, a three-year bachelor's degree, followed by a two-year master's, the promotion of student mobility and free movement, staff exchanges, student mobility, cooperation in quality, and institutional cooperation.

In general, both parents having a high level of education positively affects the likelihood that young people will participate in target countries. This cannot be said about other conventional forms of participation, e.g., a father's high level of education is negatively correlated with party membership and participation in meetings. The fact that both parents have experienced higher education matters and influences whether young people from these countries will engage in non-governmental forms of participation. A mother's higher education is positively related to protests, and higher education of both parents with singing or writing petitions and organizing informal groups. Another feature is financial status, Young people who assessed their financial situation as very good (we live very well—we can afford luxury) are less likely to vote, take part in protests and to organize them in informal groups, but they can join parties, take part in meetings and contact governmental officials, or even sign a petition. Most of the respondents who evaluated their situation as average (we enough for everyday expenses, but need to save for major purchases) and above average (we live well—we have enough with particular savings). The average financial situation is positively related to voting and signing petitions, and negatively to other forms, However above average financial situations make young people more interested in joining a party, taking part in meeting, and contacting officials just as young people very affluent backgrounds, are also interested in taking part in protests and demonstrations.

Economic or education status are predictors of participation (Verba and Nie, 1972). However scholars agree that other factors affecting political participation need to be looked at two since countries with greater participation in higher educational to not see higher participation in politics, expressed in voter turnout, for example.

Conclusion

This chapter has been about individual-level factors—opinions, perceptions, and views on democracy—as well as about political participation and civic engagement of young people in target countries. With help from the collaborative network of foreign-funded NGOs in Bosnia-Herzegovina, Georgia and Ukraine, a survey has been conducted among these potential beneficiaries. The overall goal of the survey was to answer the research question whether there is a need to provide democracy assistance via youth projects in target countries. The findings from the survey were compared with young people's views and opinions from CEE countries, who until recently were considered fully-fledged democracies, but which today find themselves at an illiberal moment.

The findings demonstrate, that there seems to be no difference regarding the cornerstones of liberal and electoral components: free and fair elections and the rule of law, and the way citizens view and evaluate democracy. Although some small differences exist between countries, there is a broad understanding of democracy by all, meaning that young people from democratizing countries have as good a knowledge of what democracy is as young people from democratized countries. These findings are similar to earlier studies (Ferrin and Kriesi, 2016; Norris, 2011) that people share a common understanding of democracy. The fact that there is a homogeneity on how young people understand democracy, with only slight differences across countries to the extent to which youth support each of the attributes of democracy, could be a good indicator showing that democratic principles and norms do spread across regions. One might derive a further conclusion that, if young people are equally knowledgeable about the principles of liberal representative democracy, contextual factors are not that important since diffusion of democratic ideas takes place.

However, support for democracy is rooted in evaluations, since support for democracy does not automatically translate into a positive assessment of democratic regimes in a given country, because, although young people may believe in the desirability of democracy, they might have little confidence in some key democratic institutions. The analysis of citizens' perspective can also tell us a lot about the quality of democracy. Evaluations of democracy shows that young people in target countries prefer democracy to any other form of government, but have little regard for actual democratic institutions as well as political elites. This can indicate that young people are not socialized enough into the political system. Therefore, in order to complete the picture, young people were tested on individual-level factors, such as individual political attitudes: trust in political actors, trust in legal institutions, trust in liberal institutions, party identification, interpersonal trust, interest in politics (watching politics on TV) as well as level of socialization and socioeconomic status.

The results of the survey show that there is very little trust and disbelief among young people from three the target countries that the government serves the needs of citizens in their countries. As regards norms of citizenship, they believe that the main duty of citizens is follow the law, pay taxes and be loyal to and respectful of the country. However, not many respondents find that "engaged citizenship" matters, and that taking part in activities of political parties or non-governmental organizations is crucial for them as citizens. The respondents only read newspapers from time to time, almost never listen to the radio in order to follow the news, and a minority watch TV, whereas online media and Internet websites as well as social media are used by young people to inform themselves about the current affairs. Individual factors and their impact on the satisfaction with democracy were tested by regression analysis and were compared with CEE countries. I have found significant differences between youth from two different groups with respect to the impact of individual-level factors on satisfaction and support for democracy. For example, in target countries, norms of engaged citizenship are not affecting satisfaction with democracy, but they do have an impact on support for democracy, whereas, in CEE, norms of engaged citizenship are important for positive assessment of democracy and for support.

While views on democracy and citizenship are important, this perception might not automatically imply participation or willingness to participate. After learning opinions and feelings about political and social life as well as an interest in public affairs in their countries, young people were also asked about their political and civic participation. They find voting an import activity. However, they do not find non-conventional forms of political actions, such as collecting signatures for petitions, participating in a protest or demonstration, as important activities in which they could take part. As regards civic engagement, country variations demonstrate some interesting findings. Ukrainian young people were less interested in participation in any type of organization. Young people in Bosnia-Herzegovina are active in organizations promoting human rights, whereas Georgian young people join organizations promoting environmental issues. However, this associational behavior is modest, and can be explained by many factors, and one of the most important could be the sense of insecurity and distrust, and weak socialization, which are shown to be important in regression analysis.

To sum up, young people in target countries are very knowledgeable about that the principles of liberal representative democracy. The lack of difference between EE and CEE regarding views of democracy means that effective ideas about democracy have spread, and citizens of different countries in different regions have similar conceptions of democracy. However, these young people in the target countries are relatively passive citizens who value higher norms of citizens' duty than norms of engaged citizens, which is also confirmed by their low participation in non-conventional forms of political participation and civic engagement. This confirms that democracy assistance to young people is needed. Young people need to be socialized into the values of engaged citizenship and human empowerment, because this will lead to changes in political culture, and will foster the demand for liberal democracy, as expressed by Inglehart and Welzel (2005) that "changes in political culture are needed toward greater self-expression and emancipation and thus toward a liberal democratic understanding of democracy."

Note

1 In order to create "Media use" variable, I have added up the answers to the question "How do you update yourself about the public affairs and how often?": (1) Newspapers and magazines (printed); (2) Radio (traditional—not online); (3) TV (traditional—not online), (4) Online media (press/radio/TV; (5) Internet websites; (6) Social media. Respondents had four possible options to choose from: "Nearly every day" (coded as 1); "About once a week" (coded as 2); "From time to time" (coded as 3); "Never" (coded as 4). These six variables were added up to create a new one, and index variable: "Media use." Each component has the same weight. Since larger values of the new variable meant more responses of "Never," the variable was recoded in order to indicate that the higher the number of the variable meant the higher consumption of media for the purpose of obtaining information about public affairs by the respondents.

5 Evaluating the impact of bypass democracy assistance

The aim of this chapter is to evaluate democracy assistance of young democracies by assessing NGO projects in a specific area of democracy assistance, youth activism. As demonstrated earlier in the book, the goal of CEE NGOs democracy assistance programs directed toward young people is not just to inculcate democratic values, but also that these values ignite subsequent political and civic engagement among young people in target countries. This chapter evaluates these efforts. There have been two programs selected for this purpose: a civic education program, and the second, derived from the former, whose goal is to inspire young people to take up leadership roles in their communities. This chapter also demonstrates the usefulness of various methods to evaluate the impact of the democracy assistance at the micro level.

It should be noticed that in the evaluation of democracy assistance, there are in general within-country analyses, comparisons between countries using a large-scale survey dataset which allows comparison between countries. Adoption and implementation of a norm may be measured at the collective level, for example legal adoption of certain norms promoted by international organizations (Schimmelfennig *et al.*, 2006). However, this can also be measured at the individual level as well, although this is more difficult than the adoption and implementation of certain norms by the states (Zürn and Checkel, 2005) because the question arises of whose habits, patterns of behavior to measure. Analysis here is based on the norm adoption at the micro level. This chapter also contributes to the discussion initiated by Horký-Hluchán̆ (2012) as well as Szent-Iványi and Lightfoot (2016) who questioned whether transition experiences of CEE countries can be seen as a comparative advantage in democracy promotion, and point out that it is difficult to draw any clear conclusions, as there have been few methodologically sound impact assessments of CEE democracy aid activities to date.

This chapter provides discussion on how organizations and researchers can measure the impact of democracy assistance programs at the individual level. Changes in young people's behaviors and attitudes can be observed at the individual level and aggregated to the societal level. I provide some suggestions on how we can go about measuring the impact of the youth programs and any programs in democracy assistance. Special attention in this chapter is given to a novel approach for studying the impact of democracy promotion by using an experimental method. I believe that, by promoting the evaluation of specific democracy promotion programs (Dodsworth, 2016; Norris, 2017) as well as randomization as an appropriate methodology to assess the impact, is important so that scholars can learn about this method, criticize, modify and use it in their research. These suggestions are drawn on practical experience with one of the NGOs with whom I had a closer collaboration during this research project. Inspired by a group of economists at Poverty Action Lab, I use a randomized controlled trails method to assess impact evaluation of NGOs' projects aimed at inspiring and educating youth. This method requires collecting information needed to clearly determine the impact of donor-sponsored NGO projects, in other words, including before-and-after measurements of key outcome variables and measurements of both the groups under discussion and control of the comparison group of young people that will be not included in the NGOs' programs.

In non-experimental research, the variation is a consequence of factors outside of the control of the researcher. The researcher only observes, but does not intervene in that process (Morton and Williams, 2006). Social experiments if they are randomized, can solve the problem of selection bias by generating an experimental control group composed of persons who would have participated but who were randomly denied access to the program (treatment) (Burtless, 1995). In experimental research, however, since subjects are randomly assigned to treatments, the experimentalist can eliminate extraneous factors that can obscure the effects (Björkman and Svensson, 2009; Duflo *et al.*, 2007; Hyde, 2015; Olken, 2007a, 2007b). The strongest argument in favor of experiments is that under certain condition they solve the fundamental evaluation problem that arises from the impossibility of observing what would happen if the democracy assistance program had not existed. An impact evaluation can answer the question of whether a program works.

Therefore, is it believed that randomization is the most credible and accurate form of impact evaluation, and the best procedure to gain knowledge regarding the effect of assistance projects. This method may help solve the problem of causal attribution of specific outcomes to NGOs' democracy assistance project. However, there is hardly any research in the democracy assistance field that employs this method. Therefore, with this novel method, this study is a contribution to research on the effectiveness of democracy assistance.

Measuring the impact of democracy assistance at micro level

This section presents different methods used to evaluate the impact of democracy assistance programs together with their advantages and limitations. These suggestions can be useful for both practitioners wishing to learn whether their programs make an impact, as well as for researchers wanting to answer the question whether and how democracy assistance efforts of organizations from foreign countries influence young people in target countries.

Before-and-after comparisons. This method entails the use of baseline survey and the same survey after the implementation of the program. The purpose of the baseline study is to provide an information base against which the project's progress and achievements can be measured later (before-and-after comparisons). It usually takes a form of surveying youth as well as other stakeholders who might be affected by the program. This method measures how program participants improved or changed as the result of their participation in the program. The outcomes of the participants are recoded before the program is implemented and these are then compared to the outcomes of these same participants after the program ends. We have to collect data on the outcomes of program participants before and after the program is implemented. This can be done through surveys conducted before and after the program.

This methodology allows comparing the outcomes before and after, and if the scores are higher than they were before the program started, it seems that the program has made a difference. Is the before-and-after comparison the right methodology for evaluating the program then? The methodology seems to be simple, but questionable whether we can be sure whether the change in scores can be attributed to program intervention, or whether something else caused scores to rise. If we simply measure knowledge and perceptions before and after the programs, we cannot be certain whether some or all of the improvement was due to the many other things that changed and influenced the learning of the young people at the same time.

For example, before the program run by People in Need and funded by the World Bank "The Youth Inclusion and Social Accountability Project (YISAP)" was implemented in Georgia, the organization conducted a survey of Georgian youth and local authorities in the Sagarejo, Terjola and Tskaltubo municipalities. The main objective of the above-mentioned PIN project was to promote youth inclusion and social accountability and to increase the participation of youth in social accountability and civic engagement at the municipal level, leading to greater youth inclusion. The survey was conducted with the object of determining the knowledge, attitudes and practices of youth among the general population with regard to involvement in civic life, perception and the extent of their use of the Internet, mobile phones and social media for civic engagement purposes. Representatives of the local authorities in the target area were included in the survey as well in order to determine their experience, attitudes and perceptions of involving the youth in local decision-making processes.

The findings from the baseline study demonstrated that there was a desire for respondents to be engaged in social and civil society initiatives, irrespective of the disbelief that they can actually change anything. It seemed that they needed more opportunities or assistance from the local authorities and other institutions. The older age groups respondents in particular agreed that they needed to overcome negative attitudes and laziness. On the other hand, local authorities needed to be more active in terms of accountability and transparency towards the youth groups, because despite authorities' perceptions that the young people have many opportunities to express their opinions, the youngsters often lack in-time information on planned developments. Thus, the findings of the base line study allowed the organization to justify that the goal of the program matched the needs of the local community.

However, the greatest limitation of the methodology has been the assumption that the program was the only factor influencing any changes in the measured outcome over time. However, many other factors other than the program we are evaluating can change the outcomes of a program over time, especially if the program lasts longer and particularly if the beneficiaries of the program are young people who, in contrast to adults, develop and change quickly. They can be activated or informed by doing something with their peers, or taking part in other parallel events, or being influenced by parents, and teachers. All other factors probably could educate and empower young people even if these young people were not given a chance to participate in the program.

In order to overcome the drawbacks of this methodology we can conduct surveys immediately after the end of the program. Also, this methodology is recommended for evaluating the programs that have a short time span. We can, therefore, limit the influence of many other factors than a program, which could influence changes. If the there is one year or more between pre and posttests than there is the risk that many factors will have influenced the learning levels of the young people who participated in the program. However, even in short-term programs, we may either underestimate the impact of the program and might even find no impact; and , we may also overestimate impact by assuming that all the improvements were due to our program.

Qualitative methods: often the before-and-after comparison method is accompanied by qualitative methods that are being used by organizations, such as interviews with the participants or focus group (FG) discussions to investigate the impact of the program. The major difference between qualitative and quantitative methods is that the latter do not attempt to reduce experiences to data. The goal of both methods is to provide more qualitative information to a mostly quantitative survey. The semi-structured interviews in addition to answering the questions prepared from the interviewers' list of topics that need to be covered, allow respondents to bring up new points or focus on some issues. Focus groups, undergo a collective in-depth interview, which follows the structure of the survey questionnaire with facilitated discussion of the reasoning behind opinions and provision of more detailed information on context. Information from interviews and FG discussions serve as data sources for the triangulation of information from the surveys. Triangulation, according to Rothbauer (2008), is "borrowed from navigational and land surveying techniques that determine a single point in space with the convergence of measurements taken from two other distinct points," and is simply the application and combination of various research methods in the study of the same phenomenon to validate the results.

The advantage of this method is that may touch upon the issues that might be discussed in closed survey questions. In other words, we may collect some rich, detailed information, that otherwise would not be collected. The difficulty in applying this method is in the interpretation and analysis of the information collected. Despite the limitations, I found that many organizations implementing citizenship education projects present tales of the former participants who became important civil activists or even politician in order to demonstrate the impact of their projects. The participants may discuss how the program has impacted them, changed their perceptions, knowledge or even lives, but it requires the participant to know what would have happened in the absence of the program.

When asking participants how a program changed their lives, we asking them to disentangle all the many opportunities that were going on it society from those that were driven by the participation in the program. This however, still might be difficult. Therefore, this method is good for simply describing a situation, but does not allow drawing conclusions about the impact of the program.

If organizations and researchers want to provide rigorous evidence, it is important to employ a rigorous methodology. This means we need to examine how the people who participated in the program performed compared to how they would have performed if they had not had a chance to participate in the program. We can never know what would have happened in the absence of the program, but we can use different evaluation techniques in attempting to make comparisons. The inspiration for the impact evolution methodology comes from the Abdul Latif Jameel Poverty Action Lab (J-PAL).

Participant–nonparticipant comparison and randomization: according to this method instead of comparing scores before and after participation in the program, we could also compare the scores of those young people involved in the program with those who did not participate in the program. Again, we conduct surveys and if we find that there is a difference between for example knowledge, attitudes, and interests of participants and non-participants, we can attribute this difference to the program.

Although this methodology more confidently allows to see the difference between what happened with the program with what would have happened without the program, this methodology also has some limitations. Usually those who were recruited to the program are often already different from those who were not. For example, an NGO I have been collaborating with in the recruitment procedure already requires students to be active and participate in different organizations. The program selects participants based on qualifications and it is quite possible that the young people are already well-motivated and inspired and care more about democratic values than those who did not apply. In other words, those who get involved in a program are already different from those who did not get involved. This tendency is called selection. If we fail to account for selection in our impact evaluation, we can introduce selection bias into our estimate of impact. This means that we may risk attributing differences in outcomes to the program when they are actually caused by differences that already existed between those selected and not selected for the program.

An impact evaluation is only as good as the comparison group that can imitate what would have happened in the absence of the program. If the comparison group is not good enough, it can ruin the evaluation and make it invalid. Therefore, the way to overcome the problem of preexisting differences in this methodology would be to employ randomized controlled trails.

The key feature of a randomized evaluation is that the people who have access to the program are selected randomly. This methodology ensures that there are no systematic differences between participants and non-participants (comparison group), and allows us to measure what impacts were caused by the program (Glennerster and Takavarasha, 2013). Randomized evolutions should be designed before the project starts. Therefore, there were many program-specific issues that we had to discuss in order to match the expectations of the organization, donor, and requirements of this methodology.

In the next sections of this chapter, I will demonstrate how these methods have been used to evaluate the impact of democracy assistance programs on young people, and what can be said about the influence of programs on infusing democratic values as well as inspiring social and political activism among them.

Inculcating democratic values and norms of engaged citizenship

As demonstrated in Chapter 3, many CEE NGOs engage in promoting active citizenship among young people through the programs that aim to educate, and to raise awareness and thus to empower young people to be active citizens and advocates of pro-democratic changes. The objective of civic education (known also as education for democratic citizenship, civic education programs, or education for active participation activities) is to teach citizens of recipient countries the basic values, knowledge and skills for being be an active and engaged citizen. Civic education has also become a popular form of empowering young people within the democracy assistance efforts of pro-democratic CEE NGOs in Eastern European countries. Civic education programs emphasize instilling the norms of liberal democracy by including "norms of engaged citizenship" which value (1) social and political responsibility in local and national affairs; (2) actual participation in political and civic life; (3) being active in social and political associations and keeping a watch on government to prevent abuses of power; (4) civic duty (including the importance of paying taxes and obeying the law); and finally (5) respecting the rights of minorities and helping those worse off in order to prevent the polarization of the country (Birzea *et al.*, 2004; Bolzendahl and Coffé, 2009, 2013; Dalton, 2006, 2008; Manning and Edwards, 2014).

These norms, which describe a shared set of expectations about the citizen's role in politics (Dalton, 2008), have behaviorally important consequences. The citizenship also becomes conscious of not only rights and obligations, but also how individuals behave on an everyday basis, what activities they are engaged in, and how they relate themselves to the smaller (city, town, village) and broader community (e.g., global community). In other words, participation has become to be perceived as an important element of citizenship. Hence "active citizenship" has been used to refer to people who feel responsible for the community, who feel the potential to make a change, who are ready to take action and who get involved in local communities (Crick and Lockyer, 2010). There is no active citizenship without participation, but is not restricted to political participation only. As various efforts of scholars and practitioners to measure active citizenship for democracy show, active citizenship is understood as participation in civil society, community and/or in political life (Abs and Veldhuis, 2006; Hoskins, 2006; De Weerd *et al.*, 2005; Ogris and Westphal, 2005). Democracy in principle demands that citizens participate, thus active citizenship and democracy are closely related and one cannot exist without the other.

There is a need to promote democratic values and activism through civic education programs among young people in Eastern Europe because post-communist countries were found to have the lowest levels of activism and party membership, and the relationship between citizenship norms and political participation in general is weaker in newer democracies (Bolzendahl and Coffé, 2013). The previous chapter also supports these findings. However, it becomes questionable if formal civic education fails or does not exist as in some post-communist non-democracies. Print and Lange (2012) and Print (2013) recognize that in addition to formal education, civic competences within schools can also take place within the informal school curriculum. The need to improve youth engagement in decision-making process through developing the skills of critical thinking, debating, and their involvement in civic and political activities by and encouraging them to actively participate and instill democratic values, challenged citizenship education as a subject at schools (Mycock and Tonge, 2014). According to Himmelmann (2013), we can observe: "a new and specified form of 'democratic citizenship education' beyond just civics', for a new way of 'teaching democracy' beyond teaching institutional political settings or a new 'education of, for and through democracy' beyond mere teacher-centered instruction in politics."

However, little is still known about whether and how citizens can be educated about responsible citizenship and participation outside of the educational system, especially in countries in which citizens' freedoms are limited. We also have insufficient knowledge of what role NGOs can play in this process, especially from neighboring countries and whether these programs are effective in influencing young people's knowledge and participation and thus transmitting democratic values. Since NGOs of CEE countries engage in this type of activity at home and abroad, we fill the gap by examining anew the effects of NGO-level civic education. In the next section, we aim to answer the questions regarding the effectiveness of the civic education programs undertaken by NGOs from CEE countries on young people from Eastern Europe.

As presented in Chapter 3, civic educational programs of NGOs from young democracies show that education for democracy does not mean learning to recognize the sanctity of democratic institutions. Rather, it means propagating the idea of democracy, citizens' rights and responsibilities and preparing people to work for the benefit of democracy. Civic education programs when communicating to students the values of democracy and developing in them the habit of political activity recognize also the differences that separate youth and adults. Many of the projects practice various forms that allow student engagement, such as discussions about fundamental principles of democracy, workshops, presentations, and lectures ways of helping them develop their opinions, judgments and to express feelings. Often, for many students from democratizing and authoritarian states, this is the first opportunity to speak freely and engage in discussion, and may lead to some inner transformation involving the desire to changing something in their lives and inspiring them to take greater responsibility for their community. Such activated young people will be better prepared to participate also in democratic institutions in the future.

Civic education is practiced either through activities organized in the partner countries with aim of supporting schools by providing teaching materials, teacher training, organizing workshops, or through activities offered in Central and Eastern European countries such as summer schools, internships, scholarships, exchange programs, and study mission programs designed to enhance participation as well through knowledge. Other activities are training and educating individual citizens in political participation, teaching political skills, increasing political awareness, conveying information on how political processes work, inspiring political discussion and interest in politics though courses, seminars and study visits.

Young people have a great potential to play important role in a society and that in order to boost their participation, a youth empowerment mechanism is required, which might not be created from within the country, particularly in an authoritarian state like Belarus. Therefore, participation in such educational programs may build young people' sense of power that they are able to make changes in their communities, region and even their country. However, the questions I am trying to answer in my research are: how can the impact of this intervention be measured, and how can we be sure that the changes we observe in the participants can be attributed to the program?

From all reviewed programs, I have chosen to evaluate the long-term civic education program that since 2004 not only aims to inculcate democratic values, but also ignites subsequent engagement in the political and civic spheres. The project recognizes that citizen participation in the political process is a defining feature of democracy, and active and informed young people are considered vital to the health and vitality of civil society and thus democracy.

This program is directed toward young people aged 18–21 from four partner countries: Ukraine, Belarus, Russia and Moldova with the aim to: (1) support the development of civil society in Eastern European countries; (2) promote democratic values and support democratic changes in the region through the impact on the individuals in accordance with the belief that broader changes are bottom-up; (3) promote knowledge about the European Union; (4) promote knowledge about Poland's transformation experience. Specifically, it is expected by the donor and NGOs coordinating the program that a visit to Poland would an opportunity for the young people from these countries not only to get to know the country, but also to broaden knowledge of the seven key areas, such as: the economy, local self-government, culture, the NGO sector, public administration, media, integration with the EU. These are the topics that should be addressed during the implementation of each visit by NGO operators.

Each year, about 240 students on the visit Poland in two sessions (spring and summer). Each session of the program is divided into groups, and each group consists of twelve participants from roughly three countries. The groups are led by NGO operators by the donor and two organizations coordinating the program.[1] NGO operators are non-governmental organizations from various parts of Poland who are responsible for the group of twelve students (the number of groups depends on the results of the recruitment process) and organize a visit for a given wave of the program. These NGOs are responsible for both the logistic side of the project and the substantive content of the visit, which should be consistent with the objectives of the program. Organizations wishing to organize a stay of students have to fulfill a number of criteria, such as experience of cooperation with Eastern European countries and youth work, employees who speak Russian, know the specificity of partner countries so that they can better communicate with participants. It is also very important for the operators to help young people get acquainted with the Polish academic environment, civic organizations, and organize meetings with significant people in public life, lectures, workshops, seminars, as well as in cultural events.

The program is promoted through several channels. First of all, information about recruitment is sent to student organizations and universities (the exception is Belarus, due to the reluctant attitude of the authorities). Second, the information is provided by the local NGO. Third, various types of Polish institutions are being reported in the East (consulates, embassies, cultural institutions). However, according to the research carried out so far, the most effective means of reaching potential program participants is promotion by people who participated in previous sessions of the program.

In order to enable assessment of the impact more information about the intervention is needed. We also need to say more about the selection procedure. This training program is meant to lead to the acquisition of specific knowledge as well as to permanent changes in the attitudes of the participants. During the visit, youth from the East learn about the functioning of the Polish economy, media, local government, public administration, third sector and integration with the European Union. In addition, young people learn more about Polish culture and academic life. Poland in the program is presented both in terms of successes achieved during the period of political transformation and those elements of Polish reality that require further development. Students are, therefore, shown the broadest possible picture of Polish reality, so that they can, based on the acquired knowledge, form an opinion about Poland and verify the stereotypes about democracy and the EU which they had when they came to Poland. The purpose of the program is not only to provide specific knowledge, but also to present the values of certain developments in various areas of social life. After the visit, the students should know about specific solutions and understand the functioning of democracy and civil society. This is intended to encourage the participants to promote democratic values and diffuse them in the local communities and countries from which they come.

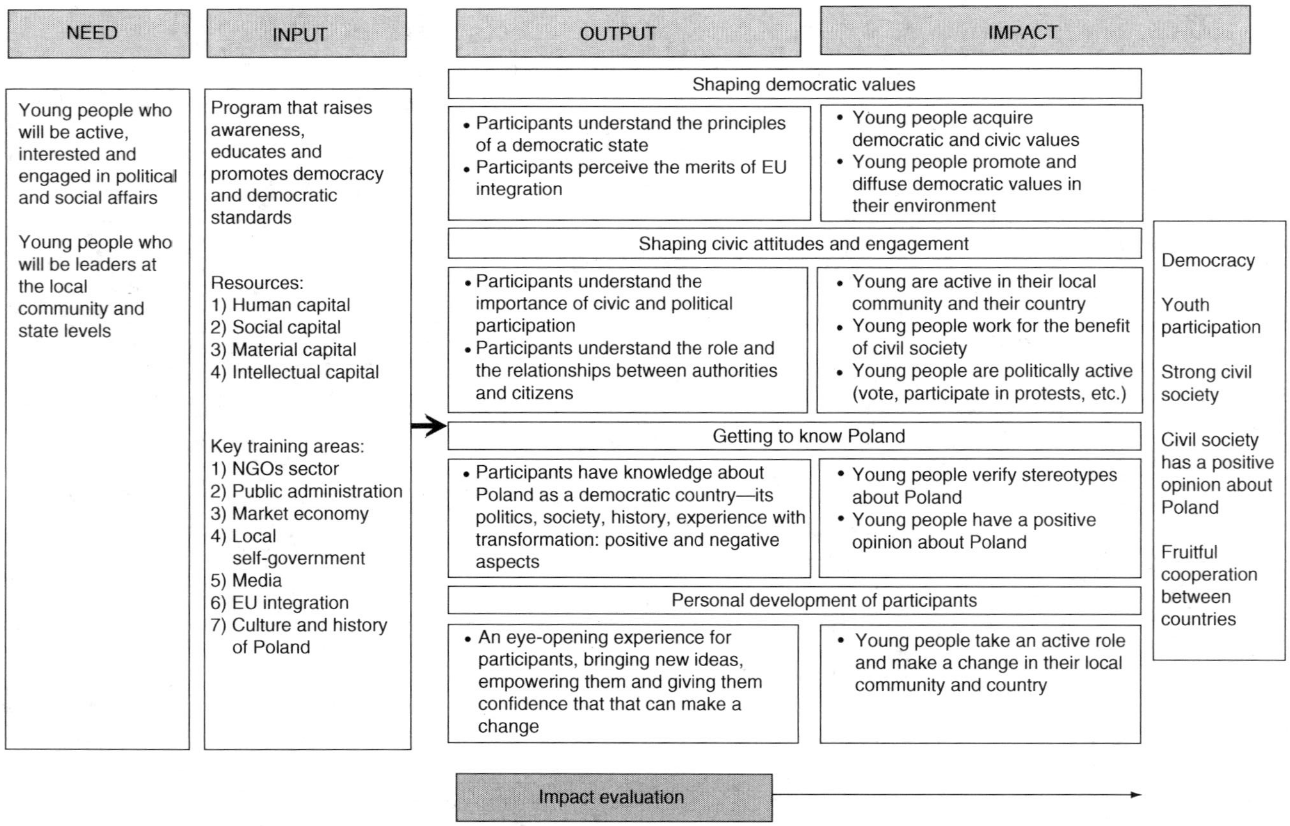

NEED

Young people who will be active, interested and engaged in political and social affairs

Young people who will be leaders at the local community and state levels

INPUT

Program that raises awareness, educates and promotes democracy and democratic standards

Resources:
1) Human capital
2) Social capital
3) Material capital
4) Intellectual capital

Key training areas:
1) NGOs sector
2) Public administration
3) Market economy
4) Local self-government
5) Media
6) EU integration
7) Culture and history of Poland

OUTPUT	IMPACT
Shaping democratic values	
• Participants understand the principles of a democratic state • Participants perceive the merits of EU integration	• Young people acquire democratic and civic values • Young people promote and diffuse democratic values in their environment
Shaping civic attitudes and engagement	
• Participants understand the importance of civic and political participation • Participants understand the role and the relationships between authorities and citizens	• Young are active in their local community and their country • Young people work for the benefit of civil society • Young people are politically active (vote, participate in protests, etc.)
Getting to know Poland	
• Participants have knowledge about Poland as a democratic country—its politics, society, history, experience with transformation: positive and negative aspects	• Young people verify stereotypes about Poland • Young people have a positive opinion about Poland
Personal development of participants	
• An eye-opening experience for participants, bringing new ideas, empowering them and giving them confidence that that can make a change	• Young people take an active role and make a change in their local community and country

Democracy

Youth participation

Strong civil society

Civil society has a positive opinion about Poland

Fruitful cooperation between countries

Impact evaluation →

Figure 5.1 An example of a logical framework of a civic education program.

By showing young people opportunities and methods of how to be active, the program is also meant be a source of inspiration and ideas, to empower young people to take responsibility for civic activity locally and nationally. This to mobilizes young people to be active and instills in them the belief that their actions can change something. It is expected that after the visit and their return home, these young people are to ready to re-evaluate their choices and to engage in social activities as ambassadors of civil society promoting the values learned during the civic education program in Poland.

Participation in this civic education program is also an opportunity for Eastern European young people to meet other participants—people from neighboring countries. During their stay in Poland, young people spend time together and exchange knowledge and experiences of their countries, which teaches them tolerance. Such direct contact between students from different countries and communities and knowledge about other countries of the region may help verify mutual stereotypes that exist in their countries about other nations.

The long-term impact of the program assumes that individuals should become a starting point for participants to achieve success in their professional lives. The program is a kind of investment in individuals, who in the future have a chance to become the elite of their countries. Regardless of the future fate of the participants and the professional path chosen by them, they should have the characteristics of so-called engaged citizens participating in the activities of non-governmental organizations and taking part in elections, and the like. The program in the long term at the macro-level is expected to contribute to positive changes in Eastern Europe—on the one hand, to the democratization and development of civil society, and on the other, to strengthening cooperation in the region. Poland, as a country supporting pro-democracy changes, should enjoy prestige among the countries of the former Soviet Union and be regarded as a positive and inspiring example of reforms.

There are two rounds of application to the program per year: between May and June and October and December through an online application form filled out by students. Candidates' forms and documents are assessed by a recruitment committee. During the selection process, the committee pays attention to the current activities of the candidates, and their average grade and short essay that they have to write. As the results of such recruitment, young participants in the program are young people who, in addition to good academic performance, are active as members of student or non-governmental organizations or of various formal and informal civic groups. Additionally, the program coordinators and a donor are interested in selecting so-called "diamonds" who are outstanding participants—the most active ones and who demonstrate leadership skills. These young people after the completion of the program session are invited again to Poland for the workshops and meetings aimed at providing them with practical tools and specific skills needed for social activities.

Given the above description of the program and logical framework, the following questions arise: how does this program affect the understanding of the rules of the democratic state and civil society by the participants? Do they identify with democratic values? How do they understand them? What do they think about them? How did the visit affect the participants' opinions on democracy? Also, given the goal of the program, the possible impact of the program leads to the following question: do the participants become active in the civic and political arenas at the local community and state levels after returning home?

Evaluation through social experiments

The programs' impact on beneficiaries has always been evaluated by the donor and coordinating NGOs through before-and-after-comparisons. Using standard program evaluation methodology, answering the above questions requires a counterfactual scenario (or, in other words, a control group not subjected to the examination). I have attempted to find counterfactual data to contrast the survey results among the participants with the survey conducted among non-participants. Therefore, given the shortcomings of the before-and-after-comparison method, the coordinating organization and donors agreed to cooperate to establish an experimental method of evaluation.

In democracy assistance, social experiments are still not popular. Scientists in democracy aid literature tend to undertake the empirical analysis either through large-scale observational methods or case studies. Randomized social experiments, however, can improve the study of politics. Experimental methods have motivated political scientists to think about causality in more rigorous terms, especially regarding the civic education programs. This section examines whether democracy promotion programs such as civic education can affect citizens' attitudes toward democracy and empower them the take civic action. I attempt to assess the impact of civic education through an experimental research design.

Finkel, Horowitz and Rojo-Mendoza (2012) show that exposure to the National Civic Education Program (NCEP) implemented in Kenya resulted in "inoculation effects" for participants when compared to non-participants affected by violence. Participants were less likely to express negative attitudes about the political system, and less likely to support ethnic violence. Also, other scholars find that civic education may be correlated with positive changes in voter behavior (Arriola *et al.*, 2017; Finkel, 2014; Mvukiyehe and Samii, 2017). Civic education, by promoting access to political knowledge increases the likelihood that voters participate in the democratic process (Finkel and Smith, 2011). Participants also tended to become opinion leaders who diffused their civics training within their social networks (Finkel and Smith, 2011). However, not all civic education programs are found to be so productive, depending on their design and implementation.

A proper impact evaluation includes efforts to establish the effects of some interventions relative to what could be observed in the absence of such interventions. This requires: (1) collection of baseline data, (2) collection of appropriate outcome data, and (3) collection of the same data for comparable individuals, groups or communities that did and did not receive the intervention. As such, impact evaluation helps determine what would have happened in the absence of the program. Randomized controlled trials (RCTs), also known as random assignment studies, randomized fielded trails, social experiments, or randomized design, are the most credible and accurate form of impact evaluation, the best procedure to gain knowledge regarding the effect of assistance projects. In development assistance, some efforts have been made to estimate the difference before and after data of selected individuals, groups and communities that did not receive assistance in order to estimate what would happen in the absence of such aid.

RCTs have been popularized in particular by a group of economists in the Abdul Latif Jameel Poverty Action Lab (J-PAL) founded in 2003 by the Department of Economics at MIT which tests and improves the effectiveness of programs and policies aimed at reducing poverty.[2] However, impact evaluations in the area of democracy assistance using randomized design are lagging behind the evaluation of development assistance. The problem with impact evaluation in democracy assistance is that evaluations lack consistent logical frameworks that carefully specify inputs, outputs, outcomes and impact, which undermines good evaluation, as the recent report by National Research Council (NRC) indicates (NRC, 2008). Also, there are not many studies that undertake these efforts mainly due to difficulties in measuring the impact of projects. However, these challenges can be overcome if impact evaluation is carefully designed before the project begins and carried out as the project itself is implemented. Therefore, within this project, the researcher would need to conduct a pilot study and use randomized evaluations to answer questions regarding the impact of democracy assistance projects.

Different randomization strategies may be used to answer different questions, and since the researcher is interested in the impact of NGO projects on youth activism, young people will be divided by random selection into treatment and control groups. The *Treatment Group* will be the group of young people who will participate in the project by random selection, and *control group* will include those young people who through randomization will not participate in the project. Then, after the end of the project (the treatment) measurement of the desired outcome will be taken for both groups. If there is a difference in outcomes between the groups, it can reasonably be inferred that the difference was attributable to the project. To enhance validity of the research, survey questions before the trail also will be collected.

Because of the comparison of the results with the control group, and thus capturing better the impact of the program on participants, the donors and a coordinating organization were willing to use randomized control trails as an impact evaluation method. However, it was not an easy process to convince the donors and a coordinating organization to randomize access since the program aims to select those with the best qualifications who are worth the investment of material resources, and who because of their engagement so far, as well as opinions and attitudes, have a great potential to be the leaders in their local community and in their countries in the future. Thus, since regular treatment was not feasible for programs that select participants based on qualifications, the solution was to conduct the treatment lottery around a cut off.

In lottery around the cutoff, randomized evaluation is still possible if we divide applicants into three groups: those who will be accepted into the program no matter what, those who will not be accepted into the program because they do not fulfill the criteria and those who will have a random chance of being accepted into the program (Glennerster and Takavarasha, 2013). As the result, access to the program still depends on a student's qualifications, because which group people fall into depends on scores and place in the ranking list. In the case of the program, the lottery around the cutoff was conducted separately for each nationality because the ranking list of students was prepared for each nationality separately and was based on the evaluation in three categories: (1) school performance (including grades and other school activity); (2) participation (in youth, civic and other organizations), and (3) answers to specific questions (essay). The figure below demonstrates the allocation of Ukrainian young people applying for the program. Since the goal was to invite 100 young people from four countries, and usually the greatest number of applicants are Ukrainians, the organization chose to accept fifty-nine young people from Ukraine. As figure shows, all those with a place on the ranking list between 1 and 35 were accepted, and those placed at 86 on the ranking list were rejected. Access to the program was randomized for students ranked between 36 and 85 on the ranking list. However, those ranked between 36 and 60 have a 60 percent probability of being accepted on the program because they had better qualifications while those

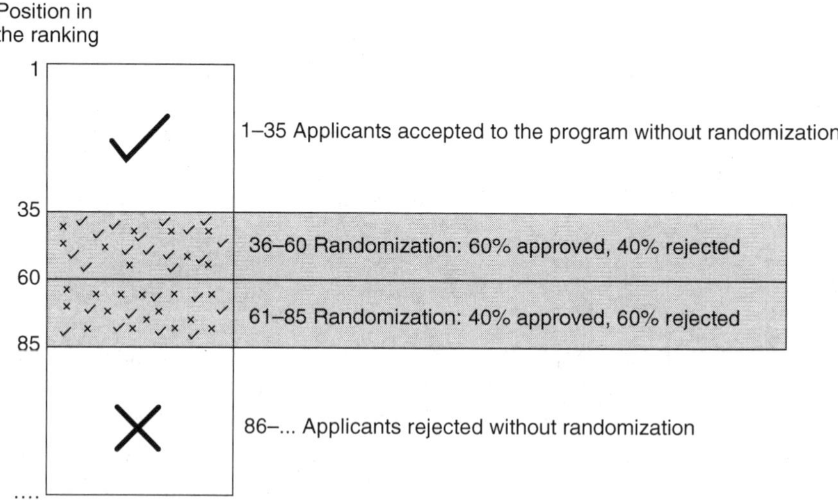

Figure 5.2 Random assignment: lottery around the cutoff for the group of young Ukrainians in Spring 2017 session of the program.

placed between 61 and 85 have a 40 percent chance of getting on to the program and they were randomly selected.

The *Output* and *impact* (primary outcome) will be measured by using surveys of both groups regarding youth attitude and behavior. The impact of the program was measured through the survey. All candidates completed the online survey when applying for the program, despite it not being obligatory. The same survey was completed by the participants on the last day of their program—the NGO operator provided computers for those who did not have them and assigned passwords to enable them to log in to the site and enable comparison of the "before" and "after" survey results. Participants accessed the website where the survey is located, log in using the password assigned to them earlier and complete the questionnaire. Table 5.1 shows the control versus treatment groups set up by the countries of origin of non-participants and participants.

As was mentioned above, not all outcomes of democracy assistance projects are easy to measure; therefore, in evaluating the impact of the program, I have focused on the outcomes that are measureable and consistent with the goal of the program. In order to achieve this, the survey was structured to meet the logical framework and included questions focusing on changes in attitudes, knowledge, and opinions concerning: (1) support for democratic principles; (2) perception of democracy and authoritarianism; (3) view of the European Union; (4) Attitudes towards citizenship norms, political trust, and political efficacy; (5) knowledge of Poland as a democracy. Also, the content of the training offered to young people from Belarus, Moldova, Ukraine and Russia served as base justification for the survey measure. The survey corresponds more or less to the topics that they learned about during the exchange.

To be consistent with the formerly adopted measures in Chapter 5 of support for democracy and the perception of democracy, the survey sought to capture opinions and attitudes of young people toward the principles of democracy. The list of

Table 5.1 Control and experimental groups in the experiment

	Selection	*Total*	*Belarus*	*Moldova*	*Russia*	*Ukraine*
Control group	Program candidates who completed the survey *at the time of applying* to the program but were *not selected* as the result of randomization process	150	22	3	4	121
Experimental group	Program participants selected (partially) *randomly*, who completed the questionnaire *on the last day of the project*	100	29	10	12	59

Note
Randomized evaluations performed on one session of the civic education program (Spring 2017).

attributes included items covering essential aspects: elections, rule of law, civil rights, and various freedoms, as well as social justice elements. The perception of democracy question asked young people to express their opinion on a set of statements regarding democracy—whether democracy has an advantage over all other forms of government, influences the quality of life of its citizens and has a positive impact on the economic development of the state. They were also asked to measure their inclination toward authoritarian standards, and they were asked whether sometimes non-democratic governments can be preferable to democratic ones, and whether governments based on strong leadership are better than democratic ones.

Free and fair elections, the rule of law, and basic civil rights are considered as indispensable in the liberal democratic template. The liberal principle identifies democracy with limited government, the rule of law and the preservation of individual liberties. Young people were asked to express their awareness regarding the importance of these specific attributes using a Likert scale ranging from 1 (Very important) to 4 (Not important). Table 5.2 shows the differences between experimental and control groups.

The results show that civic education programs do have an impact on participants' opinion regarding the importance of democratic standards related to civil liberties, such as combating social inequalities and protecting the rights of minorities (national, sexual), elections, media independence, economic freedom and the separation of the judiciary, the executive and the legislature. Also, participants more than non-participants perceive as important the need for decentralization of power in the country, the issue of transferring of state responsibilities to the local level. As less relevant as compared to non-participants, participants recognize freedom of movement, limits of state intervention in the lives of citizens. However, they are still considered to be important elements of democracy.

Overall, it should be said based on the control groups that young people from the Eastern Europe perceive the existence of democratic standards in the country positively, and that as comparison between means shows, the participation in the program seems to strengthen the belief that certain standards are important. Also, the students before coming to Poland perceived the democratic system favorably. They were convinced that democracy has an advantage over all other forms of government and that it is desirable in all countries of the world regardless political tradition and culture. The answers of the students related to the question on whether democracy leads to the welfare of the people and as well as being a good regime for their country, have demonstrated considerable differences between participants and non-participants. The majority considered that the democratic system was also associated with economic development, whereas authoritarian regimes were regarded as being inferior to democratic ones. However, although students selected to participate in the civic education program demonstrated very skeptical attitudes toward authoritarian standards after the completion of the training (and that participation in the program does have a significant impact on changing attitudes regarding the authoritarian standards), at the same young people seem to agree with the statement that sometimes undemocratic governments might be more desirable than democratic ones.

I found it important also to measure young people's attitudes toward the EU for two reasons. First, it is one of the goals of the programs, and overall CEE NGOs within their democracy assistance promote the process of enlargement and closer relations with the EU. Second, attitudes toward the EU are important, because there can be lack of trust toward domestic institutions, but if there is support for the EU, which is regarded as a "pillar of democracy," this can be an important reservoir and a trigger for political activities (Marchenko, 2016). The process of Europeanization is closely related to the building and strengthening democratic systems. Those countries that aspire to become members have to meet the Copenhagen Criteria and became democracies with a well-functioning market economy.

The young people were asked about their opinion of the EU. The results demonstrate strong pro-European attitudes. Young people had a fairly positive view of the EU. They believed that membership was beneficial, provided wide opportunities for personal development, and that the EU provided more benefits than costs. However, a significant difference can be observed between participants and non-participants. Participants clearly disagree with the statement that the European Union weakens national identity or that it is an instrument of domination of weak countries by strong countries, whereas non-participants were in the opinion that the EU could have negative impacts on its member states and their citizens. A considerable difference between two groups was that the majority of participants would like to have their country join the European community and that adopting the Western standards and norms was beneficial for the country. Also, we might observe some differences in belief that membership was beneficial, giving wide opportunities for their country's economic growth.

The bottom line is that there were many changes observed in participants' attitudes towards the European Union after the completion of the program. They continue to maintain a positive attitude and they recognize the benefits of membership, but the visit to Poland strengthened the belief that EU membership has a positive impact on the economic development of the state, and that their country should join the European community. We also cannot ignore the fact that non-participants assign some negative impact to the EU, believing that EU membership results in the loss of national identity, and that powerful countries have an impact on the weaker countries of the EU. Because of the considerable differences between participants and non-participants, the impact of the program is straightforward.

The goal of the civic education program is to encourage young people to adopt the norms of engaged citizenship and develop the sense of becoming active citizens. Therefore, the survey also intended to measure citizenship norms, political trust, and political efficacy. Researchers tend to agree that the assessment of citizenship norms is a useful way of analyzing citizens' expectations of their role in the political system. There is an assumption that these norms explain individuals' views about their own responsibilities, which, in turn may guide actual behavior (Bolzendahl and Coffé, 2013; Dalton, 2006, 2008; Hooghe, Oser and Marien, 2016).

Table 5.2 Support for democracy among youth

Elements of democracy	*Experimental group (mean)*	*Control group (mean)*	*Difference between means (95% conf.interval)*	*p values 2-tailed*
Electoral elements				
Free and fair elections	1.08	1.62	**–0.54 [–0.67, –0.40]**	**0.00**
Vertical accountability: elections give people the opportunity to punish bad government by removal from power	1.31	1.82	**–0.51 [–0.68, –0.33]**	**0.00**
Fixed-term elections: the limited number of terms a person can hold a high state position	1.61	1.19	**0.42 [0.28, 0.56]**	**0.00**
Alternative offers: the ability to choose between parties representing different political options	1.35	1.58	**–0.23 [–0.39, –0.07]**	**0.00**
Liberal elements				
Rule of law				
Equality before the law	1.10	1.21	**–0.11 [–0.22, 0.01]**	**0.07**
Independence of the judiciary	1.20	1.54	**–0.34 [–0.48, –0.20]**	**0.00**
Horizontal accountability: separation of judiciary, executive and legislative branches	1.25	1.66	**–0.41 [–0.58, –0.23]**	**0.00**

Civil liberties				
Freedom of expression	1.15	1.67	**–0.52 [–0.70, –0.35]**	**0.00**
Little state intervention	1.50	1.28	**0.22 [0.07, 0.40]**	**0.00**
Freedom of association: the independence of social organizations/NGOs from the state	1.21	1.72	**–0.51 [–0.67, –0.34]**	**0.00**
Minority protection	1.65	1.84	–0.19 [–0.39, –0.02]	0.07
Media freedom: independence of media from government	1.23	1.53	**–0.30 [–0.46, –0.15]**	**0.00**
Media pluralism	1.33	1.67	**–0.34 [–0.48, –0.17]**	**0.00**
Freedom of movement	1.29	1.12	**0.17 [0.06, 0.28]**	**0.00**
Consultation with the public on important state decisions	1.40	1.34	0.06 [–0.08, 0.2]	0.41
The delegation by the state of the broadest possible responsibilities to the local government	1.40	1.77	**–0.37 [–0.55, –0.19]**	**0.00**
Economic freedoms				
Protection of property rights	1.26	1.36	–0.10 [–0.23, –0.04]	0.16
Freedom to run a business	1.24	2.09	**–0.85 [–1.02, –0.68]**	**0.00**
Social justice elements				
Protection of workers' rights	1.26	1.44	**–0.18 [–0.34, –0.01]**	**0.03**
Equal access to education	1.18	1.54	**–0.36 [–0.53, –0.20]**	**0.00**
Fulfillment of basic needs	1.21	1.42	**–0.21 [–0.35, –0.77]**	**0.002**
Protection against poverty	1.54	1.90	**–0.36 [–0.54, –0.80]**	**0.00**
Redistribution of income differences	1.41	1.90	**–0.49 [–0.67, –0.30]**	**0.00**

Notes

Question: "Which of the following descriptions of the state you consider important, and which not, for creating a good standard of living? Instruction: Please answer all questions by choosing the answers that best describe your attitude." 1 "Very Important," 4 "Not Important." In bold: Statistically significant ($p<0.05$) difference between means in groups.

Table 5.3 Perception of democracy and authoritarianism by youth

	Experimental group (mean)	*Control group (mean)*	*Difference between means (95% conf.interval)*	*p values 2-tailed*
Democracy				
Democracy has an advantage over all other forms of government	1.66	1.60	0.06 [–0.12, –0.24]	0.50
Democracy leads to the welfare of the people	1.48	2.85	**–1.37 [–1.56, –1.18]**	**0.00**
Democracy is associated with economic development	1.48	1.77	**–0.29 [–0.46, –0.12]**	**0.00**
Democracy is desirable in all countries of the world regardless of political tradition and culture	1.80	1.96	–0.16 [–0.37, 0.05]	0.13
Democracy is a good regime for my country	1.41	2.28	**–0.87 [–1.07, –0.66]**	**0.00**
Authoritarianism				
Sometimes a non-democratic political system can be preferable	2.55	2.18	**0.37 [0.14, 0.59]**	**0.00**
Governments based on strong leadership are better	2.91	1.83	**1.08 [0.88, 1.29]**	**0.00**
You should always show *respect* to those who exercise authority	2.74	1.89	**0.85 [0.63, 1.05]**	**0.00**

Notes

Question: "How much do you agree or disagree with following statements? Instruction: Please answer all questions by choosing the answers that best describe your attitude." 1 "I strongly agree," 4 "I strongly disagree." In Bold: Statistically significant difference between means in groups. In bold: Statistically significant ($p<0.05$) difference between means in groups.

Table 5.4 View of the EU by youth (percentage of respondents in each country that responded "fully agree")

	Experimental group (mean)	*Control group (mean)*	*Difference between means (95% conf.interval)*	*p values 2-tailed*
EU membership gives more benefits than costs	1.46	1.58	–0.12 [–0.26, 0.28]	0.11
My country should join the EU	1.78	2.67	**–0.89 [–1.12, – 0.67]**	**0.00**
EU members lose their national identity after joining the EU	3.00	1.81	**1.19 [1.0, 1.38]**	**0.00**
EU has a positive impact on economic development	1.42	2.89	**–1.47 [–1.67, –1.27]**	**0.00**
EU is instrument of domination large countries over small	2.65	1.76	**0.89 [0.67, 1.12]**	**0.00**
EU strengthens ties between members	1.32	1.73	**–0.41 [–0.57, –0.24]**	**0.00**
EU creates opportunity for citizens' development (education, economic situation)	1.21	1.33	–0.12 [–0.25, 0.01]	0.07
My country should not emulate the standards of the West, but rely primarily on its own traditions and experiences	2.24	1.99	**0.34 [0.01, 0.47]**	**0.04**

Notes

Question: "How much do you agree or disagree with following statements concerning the European Union and closer integration of your country with the EU? Instruction: Please answer all questions by choosing the answers that best describe your attitude." 1 "I strongly agree," 4 "I strongly disagree." In bold: Statistically significant ($p<0.05$) difference between means in groups.

As presented in Chapter 4 citizenship norms are a shared set of expectations about the role of citizen participation in politics (Dalton, 2008). They show how individuals understand what constitutes to be a good citizen and how this citizen should behave. For example, Dalton (2008) finds that citizens who value "norms of citizen duty" are more likely to vote than citizens with a lower sense of duty, but "engaged" citizens, meaning those who value "norms of engaged citizenship" are more likely to participate in a variety of political activities—both electoral and non-electoral (e.g., signing petitions, participating in demonstrations). Also, Bolzendahl and Coffé (2013) in their analysis of twenty-five countries find that norms related to paying taxes and obeying the law, which can be compared to "norms of citizen duty" negatively predict party membership, voting, and participation in variety of political activities. However, norms such as those about the importance of being active in social and political associations were associated with a higher propensity to vote and be politically active. The comparison between participants and non-participants shows that the program makes young people more in favor of norms of engaged citizenship and less in favor of norms of citizen duty. Given this, one expects that these norms of citizenship should give some prospect that their adoption might translate into actual participation, and young people become more responsible citizens.

For being active and demonstrating that "engagement in activities designed to foster social change or, alternatively, to resist it" (Punyanunt-Carter and Nance, 2014), motivation is important together with belief in democracy, positive attitudes toward democracy, political interest as well as political efficacy and trust. Political trust which is understood as trust in domestic political institutions is related to citizens' views of democracy (Newton, 2001). It is assumed that trust in political institutions indicates a reliance on such institutions. Mistrust, however, fosters a climate that may lead to movements against the government and various unlawful acts as well. Although participants in the program show few negative attitudes, both participants and non-participants do not trust their politicians. We could infer about their attitudes to the current situation in their countries. They seemed to have negative views on politicians' work and intentions. They were convinced that the most important decisions take place behind closed doors, and that politicians, regardless of what they say, care only about their careers.

Political efficacy relates to the perception of the inclusion of a citizen within the political system, and ability to intervene in political affairs. Political; Efficacy is important because if it is low they will feel inadequate, irrelevant and powerless in influencing political outcomes in their countries. The composition between the treatment and control groups shows that the program empowers young people to believe that they can make a change and influence the decisions of the ruling elites.

Finally, to be consistent with the goal of the program, the survey also asked about the perception of knowledge of Poland. Most of the respondents in the control group declared that they knew little about the country or that they had some knowledge. The respondents declared that they knew a little Polish culture,

Table 5.5 Citizenship norms, political trust and political efficacy

	Experimental group (mean)	*Control group (mean)*	*Difference between means (95% conf.interval)*	*p values 2-tailed*
Norms of citizenship				
Norms of citizen duty				
Obedience and respect for authority are the most important values	3.04	2.69	**0.35 [0.91, 0.61]**	**0.01**
The key to a good life is obedience	2.95	2.31	**0.64 [0.42, 0.87]**	**0.00**
Norms of engaged citizens				
Strong will, being active, and engaged make people achieve something in life	2.52	2.06	**0.46 [0.23, 0.68]**	**0.00**
Political efficacy				
People like me do not have any influence on what the government is doing and politicians	3.10	2.69	**0.41 [0.16, 0.65]**	**0.00**
Political trust				
Most politicians, regardless of what they say, care only about their career	2.18	2.56	**0.38 [0.16, 0.65]**	**0.00**
Key political decisions are taken in secret situations	2.18	2.38	–0.20 [–0.43, 0.34]	0.09

Notes

Question: "How much do you agree or disagree with following statements? Instruction: Please answer all questions by choosing the answers that best describe your attitude." 1 "I strongly agree," 4 –"I strongly disagree." In bold: Statistically significant ($p<0.05$) difference between means in groups.

Table 5.6 Perception of knowledge of Poland as a democratic country

	Experimental group (mean)	*Control group (mean)*	*Difference between means (95% conf.interval)*	*p values 2-tailed*
The political transformation	3.85	2.68	**1.17 [0.93, 1.41]**	**0.00**
The process of joining the EU	3.90	2.89	**1.01 [0.76, 1.27]**	**0.00**
The principles of the functioning of the economy	3.80	2.13	**1.67 [1.42, 1.91]**	**0.00**
The principles of the functioning of NGOs	4.27	3.25	**1.02 [0.79, 1.25]**	**0.00**
Polish culture	3.75	2.29	**1.46 [1.22, 1.72]**	**0.00**
Polish history	4.05	2.02	**2.03 [1.79, 2.26]**	**0.00**
The structure and powers of self-government	4.34	3.14	**1.20 [0.97, 1.44]**	**0.00**
Relations between the media and the authorities	4.00	3.03	**0.97 [0.73, 1.20]**	**0.00**
Education system	4.20	1.81	**2.39 [2.16, 2.60]**	**0.00**
The daily life of Poles	4.26	1.89	**2.37 [2.15, 2.61]**	**0.00**
Life conditions in Poland	4.28	2.58	**1.70 [1.45, 1.96]**	**0.00**
Lifestyle of peers	4.19	3.11	**1.08 [0.80, 1.35]**	**0.00**

Notes

1 “I know very little” 5 “I know a lot,” In bold: Statistically significant difference between means in groups. Statistical significance of $p<0.05$ indicate in bold.

literature, film, theater, Polish history and the everyday life of the Poles, as well as the living conditions and lifestyles of their peers in Poland. They demonstrated less knowledge of the process of Polish accession to the EU, the functioning of the Polish economy, the NGO sector in Poland, local government, and the relationship between the media and the government. The perception of knowledge of students about Poland is significantly greater among participants in the program. Almost all of the answers were: "I know a lot." Specifically, and significantly different was a knowledge of the Polish transformation, a knowledge of the EU integration process and the functioning of the non-governmental sector and local government, as well as their knowledge of the education system in Poland.

To conclude the experiment, the experimental group (participants) performed better than control group across all measures regarding democracy. One can see that the results reveal a statistically significant difference between the groups for the main features of democracy such as separation of powers, media freedom, decentralization of power, economic freedoms, social rights and civil liberties. The results show that the participation in the program might greatly increase their knowledge of Poland as a democratic country, thus fulfilling the donor's expectations of one of the desirable impacts of the program. Whereas non-participants disagreed with the statement that democracy has an advantage over other forms of government, participants after the program believed that this statement was correct, and recognized that the democratic system definitely led to the wellbeing of citizens. Also, the opinion that democracy had a positive impact on the economic development of the country was stronger among participants. However, it should be noted that more than half of the participants after the visit still believed that there are situations in which non-democratic government can be better than democratic government. We could observe some significant difference in opinion regarding the impact of a citizen on the government, subordination, as well as in discipline and obedience being perceived as positive values.

Participants' greater interest in political and civic participation can be attributed to the project, and thus showing cause-effect is possible with randomized evaluation. Moreover, this method allows for answering what happened with the democracy promotion program and what would happen without the program. This is possible due to the key feature of this method. The people who have access to the program are selected randomly. This methodology ensures that there are not systematic differences between participants and non-participants (comparison group), and allows the measurement of what impacts were caused by the program. The experimental results by providing estimates of the mean difference in outcomes between persons receiving and not receiving some treatment are also easier to explain to practitioners in the aid community and to policymakers. In other words, these opportunities are encouraging greater use of experiment designs in democracy assistance as one of the most prominent empirical strategies that can bring new insights into the study of the effectiveness of democracy assistance programs.

Despite the merit of the method which allowed for the comparison among (partially) randomly constructed treatment and experimental groups, there are few limitations that need to be acknowledged. First, an impact evaluation is only as good as the comparison group that can imitate what would have happened in the absence of the program. If the comparison group is not good enough, it can ruin the evaluation and make it invalid. Randomization bias may occur when random assignment causes the type of person participating in a program to differ from the type that would participate in the program. Usually, those who were recruited to the program are often already different from those who were not. For example, as discussed earlier, the recruitment procedure of the civic education program already required students to be active and participate in different organizations. The program selects participants based on qualifications and it is quite possible that the young people are already well-motivated and inspired and care more about democratic values than those who did not apply. In other words, those who are accepted on the program could have already been different from those who were not accepted. If we fail to account for selection in our impact evaluation, we can introduce selection bias into our estimate of impact. This means that we may risk attributing differences in outcomes to the program when they are actually caused by differences that already existed between those selected and not selected for the program.

Therefore, in order to overcome the problem of preexisting differences, a pre-intervention survey would be valuable to make sure that the treatment and control groups are similar. It is important to answer the following questions: was there a difference between groups already before the program? Did the differences already exist between those selected and not selected for the program? I have performed a study comparing two groups, non-participants and would-be participants, when they were applying for the program to ensure myself that the groups were similar. This additional check allowed me to strengthen my conclusions regarding a positive impact of the program on participants.

However, this did not change the fact that it is possible that youth who had a greater interest in politics and a greater propensity to engage in political activism *ex ante* were more likely to apply for the program. If this is the case, it should not be surprising that these young people have a higher degree of interest in politics and political participation than the young person in these countries. We can assume that they are all very similar and therefore representative of the new elite for the country. Moreover, people recruited to such programs who are more politically minded and who are given the opportunity for socialization may strengthen their attitudes, behaviors and opinions. If people do not meet with similar people, this might restrict their personal development and empowerment. Therefore, it is also important to keep in mind that there might be other possible causal mechanism linking participation in the program to outcomes in addition to information received during the program, such as: integration and intercultural exchange.

Experiments are based on more plausible assumptions that randomization that ensures the allocation of treatment to participants (individuals or institutions) is

Table 5.7 Experimental method in democratic assistance: opportunities and limitations

Advantages
Brings new insights into the study of the effectiveness of democracy assistance programs
Suitable for assessing the impact of democracy assistance at the micro level
Possible to observe what would happen if the program did not exist
Can solve the selection problem
Results are easier to explain to practitioners
Potential disadvantages
Experiments can still provide little evidence on many questions of interest
Researcher has only limited control beyond the intervention conducted
Randomization bias
Institutional limitations of social experiments
Substitution bias
Other possible causal mechanism linking participation in program to outcomes

Sources: Based on literature (Burtless 1995; Glennerster and Takavarasha 2013; Heckman and Smith 1995) and own experience.

left purely to chance, and is thus not systematically biased by deliberate selection of participants for the treatment. However, it is not always possible. This is partially because of the nature of the field experiments where the researcher's intervention takes place in an environment where the researcher has only limited control beyond the intervention conducted (Morton and Williams, 2006). Another is reason is that it is not always possible to perform pure randomization given the objectives of the program to reach the leaders and invest resources into the most qualified young people. I call this limitation the so-called institutional limitation of the experimental method.

Critics may also ask how enduring the effect of the program is, and that follow-up study should be performed to ensure that youth from Eastern European countries that participated in the program became engaged citizens. In order to more precisely determine the *impact* of the project, indeed, such post-treatment study in the $t+1$ and then the $t+2$ period would allow one to see whether greater awareness and preferences for democratic values led to greater participation in social and political life. Although it is exciting to find out whether they voted, participated in a debate, or a protest, or became more interested in politics, and how the program affected their professional life, there is still the problem of attribution and risk of substitution bias that members of an experimental control group could also gain access to close substitutes for experimental treatment (Pospieszna and Galus, 2018). The same problem occurs if we wish to aggregate long-term impact by looking at the local indicators such as more young people registered to vote, more who actually voted, and more young people joining youth clubs or organizations, etc., as compared to the pre-evaluation period. We still cannot be sure to what extent it was due to the program if not other factors?

It is important to keep in mind that the goal of such methods is to observe the causal mechanism at the micro level, meaning that such programs can increase the political activism of their participants, but a more general question of what impact those programs can have on the participatory levels of societies as whole is not so straightforward. Certain personality traits stimulate people to join organizations and to engage in political activities. In other words, citizens who are more sociable and outgoing are more likely to engage in civic and political activities. Indeed, the civic education program under investigation searches for people with such characteristics and virtues. The goal is to look for the leaders, then to strengthen them and to empower so that they become even more engaged in their community and diffuse this activism to others. There is no easy way to generate politically engaged youth. However civic education programs create a space, a platform for civic skills and mindedness development.

Also, given the above limitations, many of them can be overcome if randomized evolutions are carefully designed before the project starts, to make sure that many program-specific issues are discussed in order to match the expectations of the organization, donor, and requirements of this methodology, and also to make sure that we will be measuring what we want to measure. The survey adopted turned out to be sufficient to measure perceptions but with the experiment we were not able to establish actual activism itself. Therefore, we could have included questions testing people's knowledge, asking them to evaluate a hypothetical case of curbing freedoms, for example, and questions that would be measuring behavioral outcome in order to better understand whether young people participating in the program would in fact become more active. Finally, not all possible impacts can be measured with the experiment. For example, given the goal of the program that it has impact on the personal development of participants making them experience a "revelation," discovering new opportunities, bringing new ideas—it was possible to achieve with qualitative methods and the participant observation method conducted.

Qualitative method

The goal of this chapter was to draw attention to how useful the experimental method can be if we are interested in evaluating the impact of the democracy assistance efforts at the micro level. Nevertheless, if we chose to narrow down our observation to the program level, it is still useful to use qualitative methods of evaluation, interviews, focus groups and participant observation methods, because they allow the impact of the program to be captured, which can sometimes be difficult to measure by traditional methods before-and-after-comparisons, as well as by the randomized controlled trails discussed here. Therefore, I have complemented the experiments with the participant observation method and as a researcher with a good knowledge Russian had a chance to get closer to the group and "blend in" so as create a unique opportunity of seeing their reactions to the material presented during the training courses and meetings with the representatives of various institutions and organizations that they visited during their stay in Poland.

The situation in eastern Ukraine and the moral aspects of war have been frequently discussed by the participants, since they were either directly affected by it or some had friends fighting in the East, even joining the Russian separatists. Topics such as war, revolution, patriotism and what it means today, despite causing disagreement between participants from Ukraine and Russia, could not be avoided and at the same time were felt to be important for them. Two female participants talked about the annexation of the Crimea, which they could not accept, and shared their reflections on Russia's "superpower" history and the fears connected with it. Discussion of these topics returned during the meeting with media representatives in Poland—"What is the attitude of Polish media to Ukraine and Russia?" asked one of the participants from Donbas in Ukraine. Participants were surprised to hear that

> there is freedom of speech and there are many public and private media whose attitudes depend on the program line adopted by a given newspaper, for example. The mainstream media supports the Polish government's foreign policy standpoint, that is, that Ukraine has been the victim of Russia's aggression.

Despite the situation of destruction and chaos, Ukrainians look positively into the future. They want to get involved and they want to go to the West to learn something and then implement it in Ukraine. They are skeptical about the changes in Ukraine, but on the other hand they highlight the importance of civic mobilization during the Euromaidan and that this event was an expression of the people's will to act and that it is better that it occurred, because it has united the nation. "We are going through changes in our mentality now"—said one of the students from Ukraine. However, the current events in Ukraine also seemed to affect the way they, as well as young people from Russia who were indoctrinated the by media and at school, perceived international relations today. During the presentation about history and the transition to democracy and market economy where young people from Eastern Europe could learn about round table negotiations, political reforms and Balcerowicz's shock therapy, to my surprise, many of them knew about Poland joining the EU. I had the impression that they admire the "normality" of the situation in Poland and that the Poles have come this long way since 1989 but it has been worth undertaking. However, a student from Russia with a negative attitude towards NATO asked: "I understand why Poland chose to join the EU but why NATO?" Also, "Why is Poland more interested in having close cooperation and economic relations with the US rather than with Russia?"

In the meantime, when Ukrainian students are wondering whether such democracy promotion programs in which they participate have a hidden agenda and why Poland helps Ukraine and what it wants in return (they ask whether in exchange for this help Poland wants Lviv), a student from Belarus says that he likes this program because it is very comprehensive and that it is not political and propagandist in contrast to the program he attended once in Moscow where there was a lot of agitation and was led by anti-West Russian nationalists. Ukrainian participants are appeased with the answer that the Poles do not think in terms of revising the borders and that there are differences in the perception of the borders between the EU and Russia, because Western countries do not seek to change borders. They feel comfortable with the borders which were established after World War II. Belarusians, however, although they admire the program are afraid of being followed by secret police officers when they return home or being expelled from university.

An eye-opening experience for all participants, also from Moldova, were meetings with the local authorities and with the police. Students were very interested and involved. the majority were asking questions, wondering how it was possible that the police managed to fight corruption and how to achieve it in the participants' countries. They are very impressed by the social trust and respect for the police in Poland, because in Russia respect for the police is not high. Although the content of the training concerning the self-government structure seemed to more challenging for students (perhaps due to the lack of analogies and references to their countries), during the visits in local authorities' offices and institutions they were impressed by the practical dimension of the functioning of the local government. Particularly, they complimented the openness, client-focus services, lack of stress when dealing with officials ("there is a greater stress resulting from contact with the officials in our country than from the case itself"), the number of women working in administration, good organization ("organized by people and for people"), transparency of information, pace of working and handling matters, comprehensiveness ("you can do many things in one place"), elevator for disabled ("there are no such facilities in our public buildings"), and finally by the presence of the local government on the Internet and social media (Facebook, Twitter). Additionally, I could learn about participants' positive and negative opinions of the program, their positive and negative impressions, and overall impact of the training courses, which I summarize in Table 5.8.

Conducting educational activity aimed at propagating the idea of democracy and preparing people to work for the benefit of democracy—improving young people's understanding about their role and ability to solve problems in their local community, region or even country—is an important element of youth empowerment mechanism but not sufficient. Analysis of the participants' profile in one of the programs allowed us to find that young people from democratizing countries or even from Belarus where civil liberties are curtailed, have a great potential to play important role in society and, that in order to boost their participation, a youth empowerment mechanism is required, which might not be created from within the country. CEE NGOs seem to recognize that full participation of young people requires adequate social and political environment that allows for such participation without fear of punishment. Therefore, in the next section I explore such a program and evaluate its impact on young people.

Table 5.8 Positive and negative opinions of young beneficiaries of democracy assistance programs

Questions	*Positive impressions*
How did the visit affect the understanding of the rules of the democratic state and civil society by the participants?	"The effectiveness of authorities in the development of infrastructure; universities are modern and very beautiful."
	"Program that has shown that living in Poland has pros and cons"
Do they identify with democratic values? How do they understand them?	"I have never dealt with Moldovans before. It was very interesting to learn more about this country."
	"Many beautiful places, number of reforms that took place—and it demonstrates that Polish people care about the future of their country, not only about nowadays."
What are they saying about them?	
How did the visit affect the participants' opinions on democracy?	"After all the lectures and seminars that we have had, I now understand that great speed with which Poland moves. Of course, there are a lot of problems, but the most important is that we saw that the people just see an aim and do not see obstacles."
What did participants know about Poland before their arrival?	"Features of self-government and education in Poland, as well as domestic tourism."
What surprised them?	"People and their attitudes toward life. We have very closed mentality, but our daily life is a sign that the same people under different living conditions have different priorities."
What did they like and what did they not like?	"I had never had interest in politics, but Poland changed my mind: senate, self-governing bodies."
What do the participants think about Poland/Poles?	"Poland's organization and history of the country, hospitality, culture, economic growth; roads, clean streets; the availability of an incredibly convenient infrastructure, especially for disabled people and cyclists."
What did the participants learn during their visit to Poland?	"Meeting President Lech Wałęsa."

continued

Table 5.8 Continued

Questions	*Positive impressions*
How did they assess various developments in Poland? Are there solutions that they would like to introduce in their countries? Which and why?	"Probably one of the most powerful and pleasant surprises is the way of presenting knowledge."
	"We did not have boring lectures. Very informative sketches about the life of Poland and its inhabitants floated before us. We analyzed and made our own conclusions. We got acquainted with different phenomena and decided what to do with them. This is very important, and I want to thank you sincerely for this. Such knowledge you want to take and learn! With such knowledge it would be desirable to start soon the realization of ideas which inspired with me."
Do they see the difference between Poland and their countries?	"The STP program is a tremendous experience, new knowledge, and the fact that you get motivated us people who like you want to change the world for the best."
What during the visit has had a special impression on the participants?	"People. Mentality. Goodwill of people. Initiative. Openness to action."
Have they discovered new possibilities for action?	"I was most surprised by the reasonable structure of the state, as well as the fact that the lecturers do not hide the problems of their organizations but honestly and openly related their problems and ways to solve them."
How did the program affect their confidence, their willingness to act, the conviction about the purposefulness of the activities undertaken?	"The beauty of nature, the cleanliness of the streets, the high standard of living and social responsibility of the population."
	"Openness of officials, the mayor."
	"People, people, people. Active, cheerful, responsive."

“The most surprising thing for me was that people, both young people and the older generation, are very proactive, full of ideas for involving the population in social projects, improving the culture and atmosphere in Poland as a whole.”

“Local government system.”

“The openness of Poland, some similarity of history, culture, to a certain level of mentality, which allows you to take experience of the Polish in relation to our country. Thus, the implementation of alternative projects and ideas seems possible.”

“Surprised that the people who occupy government posts take into account, first of all, society.”

“Even a relatively small town with a small population can be so developed, authentic, and friendly.”

“We talked with representatives of different professions, different ranks and officials, and businessmen, and so on, and they all were equally open to us, very interestingly represented their field of activity, answered all our questions and always maintained a friendly atmosphere.”

“The distribution of the budget in Poland, namely the direction of the means for development. Centralized allocation of funds to NGOs, grants for social projects from the state.”

“The initiative of people, their ability to organize their work and rest, while contributing to the life of society.”

“The most surprising thing for me was that people, both young people and the older generation, are very proactive, full of ideas for involving the population in social projects, improving the culture and atmosphere in Poland as a whole.”

continued

Table 5.8 Continued

Questions	*Negative impressions*
	"One thing that was positive and negative at the same time: Polish people look for problems even where there are no problems. Sometimes it motivates them to change but sometimes it just makes them unhappy for no reason."
	"The fact that the path of Poland lasted 10 years before joining the EU and at the initial stage, the level of development of Poland was about the same as now in Ukraine. This means that we still have a very long road of transformation."
	"Small conflicts and unpleasant situations on a political basis (between participants from Russia and Ukraine)."
	"A discrepancy between the opinions of the population and the government, which, in principle, is common in many countries."
	"Surprised by nationalist movements, prohibition of abortion, conservatism and the degree of influence of religion on politics and education."
	"Political situation."

From civic education to civic participation

The experiment set up to evaluate the impact of a civic education program demonstrated that the program has a possible impact on shaping young people's norms of engaged citizenship. Given the findings in the literature that these norms explain individuals' views about their own responsibilities, which, in turn may guide actual behavior (Bolzendahl and Coffé, 2013; Dalton, 2006, 2008; Hooghe, Oser and Marien, 2016), we may assume that participants will be more "engaged citizens." However, instead of conducting a follow-up study checking with the survey whether youth from Eastern European countries that participated in the program indeed participate in social and political life, the organization conducted the follow-up program called "ACT now!" to engage the former participants to take action as leaders in the local community. By doing so, it was believed that this would allow the long-term impact of their democracy assistance programs to be determined and to see whether greater awareness of democratic values led to the actual engagement.

The goal of the follow-up program was to providing funding for mini projects to improve the engagement of young people in decision-making processes at the local level by empowering youth to take action in their communities. The local community is most often understood as a community that can be defined by location and people are aware of its distinctiveness and have certain needs and expectations that result from belonging to a given community. In addition, the local community is associated with local democracy and with the following values: social inclusion, independence and self-governance, shared responsibility, freedom of articulation of values and interests, commitment to community affairs, striving to identify and implement the common good. On a wider scale, local democracy can be defined as a system of values, rules, institutions, mechanisms and tools allowing for formal influencing and participation in local affairs processes and processes of appointing representatives to decision-making and consultative bodies in local entities and political and administrative structures.

Activation at the local level is important for the development of democracy, because the bonds built by social capital and trust foster the development of civic participation that is necessary for the development of the civic community (Putnam, 1995). Thanks to civic participation, a system is created that can satisfy the necessary needs in society in an effective and efficient manner, a system in which citizens participate in making decisions regarding problems that concern them. In addition to co-decisions, a better flow of information between citizens and local authorities takes place, as well as consultation, and overall dialogue improves between members of the local community and its authorities. However, it is necessary to find and adapt tools that will motivate social interaction at the local level, and involve citizens by solving their own problems and satisfying their needs in an independent manner. An important role in this process is played by so-called social leaders.

The program aimed to reach those who want to be engaged or already have some idea about what to improve in the local community, as well as someone who also understands what local community is, and its importance for building social bonds between various actors. In the first round of the program, the

Who is the local leader?
- takes responsibility for local actions
- through activities becomes an authority in the local community
- motivates social interaction at the local level
- activates others to solve local problems and address needs
- has leadership predispositions and appropriate personality traits
- strives for personal growth and to be a lifelong learner

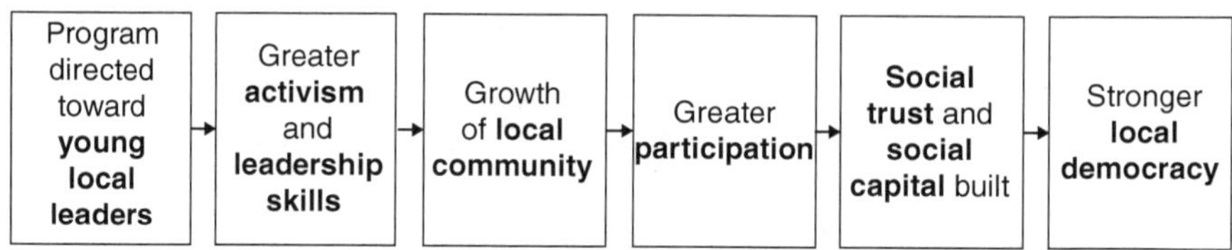

Figure 5.3 Logical framework of civic engagement programs.

organization and donor decided to only admit young people from five oblasts in Ukraine: Zaporizhia, Dnipropetrovsk, Kharkov, Mykolaiv and Odessa, who submitted mini local projects for the competition. Young people were required to diagnose the needs of the local community in a way chosen by them and send the description of the project to the grant-giving organization together with specified recipients/beneficiaries as well as entities for cooperation, such as non-governmental organizations, local authorities, state administration, the media, educational institutions, cultural centers, libraries, museums, as well as companies from the private sector. The plans of the mini projects included a minimum project duration of two months necessary for project implementation, preparation, public consultations with the stakeholders, advertising among members of the local communities, actual implementation, and reporting.

Six projects qualified for funding: (1) supporting the local community through creative activities; (2) improving the safety of cyclists in Kharkov; (3) increasing safety in children; (4) increasing ecological awareness; (5) health protection for young people (cancer prevention); (6) a project on integrating the local community (street practices) mainly through young people and NGO activists. The first of the projects was directed towards the cycling community and its aim was to promote a healthy and active lifestyle and to protect the environment by increasing the share of cycling paths with road traffic. Professional organizations, members of the cycling community, school pupils, university students and the physically active, as well as photographers were invited to participate in its implementation. The second project was also related to the dissemination of knowledge and promotion of a healthy lifestyle. It raised the issue of youth health and was concerned that young people are not taking care of their own health. The project offered classes in schools that would address education in the areas of healthy habits, diet and medical examinations. The project aimed to attract young people with the help of effective teaching techniques, which would not be possible without close collaboration with schools, as well as doctors.

Another project implemented as a part of the "Act Now!" in Ukraine, was a project devoted to the activities of emergency services, the police and health care services. The author if the project saw that distrust of authorities and social structures was the problem of the modern community. The project was aimed at children and adolescents and was coordinated with medical staff and police offices helping to build a positive image of social workers and increasing social trust. The fourth project, similar to the aforementioned one, concerned the improvement of the image of the authorities and aimed at improving the circulation of information, resulting in raising the quality of policies produced by the state and local authorities in the energy sector and natural environment. According to the author of the project, the low level of information from the authorities contributed to the lack of public confidence in state programs and, consequently, to search for unauthorized, often unreliable information. The creators of the project have proposed creating a team of young journalists that will allow the public to be informed about the real state of energy efficiency in the region, plans for the future at both local and national levels. The main goal of the fifth and last project funded within program "Act Now!" in Ukraine, was to strengthen local communities in relations to problems arising from them. The priority was to initiate joint action in the transformation of the local environment, which will become safe and oriented to people's needs. The authors noted that previous campaigns to support civil society were too theoretical and lacked the use of cultural potential and social impact. Attention in this project was focused on improving participants' competences in the field of managing non-governmental organizations and on issues related to the organization and training of volunteers participating in social initiatives. The project was supposed to solve the problems of the local society through a series of local events, creating permanent groups of the same character and also by increasing competences in the field of active learning. Ultimately, the project aimed to strengthen the ability to work with volunteers, social partners, institutions and to create best practices in the field of joint local activities.

The mini projects implemented in the local community were aimed at activating young people and also to strengthen their position in the community in which they live so that they become perceived as local leaders by the community. More importantly, the goal was to make them more confident and to strengthen their leadership skills. The local community solves its social problems well if there are social bonds, and where local leaders aim to engage the members of a given community to build the community. Who is a local leader? A local leader is a person who feels responsible for running, directing and leading a community. Often the level of development and life of the local community depends on them. The leader is the authority for others in the community thanks to what he or she does, and the person is distinguished by certain predispositions and personality traits. The leader can be defined as an individual who is self-confident, responsible, persistent in pursuing goals, knows how to search for resources, has problem-solving skills and the ability to cope with stress. Being a leader means also the willingness to constantly increase knowledge, to serve others, and be able to influence others. However, the presence of leaders in the community is not enough and it is necessary to help them strengthen their potential. Polish organizations seem to understand well the role of the local leader in the development of local communities.

The evaluation produced an answer to the question of whether the selected NGO program has an impact on the participants and contributed to their greater activity by strengthening their leadership potential. Has the project developed leadership skills? Did the project engender self-confidence and encourage them to take similar actions in their community also in the future? In a focus group meeting, which took place in Kharkov led by the program coordinators and myself, the participants agreed that thanks to the activities of the project, they increased and developed communication skills, learned to manage time and self-discipline better, learned how to properly manage the budget and not postpone matters for later. They also gained experience in establishing contacts with various institutions and stakeholders in local communities, although they frequently encountered barriers in project implementation, such as obtaining consent for project implementation from conservative educational institutions, misunderstandings, bureaucracy, problems with recruitment of participants, high financial requirements of trainers, problems with a place for the implementation of the project and in some cases also problems related to corruption inside educational institutions.

Regardless the obstacles, the essence of this program was to draw the attention of young people to how little it takes to come out with initiative and implement their own ideas for the benefit of the local community, in addition, to activate them to take similar actions in the future. Since the goal of the program was to stimulate people who could become potential leaders in local communities, the survey included questions about leadership competences, and the comparison of responses allowed us to observe quantitatively the impact of the program. The respondents were asked about their opinions regarding a project team building process; communication with members of the local community; searching for partners in the local community, etc. In the survey afterwards, the project respondents said that their understanding and knowledge improved in the following fields.

Table 5.9 Young people's assessment of the civic engagement program's impact on their leadership skills (percentage of responses to "Improved")

Ability to act as a leader	100.00
Ability to understand the emotions in different situations (emotional maturity)	71.43
Understanding of how and when leaders must be able to manage change	85.72
Knowledge of methods and tools that can be used by people who make decisions	71.43
Ability to lead a group project and to understand a group dynamic	71.43
Ability to understand what it means to be responsible	42.86
Ability to present ideas to the public	100.00
Understanding of the needs of the local community	85.71
My position and reputation in the local environment improved	85.71

In comparison with answers in the pre-test, the changes were noticeable, in particular, the responses regarding their public performances and presenting ideas to the others (an increase of 30 percentage points), as well as knowledge of the team building process (an increase of 30 percentage points), and the ability to search for the right partners for cooperation in the local community (an increase of 30 percentage points), and how to make changes in local communities (an increase of 18 percentage points). Subsequently, the participants positively responded to the questions, which are important for the role of a leader in the local community, whether they had an influence on decisions relating to the local community, and whether it gave them self-confidence. When asked if they had a great impact on their changes in the local community, in order to make it a better place to live, the respondents answered that they felt that they had an impact on such changes and that this even strengthened the participants' faith in themselves. Another question concerned the sense of community and closeness with the local community. In the survey before the project implementation, 44 percent of the respondents described their relationship as strong. In the survey after the project implementation, as many as 71 percent declared a strong sense of community and closeness. Interesting results brought and answer to the question regarding trust in officials and employees of various professions. The largest increase in trust occurred towards the following entities: state administration (an increase of 30 percentage points); local media: radio, TV, press (an increase of 20 percentage points); health care providers: doctors and nurses (an increase of 50 percentage points), and the police (an increase of 22 percentage points).

To sum up, a positive impact of the civic engagement program on the participants has been observed, on the basis of widely used evaluation tools such as surveys examining the development of leadership competencies, monitoring and reports, complemented by interviews with participants and their presentations at the workshop in Kharkov. Such activating programs seemed to have great potential in encouraging young people to get involved in working for their own local community and to develop their leadership competences. By creating such programs, Polish NGOs can influence the development of civil society in partner countries. This was evidenced by the positive results of the surveys carried out, general satisfaction of participants, and, above all, their willingness to continue to act for the benefit of the local community. The program shows how little it takes to come out with an initiative, fulfill one's own idea to achieve better development of civil society. The initiative of creating projects involving the local community may contribute to increasing local activity in the future, because young people will pass on values related to the activation of the local society from generation to generation, which is a priority issue, especially in democratizing countries such as Ukraine.

Undoubtedly, the willingness to change the current situation in localities from where the participants came, gave a good foundation for creating original mini projects which were adapted to the problems and needs of a given community. The young Ukrainians showed a great willingness to act. They created innovative ideas that in the future may result in increased interest of other youth or translate into the involvement of other age groups.

Conclusion

In this chapter, I have presented some possible impact evaluation methods based on experience with partner organization in evaluating specific type of democracy promotion programs, such as civic education program and programs engaging citizens to take action. These are some practical suggestions for the organizations wishing to find out the impact of their programs. However, the impact evaluation methods may also allow researchers to understand better how citizenship education is being practiced through venues other than schools and what the role of NGOs can play in this process. Measuring the impact of intervention requires comparison of what has happened with the intervention with what would have happened had the intervention not taken place. Nevertheless, it should be noticed that the ability to generalize from my findings is limited by both the nature and size of the sample and I do not aggregate individual-level values to the national level since the focus is on possible beneficiaries of the programs.

CEE organizations are aware that a strong and integrated local community not only knows how to solve problems and meet their needs by, but is also a better and more reliable partner for cooperation with local or national authorities. Nevertheless, a group without a leader is not able to actively participate in social life. Social leaders are an important part of the local community. Polish NGOs with knowledge and experience related to the development of local democracy in Poland, communicate it to their eastern neighbors. The aim of this chapter was to evaluate those efforts aimed at educating and then activating local society in target states. It is thanks to the programs of non-governmental organizations that young people in other post-Soviet countries have had the chance to learn how they can take actions that bring their country closer to democracy, and from experts to gain the knowledge and inspiration they need to act in their countries.

There are two main conclusions from this study. First, this study has also demonstrated the usefulness of experimental method of evaluating the impact of democracy assistance efforts on young people, by narrowing down the observation to specific civic education and civic engagement programs. It has been shown that carefully designed randomized experiments may allow for a more rigorous evaluation for solving the problem of causal attribution of specific outcomes to the program in democracy assistance. However, it also suggests using a combination of techniques to complement measuring the effects of these programs, such as qualitative methods surveys, behavioral activities, etc.

Second, it has been demonstrated in this chapter that citizen-oriented democracy promotion seems to have had a positive impact on the beneficiaries, thus it should become the main component of democracy assistance rather than aid that goes to and through governments. If well-designed it may make young people become effective in norm adoption and implementation and not only change young people's attitudes and opinions but also empower them to take civic action, create a culture of democracy, where civil society's voice is listened to, and participation in decision-making takes place. Thus, rather than trying to get "better politicians" and institutions to instill and strengthen democracy, as suggested by Vráblíková (2017), it may be more effective if there a process, which precedes or goes in parallel, that produces "better citizens" via democracy assistance programs.

Notes

1 Since 2004 the donor of the program is Polish American Freedom Foundation. However, NGO operators, organizations that conduct visits, are required to provide 20 percent of the total cost of the visit in the form of own their contribution, and incoming students partly to cover the costs of travel. The main coordinators have been two organizations The Leaders for Change and the Borussia Foundation, which are responsible for the substantive and organizational side of the program. Employees of both organizations form the "STP Team" consisting of people with experience in the implementation of Eastern programs, knowledge about the specificity of the region and contacts in the countries from which beneficiaries of the program come from (Russia, Belarus, Moldova, Ukraine).

2 For more information about this research center see www.povertyactionlab.org/about-j-pal.

6 Closing space for bypass democracy assistance

Democracy-promoting countries' commitment to aiding democracy overseas has started to wane with the decline in influence of the liberal democratic model of political, and economic development. The CEE countries not only have been revising purposes and direction of their official developmental assistance but also the anti-democratic offensive taken by governments against CEE NGOs engaged in democracy assistance undermines overall efforts to spread liberal democracy values elsewhere. The chapter demonstrates that the current developments in the political arena are hazardous for the civil society to function. On the example of the specific regulations and measures taken by the governments in Poland and Hungary, I show how these constraints has affected the way NGOs in Hungary and Poland are involved in democracy assistance both domestically and abroad in post-communist regions.

Illiberal democracies of CEE are at the center of scholarly debate today (Holzer and Mareš, 2016), since their governments are moving countries backwards by punishing freedom of speech, and the freedom to organize and to assemble, as well as to receive funding from foreign entities. However, illiberal, nationalist, and anti-immigrant appeals emerge in the politics of other European (liberal) democracies, such as France, Switzerland, and Germany, as well as of the United States, causing damage to the image of democracy.[1] Moreover, scholars and practitioners talk in terms of overall democratic recession (Burnell and Youngs, 2010), a backlash against external democracy promotion (Carothers, 2006; Gershman and Allen, 2006), and policies of closing space (Carothers and Brechenmacher, 2014; Mendelson, 2015). Although probably almost three decades later no one would have predicted that would be a repeat conflict between the state and society in CEE (Ekiert, 1996). for civil society in CEE This is not the first time and probably the last time when states and society are in conflict again. This chapter shows how in alarming democratic deterioration, especially in Hungary and Poland, civil society fights back and more importantly how those CEE NGOs engaged in spreading liberal values abroad struggle to survive.

State against civil society and civil society against state again

Hungary and Poland are certainly facing populist threats and are seen as the core of the "EU's illiberal democracies" (Applebaum, 2016; Tomini, 2015). However, not only Hungary and Poland but also recently the Czech Republic and Slovakia began questioning their previous commitment to liberalism.

Populism is hostile to the idea and institutions of liberal democracy, and one form of what Zakaria (2003) popularized as "illiberal democracy." Although the developments in CEE might be perceived as shocking, right-wing populism is a normal pathology of western democracies (Mudde, 2004), which has become a regular feature of politics since the early 1990s, but only now consolidated democracies are faced with this "populist Zeitgeist" (Mudde, 2004). Following elections in September 2005 and June 2006, we have witnessed the success of populist movements in CEE with liberal ideology ebbing. Populism is a normal pathology, because, as Canovan (1999) said, populism critiques the democratic limitations within liberal democracy. Many aspects of the liberal heritage are fundamental to the persistence of democracy itself, and among them is freedom of expression and the rule of law. However, liberal principles place restraints on democracy, and populist democracy is a version of democracy uninhibited by these liberal constraints (Canovan, 1999).

Recognizing these constraints of liberal democracy as obstacles in Poland and Hungary, both governments have consolidated power and moved to gain political control over key institutions like the media and the judiciary while muting checks and balances on government power. Independence of judiciary, central banks, organizations, means for populists independence from democratic control. Thus, in Hungary, since the 2010 victory of the conservative Fidesz party, and the later re-election in 2014, Prime Minster Victor Orbán has concentrated power in his hands and his Fidesz party, undermining the independence of judiciary,[2] press, organizations, and other liberal practices and norms. In 2013, Orbán managed to rewrite the constitution in an unconstitutional way, in Poland, a populist-nationalist Law and Justice party (Prawo i Sprawiedliwość—PiS), led by the Jarosław Kaczyński, following Hungarian steps upon taking power, embarked on destroying the country's democratic and state institutions: the Constitutional Tribunal, a crucial piece of the checks and balance system, which was disregarded and then paralyzed and brought under control of PiS-friendly appointees, the independent prosecutor, the independent civil service, and the public media.

Slovakia is also becoming the next area for testing the state of liberal democracy in Europe. Slovakia's extreme right-wing parties have been a part of a broader political current that began to form in CEE after 1989. These parties range from established parties in mainstream politics (for example, the Slovak National Party, SNS) and their splinter parties (the Real Slovak National Party, PSNS) (Kluknavska and Smolík, 2016). In the Czech Republic, however, a populist Babisz won the parliamentary elections, and the extremist Okamura, which wants to expel "strangers" and rejects all elements of the current system, won over 10 percent of the votes. The Civic Democratic Party (ODS) blamed the then ruling Social Democratic Party (CSSD) for having "betrayed the people" by settling unfavorable conditions during the negotiation process with the EU.

Populists see themselves as true democrats (Canovan, 1999), who appeal to "the people," the "united people," "our people," as well as "ordinary people," and who claim to speak in the name of these "oppressed people." Although "the people" are neither real nor all-inclusive but are in fact "a mythical and constructed sub-set of what whole population" or an "imagined community" (Canovan, 1999), the term is contrasted with word "the elite." Populism considers society to be divided into two homogenous and antagonistic groups, "the pure people" and the "corrupt elite" and argues that politics should be an expression of the general will of the people (Mudde, 2004). Populism draws its strengths from the confused and often opportunistic promises of the political elites. For example, in Poland in late 2015, Polish citizens went to the polls and ousted the center-right ruling party, Civic Platform, which had been in power for nearly a decade then. The main reason for Civic Platform's failure was that the Poles had become incensed by corruption scandals, although the country had experienced remarkable economic growth when the party was in power. The PiS narrative was that the country would once again gain legitimacy and power on the world stage, and that it would at last dismantle the semi-mythical "*układ*," a group of corrupt elites who held the levers of power.

In fact, all CEE countries have corruption scandals (Sprinz, 2007; Tupy, 2006), which discredited the ruling class and undermined confidence in democratic institutions. Corruption is a persistent problem across Central Eastern Europe, according to Freedom House's Nations in Transit report[3] and Transparency International.[4] Only recently, in Slovakia, thousands took to the streets of Bratislava to protest corruption and called for the resignation of Slovakia's interior minister, a close ally of social-democratic Prime Minster Robert Fico.

The emergence of right-wing parties was considered to be a result of the political, economic and socio-cultural changes (Beichelt and Minkenberg, 2002). Orbán used economic failures as a sign that Hungary needed to seek alternative ways of political and economic governance. Hungary was hit hard by the 2008 economic crisis which saw a decrease in private consumption, gross capita decrease and cuts in government expenditures (Dutkiewicz and Gorzelak, 2013). However, there was virtually no negative impact in terms of GDP or labor market indicators in Poland, the Czech Republic, and in Slovakia, but severe impact in Hungary (Verick and Islam, 2010). Hungary's economy shrank 7 percent in 2008, worse than most other Central and Eastern European countries. In order to deal with the economic collapse, Hungary went to the International Monetary Fund (IMF). As a condition for getting IMF assistance, Hungary had to implement a very unpopular austerity plan. The economic crisis was an opportunity for Fidesz. The party ran on a platform of raising taxes on multinational corporations operating in Hungary. Populism also aims to quickly please the voters and buy their support (Mudde, 2004), just like the PiS in Poland did with the "Family 500+ program" which is an income-support benefit for Polish families earning 500 PLN monthly.

"The people" the populist propaganda should be against the established structure of power. Merely that what makes populists is their reaction to the structure of power (Canovan, 1999). Because Fidesz obtained a two-thirds majority in parliament in 2010, it gave Orbán the opportunity to begin the process of making profound changes to the Hungarian government and political system and consolidating power by attacking institutions that could threaten his power, by making a dramatic U-turn (Kornai, 2015). In 2011, a number of European intellectuals and others including the late Václav Havel, the former Czech president, published an open letter that criticized the Hungarian government's misuse of power, such as the elimination of checks and balances. A common comparison is Kaczynski's plan to introduce a populist electoral autocracy in Poland along the lines of Prime Minister Viktor Orbán's in Hungary. Law and Justice (PiS) have a mandate to rule, having a slim parliamentary majority, which was won with just over a third of the popular vote. Although, the party does not have a constitutional majority and do not have the popular backing of the majority, the party has a mandate to change the political system, and thus making an impact on the different spheres of society: political institutions, the rule of law, the free market, as well as the life of civil society.

However, "the people" according to populists should not only be against the established structure of power but also the dominant ideas and values of the society. Thus, populism challenges not only established power-holders but elites in general (Canovan, 1999). The elites are intellectuals, representatives of civil society organizations and the media. In Poland, politicians of the ruling PiS, have consequently questioned the legacy of Lech Wałęsa and argued that he collaborated with the Communist secret police and informed on other dissidents before becoming renowned leader of Solidarity (BBC, 2016b). The Hungarian government also attacked journalists and the media and imposed regulations on media outlets that are critical of the government, e.g., a commission that fines journalists for vague attacks on "human dignity" whereas state-supported media outlets were filled with Fidesz loyalists. The PiS seems to use the Hungarian model for its reforms, and introduced controversial media laws, and the boards of state-owned media have been replaced with friends, and family.

"The elites" who stand against "the people" are also bureaucrats of the EU. Prime Minister Orbán also was calling for Hungarians to "retake control of their country" criticizing the European Union and claiming that Hungary was a victim of foreigners, and has been mistreated by Brussels. As the refugee crisis became more of a pressing issue for the European Union, including Hungary, Orbán made Euroskepticism an acceptable form of Hungarian foreign policy allying with European right-wing parties. He put himself and Fidesz at the forefront of the European anti-refugee movement, calling refugees "rapists, criminals, and terrorists" and sealing the borders (Puddington, 2016). Instead of praising the EU old member states, Prime Minister Orbán in the summer of 2014 in a famous speech in the Transylvania (a region of Romania with a large Hungarian minority) praised "non-liberal democracies" and referred to Russia and Turkey as models for imitation. Hungary's Prime Minister Viktor Orbán stated that he wants to transform his country into an illiberal state (Simon, 2014). Such an attitude might seem shocking given that Central Europe has been commonly seen as a region of successful democratization. These countries legitimated market economy, and democratization has fueled a vibrant civil society that was central to the collapse of communism in 1989 (Ekiert and Kubik, 1999; Osa, 2003).

Civil society and protests

Shortly after the breakthrough of 1989 and the fall of communism, two researchers studying civil society in post-communist countries, Grzegorz Ekiert and Jan Kubik, noted the emergence in Central and Eastern Europe of "rebellious civil societies." Today demonstrations have been taking place, which are the largest since the collapse of communism in 1989; especially in Poland, we can observe serious political crisis, the accumulation of grievances and the emergence of collective protests. The first type of protests in Poland against the PiS began in December 2015 and were organized by the "Committee to Defend Democracy" (KOD—Komitet Obrony Demokracji)[5] associated mainly with Mateusz Kijowski. KOD organized a picket supporting the role of the Constitutional Tribunal as a body controlling the compliance of lower-order legal norms with higher-level legal norms, primarily the constitution and some international agreements. The Polish protests took place under the banner "defend the constitution." Shortly, after KOD organized demonstrations under the slogan "Free Media" that took place in many Polish cities as well as abroad, in Prague, London and Stockholm. The participants protested against the changes made in the Radio and Television Act, and consequently made changes the boards of TVP and Polish Radio. Other types of protests were in defense of the honor of Lech Wałęsa, inspired by the activities of the Institute of National Remembrance, which published the content some files from the home of General Czesław Kiszczak without prior verification.

Marches and meetings in Poland inspired people and they kept their distance from political parties. In addition to protest organized by KOD, there have been women's protests. Women took to the streets in a massive protest over abortion rights for the first time in October 2016 (the so-called Black Monday). Hundreds of thousands of Polish women marched through the streets wearing black joined a national protest against a very harsh proposed abortion law, which was a well-organized, single-issue protest having far more impact than the general marches. This women's protest held in dozens of cities did succeed at least in stopping a proposal to criminalize abortion. Nevertheless, women continue to oppose interference in their reproductive rights.

Although opposition to PiS is still weak, however, opposition parties in Poland also protested against an attack on free media and later also engaged in protests against the reform of the National Council of the Judiciary and the Supreme Court conducted by the PiS. Poland's opposition parties protested in

Parliament against planned media restrictions and the perceived mistreatment of its MPs by the speaker of Parliament who excluded an opposition MP for objecting to rules that will make it harder for journalists to report on Parliament. Kaczyński was accusing them outright of trying to stage a coup d'état.

It is difficult to name opposition protests in Hungary, because Viktor Orbán has cemented his power by destroying very effectively the power of traditional democratic parties. His biggest challenge is the xenophobic, nationalistic party Jobbik (the second-biggest national political force), which in recent years has moved from the Right to the Center. Jobbik also had its campaign in which Viktor Orbán and a group of his advisers were presented as thieves: "You work, they steal," proclaimed the slogan of this far-right party, Kim (2016). Before the April parliamentary elections in 2018, the Fidesz party began to interfere with opposition. For example, the State Audit Office (ASZ) unexpectedly imposed on the opposition parties multimillion penalties in connection with the alleged irregularities in their financial settlements. Jobbik has been treated particularly harshly. Demonstrations organized by the opposition have an ever-lower turnout, and crowds do not come for anti-government rallies, although many want a change of government.

Hungarian sociologist Borbala Kriza believes young people in Hungary "are either completely apolitical or are active in the far right. The far right has been able to not just build a party, Jobbik, but also a political subculture" (Schleifer, 2014). Whether or not this is an accurate reflection of all of Hungary's youth culture, it is an indication of a problem and not good news for the future of Hungarian democracy (Ágh, 2016). Nevertheless, when Orbán's targeted CEU University, which was founded in 1991 and sponsored by an American billionaire and a philanthropist of Hungarian origin to educate political leaders and support democratic processes in Europe, the Hungarians were fighting for it in the streets. Under the new regulations, this university would have to suspend its activity if it did not conduct teaching in its country of "origin" (in this case, the United States). In practice, this means the liquidation of CEU, which currently teaches 1,300 students. In April 2017, there were demonstrations for four days organized in the city's main squares where young people demonstrated against these regulations.

In Slovakia, although the Direction—Social Democracy (Smer-SD) party won the March 2016 parliamentary election, forming a coalition government with the Slovak National Party, Most-Híd, and Network, civil society disapproved corruption scandals. Thousands of Slovaks took to the streets of Bratislava to protest corruption and call for the resignation of Slovakia's interior minister. The march was planned not by opposition politicians, but by secondary-school students, who were inspired by protests of this kind in Romania earlier in 2017 (Tamkin, 2017). These protests could be viewed as successful at least because Fico issued a statement saying his government takes corruption seriously and will continue to do so.

Nevertheless, one of the most spectacular, powerful, and widespread protests of civil society took place again in Poland in summer 2017, when civil society reacted to proposed reforms from the populist Law and Justice party (PiS). More than a week of demonstrations across the country, in which hundreds of thousands of Poles took to the streets in towns and cities, held vigils in front of courthouses, and organized rallies at the Presidential Palace. Protestors considered the reforms, which allowed the government to sack Supreme Court judges and giving the justice minister the power to appoint new ones to be, an unashamed power-grab by the PiS, and violation tripartite elements of power.

Demonstrators wielded Polish and European Union flags and carried placards saying "constitution" and "I love and understand freedom," and shouted "we want a veto," a "free court" and a "free Poland." After the lower house voted, the Parliament's upper house, the Senate, approved the bill after sixteen hours of debate, sparking mass protests across the country, calling on President Andrzej Duda to veto the bills. Andrzej Duda bowed to the pressure of nationwide protests and used one out of three vetoes. He blocked proposed legislation that would have put the Supreme Court under the control of the ruling party (wiping out the Supreme Court's independence and allowing the justice ministry to appoint judges) (Connolly, 2017). Among the experts, Duda said he had consulted with lawyers, sociologists, historians, philosophers and anti-communist dissidents. He admitted that the person who had given him most guidance was Zofia Romaszewska, a prominent campaigner of the 1970s and 1980s, who had said to him: "Mr President, I lived in a state where the prosecutor general had an unbelievably powerful position and could practically do anything. I would not like to go back to such a state" (Mortensen, Sterling and Dewan, 2017).

As the war on rule of law moved to a larger theater, Poland became the first country in EU history to face sanctions. The governments of Hungary and the Czech Republic have backed Poland in its dispute with the EU, showing solidarity against EU criticism of their countries' joint backtracking on democratic values and the rule of law. Viktor Orbán said that Poland is the "guardian of the European treaties," and allegations of violation of the rule of law are "inquisition" and they come from the fact that Poland protects its Christian identity (Orlowski, 2017a).

Nevertheless, there have been a great civic awaking in Poland showing that civil society is mature and has deep roots within society, which does not "buy" PiS or other populists' rhetoric and will not give up its freedoms and linkages with the EU so easily, as one of the interviewed activists said. When hundreds of thousands of young people took to the streets all over Poland to defend the constitution and independence of the courts, an important phenomenon was taking place: in parallel with the demolition of the political system by PiS, a process of deep democratization and awaking of civil society in Poland was observed. Undoubtedly, civil society is back on the streets in CEE, and we witness the reappearance of civil society protesting after a period of withdrawal and low social engagement (Howard, 2003).

Emergence of uncivil society

One also has to acknowledge the fact that parallel with the rise of civil society in CEE, there is the emergence of uncivil society that endangers democracy and raises fears of deeper backsliding. The concepts of civil society have been at the forefront of research in the social sciences for several years. A focus on uncivil society is important to understand the sources of impact of populist, xenophobic and Eurosceptic parties, particularly those of the extreme right. Extreme right-wing organizations are often linked to various social networks and associations (e.g., football clubs, cultural associations, media) that openly express discriminatory views and behavior. However, these associations of violent, anti-democratic and xenophobic groups are not reaching out to others. Uncivil societies are based on organizations that are exclusionist. They do not produce solidarity but external aggression, manifest hostility towards liberal democracy and some of its practices. They share the view that conventional politics alone is inefficient and these anti-political sentiments have emerged in Europe as a result of a set of corruption scandals involving incumbents. These sentiments are also linked to anti-elitism. Mudde (2007) considers several typologies of extreme right parties: xenophobic (racist organizations, neo-Nazis fit into this category), nationalist (main concern is territory—territory is a proxy for a community that share a notion of common belonging, also Eurosceptic, nationalist fascist), populist (against the elites).

Populism is a thin-centered ideology and rarely exists on its own and mostly attaches itself to other ideologies (Akkerman, Mudde and Zaslove, 2014). The extreme right political parties in CEE have relied on issues that fall into the ideological definition of extreme right groups identified by Mudde (2007). They frame their ideology through the populist and xenophobic criticisms of perceived enemies.

The whole region has been swept by populism underpinned by nationalism. Xenophobic discourse is based on ethno-nationalism, on opposition to immigration (also fueled by the ongoing refugee crisis). However, whereas such framing has been gradually taken up by the extreme right parties in in CEE, it has been present Western Europe for longer time (Rydgren, 2005). Although current nationalism revolves around the national interests and might seem not to be as dangerous as it was in the 1930s, attacks on migrant by skinheads is becoming commonplace. For example, tens of thousands of Poles marched across downtown Warsaw one Saturday, in an independence-day procession organized by a nationalist youth movement that seeks an ethnically pure Poland with fewer Jews or Muslims (Hinshaw, 2017).

Populism, xenophobia, racism appear frequently in the mass media in the context of attacks against refuges and LGBT people in the new EU member states and are spread by extremist groups. In recent years, right-wing parties achieved electoral success, which allowed for such extremism to grow and to support or even justify their verbal and non-verbal violence and discriminatory actions. Right-wing groups from networks of like-minded people who engage in extremist undertakings (Ruzza, 2011), encourage and support racist movements. These are a distinct type of associations which scholars and practitioners have called uncivil society. In this sense, uncivil society is a community that is incompatible with the modern democracies. In principle, uncivil society activities can also be undertaken by left-wing groups, but in CEE countries, the most contemporary instances of uncivil society emerge in relation to the activities of the extreme right.

As Ruzza (2009, p. 87) has put it

> membership in uncivil society organizations is an alternative type of political participation which articulates growing anti-political sentiments, and that the emergence of uncivil society activities is rooted in newly relevant conceptions of social and political life which are anti-modern and based on ascriptive criteria of membership.

They react to a perceived ineffectiveness of the relationship between politics and society in the liberal democracies, based on social marginalization, and reaction to the ills of globalization. They also may produce models of participation that deny the spirit and practices of liberal democracy. The National-Radical Camp "Podhale" in Poland recruited people from all over Poland on a trip organized "together with friends from the People's Party of Our Slovakia," who considered themselves the heirs of the Slovak People's Party, led by Fr. Jozef Tiso, who ruled Slovakia during World War II under the auspices of Nazi Germany.

Today civil society is being made weak by the efforts of the Polish populist right which substitutes "nation" for civil society and discredits civil society. Nationalist discourse had been adopted by right-wing political parties in Poland, but it became evident in the 2005 electoral victories of the Law and Justice Party led by Jarosław Kaczyński, who became prime minister, and his twin brother, Lech was elected president. Poland's divide was fueled by some of Kaczyńskis' rhetoric, that those who oppose the PiS are the "Poles of the worst sort." It has been presented as a struggle between "us" and "them." Because electorates are less stable, parties try to improve their connections with society through channeling state resources to associations in exchange for electoral support. The relationship becomes more like a service because civil society organizations perform in society for the benefit of parties. The emphasis on civil society is in the political programs. Political elites are manufacturing civil society organizations to improve their brokerage power. This political crisis undoubtedly alters relationships between the state and various groups and organizations within society, which has consequences for democracy promotion efforts coming from the governmental programs of CEE countries. Therefore, it is important to address these changes in the next section.

Changes in democracy promotion in CEE countries

This section presents governments' attempts to provoke scandals to discredit civil society organizations, curtail their financial resources, and to silence the civic sector by introducing legislation to limit the space available for its activities in Central and Eastern European countries. Such practices so far were known in (semi-) authoritarian states, such as Russia, Belarus and Venezuela, where there has been a history of backlash against democracy promotion as well as intimidation or harassment of foreign-funded NGOs, which are now called "foreign agents" and international organizations that provide civil society support to them (Applebaum, 2015; Rutzen, 2015; Walker, 2016). The turning point in the offensive against NGOs came after the "Color Revolutions" in Ukraine, Georgia, and Kirgizstan. NGOs that were receiving funding came to be regarded as foreign-sponsored agents, Trojan horses serving the West. Governments stripped NGOs of financial aid from the West, and also passed laws that limited the right to free assembly. Such practices took place in Russia, Belarus and Venezuela, but also later in Hungary, and now in Poland. Foreign-funded NGOs were squeezed whereas pseudo-NGOs or NGOs favored by the governments were given some financial privileges. The governments of these countries have started to limit the amount of foreign funding that NGOs are allowed to receive. They also even openly harass groups that receive external support, creating burdensome requirements on foreign funding that include obligatory government approval, for example. However, these phenomena can be observed today in Poland and Hungary where the governments create the centers through which funding would be disbursed to the society.

The policies in CEE today gradually shifted and in Hungary, as well as partially in Poland, where foreign-funded NGOs are gaining status as foreign agents, and the governments adopt the legislations as well as establish entities that make financial flows to NGOs more difficult. Civil society organizations' capacity to act as a watch-dog of political power and to mobilize protest against its abuse have not escaped the attention of ruling right-wing political elites. These measures pose a considerable challenge to civic organizations in CEE countries, forcing some to withdraw from open engagement in public affairs. Some changes that are taking place in governmental development cooperation programs, may take many years to be reversed.

Therefore, based on Poland's and Hungary's examples, I am presenting how governments in democratic countries are attempting to control civil society, in order to better understand this phenomenon. These two countries, because there is no good news of the fate of Hungarian democracy today, and Poland, which is a showcase country for successful transformation, today is a country where democracy is in peril. It is the second country after Hungary in Central and Eastern Europe where there is fear of backsliding.

NGOs under attack

CEE NGOs that emerged in the 1990s and which were active abroad survived mostly because of financial support from abroad. Today it makes them vulnerable vis-à-vis the authorities. The third sector is being undermined not only by exposing such organizations, how much money they received and from whom and for what purposes, but also by condemning' personal and political ties, in order to discredit NGOs. A such scenario of "unmasking" non-governmental organizations began in Poland in the autumn of 2016. The public channel TVP's news programs made allegations of uncontrolled financial flows to NGOs, and about personal relationships between major non-governmental organizations and political elites. The public media attacked Association 61 (Stowarzyszenie 61) whose president is Róża Rzeplińska, a daughter of the former president of the Constitutional Tribunal) or Pracownia Badań i Innowacji Społecznych "Stocznia" (the director is Zofia Komorowska, a daughter of the former president).

Deputy Prime Minister and Minister of Culture Piotr Gliński, referred to this media information concerning persons operating in the non-governmental sector and the issue of family relations or political activity of some sector activists as follows:

> I think that they were too far-reaching, sometimes harmful to these activists (…). It really has nothing to do with anyone being related to someone. We should not drive this type of polemics. These people were put in a critical light due to the fact that the non-governmental sector sometimes implements things in a wrong way.[6]

He apologized to those who might have felt offended, mentioning Zofia Komorowska, Róża Rzeplińska and Jan Jakub Wygnański, meritorious civil society activists in the organization. However, while apologizing at the same time the minister of culture, who is a professor of sociology and who studied civil society and knew what too much government might mean for the third sector, announced the establishment of the so-called the National Freedom Center for the Development of Civil Society, a public institution that will "take care" of matters of non-governmental organizations, as discussed later in this chapter.

The elements of Law and Justice's populist programme of so-called "good change" (*dobra zmiana*) began in the third sector. The way the public media tried to discredit non-government organizations was met with strong opposition from organizations that resulted in petitions and letters. The representatives of NGOs, as well as academia and opposing parties expressed their strong disapproval to the way in which the editors and journalists of TVP presented non-governmental organizations, undermining the credibility and offending people working in them.[7] When the Democracy Action (Akcja Demokracja) was also targeted by the government, this initiated the July 2017 "chains of light" protests. TVP alleged that the protests were "financed from abroad," perhaps by George Soros, although this action was in fact financially supported by individual donors from Poland, and the pro-government *Gazeta Polska* claimed that it is preparing the "autumn coup."

In the Czech Republic and Slovakia, "neziskovky" (non-profit organizations) have also been under attack. Similarly to Poland, it has been stressed in the Czech Republic that such organizations are working with children or spouses of current or former ministers (mostly dissidents, who after 1989 became ruling elites), which constitutes evidence of a "clique" that supports only its own members. The Czech President Milos Zeman known for his pro-Russian stance, called the NGOs representatives of *pražská kavárna* (Prague café) which he used to define a group of urban intellectuals who are publicly active and interested in politics, seeking to build on the of policy Václav Havel. The word "café" refers to a meeting place for intellectuals in Prague regarded as a symbol of a city of intellectuals divorced from reality of ordinary people.[8] He was called "an architect of hatred that is poisoning society" as five NGOs wrote in an open letter in April 2016. The letter was an analogy of the letter of former president and Czechoslovak dissident Václav Havel who wrote to Communist President Gustav Husak in 1975, which described the fear, apathy and humiliation that Czechs and Slovaks faced in the first years after the Soviet-led invasion of 1968, and which was signed by the Prague Academic Club 48, the Edvard Beneš Society, the Antonin Svehla Society, Mene Tekel and the Center for Documentation of Totalitarian Regimes. However, President Václav Klaus had been a longtime critic of NGO involvement in policymaking, and NGO initiatives had often been labeled as lacking legitimacy or motivated by party politics.[9] In his opinion, non-governmental organization often interfere in normal life, creating political pressure, despite the fact that they did not receive an electoral mandate. His statement provoked outrage among activists in the third sector, and some organizations sent a letter to the president calling for an apology.

The third sector also fell out of favor in Slovakia. In Spring 2016, Robert Fico, who was the leader of the center-left Direction-Social Democracy (Smer-SD), won the election for the third time and became prime minister, but to stay in power he had to form a coalition with small parties, including those on the far right. As the result, Fico emerged severely weakened and the far-right and populist parties did well in the Slovak election (POLITICO 2016). In his first media interview he said that the fight for victory was difficult and unusual, because the main enemy, paradoxically, was not the political opposition but non-governmental organizations, which, as he maintained, were sponsored from abroad. However, he is less determined to deconstruct institutions as Kaczynski and Orbán.

In Hungary, the attack on NGOs was earlier. After the making constitutional changes, as well changes in media outlets and law and in state-controlled businesses, the government targeted the third sector which, in order to work as was predicted, should be subordinated to the government, according to Orbán's government. The largest non-governmental organizations in the country that track corruption and monitor the government and which do not depend on state subsidies, but are financed by national and foreign subsidies in Hungary were attacked by the government. In 2013, the pro-government daily "Heti Valasz" published an article about a dozen or so organizations co-financed by George Soros, an American billionaire and a philanthropist of Hungarian origin, as well as those using funds from the Norwegian fund. The authors of the articles wrote that the opposition is supported with money from abroad (Wyborcza, 2017). Third-sector organizations were first called by "paid political activists who are trying to help foreign interests" (Otarashvili, 2014). During a year-long investigation, Fidesz's politicians spread visions of NGO activists, who were heavily paid by the West, who want to overthrow the government.

Autumn 2014, saw the first wave of intimidation and harassment of NGOs, with tax office officials entering the offices of several organizations accompanied by the police, who were supposed to scan the organization's finances and find evidence of irregularities. The authorities also presented a new bill, according to which the heads of non-governmental organizations were to publish their property declarations. Persecution stopped in 2015 when the tax office withdrew all allegations against the organization, not being able to find any irregularities. It was a government failure, which, however, was not going to give up at all. In interviews with NGOs it has frequently been pointed out to me that they are being marginalized in Hungary if they criticize governmental positions.

The heaviest attack against foreign-funded NGOs began in January 2017. Hungary's government spokesperson Zoltán Kovács accused some NGOs of being foreign agents financed by foreign money, and critical of Hungarian-American philanthropist and civil-society supporter George Soros, saying he was fostering chaos in Hungary by funding non-governmental organizations. Soros became a public enemy for the government in Budapest (Simon, 2017). Prime Minister Orbán publicly accused Soros of supporting immigration to Europe and exposing Hungary to terrorist attacks. He launched an anti-migrant billboard campaign using the image of US financier George Soros. Everyone traveling to Budapest could see, especially on the way from the airport to the city center many billboards with the smiling face of Soros with the caption: "Don't let Soros have the last laugh."

As the first steps to liquidate NGOs failed, the Hungarian government held two "national consultations" among Hungarians regarding the fate of organizations in 2017. They were to say in the survey whether they agreed to the "risky activity of non-governmental organizations." One of the questions was framed

> More and more organizations supported from abroad operate in Hungary in an improper way, meddling in the internal affairs of our country. These organizations may threaten our independence. What do you think Hungary should do? a) Force them to register, disclosing their business goals and sources of funding; b) Allow their risky activities without any supervision.
>
> (Kokot, 2017b)

The authorities accused their representatives of harming the government because they were writing reports stigmatizing corruption and a lack of respect for human rights. For Fidesz politicians, this is synonymous with political activity, and they call civic activists "political activists."

The government again sent a second questionnaire in Fall 2017 to four million households, this time with seven questions. In the second "consultation" citizens were asked whether they agreed with the plan of the American billionaire and philanthropist George Soros, who wants to bring millions of immigrants to Europe. It was preceded by an electoral campaign in which the government was encouraged "to say 'stop' Brussels!" In the streets, in the subway and on the billboards, there are government posters with slogans saying "stop Brussels."

One of questions in the survey was this: "Together with officials in Brussels, George Soros plans to dismantle the fence on the Hungarian border in order to allow a million immigrants to enter the European Union, including Hungary. Do you agree with this?" Citizens were also asked to state to whether they agreed that immigrants should be punished less severely for the crimes they commit, as Soros's plan foresees (Kokot, 2017a). All these actions against NGOs and George Soros could be perceived as politically motivated in order mobilize conservative voters, who in the Spring 2018 will vote for Fidesz party to help it win the parliamentary elections.

Government attempts to provoke scandals in order to discredit civil society organizations (in all CEE countries) are only some of the measures taken. Additionally, in Hungary there have been efforts to silence the civic sector by introducing legislation to limit the space available for its activities. Also, in both Poland and Hungary, there have been actions taken by the government to curtail NGOs' financial and resource bases and to bring NGOs under control.

Introducing state mechanisms controlling foreign-funded NGOs

In Hungary as well as in Poland, non-governmental organizations, particularly those fighting for democracy and human rights, and being foreign-funded are disliked by governments. At the time when public TV broadcast discrediting information about Polish NGOs, the former Prime Minister of Poland, Beata Szydło announced the establishment of a special institution to monitor grant money because—as she claimed—the government needed to sort out the situation of the third sector. In her opinion, money went to the "wrong" organizations. The government also argues that it needed to provide support for civil society, addressing needs of small, weak organizations that have had problems functioning so far.

The new National Institute of Freedom—Center for the Development of Civil Society was supposed to allocate funds from the Civic Initiatives Fund FIO (PLN 60 million a year) and EU programs. Public funding for NGOs has so far been distributed by open competition on a transparent basis which guaranteed the suitability of the applicants for funding and the transparency of competitions. Meanwhile, the government wants to make an exception to this rule. The Center will be able to assign tasks without a competition if it considers that this requires "job specificity." In this way, the center will be able to donate money not only to selected organizations, but also to companies or religious associations.

However, the changes mean a stronger centralization. According to the law, the Institute will set the goals for NGOs and will distribute funding to organizations, which will be supervised by the chair of a specially created Public Benefit Committee. The committee, however, will be "a government administration body" and its chair will be a member of the government. The director of the institute, appointed by the chair, will determine the rules of the competition. The council, which will be of composed of NGO representatives, will only act an advisory capacity. Organizations are aware that the director will have a very important role, and the council only a marginal one, which will include NGO representatives. They stress that the director of the institute will not only determine who can apply for grants, the conditions for the allocation of funds and financial settlements but will also be able to discretionally subsidize an organization within the framework of undefined "institutional development."

The parliament ignored the appeals by non-governmental organizations. The law on the National Institute of Freedom—Center for the Development of Civil Society, which is to decide on the distribution of funds for NGOs, was adopted by the lower chamber of Parliament, the Sejm, in mid-September and then—without any amendments—by the Senate. This has happened despite many remarks made by the Legislative Office of the Senate and numerous amendments suggested by the opposition parties. As Adam Michnik's "Gazeta Wyborcza"[10] put it well (Zakrzeweski, 2017):

> the name of the institution itself, which is supposed to control the world of non-governmental organizations, is like in George Orwell's "1984" in fictitious Oceania, where the Ministry of Truth censored the truth and produced disinformation, the Ministry of Peace waged war, and the Ministry of Abundance meddled the subjects into misery and hunger.

The law also consistently opposed the non-governmental organizations. The Polish Federation of Non-Governmental Organizations (OFOP brings together 127 coalitions of associations from all over the country) appealed first to the prime minister and then to the MPs not to pass the Act. The Federation also wanted to organize a public hearing, but this request was rejected. After the bill was passed by the Sejm, NGOs appealed to the president to veto this law. In a special letter[11] NGOs wrote that the law "poses a threat to the independence of civil society, destroying the existing system of cooperation between the public administration and non-governmental organizations." According to NGOs, the law introduces a system "both opaque and fraught with the risk of strong politicization" and "introduces the possibility of differentiating relationships with selected organizations based on faith and worldview." However, President Andrzej Duda signed a law on the National Institute of Freedom.

It should be mentioned that not all organizations were against this law. The bill was recently praised by the Confederation of Non-Governmental Initiatives of the Republic of Poland (*Konfederacja Inicjatyw Pozarządowych Rzeczypospolitej*), which was founded at the beginning of 2017 and brings together conservative and right-wing organizations. One example of a member of this Confederation is the Service for an Independent Foundation (*Fundacja Służba Niepodległej*) which was founded in order to promote Polish national heritage based its Christian heritage, the ethos of patriotism among young people in Poland. The Confederation attacked the Batory Foundation, which distributes so-called Norwegian funds, for "supporting organizations with a clearly ideological profile of action and questioning the basic principles of the Polish constitutional system." Several organizations, like the Solidarni 2010 association, which promotes the development of Poland on the basis of "historical truth and national identity" and aims "to preserve the Catholic identity of Poland by cultivating historical memory, the distinctiveness of the tradition and culture of the Polish nation," and *Gazeta Polska* which is a right-wing, conservative news magazine wrote a pro-government letter to the wider public.

The government would like to see the newly created institution also distributing Norwegian funds to NGOs. Norwegians oppose this, believing that it violates the principle of independence. It was the same in Hungary. Also, the government wanted to reduce Norwegian funds, but the Norwegians said no. As a result, Hungarian NGOs can no longer receive money from these funds and have to end their programs. In October 2017, President Andrzej Duda signed the Act on the National Freedom Institute—the National Center for the Development of Civil Society of Poland,[12] which is to give money to NGOs. The National Freedom Institute's tasks were to promote the involvement of citizens and civil society organizations in public life and decision-making processes and civic control over public institutions. In fact, it will create a situation where, in practice, the responsibility of distributing the great majority of public funds or resources to civil society organizations would be assigned to just one entity.

Citizensobservatory.pl (2017) issued its opinion on the draft bill in which several aspects of the National Institute were criticized. Especially, the fact that the executive branch appears to have a direct, or indirect, decisive influence on the governance and operation of the National Institute, including its programs, financial planning and reporting. Also, the executive would also have a direct influence on the identification of priorities to support civil society organizations. citizensobservatory.pl (2017) referring to international standards on the right to freedom of association and public support to associations, suggested that the National Institute should complement other public funding schemes rather than be established as a centralized body responsible for the distribution of the great majority of funds or resources provided by central authorities to civil society organizations. citizensobservatory.pl (2017) also recommended a reconsideration the supervisory and organizational structure, and to provide measures or safeguards limiting potential government interference, for example by increasing the number of civil society representatives on the Board (the criteria for becoming a Board member who should be of "untarnished reputation" are also vague and broad) so that they make up at least half of the total number of Board members and "ensuring that such participation of civil society organizations is inclusive and non-discriminatory, and based on a fair, public, transparent, open, non-discriminatory, inclusive and competitive selection process". Ideally, civil society organizations should participate in the management, decision-making and programming of the National Institute through partnership and joint decision-making. Unfortunately, none of the suggestions was considered.

Law and Justice, centralizing politically the distribution of public funds, gained enormous power over civil society organizations. What would be the consequences of such actions? It is worth looking a the "big brother" in Hungary.

The government of Viktor Orbán introduced a similar center in 2012 when changing National Civic Fund into the National Solidarity Fund (NEA) (Szurovecz, 2014). In this way money from the budget was to be distributed fairly, but it soon turned out that this only concerned a few organizations. László Csizmadia, the chairman of the Hungarian Civil Union (CÖF), financially supported by the ruling Fidesz, stood at the head of the institution. Since then, money from the NEA began to flow in a wide stream to the organizations headed by politicians. Fidesz youth and their families, associations organizing rallies with the participation of members of the ruling party as well as CÖF itself. Before the 2014 elections, CÖF took part in the Fidesz campaign. The organization sent four million letters to Hungarians, asking for support in the elections for the Orbán's party, and posting billboards on the streets of cities disparaging the opposition. Recently, the association received 500 million forints (about seven million PLN) of support from the state-owned energy company (Szurovecz, 2014; Kokot and Kośmiński, 2017c).

However, in Hungary, things were even further and the question is whether Poland will follow in its "big brother's" footsteps. The situation of foreign-funded NGOs has deteriorated as the results of the law that was passed in Hungary in June 2017 (bill took one day to pass through Parliament, and three days later it was signed by the president), which was similar to the law that is in force in Putin's Russia. The law requires these NGOs to admit "getting money from abroad." Specifically, organizations that receive more than 7.2 million forints annually from abroad have to register as "an organization financed from abroad," and a notice reflecting this has to appear on every public statement, in reports or media materials. There are various sanctions for non-compliance with these regulations, such as a fine of up to one million forints or to be struck off the register as a non-governmental organization (Kokot, 2017c).

The government claims that this will increase the transparency of these organizations. However, organizations publish financial data every year, whereas a new status is perceived by the government and its media as a stigma, which makes it harder for them to gain the confidence of the Hungarian people. Almost identical laws were passed in Russia a few years ago. Representatives of Hungarian NGOs are afraid that that the law and new the "foreign agent" status, may significantly impede their activities and result in a reduction of funds from social donations. The Act has been criticized by the European Commission (which initiated the infringement procedure) and the US Department of State. Also, Hungarian organizations (about twenty-three) complained to the Hungarian Constitutional Court, which was dominated by Fidesz appointed judges, the about a bill. The party has since increased the composition of the judges, appointed loyal judges and increased their term of office to twelve years, guaranteeing favorable judgments even in the event of losing the next parliamentary election.

NGOs intend to complain to the Human Rights Tribunal in Strasbourg, even though a lot of harm has already been done, because of the hostile atmosphere created around us these organizations, people are still afraid to seek legal advice, for example, as they do not want to risk problems with power. The Hungarian

Union for Civil Liberties (TASZ), defending human rights, has already announced that it will not comply with the law. The Hungarian branch of the Helsinki Foundation for Human Rights will do the same. The new regulations criticize the Venice Commission, Germany and the United States.

The end of democracy promotion through development cooperation?

In Poland and Hungary, it is difficult to rely on foreign funding, but it is also problematic to obtain domestic money for activities related to democracy and human rights. In this section, I am focusing on those organizations that used to cooperate within their governments within developmental cooperation programs established at the Ministry of Foreign Affairs. I am mainly giving voice to social activists in Hungary as well as to the Department of International Development at the Ministry of Foreign Affairs and Trade in Hungary. I also discuss changes that have already taken place regarding new donors' democracy promotion, and in the end draw some conclusions also for the future of bypass democracy assistance for CEE NGOs.

As discussed in Chapter 2, many CEE NGOs active abroad, especially those associated with umbrella organizations in their countries, who are members of the EU-level CONCORD platform, have received money for their projects through appeals by the entities responsible for development cooperation at the Ministries of Foreign Affairs. A lion's share of the aid from the region is deployed to neighboring countries. Most of the Hungarian ODA is channeled to neighboring countries, with particular emphasis on the Balkan states. In Slovakia, a large chunk of the aid goes to Serbia and Montenegro. In the Czech Republic and Poland, most aid goes to Belarus, Ukraine and Georgia, who are foreign policy priority partners, and the priorities in the CEE include regional stability, economic cooperation, etc., and sharing transition experience.

However, after almost fifteen years of these programs, there have been some differences emerging between the CEE countries in the ways the government cooperates today with organizations that are active abroad in developmental cooperation and democracy assistance, and which are members of umbrella organizations belonging to the CONCORD platform. The situation of non-governmental development organizations in the Czech Republic seems to be the most influential, and those in Hungary the least. Polish and Slovak NGOs, however, are located between these two extremes.

In the Czech Republic, organizations associated in FoRS, of which there are over forty, seem to speak with one voice, and are relatively effective in their cooperation with Czech Ministry of Foreign Affairs, which is very open and sees the benefits of mutual partnership. There have been no restrictions and limitations implemented that would jeopardize the work of NGOs and their ability to obtain funding for their work abroad from MFA. Jan Latal from the Ministry of Foreign Affairs of the Czech Republic stressed during an interview that the fact that Transition Program under MFA was created, shows how important it is to share the Czech experience of political and economic transition with other countries. Although the budget has been modest since 2004, there is an uninterrupted cyclical annual grant scheme to NGOs to incorporate projects with partner countries. Calls for proposals are also broadly defined so that all NGOs could suggest anything that strengthens civil society, focuses on promoting civic participation and the learning by doing process. More than 90 percent of bilateral aid goes through Czech NGOs, because legal provisions and budget rules do not allow sending money directly to other actors, "but at the same time we understand that NGOs are important partners, who also seeks other partners in recipient countries, so that they can learn from Czech NGOs about youth engagement, student debates, etc."

The Polish umbrella organization Grupa Zagranica, which counts the largest number of associated organizations in comparison with other countries, consists of more than sixty organizations, which, although not always living in harmony with the Ministry of Foreign Affairs, are quite cohesive and are treated as a serious partner. The Slovakian federation, despite obtaining direct financing from the Ministry of Foreign Affairs, believes that it is not considered a serious partner. The most difficult situation is in Hungary, because there are very few organizations associated with HAND. Currently, ten or less are active. Their activities are very fragmented and organizations use EU funds in a moderate way, while relations with the development aid unit in the Ministry of Foreign Affairs and Trade are quite tense and there are no clear signs of improvement.

In Slovakia, and in particular in the Czech Republic, the positive attitude of the Ministry of Foreign Affairs in the Czech Republic or the agencies that deal with development aid to non-governmental organizations results from the fact that the government realizes that without cooperation with these organizations, the implementation of development projects, including those aimed at promoting democracy becomes impossible. Positive perception of non-governmental organizations also results from professionalism and strengthening their position outside the country. When I was interviewing representatives of Polish Aid in 2008, I received the same impression. However, at this moment, the Department of Development Cooperation at the Ministry of Foreign Affairs of the Republic of Poland, is affected by the decisions taken at the higher level and the political discourse in Poland regarding civil society organizations.

Whereas priorities of Polish Aid have not officially changed,[13] and the support to civil society continues to flow via Polish NGOs, there have been other measures taken by the government that might lower trust in public institutions and have negative consequences on activities taken within development cooperation in the future. In 2016, the Solidarity Fund, whose activity in the field of democracy assistance has been described in Chapter 2, had an unexpected change of president. Based on the new regulations that were passed, [14] the minister responsible for foreign affairs within three months from entry into force of the Act on the Management of State Property, had a right to appoint the new President of the Board of the Solidarity Fund. As the result, Krzysztof Stanowski, who was the president of the Solidarity Fund between 2012 and 2017, was dismissed.[15]

There have been also other murky actions taken by the PiS government. They refer to unjustified funding for the government-friendly *Gazeta Polska* foundation, Solidarni 2010 and the Rydzyk foundation, who do not give money to those who "look at the hands," promote equal rights for women, sex education, or the rights of LGBT people. Unfriendly and often foreign-funded NGOs become squeezed whereas pseudo-NGOs or NGOs favored by the governments are given some financial privileges. For example, in 2016, the Ministry of Foreign Affairs announced an appeal to various entities in Poland who were supposed to form intersectoral consortia in order to create a "Regional Center for International Debate 2016–2018." One of the Polish newspapers *Rzeczpospolita* did an investigation and raised an objection regarding the amount of money that the nine entities received.[16] The most astonishing was, according to *Rzeczpospolita*'s journalists, the fact that among the beneficiaries was the Election Control Movement (*Ruch Kontroli Wyborów*), which is closely related to the Law and Justice party, as well as the College of Communication and Media at the University of Toruń. Both institutions seemed to be underqualified to lead the center for international debates. One of the activists complained in the interview that although two organizations applied from Olsztyn, they did not receive funding:

> it turned out that the Regional Center for International Debate in Olsztyn—the capital of the region with over 200 km of border with the Kaliningrad region of the Russian Federation is not necessary from the perspective of the Polish Ministry of Foreign Affairs, and our competences in the sphere of international debate, in contrast to the Election Control Movement or the College of Communication and Media from Toruń, are insufficient.

I was told that the application of this activist was rejected, based on trivial justifications.

In Hungary, pressure from the private sector as well as government policy aimed at limiting the negative effects of the impact of the economic crisis has led to the emergence of new trends in development policy. These changes can be observed in the aid directed to more traditional sectors that bring better economic cooperation, greater pressure for cooperation with the private sector and non-governmental organizations, which results in a diminishing number of non-governmental organizations that deal with development aid. The greater focus on economic issues was also manifested by the fact that the Hungarian Ministry of Foreign Affairs was merged with the Ministry of Trade, creating the Ministry of Foreign Affairs and Trade of Hungary (MFAT).

During my interview at the Department of International Development of MFAT, I was told that Hungary is less visible and engaged in democracy assistance, because there is not sufficient awareness among the public sector as well as private sector. Another reason is that there are no sufficient financial resources mainly because of the economic crisis that took place in 2008. Also because of this crisis, Hungary is not able to meet ODA/GNI portion of 0.33 percent. Finally, since the institution that disburses bilateral money is the Ministry of

Foreign Affairs and Trade (MFAT) it gives new challenges and new task, but as the representative expressed

> I don't think that democracy would play an important role [for Hungarian MFAT] (...) this year there are opportunities and financial framework for development aid. We cannot be active in every important field of development cooperation but in our strategy, which is for the period between 2014 and 2020, it [democracy assistance] is an important part.

Hungary became a member of the OECD Development Assistance Committee in December 2016 and I was told that it was the result of long-term initiatives taken by the non-governmental organizations as well. An international development strategy was accepted by the government in 2014, and it was the first policy document since 2001. When asked about why Hungary was the last to adopt it, I was told that the first measures were taken in around 2001/2002. However, it was a subject of broad consultations between stakeholders in international development cooperation, and needed to be carried out in compliance with foreign and security policy and economic policy as well as fully being supported by the public, private and third sectors: "We really needed to learn the framework of this policy so maybe this is why it has taken so long" (Interview, July 14, 2015, Budapest). The Department also turned to Slovak Aid as well as to the MFA of the Czech Republic for the consultation regarding strategy.

Hungary within ODA is mostly active in the Western Balkans and Eastern Europe with the goal of share experiences regarding the EU integration process or transition experience. When the Department says "we are active in those countries," it means MFA through NGO projects, because bilateral aid cannot take the form of direct assistance to CSOs in recipient countries that do not go through CSOs or through embassies. The MFAT supports those civil societies that are active abroad through calls for proposals. The representative expresses the opinion that support for the governmental and civil institutional reforms are the most effective. However, at the same time, while the interview was taking place there was no general call for proposals in 2015 announced by Department of International Development at the MFAT, but a more specialized one with the goal to help the Western Balkans with flood damage and reconstruction work. My interviewees argued that there is a strong connection with awareness raising, because Hungarian people really do not have the chance to meet civil organizations such as the fourteen or fifteen NGO that are acting abroad, and do not have information about their work. Therefore, for future and fruitful cooperation as well as the realization of ODA, the Department would like more opportunities for NGOs to raise awareness among the Hungarian people because once people to get to know NGOs and trust them, they feel they would like to donate some money for their work.

Whereas the Department at Hungarian MFAT blames NGOs and would like to see them more active in civil society, and get a better idea of their work, the Hungarian Association of NGOs for Development and Humanitarian Aid

(HAND) is of a different opinion. HAND was officially established in 2003 by fifteen members, with the assistance from the Canadian Developmental Agency (CIDA). Interestingly, CIDA was providing financial support and policy development recommendations for both the Hungarian government, which was establishing its official development assistance structures, as well as the NGOs. Since the establishment of bilateral aid and HAND, it was growing organizationally and financially and "more and more NGOs could apply for funds from the ministry and could go abroad, so everything was bright" (Interview, July 14, 2015, Budapest, Hungary). But at the same, time when the financial crisis hit in 2008, humanitarian and developmental funds of the Ministry of Foreign Affairs immediately decreased to a tenth of the previous year's budget, and thus NGO activities could not really expand. The crisis of 2008 was the main reason, but not the only one, because "on the other hand it is true that even previously the Hungarian government did not think of us as priority, it was not at the top of the list" (Interview July 14, 2015, Budapest). Also, the development cooperation strategy that was adopted in 2014 was not clear. It was not clear who was responsible, who was coordinating or which institution was coordinating in Hungary. That is why it was such difficult context.

Since 2008, the scope of development intervention of NGOs in the Western Balkans and Eastern Europe is shrinking due to less funding, caused by the financial crisis, and the lack of commitment from the governmental side. There was no strategic thinking, and even the Department became more responsible and charged for development cooperation within MFA. The external policy is also transferring funds to another priority which is economic growth, especially that the MFA was merged with Ministry of Trade and now priorities of external economic relations have to be taken into account as well. The economic issues are now the priority and the main actors who were invited, are focusing on economic issues, not development cooperation.

HAND has monthly meetings with the Department of International Development just like their counterpart in Poland, Grupa Zagranica with Polish Aid, where the can discuss important issues. The meetings with this Department of the MFA take place in a friendly atmosphere, because they had a good relationship for years. The decisions of those meetings at this level are not sufficient, because "important decision is taken somewhere else." The representatives of HAND realized that in order to have influence they have to make connections with other government offices, especially the Ministry of Economics and even the prime minister's office because that is where matters regarding bilateral aid allocation are decided. Even in past ten to fifteen years, the Hungarian government did not see the importance of this issue, and politicians did regard this as an investment for further business opportunities for other partners and actors: "when it comes to the questions of political issues and even funding, then you have to influence higher-level bodies and that's a challenge for us for sure" (Interview with a representative HAND that prefers to be anonymous, July 14, 2015, Budapest).

When Hungarian NGOs were being attacked, some of the members of CONCORD, and other umbrella organizations, got very active in Croatia or

Ireland. Through CONCORD, they can inform and make other associations aware of their situation, and keep following the what is going on—

> When it comes to development policy questions and issues, specifically at the European level, that's our entry point (…) we can talk to them when there's an issue such funding, also through them we could get our interest represented (…) in the confederation there are always gaps and different interest so you have to always struggle, but at the same time it is absolutely the kind of forum where we can express our interests.

Since the income from membership fees is limited, HAND needs other sources of funding, which come mainly from the EU since the association is a part of three big international projects funded by Europe Aid. One is "Trialog,"[17] which focuses on spreading awareness and greater involvement of civil society organizations in Europe, the second one is concerned with policy coherence development,[18] and the third, Beyond 2015,[19] is a global civil society campaign.

When I asked HAND about the current general situation of NGOs in Hungary that are engaged in democracy promotion, I was told that they are weak in financial and political terms, and that anything can happen to them and they can be attacked by the government. NGOs might be regarded as a threat for political reasons, because they are critical and that they have monitored the sector which favors democracy, transparency, and government accountability for the past five years.

A reliable source of funding for NGOs was the National Civic Fund (NCF), which became National Cooperation Fund (NCF). The NCF was coming from the 1 percent of personal income tax that people donated to NGOs. It was a matching fund because the same amount of money from the government raised through taxation was put into this fund. This fund was established in 2003 and operated until 2010/2011. One advantage of it was that the work was divided between boards and councils and the CSOs were represented. There were dialogue between these elements and they decided on the applications. About 60 percent to 70 percent of the fund could have gone towards operational costs and financing. The remaining 40 percent went to the projects which helped small-scale organizations to be set up and to start working. In 2010/2011, Orbán's government changed the name of the fund. Everything began to have "national" in its name, so it became the national cooperation fund. This meant that that the decision-making mechanism was changed, and not that many representatives of CSOs were involved. Decisions were increasingly made at ministerial level. The same amount of money was given out but distributed differently. More went to organizations that were linked to the government. Nevertheless, the situation of GONGOs, like International Center for Democratic Transition (ICDT) which used receive 50 percent funding from MFAT (and thus did not fulfill criteria to be a member of HAND) was also not favorable. Now, these organizations have to obtain money from outside donors for their work. It was different but it has changed. Because of the problem with the budget and decreasing amounts allocated to the Department of International Development at the MFAT ICDT work was affected. Instead of a twice-yearly call for NGOs projects, now small and medium enterprises dealing with developmental cooperation projects.

It has been pointed out by HAND representatives that in past twenty years NGOs could not really organize themselves very well as organizations to stimulate interest. However, the difficult situation in which are NGOs engaged in development assistance today, is "good in a way because people are starting to be more and more aware, and they start to donate. There's a big issue so-called development awareness and development education in Hungary" (Interview with representative of one of the Hungarian organizations that prefers to be anonymous, July 14, 2015, Budapest). The representatives said that from their point of view, more and more Hungarian NGOs work in awareness raising in Hungary because development cooperation and assisting other countries and developing countries in general is perceived by the Hungarian public as something not important.

> We have the feeling that there's a lot to do about awareness here in Hungary, so even though there are many small NGOs working in developing countries, they are like islands who are not connected, working in one specific country or area, there are not the usual type of NGDOs. We're really behind for example Slovakia, Czech Republic and Poland.
>
> (Interview, July 14, 2015, Budapest)

Despite many obstacles associated with financial stability, the organization continues to be present in other countries. It manages some funds from the International Visegrád Found (IVF), like Demnet, for example. Demnet is one of the oldest and the largest NGDOs (non-governmental development organization) in Hungary. It is one of the founding members of HAND platform and also actively participates through HAND in CONCORD's initiatives. The person interviewed highlighted the fact that the IVF typically requires more partner organizations to apply together so by definition the organization has another partner organization from a partner country. Demnet is also one of the four foundations that manage the Norwegian funds, and thus is not a recipient but a manager. Sometimes embassies in the field are easy to work with but it is not always possible to find follow-up money.

In the case of the European Commission EuropeAid, interviewees in Hungary agree that it is more likely to finance big development cooperation projects, and small NGOs cannot really apply because they are unable to prepare mega projects, especially as the main applicant and these funds are diminishing within the budget of those NGOs. I was told that it is always very difficult for a new NGO from the new member state to start development cooperation, and Western NGOs are not interested in the cooperation, because they have their own postcolonial large-scale programs. Therefore, the European Commission instead of spreading awareness, should announce a

> call for the proposals in which Western NGOs participate together with new member states as partners, not just as someone who participates in their

> workshop, but doing something together in the field—but they are reluctant to do it. But for that we need committed people in the European Commission.
>
> (Interview with ICDT representative, July 14, 2015, Budapest)

The organization also receives money from MFAT, but it's not a large amount, and what they receive is more or less used to co-finance other projects. They claim that they have a good relationship with the Department of International Development at MFAT, and consider them as partners, and that there is a massive information exchange between them, therefore

> it's like a schizophrenic situation—on the one hand Demnet is fighting with the government due to all of those issues regarding our region, but on the other hand we're getting well with the MFAT because development cooperation is kind of neutral area and MFAT are professionals so they are fully aware that civil society needs to have visible and efficient development cooperation.
>
> (Interview, July 14, 2015, Budapest)

The interviewee of organization also sat on the Board of HAND, and within this umbrella organization they try to convince the MFAT about the important role of civil society organizations active abroad:

> What we experienced is that even though MFA values our work and perceive us and HAND members and HAND in general as partners, more engagement would be essential and more money definitely. What we keep telling MFAT colleagues is that without NGOs, giving cooperation in development and raising domestic awareness cannot be successful because it's not the government delivering to the civil society. So governments and governmental programs may leave, but civil society remains (…).

Also, one of the long-term civil society activists in Hungary is not optimistic about the relationship with the MFAT and prefers to be anonymous. This person was engaged in establishing HAND, and underwent training in the 1990s offered by Western donors to civil society activists, and was also involved in sharing transition experience. For people like this, the situation that is taking place in Hungary is a personal failure, because they know how it was in the past. They know what Hungary went through to be where it is today, and they feel responsible, but at the same time are not able it to do anything. "How can we influence the government, with demonstrations in the street? People do not care about the work of NGOs; public interest is low, especially now, because there are millions of other problems." Another activist also complained that the new minster of MFAT would like to promote ethical business and investment, and he does not understand development cooperation, and in order to fulfill ODA obligations is focusing more on multilateral ODA than bilateral aid that is distributed through NGOs, she claims. "In the end who will complain, if not NGOs, nobody else will care, international organization if they receive money through multilateral aid that's the most important for them." She worked against the communist regime and the she learned from the Americans who trained her about non-corruption, the role of NGOs, democracy, transparency, but also know-how regarding the organization's management, its very strict way of implementing things, financial management, preparing manuals, guides, strategic thinking and implementation, the frame that she was able to apply to her work as an activist. in NGOs. "It was like imprinting for the birds when they born." The transition period, and membership of the EU, the logic of the EU and pre-accession funding shaped her work. However, she did not anticipate that things might look different in Hungary one day:

> The only thing that I am not happy about is that we have very difficult time now and we have to change it, and do not know what to do. It did not happen before. I have no idea what to do and how to influence this horrible situation. This is a special experience we are going through, and we have to deal with it, not just only 25 years ago but right now, is something happening, which is also very interesting and important to understand, to monitor, to follow, and to act. Because it is going to happen also in other countries around the world that have stabilized their pro-democratic initiative.

The new stance of the Hungarian and Polish governments regarding bilateral aid affects not only cooperation with organizations engaged abroad, but also destroys the image that NGOs and former elites have worked so hard to establish, an image of new donors sharing their own experience of transition. Recognizing this knowledge and experience of the new member states in the field of transformation is reflected in the most important EU documents on development policy and the special European Transition Compendium.[20] What is more, the whole EU policy focuses heavily on supporting democracy, the activity and greater lobbying of the CEE countries has meant that the promotion of democracy from the periphery has become a focus of EU development cooperation policy. In addition, membership of the EU has given non-governmental organizations the chance to be noticed as important actors involved in the implementation of the EU foreign policy, which can also shape it directly by lobbying the EU institutions.[21] Nevertheless, a different Hungarian policy causes difficulties in cooperation between the CEE countries in the area of supporting democracy, which could have been observed in reaction to Russia's policy in Ukraine. The CEE countries did not condemn Russia's aggression jointly. The sanctions were different, and they did not prepare a joint package to support democratic changes in Ukraine. In addition, the CEE countries have become more aware of the limitations of cooperation under the International Visegrád Fund, in particular Visegrád 4 Eastern Partnership Program or Visegrád+. The implementation of joint projects carried out by non-governmental organizations showed that the V4 countries perceive each other as competitors rather than partners.[22]

In addition, pragmatism, which guided Hungary's as well as Poland's development policy, may result in the Czech Republic and Slovakia analyzing the experience of more than ten years of development cooperation. Instead of supporting democracy, they will invest in other areas of development aid that will generate sales markets in developing countries or aimed at promoting nationalism. If in fact the other CEE countries change their approach to democracy and development, this can be a challenge for the main actors involved in supporting democracy, i.e., non-governmental organizations, as happened in the case of non-governmental organizations in Hungary. For many non-governmental organizations in the Czech Republic, Slovakia and Poland that specialize in the democracy support sector, this can pose serious challenges and difficulties in adapting to the new approach.

Undoubtedly, the CEE countries have taken up the challenge of being leaders in supporting democracy in the EU at a time when the promotion of democracy is treated with suspicion, and several recent events are associated with growing destabilization, which further undermines faith in the need for democratic change. In addition, when choosing democracy support as the main policy area for development cooperation, the CEE countries have taken on the responsibility of being exemplary democracies, the omission of which may make these countries no longer credible in supporting democracy.

When CEE countries' governments do not adhere to liberal democracy anymore, liberal democracy as a model can be promoted both domestically and abroad only by CEE NGOs. NGOs act as downloaders of democracy norms. It should be remembered that these organizations started investing in democratization processes in the neighborhood, when they were still struggling with their own challenges related to political and economic changes in their countries. Supporting democracy for many of these organizations is their main pillar of activity and changing the country's strategy in development policy will mean that they will either be forced to cease operations or develop new competences in the areas of more traditional development assistance. For other organizations, however, it will mean a return to seeking funds for their activities in the area of supporting democracy from foreign sources—government and quasi-governmental organizations as well as private donors and the European Commission. Nevertheless, the experience of Polish and Hungarian NGOs demonstrate that both reliance on domestic funding as well as foreign funding of local NGOs raised the suspicion that funding can be politically motivated and may compromise the institutional autonomy of NGOs. It is important to find a balance, and as one of the activists in Hungary put it nicely "an awareness rising among people and education, it is all NGOs need for their work to be appreciated by the society and willing to donate some money for their work."[23]

Conclusion

It is an important and volatile time for democracy in the world, when pessimism and despair regarding the promotion of democracy is widespread. Given recent democratic erosion and backsliding (since 2010) in the CEE countries: Hungary, Poland, Slovakia, and the Czech Republic, liberal democracy is under threat. However, the key feature of democracy is the ability to self-correct. Therefore, civil society mobilization is important, but the greatest danger is indifference.

After short period of passivity and low social engagement, civil society is eager to protest and march in the streets, and is again the most natural form of civic engagement. Just as civil society was rising up against post-communism, there are civic protest against the new abuses of power in CEE region. What is important is that in the big-city demonstrations, in Poland, Hungary and Slovakia, young people and women came to the streets of cities. Some are more effective than the others, for example, under the pressure of striking women in 2016 in Poland, the president withdrew from the tightening of the anti-abortion law. Due to the pressure of civil society in 2017, the Polish president vetoed only one out of three drastic measures of the ruling party to curtail the separation of powers. However, it was important that people disagreed, and that they felt empowered to stand up against their offensive governments. The legitimacy and the room for maneuver of the pro-democracy organizations have shrunk.

CEE NGOs are facing challenges from the governments due to their connections with the foreign donors. Reliance on foreign funding raises suspicion and leads to government oppression of the NGO community. Organizations rely on foreign grants as there are sometime no other resources available. This is viewed by governments in CEE as interference by external powers, because external donors and national states can have different goals and agendas regarding civil society. Donors would rather see civil society as a body checking the power of the government (by also acting as a counterweight to state power) and thus bringing about democracy or sustaining it, knowing that (authoritarian) regimes target these groups and repress them throughout the world, both within and outside the borders. Moreover, national governments may have different agendas regarding civil society than external actors.

One could have an impression that the period after the fall of communism, was a paradise for CEE NGOs to operate. Indeed, although they were struggling with financial sustainability, and suffering from miscommunication with the government, and lack of adequate protection from the state, they were not dependent on the government, and were not repressed in direct or indirect ways. When domestic funding was scarce, the CEE NGOs relied on foreign funding, nevertheless fragmenting their budget in order to not be heavily dependent on one source of income. Today, the current efforts in Poland to create a center through which all foreign funds will be disbursed may jeopardize the independence of Polish NGOs. This dependent relationship will prevent organizations in Poland and Hungary from engaging in any activities that might compromise their financial status. It is a hard choice between working along the lines of the government's approach and receiving financial support for their activities, or developing something alternative.

This is a test for CEE NGOs whether they can uphold the norms, and survive and prolong their activity in democracy promotion domestically and abroad.

Perhaps, those organizations that belong to networks are more likely to survive and adapt to the new situation very quickly. Thus, the next step in research on non-state actors in democracy promotion should be the analysis of networks, and research on whether CEE NGOs seek opportunities to gain leverage upon their government from social groups and networks to which they are already tied. Possibly, these networks developed through bypass democracy assistance that they were engaged in for years. It will not only will help them to survive but also promote and sustain democracy in their own countries in CEE.

Notes

1 The Fidesz Party in Hungary and the PiS in Poland, who dominate their respective governments, are only a sample of the growing right-wing national populist movement in Europe. The French National Front—the most popular party in France at the moment—has adopted the anti-immigrant, nationalistic approach. The Austrian Freedom Party is an ultranationalist party, and there are right-wing national populist parties that are part of governing coalitions in Finland, Norway, and Lithuania (Mudde, 2016). Moreover, the UK Independence Party (UKIP) has a similar approach to politics and policy as its counterparts elsewhere in Europe. The new Alternative for Germany Party (AfD), Party and the Party for Freedom in the Netherlands are other examples of ultranationalist parties. Hungary's anti-Semitic Jobbik Party is also the nation's largest opposition party, and there is the neo-fascist Golden Dawn Party in Greece.

2 Changes to the Constitutional Court of Hungary led to the situation that in the nation's highest court, the majority party in Parliament—Fidesz—can appoint judges without consulting the opposition. Also, the number of judges in the Constitutional Court was increased and the posts filled with Fidesz loyalists.

3 https://freedomhouse.org/report/nations-transit/nations-transit-2017.

4 www.transparency.org/news/feature/corruption_perceptions_index_2016.

5 KOD which intentionally refers to the legendary KOR (Workers' Defense Committee), as mentioned earlier, was one of the core elements of the Polish dissident movement in 1970s.

6 www.rmf24.pl/fakty/polska/news-niespodziewane-przeprosiny-ministra-kultury-piotra-glinskieg,nId,2312973.

7 The text of the protest letter of non-governmental organizations can be viewed [in Polish] at ngo.pl website http://wiadomosci.ngo.pl/wiadomosc/2001353.html.

8 See http://archiv.ihned.cz/c1-64829520-barvy-moci-jindricha-sidla-posledni-text-o-prazske-kavarne.

9 Nation in Transit 2014 https://freedomhouse.org/report/nations-transit/2016/czech-republic.

10 *Gazeta Wyborcza* is a private newspaper. The private media in Poland is divided between the established liberal outlets and the conservative media. The divide between them has always been significant. The PiS maintains that private media represents foreign interests, and so does *Gazeta Wyborcza*.

11 A full text of the letter is available in Polish at http://obserwatoriumdemokracji.pl/wp-content/uploads/2017/09/Apel_OFOP.pdf.

12 See the full text in Polish at http://dziennikustaw.gov.pl/du/2017/1909. An unofficial English translation of the Draft Act commissioned by the OSCE Office for Democratic Institutions and Human Rights can be found at www.legislationline.org/documents/id/21176.

13 In 2018, development cooperation focuses on achieving objectives under the six thematic priorities set out in the Multiannual Development Cooperation Program for

2016–2020: (1) good governance; (2) democracy and human rights; (3) human capital; (4) entrepreneurship and the private sector; (5) sustainable agriculture and rural development; (6) environmental protection. Polish development assistance continued to be targeted at Belarus, Georgia, Moldova and Ukraine, since it is in line with Polish priorities under the Eastern Partnership policy and consistent with the wider involvement of the EU in its relations with the Eastern Neighborhood. In 2017, as the result of an appeal, the minister of foreign affairs, co-financed thirty-two programs, the list of organizations receiving funds can be found at www.polskapomoc.gov.pl/Wyniki,konkursu,Polska,pomoc,rozwojowa,2017,2610.html.

14 A text of the law http://orka.sejm.gov.pl/opinie8.nsf/nazwa/1054_u/$file/1054_u.pdf.

15 Krzysztof Stanowski is an important figure in the field of democracy in Poland, sharing transition experience and promoting democracy and civic education in other post-communist countries. He was a co-founder of underground structures of Solidarity and from the beginning of the 1990s was in charge of many non-governmental organizations. He was also a former long-term president of the Education for Democracy Foundation and a member of the Executive Committee of the Zagranica Group. Between 2007 and 2012, he was Undersecretary of State in the Ministry of National Education, and then the at Ministry of Foreign Affairs. He was Co-author of the Development Cooperation Act, and a signatory of the intersectoral agreement on global education. Between 2012 and 2017, he was President of the Solidarity Fund. An interview with him after his dismissal is available at http://wiadomosci.ngo.pl/wiadomosc/2051690.html.

16 The note on this can be found at https://wpolityce.pl/polityka/299779-rz-zdziwiona-wynikami-konkursu-msz-niepokoj-dziennikarzy-budzi-dotacja-dla-rkw-w-wysokosci-prawie-14-mln-zl published on July 7, 2016.

17 www.trialog.or.at/.

18 http://hand.org.hu/en/projects.

19 http://hand.org.hu/en/projects.

20 The European Transition Compendium Report—ETC available at the European Commission website at https://ec.europa.eu/europeaid/european-transition-compendium-report-etc_en.

21 See Börzel and Buzogány (2010).

22 See also Kugiel (2001).

23 Interview with a representative of one of the Hungarian organizations that prefers to be anonymous, July 14, 2015, Budapest, Hungary.

Conclusion

> We put together the project ideas and apply; three of ten submitted get funding. We never do anything without local partners. This is different in the EU new member states when they are doing development cooperation; it is easier to communicate with partners in Eastern partnership countries and in the Balkan states; we have a similar history and grandparents' stories; it is more important than the money that is coming in. It is a mutual understanding, a mutual-learning process, and this is what we are doing it. It is difficult, because the donors' attitude is different—they prefer these high-skills projects, which are impossible for the small to medium-size NGOs.[1]

The goal of the research project has been to provide answers to four research questions regarding why and how the young people are supported by the non-state actors involved in democracy promotion, whether they need to be supported, and whether this youth support is effective. I briefly revisit the puzzle that stimulated my inquiry and remind the reader why solving this puzzle has been important for the greater body of political science: democracy promotion literature, democratization, and aid effectiveness, as well as for practitioners involved in democracy promotion. Then, I discuss where this research might be taken subsequently.

This book is about democracy promotion. Democracy promotion is a broad process through which external actors intervene to install or assist in establishing democratic government in a target state. It can entail coercive measures as well as various positive and soft measures such as democracy assistance which encourages the spread of democratic ideas and institutions by means of various programs and initiatives. A wide range of states (national governmental agencies' programs), party foundations, international organizations, and NGOs participate in these practices. Nevertheless, the research on democracy promotion has primarily been state-oriented, dealing with single actors. Thus, this book demonstrates the efforts of the NGOs as senders of democracy assistance contributing to a better understanding of *what type of democracy* they are promoting and *how* and also *what* exactly these actors are doing when they are promoting democracy. Democracy assistance should be designed in ways that will produce meaningful change. Therefore, I also examine *whether* and *how* democracy assistance works on the ground, and what is the *impact* of these efforts. The study has focused on the engagement of NGOs from Central and Eastern Europe in supporting young people in in Eastern Europe, the Western Balkans and Georgia.

Democracy assistance faces many challenges today. There is the rise of populism that undermines liberal democracy norms and authoritarianism is also staging a comeback closing the space of civil society, as well as an overall backlash against the promotion of democracy. In these difficult and uncertain times, scholars ask how democratic conviction can be rebuilt and how democracy promotion can be made more effective (Diamond, 2017; Hobson and Kurki, 2012; Jahn, 2012; Youngs, 2012). This book contributes to this debate by demonstrating the strength of bypass democracy assistance delivery mechanisms of democracy promotion, which avoids the governments of recipient countries and links civil society actors across the countries, allowing for networking and reaching direct beneficiaries. These are various civil society groups, for example young people, who can be reached directly or via domestic NGOs, through which the diffusion of democracy norms can take place. Although, there has been substantial increase in research on evaluating democracy aid, surprisingly little is known about the effectiveness of bypass democracy assistance. I embarked on this effort to evaluate these efforts by answering the questions whether there is a need to support young people by measuring their perceptions regarding democracy, the role of the state and citizens, and their knowledge of democratic standards, as well as changes in their views and opinions caused by participation in a democracy assistance program.

Contributions to democracy promotion scholarship and implications for practitioners

What actors? Why, what and how are they promoting democracy?

This study has demonstrated how non-state actors from CEE countries that were recipients of aid from Western donors in the 1980s and 1990s as a means to support democratization in the region, dominated by the liberal agenda, became active in democracy promotion. Many of these organizations are active in umbrella organizations that are engaged in so-called developmental cooperation, which are also linked to European-level associations, such as CONCORD. The democratic community in these countries had maintained communication with their counterparts and experts in other CEE or Western democracies. They have had partners from national umbrella organization and also maintain relationships with international organizations and independent media, and academia. They identify themselves as global civil society.

Many of these NGOs established links with other civil society actors in neighboring countries already in the 1990s and with national or foreign funding. These non-state actors played an important role in transforming CEE states from the recipients to donors and lobbied to make sharing transition experience within democracy assistance an important component of their bilateral development aid once they became OECD DAC members. They also seek to influence the way the EU and other donors support democratization and democratic consolidation, in the Eastern Partnership countries and in the Western Balkans. In fact, the CEE NGOs have emerged as the major non-state actors involved in public diplomacy in the field of development aid and democracy promotion in their countries, as Chapter 2 in this book shows. As the result, recognizing the importance of civil society, the governments of the CEE countries engaged financially to support civil society in neighboring countries of the in 2003/2004 through establishing separate departments at ministries of foreign Affairs. From the beginning of these programs' existence, it became clear that a great portion of bilateral aid coming from these countries would be used for democratizing purposes in other post-communist countries in order to fulfil foreign policy goals of having democratic and peaceful neighbors. The major domestic partners in democracy assistance have been NGOs who were recipients of democracy aid in the past and played the important role in CEE countries' transition, without which the ability of the governments to reach civil societies in other countries would not be possible. In addition to funding from their governments, which is decreasing at present, as demonstrated in Chapter 6, CEE NGOs have for a long time been able to secure their funding from various sources, including the foreign ones.

These entities implement projects often in cooperation with their counterparts in recipient countries. Hungarian organizations due to geographical and cultural closeness prefer to cooperate with organizations from the Western Balkan countries. The Czech Republic as well as Slovakia has a number of recognized NGOs operating in Georgia and in the Western Balkans. Slovakian NGOs are active in Moldova, the Republic of Macedonia and Montenegro. Polish NGOs, however, are engaged in Ukraine and Belarus, since these countries are foreign policy priority countries. They assist civil society in these countries because they feel obliged to help resulting from the fact that CEE NGOs were themselves recipients of aid in the past, but also because they received an impulse from Western donors to conduct activities in other post-communist countries and to share their experience. Geographical proximity and a higher probability that the help will be well used are also other factors and finally demand for CEE transition experience, which is perceived as adequate to social and political realities in other post-communist countries and complementarity with diplomatic actions within the framework of foreign policy in which the post-communist countries have always been perceived as priority countries. For example, Ukraine is at a pivotal point in its history since the Euromaidan and annexation of the Crimean Peninsula. It is struggling with bad governance and weak institutions, but has many non-state actors that are very active, such as journalists, and civil society organizations which, according to the Polish NGOs, should be supported and their activities strengthened.

The comparative advantage of these organizations is capacity building, the ability to survive and adapt to changing circumstances, and that they have partners in the target countries and work together while implementing the projects that respond to the needs of the community in recipient countries. Thus, they believe that bypass democracy assistance as become their powerful device that guarantees that the project is successful. CEE non-governmental organizations have chosen a specific way of implementing democratization programs, which is based on the principle of partnership, as it has been demonstrated based on the youth programs in Chapter 3. As part of partnership relations, many projects are created as a result of arrangements with partner organizations, and then, after obtaining finance, they are jointly implemented. Through cooperation based on partnership, NGOs understand better the current situation of partner non-governmental organizations as well as that of direct beneficiaries, which increases the effectiveness of democracy assistance.

Diffusion of norms via (transnational civil society) networks

This book has contributed to the literature on networks, which comes from sociology. The sociological literature on networks examines the various links between organizations and individuals (both private and public), domestically and internationally (Karnst and Mingst, 2010). Transnational advocacy networks have become increasingly important to global governance through "the centrality of values of principled ideas, the belief that individuals can make a difference, the creative use of information, and the employment by non-governmental actors of sophisticated political strategies in targeting their campaigns" (Keck and Sikkink 1998, p. 2).

Specifically, this study has contributed to a better knowledge of the role of value-driven organizations involved in networks that aim to spread democracy norms. The role of transnational civil society which includes groups that are not governments or profit-seeking private entities, in the international arena cannot be ignored (Finnemore and Sikkink, 1998; Florini, 2000; Lipschutz, 1992; Tarrow, 1998). The role involves linkages across national borders and many connections that aim to have a more practical and concrete role, such as those oriented toward environmental issues. CEE NGOs have been able to create transnational social networks with other partners in Europe and in the US, and are now extending them to include other partners in post-communist countries.

The emergence and growing strength of transnationally allied civil society organizations was visible especially in the international adoption of norms on human rights, and the environment (Clark, 1995; Finnemore and Sikkink, 1998; Florini, 2000). This book provides an example of how networks in democracy promotion began and how they are being expanded. As shown in Chapter 2, Polish NGOs as recipients of support from the West socialized themselves as "norm takers" (Flockhart, 2005) since they perceived these rules as desirable and they are interested in "belonging to the club," and being incorporated into the cohort of democracy promoters. Today, the CEE NGOs, as transnational agents, want to diffuse these norms and to be norm entrepreneurs.

The CEE NGOs are forming a vast number of connections across national borders with informal associations and various civil society organizations in target countries, with other organizations from the CEE regions, as well as with donors. The reciprocal and positive relationship creates more interactions and activities and through durability of close cooperation and links, civil society has a greater chance of survival. As demonstrated in Chapter 2, the CEE NGOs that were created and sustained mainly through foreign sources were able, thanks to porous international borders, implemented liberal policies in their own countries and continued their work beyond national frontiers, as well as advancing the agendas and values of liberal democracy that influenced them. The CEE NGOs operate via an organization platform through which they are able to promote norms. Aid programs in CEE countries were constructed for the purpose of delivering bilateral aid and from the beginning of their existence, the CEE NGOs use this aid to promote democracy norms. They are also involved in large transnational advocacy networks of which these NGOs are a part and through which they continue supporting and reaching civil society which allows them to be independent of governments, as shown in youth program examples in Chapter 3.

The awarding institutions that funded civil society during the transition period, and some of them are still funding many the CEE NGOs projects abroad, include various international governmental or quasi-governmental organizations, international non-governmental organizations, private donors, foundations, international organizations, and US-based non-profit organizations, such as the World Bank, and the Organization for Security and Co-operation in Europe (OSCE), the United States Agency for International Development (USAID), the Open Society Foundation, Germany's Stiftungen, the European Commission initiatives, such as European Initiative for Democracy and Human Rights (EIDHR) and earlier Civil Society Development Foundation financed by the European Union's PHARE Program, the Charles Stewart Mott Foundation, the German Marshall Fund of the United States, the Jan Hus Educational Foundation, the British Know How Fund, the Fund of Canada, the United States Information Service (USIS), the National Endowment for Democracy, and the others. These linkages show that a long history of close, interpersonal relations characterized by trust, reciprocity and learning, preserve those links.

The research has demonstrated how the CEE NGOs that were incorporated into the network of organizations are reaching civil society in partner countries, through partnership with grassroots organizations in recipient countries bypassing governments, and how are advocating or promoting liberal values and norms, as well as are how they are spreading these connections across national borders. In this network, the CEE NGOs are intermediary institutions through which funding goes to NGOs and civil society groups to protect them from excessive donor influence. The CEE NGOs do not engage directly with decision-making processes like organizations that work in the area of international security, human rights or the environment. Nevertheless, CEE NGOs spread democratic norms that are severely weakened and ignored by the governments in CEE countries, as well as those countries where democracy has never been secure. Rather than trying to shape the norms directly by perusing policymakers to change their minds, they work indirectly by altering civil society's perception, as variety of youth programs demonstrated in Chapter 3, and their impact in Chapter 5.

This is not to underestimate authoritarian regimes in limiting the role of transnational networks. On the contrary, CEE NGOs are aware of the fact that authoritarian regimes can successfully impede democratization. However, external actors by streamlining and improving the mechanisms of democracy assistance can help civil society in these regimes slowly work from within. As demonstrated in Chapter 2, an authoritarian regime, like that in Belarus, can create a real challenge even for the non-state actors to support civil society actors. However, as presented, it is not impossible, because despite the repressive NGO law in Belarus, NGOs have been still able to cooperate with teachers, young people, students and other civil society representatives, forming with them linkages.

The strength of bypass democracy assistance lies in networks. It provides resources in form of programs that are not available locally, social, cultural and educational, in the field of human and minority rights, monitoring government agencies and political actors, the fight against corruption, etc. All of them include civil society as a specific target for the support. CEE NGOs are external actors, who are dedicated to help growing world citizenry (global civil society) that upholds liberal democracy values, and it is justified in Chapter 2 which shows opinions of CEE NGOs' representatives regarding their work, and Chapter 3 which analyses youth programs conducted by these organizations in post-communist countries between 2000 and 2017.

Youth assistance and micro-macro link

This book has been a first attempt to demonstrate efforts of external actors in the area of youth assistance, which as compared to other areas of democracy assistance, such as election assistance, human rights assistance, and media assistance, has received little attention. In Chapter 3, I have offered a typology of youth assistance, the development of which has been guided by the scholarly literature on youth, student activism, and political engagement of youth in democracies (Diuk, 2012; Flanagan, 2013; Hensby, 2017; Roberts, 2009), as well as on the role of young people and overall non-state actors in democratization processes (Barrett and Zani, 2015; Dalton, 2014; Norris, 2002; Vráblíková, 2017). These five categories of youth programs (Civic Participation; Political Participation; Civic Education; Economic Empowerment; Capacity Building of Youth Organizations) allow for linking the concepts offered in the literature with those used by the practitioners. This typology is disaggregated into more detailed categories based on interviews with practitioners, donor officials and project description as well as on democracy promotion literature, allowing the researchers to compare youth assistance across countries or donors.

Moreover, the categories of youth assistance demonstrate what kind of norms are being promoted to young people through the programs of the CEE NGOs. Citizens' participation and involvement in politics are the most promoted behaviors through the programs, and these two concepts are also central to the study of political systems and liberal democracy. Youth programs encourage young people to be active citizens through their participation in civil society organizations. According to the liberals, organizations remain crucial vehicles for citizen participation and for providing a basis for mobilization and aggregation of interests. They also are establishing channels of communication between citizens and the state and facilitating consultations and discussions. The programs also emphasize any form of civic participation—an activity which is focused on helping others within the community, solving a community problem, participation in the life of community or undertaking organized voluntary work—since it is believed that such participation fosters networks of colleagues, creating bonds, norms, and thus encourages broader engagement in community affairs as well as shaping leadership skills, political awareness and identity.

The norms which are promoted by the CEE NGOs are norms of engaged citizenship (participation in political and civic life): meliorism; social and political responsibility in local and national affairs; participation in political and civic life; monitoring on government to prevent any abuses of power; respecting rights of minorities and helping those worse off in order to prevent polarization in the country. The CEE NGOs promote collective understanding, increased citizen participation and active citizenship participation and promote these principles in their youth programs. The goal of many youth programs implemented by the NGOs from CEE is to encourage young people to be more socially responsible for their local community, region and country, believing that a democratic country requires such active participation. I have found that many programs targeted at these groups aim to educate them about the citizens' rights and role they can play in the society, and about the functioning of democratic institutions and authorities' responsibilities.

Transnationally, allied CEE non-state actors promote liberal democracy norms because the goal is "freeing of the people" and empowering them. CEE NGOs find it important to invest in individuals and target the so-called young leaders, who might become future political elites willing to introduce changes in their countries, maintain and consolidate democratic institutions, norms, and practices. The representatives of interviewed NGOs believe that political leaders in the first place should become local social leaders. Therefore, many projects aim at improving leadership skills, teaching technical and organizational skills, helping young people find the way and resources to be proactive in their communities, and enhancing communication and creating a network of support to mobilize the community to address concerns. Given the potential especially of young people in observable democratization processes and in newly established democracies as well as the role of external support to influence youth in these countries, the CEE NGOs find it crucial to work with young people. Activation of young people is about increasing the quality of citizen competencies through rising awareness and empowering them so that they can be included in public life, especially decision-making processes at the local level. The support for youth is also justified for more practical reasons—to create a more secure, stable and friendly neighborhood that in turn may lead to mutually fruitful political and economic cooperation between the countries.

By demonstrating efforts to support young people, I have contributed to building a theory of democratic change in which agent empowerment plays a crucial role. The evidence provided is based on the analysis interviews with CEE NGOs, the analysis of the programs, and perceptions, opinions, and behaviors of young people's in target countries, as presented in Chapter 4, as well as on evaluating the impact (Chapter 5). The CEE NGOs admit that they were impacted by the liberal view of civil society, based on the concept of the importance of the individual, and believe in internalization of these norms and emergence of active citizens willing to engage with the state directly and/or through organized civil society. CEE NGOs engaged in democracy promotion have learned over the past 25 years that plurality tends to be better than any form of one-party or authoritarian rule, and thus promote freedom of expression and association, encourage contributions to the voluntary sector, as well as oppose oppression and human rights violations.

Welzel (2013) equates human development with the empowerment of people to exert their freedoms. Liberal democracy is a legal component of empowerment. CEE NGOs recognize that liberal institutions create legal protections that allow citizens to participate in various associations and in fact to practice individuals' freedoms like freedom to associate. Nevertheless, in the situation when liberal democratic institutions are not in place, and when resources are unevenly distributed in target countries, which explains the differences in political participation, the CEE NGOs find it important to fill the gap through their programs. Indeed, as demonstrated in Chapter 3, these non-state actors provide via the programs access to social resources (time, money, and skills), education and civic awareness that allow young people to comprehend better the political world, that might facilitate political action. These programs create an opportunity for young people to learn about the importance of their engagement and participate in democratic processes and civic life as adolescents, who may continue this participation in adulthood.

The study offers to link micro and macro perspectives through individual empowerment that might lead to the changes in political culture. A fundamental issue in social science is the relationship between the individual and society, the relationship between micro and macro. As was pointed out by Flanagan (2013): "the full promise of democracy cannot be realized through laws, elections, or institutions but only through the collective will of people committed to its ideals." CEE NGOs find it important provide support to young people, because resources available within the country are inadequate, but also because in many post-communist target countries a culture of active participation is weak often because of co-optation, forceful connections between the ruling elites and population, and because national governments regard civil society as an object of their policies and political action. Scholars point out that there are two factors that prevent the proper development of a strong civil society: culture and authoritarianism (Mathews, 1997). In countries with conservative, patriarchal, and a subject political culture, in which the role and power of non-state actors have increased relative to those of governments, citizens do not participate and this in turn only strengthens the authoritarian system. Participant political culture in which citizens participate in political affairs and support political affairs promote a stable democratic system (Almond and Verba, 1963). Therefore, such a culture should be encouraged and strengthened from outside by the external actors, and youth assistance programs, which offer an opportunity through empowering young people to change the political culture in target countries.

This study shows that faith in the role of individuals in democratic changes, and that actors' identities, goals and aspirations are themselves subject to change. They arise and are sustained through interaction, and that the human subject must be regarded as an ongoing developmental process. Also, agency and structure interpenetrate one another and redefine themselves. This is not to say that institutions do not matter. They do, and different kinds of institutions provide different spaces for civil society to function. Nevertheless, they can be altered through changes in political culture. According to this logic, empowered citizens participate more and then search for interactions, which in turn strengthens social capital and the norms of reciprocity and trustworthiness that arise from them. Social capital which emerges in civil society, especially in organizations, fuels changes in political culture (Putnam, 2000). This study contributes to theories that explain that changes result always from the mixture of individual characteristics and structural factors.

In Chapter 4, I have embarked on testing whether there is a need, as CEE NGOs claim, to support young people in target countries. By means of established NGO collaborative networks in Bosnia-Herzegovina, Georgia and Ukraine, I was able administer the surveys especially among young people who were participants in actual programs or potential beneficiaries of these programs. The NGOs selected to conduct surveys were recommended by the Czech, Slovak, Hungarian and Polish organizations engaged in democracy assistance programs. The survey measured young people's views and support for democracy, opinions and feelings about political and social life, interest in public affairs, as well as being asked about current and future civic and political participation with the aim of explaining not only *how* people participate but also *why* they participate or do not participate. The same type of study was conducted among young people in CEE countries in order to provide comparisons.

The results show that there are no major differences between young people regarding individuals' attitudes to democracy. There is a broad understanding of democracy by all, meaning that young people from democratizing countries have a good knowledge of what democracy is, as good as young people from democratized countries. These findings are similar to earlier studies (Ferrin and Kriesi, 2016; Norris, 2011) that people share a common understanding of democracy. Also, the lack of difference between Eastern European and CEE regarding the view of democracy can mean that diffusion is effective. Ideas about democracy have spread, and citizens of different countries in different regions have similar conceptions of democracy.

Nevertheless, although young people in target countries positively evaluate democracy, there are some differences in satisfaction with democracy. Young people, although they have a good understanding of specific democratic principles they do not link their satisfaction or lack of satisfaction with any specific components. It could be because these elements of democracy are not fully provided in these countries, and young people have not had a chance to practice them yet. Moreover, for satisfaction with democracy and overall support for democracy have also to impact other individual-level factors, such as individual political attitudes: trust in political actors, trust in institutions, party identification, interpersonal trust, interest in politics as well as the level of civic and political engagement. Young people in target countries show apathy and low trust in politicians, political institutions and politics in general. Norms of citizenship are for them "norms of citizen duty" which indicate passivity, obedience, and a limited participatory role of citizens, whereas in the case of young people in CEE countries, the "norms of engaged citizens" dominate which highlight the participatory role of the citizen. Moreover, the study shows that out of all possible forms of political participation, voting seems to be a dominant form of political engagement of young people from the three target countries. Lack of associational behavior in post-communist societies can be explained by many factors, and one of the most important could be the sense of insecurity and distrust. The results, allow one to conclude that democracy assistance to young people is needed because democratic political culture—interest in politics, confidence in political institutions, satisfaction with democracy, social trust social capital—is low, and in order to change their perceptions regarding their role as citizens, to empower them and thus to influence the others, support from outside can facilitate this process. If young people are socialized into the values of freedoms and human empowerment, this will foster the demand for liberal democracy.

The results of surveys conducted among young people are important contributions to the literature on participation in general (Horowitz *el al.*, 2003; Newton, 1999; Norris, 2011) but also in particular on youth participation (Diuk, 2012; Flanagan, 2013; Roberts, 2009), as well as on the current rise of populism in Central and Eastern Europe. Young people in the post-communist region are a new generation. At this moment in 2018, when a crisis of liberal democracy became evident, it is worth exploring whether citizens' beliefs explain and also justify the political arrangements and whether young people want to reinterpret the social contract or to create a new one (Mannheim, 1952). In times of populist democracies, as well as the rise of nationalist appeals, such snapshots of young people show that this is a unique generation at a pivotal turning point, in which new views on life are reflected in the formation of new movements, bringing new issues onto political agendas that might lead to transformation of their countries.

Effectiveness of bypass democracy assistance

The central argument of this study has been that bypass democracy assistance, which offers an opportunity for the linkages between non-state actors across borders to be formed, makes democracy promotion more effective in the sense that it makes diffusion of the norms of democracy more likely to take place. The following strengths of the bypass democracy assistance that were demonstrated in Chapters 2 and 3 of the book are: a greater likelihood of adapting to the political situation, context and situation of the partner and of respecting the cultural specificity of countries, long-term cooperation, and geographical proximity which facilitates the diffusion of norms, attitudes and democratic values. The findings regarding bypass democracy assistance provide responses to the questions that scholars and practitioners ask "How to improve democracy assistance?" and more especially: "How to rebuild democratic conviction and thus to make democracy promotion more effective in times where the spread of democracy is facing challenges?" (Basora, Marczyk and Otarashvili, 2017; Kramaer, 2017).

One of the arguments was that given close linkages and knowledge on the ground, non-state actors in CEE developed the ability to respond to the needs of recipient countries. In Chapter 2, the study shows that support is relevant and useful, because it is locally owned, adjusted to the needs of the recipient and based on long-term cooperation. As shown in the example of Polish NGOs' engagement in Ukraine and Belarus, the programs are tailored to the country's context since they are not only targeting different topics but also taking into account their different political conditions, avoiding ready-made solutions when sharing knowledge. Cooperation between Polish democratic society and pro-democratic groups in Belarus shows that flexibility of actions and experience of Polish NGOs to operate in repressive environment is useful. Connections between communities are conducive to the introduction of new solutions in Belarus, without which such a cooperation would never have been created.

The analysis of the interviews and collected documents shows that CEE NGOs recognize that the success of efforts related to supporting civil society in other post-communist countries is possible only in cooperation with domestic entities in the partner country. CEE NGOs have close ties to the local population in partner countries, have sensitivity to local needs and flexibility of actions and experience that is suited to perform certain tasks. Thus, geographical proximity is an important factor contributing to the effectiveness of bypass democracy assistance. For example, Hungarian organizations are engaged in democracy promotion in the Western Balkans because they know this region better. Traveling there is much easier and there are no significant barriers like, for example, language ones, which means meetings and face-to-face discussions are much easier to organize there than in other countries.

Organizations, because of cooperation with other organizations in partner countries, have knowledge of the needs of society and insight into the possibility of carrying out certain projects, and so foreign assistance can be better adapted to local conditions. In contrast to ways of promoting democracy by Western countries, and the critique of traditional civil society assistance, bypass democracy assistance allows for taking into account separate needs and conditions of partner countries. Context sensitivity entails deciding with local actors what type of programs respond to community needs, and what form the transfer of expertise and values should take, which makes external actors not only norm promoters but also norm localizers. CEE NGOs are outsiders who become insider proponents. they are physically present in the region or keep close linkages with local agents and work through them, and their primary commitment is to localize norms. These findings also contribute to the literature on norm diffusion and localization (Acharya, 2004, 2011; Hobson and Kurki, 2012; Zimmermann, 2017).

This book has carefully matched theory with the choice of evaluation method of democracy assistance. The aim of this book has been to evaluate democracy assistance efforts directed towards young people at the micro level, that is the impact of democracy assistance programs on beneficiaries' opinions, perceptions, capabilities of participation, etc. Often, practitioners and researchers operate at different levels when assessing the impact of democracy promotion efforts—practitioners at micro level, and scholars at macro level, although they can employ micro perspective in order to explain the possible impact. If we operate at the micro level in democracy promotion, we should stay at this level and there is a good theory that will explain developments at the micro level and how these micro developments may contribute to the macro-level. I believe that the literature and practice can benefit if we take theoretical positions or the ranking of theoretical sub-positions and narrow the focus of work to achieve the best way to test theory.

The theory employed in this book has been that democracy is a consequence of individuals' actions, but for the changes to be ignited by those actors there must be always some motivational forces—a theory that connects micro with macro has been through "human empowerment" as the most important driving force behind effective democratization. Micro are young people as agents of change who need to be empowered in order to act, and macro is a culture, a new domestic structure created by the efforts of actors. The empowerment comes from outside, from the external actors, which in this book are CEE NGOs. However, one should not presume that all the different actors involved in democracy promotion, international organizations, NGOs, and other donors conceive democracy and support to civil society in a comparable way. For CEE NGOs, a vibrant civil society has been regarded as a symbol of liberal democracy. Civil society needs to have local roots in its own society and internal democratic structures, since only civil society groups with local roots are best at advancing lasting democratization. Youth is considered an important part of the civil society and youth especially in transition countries can make a difference if it is strong and engaged.

Empowered civil society groups, equipped with information as well as money by the transnationally operating CEE NGOs is more likely to pressure governments. My assumption has been confirmed by analysis of the interviews with representatives of NGOs. Rather than approaching governments in recipient countries, they aim through various programs—youth exchange programs, scholarships, internships, training seminars, workshops or even study visits—to foster the demand for liberal democracy among young people, to empower domestic groups by legitimating their claims, informing, arousing awareness that they can be included in public life, especially decision-making process at the local level, educating as well as by allowing them to feel their independence and physical integrity with other people who think and behave alike. The analysis of the experiment conducted to test the impact of civic education programs in Chapter 5 shows that young people are socialized into the values of freedom, are more in favor of democracy, make a positive assessment of their role in a society and show greater interest in participation. However, although civic education might be an important part of the youth empowerment mechanism, the CEE NGOs seem to recognize that full participation of young people requires an adequate social and political environment that allows for such participation without fear of reprisal. Therefore, I also explore such a program and evaluate its impact on young people.

In times of "authoritarianism staging a comeback" (Burrows and Stephan, 2015) targeting civil society became even more important and thus the need to investigate this type of aid even greater. However, given the reduction of freedom and space for pro-democratic civic activism and the backlash against promoting democratic development worldwide (Carothers, 2016; Cooley, 2015), this creates obstacles for international donors to support democracy (Christensen and Weinstein, 2013) and a question is how the donors respond to the crackdown. Dupuy and Prakash (2018) find that those Western donors who rely on non-governmental organizations tend to withhold aid from countries with restrictive NGO laws. Support through networks rather than penalizing civil society whose governments enacted restrictive NGO laws with reduced aid flows, are finding different channels and tactics to deliver democracy aid, as demonstrated in Chapter 2, such as other civil society groups—young people, teachers, parents, writers, and so-called leaders in their local communities—bypassing not only governments but also GONGOs.

Findings of the book regarding the features of bypass democracy assistance—the ability to respond to local needs, the ability reach civil society and forming networks—imply that assistance coming from the Western donors, such as the US (NED, the Open Society Foundation, USAID), but also German Stiftungs, the International Visegrád Fund, would be more efficient if it went through NGOs that share their knowledge and experience with their counterparts abroad. These NGOs know how to adjust their programs, and who to work with in various fields such as, civic education, women's rights, press freedom, and today even conflict resolution.

Usefulness of experimental method as impact evaluation

The contribution of this book has been to demonstrate the usefulness of this as well as various methods to evaluate the impact of the democracy assistance at the micro-level. Inspired by the impact evolution methodology developed by the Abdul Latif Jameel Poverty Action Lab (J-PAL), I used a social experiment to test the impact of one of the long-term civic education programs. Randomized controlled trails methodology can provide organizations and researchers with rigorous evidence, and to examine how the people who participated in the program performed compared to how they would have performed if they had not had a chance to participate in the program. We can never know what would have happened in the absence of the program, but we can use different evaluation techniques in attempting to make comparisons. As demonstrated in Chapter 5, such a methodology of impact evaluation allowed me, as a researcher, as well as donors and NGOs to see whether young participants from post-Soviet countries have the chance to learn how they can take actions that bring their country closer to democracy, and from experts gain the knowledge and inspiration they need to act in their countries. The democracy assistance program has changed young people's attitudes and opinions and also empowered them to take civic action, thus giving hope that the programs contribute to change in a culture of democracy, where civil society's voice is listened to, and participation in decision-making takes place.

In Chapter 5, I have demonstrated the research design and the results, as well as the limitations of this methodology. It shows that randomization can be a credible and accurate form of impact evaluation, and the best procedure to gain knowledge regarding the effect of assistance projects, because it can help solve the problem of causal attribution of specific outcomes to NGOs' democracy assistance projects. Nevertheless, this impact evaluation is only as good as the comparison group that can imitate what would have happened in the absence of the program. If the comparison group is not good enough, it can ruin the evaluation and make it invalid. I also discuss the difficulties that researches can encounter when establishing the experiments, such as randomization bias, or selection bias and how they can be overcome. Moreover, it should also be noticed that the ability to generalize from my findings is limited by both the nature and size of the sample and the fact that I do not aggregate individual-level values to the national level since the focus is on possible beneficiaries of the programs. Finally, a combination of techniques to complement measuring the effects of these programs, such as qualitative methods surveys, behavioral activities, etc., are recommended.

There is one more implication for the practitioners regarding the evaluation of democracy assistance efforts, which I believe is well-put by a representative of one of the Hungarian NGOs. This statement indicates that, in democracy promotion, it is worth acknowledging that it takes time to evaluate the efforts of programs, and that sometimes what is not tangible is important. Therefore, is important for the donors to be forgiving, more flexible, and to understand the work of local organizations:

> Impact of democracy assistance is one of the factors, but [we should] do not overestimate this influence. It is complex. You cannot get knowledge in two weeks, but you can have a different picture; this is a kind of hook; they also build a network; they can have people to contact later and use it. But it is complex, it is about personality. I saw so many people who participated in all the available short-term technical programs in the US, in Europe, and

> they are always traveling somewhere, and now they are in their 50s and they still participate in such initiatives. This is happening many times in Eastern Partnership countries that these poor people are living in poverty, living without hope, but speaking good English and have a career funded by a scholarship. They are always around. They go round the Europe and the US and nothing happens, and then in the end they emigrate. Instead of those, who participate in small but engaged communities, they do things in their own countries. Thus, development of leaders is very important. Lack of donor coordination is a failure of development cooperation.

Recommendations for future research

There are two suggestions for future research that arise from my study. First, there is an analysis of bypass democracy assistance as a two-way process, and second, which is connected with the previous one, the analysis of sustainability of liberal norms through networks.

Bypass democracy assistance can be a tool for vulnerable civil society to fight powerful or misguided governments on both sides, especially that freedoms given to civil society are not given for good, as the situation of CEE NGOs shows, since NGOs engaged in democracy promotion can face the same or similar challenges as civil society in recipient countries. Thus, bypass democracy assistance is a promising response to the spread of restricting space, intimidation or harassment of foreign-funded NGOs (now called "foreign agents") and the targeting of international organizations that provide civil society support. Authoritarian states openly harass groups that receive external support. However, today democracies are also using restricting space techniques as demonstrated in the examples of NGOs in Hungary and Poland in Chapter 6. The techniques might include more indirect measures to pursue those foreign organizations that deliver civil society aid, some of which even started to limit the amount of foreign funding that NGOs are allowed to receive or created burdensome requirements on foreign funding that include obligatory government approval to more direct measures like the adoption of laws and decrees that criminalize the work of civil society organizations and the acceptance of foreign. In other words, stifling freedoms of speech and association through laws is no longer the only preserve of contemporary authoritarian regimes, but also consolidated democracies in CEE are using such measures.

Given the fact that in the contemporary global political system states do not remain the predominant actors, and CEE NGOs active in democracy promotion have linkages with Western organizations, and donors, as well as other actors, through these contacts they can exert pressure on government. The interesting question, which is worth further analysis, is too what extent those NGOs are linked to a number of interesting developments throughout CEE that took place in the recent years. We have witnessed the actions of ordinary citizens that have challenged the political order. Grassroots movements and various forms of mobilization have inspired civil society in Western Europe and in the US (e.g., the Black Monday women's march in Poland that inspired women's marches in the US). The example of Slovakia and its strong civic engagement and objection expressed on the streets in March 2018, serves as a positive example as well.

The current instances of greater political participation in such countries as Poland, Hungary, Slovakia represent a new phase in the development of civil society. We cannot say any more that in comparison to Western Europe, the level of political participation in Central and Eastern Europe is lower (Bernhagen and Marsh, 2007; Hooghe and Quintelier, 2013; Howard, 2003; Kostelka, 2014), because protests and overall movement of civil society to be more engaged can be interpreted as proof of changes in politics and the relationship between society and the government. Different types of non-institutional forms of political action have been gaining importance. People express their anger in the streets (Falkowski, 2016), and thus parliamentary politics has become more strongly intertwined with the activities that are taking in the streets. Of course, it should be noted however that the mobilizing of supporters through street protests is not only a strategy of the opposition but also of the ruling parties, such as Fidesz in Hungary, or the PiS (Law and Justice) in Poland. Ekiert and Foa (2012) show that civil society in CEE has the potential to be strong because active civil society organizations are strongly connected to transnational civic networks—thus the important question worth investigating is whether those CEE NGOs active in the field of democracy promotion have deep roots within society and are indeed the motor of all changes we observe today.

The CEE countries as democratic success stories are facing serious problems in democratic consolidation, however CEE civil society including NGOs seem to play an important role in an era of democratic backsliding across the region (in particular Poland and Hungary) as an arena for contestation of populist governmental reforms. My argument is that CEE NGOs have become a conduit for ideational democratic norms in times of the growing populist ideologies; facilitating pro-democratic citizen mobilization and participation, not only abroad but also in their countries. The question is to what extent those CEE NGOs active in democracy promotion redirect their activities inside their countries, and whether they try indirectly, through influencing society, to alter the civil society perception of what governments should be doing to have impact on changes. This will require additional research.

Social movement researchers argue that movement emergence depends not only on political opportunity but on organizational networks (McAdam and Snow, 1996). In non-democratic states, the political system is closed, the media is controlled and societies lack the mechanism for regular, legitimate transfers of power sanctions by those subject to the state and higher degrees of coercion. This was how it was in Poland and other communist countries. Political opportunities were limited because the state did not permit access to policymakers, the media and the courts, and the sphere of civic associations was restricted to a narrow range of non-political organizations. Many forms of associations were illegal and the public sphere was replaced by the official one. However, despite these limitations, protest and mobilization did occur, and it was thanks to the social networks, since one of the ways in which challengers circumvent state power is through social networks (Osa, 2003). I believe that the networks between civil society groups across borders, not only with CEE NGOs with Western entities, but also with organizations in democratizing countries, are important.

Given the fact that many organizations in Bosnia-Herzegovina or Ukraine became professional in applying for grants and have good connections with the donors, they can help CEE NGOs survive and continue they work through joint implementation of the projects empowering them financially and mentally. In other words, it seems that bypass democracy assistance is a two-way process, which in times of backlash against NGOs in the wake of populism and other threats to liberal democracy can be an effective strategy in democracy promotion. The roles of donor and recipient countries in the case of CEE NGOs and countries from other post-communist countries at some point may intertwine. Allowing individuals and organizations to get access to the social capital of the networks can create an agency that affects structure, which in turn leads to gradual change. Democracy promotion through networks rather than direct donor to beneficiary should work better and can be explained through social network and social capital theories.

Hungary's government spokesperson Zoltán Kovács accused some NGOs of being "foreign agents financed by foreign money" who are organizing "networks and frameworks" in an attempt to influence political decision-making. The bypass democracy assistance model creates and opportunity for the domestic groups (opposition groups, NGOs and social movements) to bypass their government and directly search out international allies to bring pressure on their states from outside. CEE NGOs are members of the transnational network and they link with domestic groups bypassing the governments both in their own countries and others, and the empowered civil society groups themselves, which are equipped with information, often also money (to finance protests) by transnationally operating CEE NGOs, put pressure on governments. In addition to initiating bottom-up activities, and changing civil society, CEE NGOs as demonstrated in Chapter 6, attempt to shape the deteriorating situation of civil society organizations and policies affecting them by directly perusing policy makers to change their minds. The questions worth investigating are whether those NGOs that are well-embedded in networks, use them for these purposes, and why some NGOs are more successful than the others in influencing the governments.

As observed by Keck and Sikkink (1998), networks are bound together by shared values, a common discourse, and dense exchanges of information and services. These networks in which CEE NGOs participate can set the terms of international and domestic debate regarding the setbacks in democracy and to influence international and state-level outcomes, and to alter the behavior of states. Thus, because of CEE NGOs' regional, issue-specific character, they are useful link between the subnational community and national and international communities and institutions. One can hypothesize that the stronger the links between civil society organizations and transnational civil society, the more likely it is that the government will be forced to change the course (Risse, 2000). The bypass democracy assistance model established through networks enables domestic civil society to challenge to their governments. Through transnationally derived knowledge, domestic non-state actors can acquire knowledge if how to influence the government on certain issues. Challenging governments through greater public engagement is crucial for holding governments to account, and the role of CEE NGOs as transmission belts in current political developments could be an important field for scholars to explore.

If democracy is an open-ended process and can never be finished, because it should respond at all times to the needs of society as well as external conditions—global and regional—this means that the two-way perspective in bypass democracy promotion is compatible with such a viewpoint. Linkages formed with civil society organizations across borders allow for two-way learning or so-called peer-to-peer learning. Civil society organizations can learn from their counterparts how to overcome similar problems in the future. For example, xenophobic and populist as well as nationalist movements are on the rise throughout the whole Europe. They have challenged and reshaped political context in CEE countries, especially those hit by the economic crisis which many link with the failure of economic liberalism. The new elite allows those who disagreed with the former to reject the latter as well, and the consequences was to compromise the idea of liberalism, and to push former supporters to the political right (Ost, 2005). Arato (2011) agrees that the rightward turn killed off the discourse of civil society and discredited political liberalism in Poland, and destroyed it in Hungary. For him "political liberalism should have been socially liberal, preserving the discourse of civil society and institutionalizing the active political role for its associations and movement," whereas economic liberalization is only a short-term policy without which structures of command economy could not be dismantled (Arato, 2011, p. 195). Nevertheless, as currently observed in Hungary, economic problems caused by economic liberalism motivated large numbers of people to support Orbán's policies, and him to use this opportunity to turn the public against civil society. This experience in Hungary can be transmitted through civil society to make other states avoid a similar experience.

Democracy is a training school where people have to practice and learn. Thus, it is important to look at democracy promotion in general as a two-way process and bypass democracy assistance creates such an opportunity. Recent developments in Central and Eastern Europe show that the liberal democracy is not perfect and can be improved, both in the quality of participation and contestation as well as in the protection of liberties (Diamond, 2003). CEE NGOs and civil society in post-communist countries by maintaining transnational information channels can provide each other with training, educational opportunities, and offer each other problem-solving expertise. Socio-economic issues have come to the fore because pluralist politics has not made much improvement causing disappointment among citizens in many young democracies. The results of the survey conducted among young people in CEE countries in Chapter 3 show that there seems to be movement towards a social democratic model which is currently important for the new generations whose own experiences are necessary to achieve consolidation of democracy in these countries, and maybe we are even observing the historical destiny of Central Europe. Therefore, the dominance of the donor-recipient relationship should not blind us to the diversity and varieties of assistance that exist today within democracy promotion practice as well as it is a two-way process in which the promoter and recipient switch roles.

The book also opens another interesting avenue of research in democracy promotion. The survival of pro-democratic NGOs and their ability to spread the liberal norms and the spirit of democracy within and outside a country may depend on their ability to spread the network and keep linkages with other civil society actors across borders. Gershman (2017) said that in current times in order to rebuild democratic conviction it is important to connect people on the "frontlines of democratic struggles around the world." In other words, strengthening links and networks between civil society actors not only those in target countries that are democratizing and struggling with democracy, but also with countries that were once considered stable and are now experiencing an anti-democratic offensive and alarming democratic deterioration, such as the Central and Eastern European countries. Although it might seem that today liberal views are less attractive to societies in CEE countries than when they were fighting communism, and less attractive than populist alternative, there are individuals as well as formal and informal non-state actors who oppose right-wing parties and condemn the regression. For liberal and pro-democratic foreign-funded NGOs, as demonstrated in Chapter 6 of the book, it is a new context in which they are forced to work, since populist forces adopt anti-democratic promotion rhetoric and create their own organizations as an instrument for promoting their agendas to influence the relationship between the state and the people.

Civil society organizations need to be preserved, and they can be preserved in networks and expanding the network. They might be the only conduit of liberal democracy given the collapse of liberal-democratic or the Tocquevillian perspective. The CEE NGOs might be able to deal with the new situation and sustain it because they retain the networks they had inherited from the past. Although ill health of democracy has been observed in their countries today, and the danger coming from regimes because of shrinking space is increasing, these democracy activists are reservoirs of liberal and pro-Western values in the region. Civil society organizations remain a crucial vehicle for citizen participation and for providing a basis for mobilization and aggregation of interests. They are establishing channels of communication between citizens and the state and facilitating consultation and discussion. CEE NGOs are a piece of transnational civil society that solves problems of global governance. These organizations are needed in order to spread democratic norms that are severely weakened and ignored by the governments both in CEE countries as well as those were democracy has never been secure. Through their networks, they can be an effective instrument of democracy promotion across the territorial boundaries, linking civil society organizations and individuals.

Relatively few analysts have looked at networks and transnational civil society as protagonists of democracy, and its role not only for developing or democratizing countries but also for established democracies. The current developments in Europe encourage one to investigate the strength of building networks, inclusion and achieved synergy. Networks of collective liberal-minded and Western-sponsored NGOs can help to challenge the structure and bring about or maintain democracy. Demands for adherence to civil rights, political liberties, greater citizen participation in decision-making processes is something that these organizations highlight in their activities and they exercise their influence through their ability to make policymakers listen. So, their powers lie not in force, but in moral authority as well as credible information. Thus, pro-democratic political and civic engagement should be encouraged and fostered.

This is not to underestimate the role of the state and institutions. Autocratic leaders can limit exposure to and reduce receptivity to democratic diffusion (Vanderhill, 2017) through the use of coercion, patronage and economic growth in order to counter both internal and external threats to their rule. However, as presented in Chapter 6, such tactics are also used by Hungarian as well as Polish governments. This means that also in democracies, the governments have the capacity to both facilitate and impede the growth of the non-profit sector within the territories under their control. Thus, we have to realize that there are limits to civil society's influence. In the end, the states guarantee civil and political rights. However, just as civil society needs democracy, democracy needs civil society in order to grow and sustain. Structure determines and is also in turn determined by the actions of individuals; as has been implied in my book, the norms are inserted in civil society (young people), and the consequence of such insertion is empowerment and greater activity of individuals which eventually changes in political culture.

In times when values and freedoms are undermined, democracy promotion via networks provides hope to "bet heavily on this battle of information and ideas, because this is a battle we can win" (Diamond, 2017). Even in authoritarian states bottom-up forces are possible, as Osa (2003) pointed out:

> The absence of collective action and civic association in an authoritarian state is the norm. Yet, the barriers to autonomous social action are sometimes surmounted, protests are organized, and occasionally social movement emerge. Under difficult, risky conditions, people do form organizations with challenge the state power.

Therefore, it is important for the donors to support front-line activists, to keep linkages with NGOs, work through them, and finance their activities. Especially, in developing and newly democratizing countries where grassroots and national NGOs depend on international funding, democracy activists should not pay for the consequences of the actions taken by their governments, and thus it is important to protect them so that liberal democracy can be preserved. Such collaboration between donors and NGOs helps to avoid corrupt recipient governments as well those that represent different norms. Today, it is up to NGOs to maintain and support diffusion of liberal democracy. CEE NGOs consider themselves Western liberal, pro-democratic and pro-capitalist. For them, the support they give to other post-communist countries is recognition of the critical role they have played in bringing about democratic change. Without the support of Western donors, the NGOs engagement in democracy assistance would be less apparent. If donors fail to recognize the importance of bypass democracy assistance, the linkages and networks, and choose to cease support, this book might be the last evidence of non-state actors spreading democratic norms elsewhere.

Note

1 Interview with a representative of one of the Hungarian organizations that prefers to be anonymous, July 14, 2015, Budapest, Hungary.

Appendix

Youth participation study

Part I Regime, society and authority

We would like to know your opinion on the rules of organization of the state, media and authorities. We are also interested in your opinion on democratic regime, and in your attitude toward some aspects of social and political life.

1 Which of the following descriptions of the state do you consider as important, and which are not, for creating a good standard of living?

Instruction: Please answer all questions by choosing the answers that best describe your attitude.

Table A

Elements of democracy	*Very important*	*Rather important*	*Rather not important*	*Not important*
Electoral elements				
Free and fair elections				
Vertical accountability				
Fixed-term elections				
Alternative offers				
Liberal elements				
Rule of law				
Equality before the law				
Independence of the judiciary				
Horizontal accountability				
Civil liberties				
Freedom of expression				
Little state intervention				
Freedom of association				
Minority protection				
Media freedom				
Media pluralism				
Freedom of movement				
Economic freedoms				
Protection of property rights				
Freedom of running business				
Social justice elements				
Protection of workers' rights				
Equal access to education				
Fulfillment of basic necessitates				
Protection against poverty				
Redistribution income differences				

2 How much do you agree or disagree with following statements?

Instruction: Please answer all questions by choosing the answers that best describe your attitude.

Table B

	Fully agree	*Rather agree*	*Rather disagree*	*Fully disagree*
Democracy is the best form of government				
Democracy leads to the well-being of citizens				
Democracy leads to economic growth				
Democracy works everywhere				
Democracy is a good regime for my country				
Sometimes non-democratic government is preferable				
Strong leadership is better than democratic leadership				
Democracy the best form of government				
Democracy leads to the wellbeing of citizens				

3 How much do you agree or disagree with following statements.

Instruction: Please answer all questions by choosing the answers that best describe your attitude.

Table C

	Fully agree	*Rather agree*	*Rather disagree*	*Fully disagree*
You should always show respect to those who exercise authority				
People like me do not have any influence on what the government and politicians are doing				
Most politicians, regardless of what they say, care only about their career				
Key political decisions are taken in secret situations				
My country should not emulate the standards of the West, but rely primarily on its own traditions and experiences				
A strong leader can do more for the country than the law, discussions and consultations				

4 What is your opinion about the role of the national and local government?

Instruction: Please answer all questions by choosing the answers that best describe your attitude.

Table D

	Fully agree	*Rather agree*	*Rather disagree*	*Fully disagree*
The activities and the laws passed by the *national* government have a great effect on your day-to-day life in your country				
The activities and the laws passed by the *local* government have an important effect on your day-to-day life in your country				
On the whole, the activities of the *national* government improve conditions in your country				
On the whole, the activities of the *local* government improve conditions in your country				
|If you had some questions to ask a *government officials*, for example, a tax question or a housing regulation question, you would be given and an equal treatment				
If you explained your point of view to the *governmental officials*, you would be given serious consideration				
People like me do not have any influence on what the government and politicians are doing				
Most politicians, regardless of what they say, care only about their career				
Key political decisions are taken in secret situations				

Part II Citizenship: my role as a citizen

We would like to learn about your opinion and feelings about political and social life as well as your interest in public affairs in your country.

5 Are you proud to be a citizen of your country?

Instruction: Please choose one answer that best describes your situation.

Completely yes

Mostly yes

Mostly not

Completely not

Don't know

6 What are the things about your country that you are most proud of?

Instruction: This is a multiple-choice question. You can choose up to three answers.

Characteristics of people

Contribution to science

Contributions to the arts

Economic system

Educational system

Governmental and political institutions

Military

Physical attributes of country (landscapes, etc.)

Position in international affairs

Social legislation

Spiritual virtues and religion

Nothing

Don't know

Other, please specify……………………………………………………

7 What should be citizens' obligations and activities?

Instruction: Please answer all questions by choosing the answers that best describe your attitude.

Table E

	Fully agree	*Rather agree*	*Rather disagree*	*Fully disagree*
Displaying the flag during national days				
Following the current affairs				
Following the law				
Homeland defense (military)				
Knowing the history of your country				
Loyalty and respect for you country				
Paying attention to the natural environment				
Paying taxes				
Taking part local government activities				
Taking part in activities of political parties				
Taking part in non-governmental activities				
Volunteering				
Voting				
Working honestly				

8 In your opinion what is most important for a young person to enter politics successfully?

Instruction: This is a multiple-choice question. You can choose up to three answers.

Personal qualifications (e.g., education, skills)

Personal characteristics (e.g., charisma, leadership skills)

Experience in politics

Experience in various organizations (e.g., non-governmental, student organizations)

Financial support

Informal connections

Political program

Nothing

Don't know

Other, please specify..

9 In your opinion, how quickly you would be able to provide the surnames of the political figures in your country, if you were asked to give them?

Instruction: Please answer all questions by choosing the answers that best apply to you.

Table F

	In 1 second	*In less than 10 seconds (after a short time to think)*	*In 10–60 seconds (after a longer time to think)*	*More than 60 seconds (only after checking on the Internet/books)*
President				
Prime Minister				
Minister of Foreign Affairs				
Minister of Internal Affairs				
Leader of the ruling party				
Leader of the biggest opposition party				
A well-known human rights defender				

10 How do you update yourself about public affairs and how often?

Instruction: Please answer all questions by choosing the answers that best apply to you.

Table G

	Nearly every day	*About once a week*	*From time to time*	*Never*
Newspapers and magazines (printed)				
Radio (traditional—not online)				
TV (traditional—not online)				
Online media (press/radio/TV)				
Internet websites				
Social media (e.g., Facebook, Twitter, blogs, etc.)				
Talking to other people (e.g., friends, family)				

11 If you had a chance to influence the national government, what would you do to try to influence the national government about an unjust regulation or action?

Instruction: This is a multiple-choice question. You can choose up to three answers.

Consult a lawyer and appeal through the courts

Directly contact administrative (non-elected) officials

Directly contact political leaders (elected officials) or the press; write a letter or visit a local political leader

Protest

Organize an informal group; inform friends and neighbors and get them to write letters of protest or to sign a petition

Take some violent action

Vote against offending officials at next election

Work through a formal group (union, church, professional association to which I belong)

Work through a political party

I would not try at all

Don't know

Other………………………………………………………………………

12 If you had a chance to influence the local government, what would you do to try to influence the local government about an unjust regulation or action?

Instruction: This is a multiple-choice question. You can choose several answers.

Consult a lawyer and appeal through the courts

Directly contact administrative (non-elected) officials

Directly contact political leaders (elected officials) or the press; write a letter or visit a local political leader

Protest

Organize an informal group; inform friends and neighbors and get them to write letters of protest or to sign a petition

Take some violent action

Vote against offending officials at the next election

Work through a formal group (union, church, professional to which I belong)

Work through a political party

I would not try at all

Don't know

Other..

Part III Social and political participation

We would like to know about your political and social participation.

13 Did you vote in any political election at the local or national level?

Instruction: Please choose one answer that best describes your experience.

Yes

No, I didn't

No, because I was too young to vote

Don't know

14 Will you vote in any upcoming political election at the local or national level?

Instruction: Please choose one answer that best describes your intention.

Yes (please answer question 15 and omit question 16)

No (please go to question 16 and omit question 15)

Do not know (please go to question 17 and omit questions 15 and 16)

15 Why will you vote?

Instruction: This is a multiple-choice question. You can choose up to three answers.

Please answer this question only if you answered YES in question 14.

I believe that my voice will change something

I consider voting as my civic duty

I feel responsible for my country and/or region

I want to express my dissatisfaction with a party or candidate

I want to express my support for a party or candidate

I'm interested in politics

I always vote

Don't know

Other, please specify..

16 Why will you NOT vote?

Instruction: This is a multiple-choice question. You can choose up to three answers.

Please answer this question only if you answered NO in question 14.

I don't believe that my voice will change anything

I don't consider voting as my civic duty.

I don't feel responsible for my country and/or region

I don't want to express my support for a party or candidate

I sometimes find campaigns silly or ridiculous

I don't always vote

I'm not interested in politics

Don't know

Other, please specify……………………………………………………………

17 Have you participated in any activities of listed organizations?

Instruction: This is a multiple-choice question. You can choose several answers.

A cultural organization

A faith-based organization

A leisure-time/sport organization

A political organization

A trade union

An informal organization (e.g., neighborhood group, interest circle)

An organization aimed and improving the local community

An organization promoting democracy

An organization promoting environmental issues

An organization promoting human rights

None

Other, please specify……………………………………………………………

18 What kind of actions did you take during the last year?

Instruction: This is a multiple-choice question. You can choose several answers.

I volunteered for a social project

I organized meetings focused on the matters of the local community

I participated in meetings focused on the matters of the local community

I wrote a petition

I signed a petition

I organized a demonstration/collective action

I participated in a demonstration/collective action

I contacted governmental officials or politicians on the local level during my social activities

I contacted governmental officials or politicians on the national level during my social activities

I organized my neighbors, co-workers or other groups around of some common interest

None

Other, please specify..

19 How important is the role of NGOs for creating a good standard of living?

20 Instruction: Please answer all questions by choosing the answers that best describe your attitude.

Table H

	Very important	*Rather important*	*Rather not important*	*Rather not important*
The delegation by the state of the widest possible competence to social organizations/NGOs				
Consultation with the interest groups on important state decisions				

Part IV Your profile

Finally, please answer a few questions concerning you and your family. This data will be used for statistical purposes only. We pay special attention to ensuring its confidentiality.

21 What is your country of origin?

Bosnia-Herzegovina

Georgia

Ukraine

The Czech Republic

Poland

Slovakia

Hungary

Other, please specify..

22 Gender

Female

Male

23 Age: ....

24 Education: Academic Major

Humanities

Technology

Life Sciences

Medicine

Art

Other major

I am not a student

25 What is educational level of your mother?

Incomplete secondary education

Secondary education

Secondary vocational/technical

Incomplete higher education

Higher education

Technical higher

Academic degree

I do not know/hard to say

26 What is education level of you father?

Incomplete secondary education

Secondary education

Secondary vocational/technical

Incomplete higher education

Higher education

Technical higher

Academic degree

I do not know/hard to say

27 How do you evaluate the financial situation of your family?

We live very frugally—we do not have enough money even for basic needs

We live modestly—we manage our budget very carefully to provide what we need on a daily basis

We live averagely—we have enough money for day-to-day expenses, but we need to save for major purchases

We live well—we have enough to live on without special savings

We live very well—we can afford luxuries

No answer

28 What is your place of residence?

Village

Town of up to 20,000 inhabitants

Town of 20,000–50,000 inhabitants

Urban area of 50,000–200,000 inhabitants

Urban area of 200,000–500,000 inhabitants

Urban area of 500,000–1 million inhabitants

Urban area of 1–5 million inhabitants

Urban area with more than 5 million inhabitants

References

Abs, H. and Veldhuis, R. (2006). *Indicators on Active Citizenship—The Social, Cultural and Economic Domain.* Ispra: Joint Research Centre.

Acharya, A. (2004). How Ideas Spread: Whose Norms Matter? Norm Localization and Institutional Change in Asian Regionalism. *International Organization*, 58(2), pp. 239–275.

Acharya, A. (2011). Norm Subsidiarity and Regional Orders: Sovereignty, Regionalism, and Rule-Making in the Third World. *International Studies Quarterly*, 55, pp. 95–123.

Acharya, A. (2016). The Future of Global Governance: Fragmentation Maybe Inevitable and Creative. *Global Governance: A Review of Multilateralism and International Organizations*, 22(4), pp. 453–460.

Adler, R. and Goggin, J. (2005). "What Do We Mean By 'Civic Engagement'?" *Journal of Transformative Education*, 3(3), pp. 236–253.

Ágh, A. (2015). De-Europeanization and De-democratization Trends in ECE: From the Potemkin Democracy to the Elected Autocracy in Hungary. *Journal of Comparative Politics*, 8(2), pp. 4–26.

Ágh, A. (2016). The Decline of Democracy in East-Central Europe. *Problems of Post-Communism*, 63(5–6), pp. 277–287.

Akkerman, A., Mudde, C. and Zaslove, A. (2014). How Populist Are the People? Measuring Populist Attitudes in Voters. *Comparative Political Studies*, 47(9), pp. 1324–1353.

Aksartova, S. (2005). NGO Diffusion in the Former Soviet Union and its Effects. In: *Civil Society from Abroad: U.S. Donors in the Former Soviet Union*. PhD Dissertation, Department of Sociology, Princeton University.

Alcock, P. and Kendall, J. (2011). Constituting the Third Sector: Processes of Decontestation and Contention under the UK Labour Governments in England. *Voluntas*, 22, pp. 450–469.

Alexander, A. and Welzel, C. (2011). Measuring Effective Democracy: The Human Empowerment Approach. *Comparative Politics*, 43(April), pp. 271–289.

Almond, G. and Verba, S. (1963). *The Civic Culture: Political Attitudes and Democracy in Five Nations.* Newbury Park, London and New Delhi: Sage Publications.

Almond, G. and Verba, S. (1980). *The Civic Culture Revisited.* Boston, MA: Little, Brown.

Almond, G. and Verba, S. (1989). *The Civic Culture: Political Attitudes and Democracy in Five Nations*. London: Sage Publications.

Alonso, S. (2016). What Type of Democratic Commitment Lied Behind the Importance of Living in a Democracy? In: M. Ferrin and H. Kriesi., eds., *How European View and Evaluate Democracy*, 1st ed. Oxford: Oxford University Press.

Amnå, E. and Ekman, J. (2013). Standby Citizens: Diverse Faces of Political Passivity. *European Political Science Review*, 6(2), pp. 261–281.

Anheier, H., Glasius, M. and Kaldor, M. (2001). Introducing Global Civil Society. In H. Anheier, M. Glasius and M. Kaldor, eds., *Global Civil Society 2001*, 1st ed. Oxford: Oxford University Press.

Applebaum, A. (2015). Authoritarianism Goes Global (II): The Leninist Roots of Civil Society Repression. *Journal of Democracy*, 26(4), pp. 21–27.

Applebaum, A. (2016). *Illiberal Democracy Comes to Poland.* [online] *Washington Post.* Available at: www.washingtonpost.com/news/global-opinions/wp/2016/12/22/illiberal-democracy-comes-to-poland/?utm_term=.d309ea8aa438 [accessed December 22, 2016].

Arato, A. (1981). Civil Society Against the States: Poland 1980–81. *Telos*, 1981(47), 23–47.

Arato, A. (2011). Afterword: Revis(it)ing Civil Society. In: U. Liebert and H. Trenz, eds., *The New Politics of European Civil Society.* Abingdon and New York: Routledge, pp. 195–208.

Armingeon, K. (2007). Political Participation and Associational Involvement. In: J. van Deth, J. Montero and A. Westholm, eds., *Citizenship and Involvement in European Democracies: A Comparative Analysis*, 1st ed. London and New York: Routledge, pp. 358–383.

Arriola, L., Matanock, A., Travaglianti, M. and Davis, J. (2017). Civic Education in Violent Elections: Evidence from Côte d'Ivoire's 2015 Election. [online] Webbly. Available at: http://manuelatravaglianti.weebly.com/uploads/2/2/8/8/22888518/amtd_civic_education_june_2017_v5.pdf [accessed June 2017].

Badelt, C. (1997). Entrepreneurship Theories of the Non-Profit Sector. *Voluntas: International Journal of Voluntary and Nonprofit Organizations*, 8, 162–178.

Bahry, D. and Silver, B. (1990). Soviet Citizen Participation on the Eve of Democratisation. *American Political Science Review*, 84, pp. 821–847.

Banerjee, A. V. (2007). *Making Aid Work.* Cambridge, MA: MIT Press.

Banks, J. (2004). *Diversity and Citizenship Education: Global Perspectives.* San Francisco: Jossey-Bass.

Barnes, S., Allerbeck, K., Farah, B., Heunks, F., Inglehart, R., Jennings, M. Klingemann, H., Marsh, A. and Rosenmayr, L. (1979). *Political Action: Mass Participation in Five Western Democracies.* Beverly Hills, CA: Sage Publications.

Barnes, S., Kaase, M. *et al.* (1979). *Political Action: Mass Participation in Five Western Democracies.* London and Beverly Hills, CA: Sage.

Barnett, C. and Low, M. (2004). *Spaces of Democracy: Geographical Perspectives on Citizenship, Participation and Representation.* London: Sage Publications.

Barrett, M. and Zani, B. (2015). *Political and Civic Engagement: Multidisciplinary Perspectives.* New York: Routledge.

Basora, A. Marczyk, A. and Otarashvili, M. (2017). *Does Democracy Matter? The United States and Global Democracy Support.* Lanham, MD: Rowman & Littlefield.

Basora, A. and Yalowitz, K. (2017). Introduction. In: A. Basora, A. Marczyk and M. Otarashvili, eds., *Does Democracy Matter? The United States and Global Democracy Support*, 1st ed. Lanham, MD: Rowman & Littlefield, pp. ix–xxii.

bbc.com, (2016a). Black Monday: Polish Women Strike Against Abortion Ban. [online] BBC News. Available at: www.bbc.com/news/world-europe-37540139 [accessed October 3, 2016].

bbc.com, (2016b). *Lech Walesa "Was Paid Communist Informant."* [online] BBC News. Available at: www.bbc.com/news/world-europe-35602437 [accessed June 4, 2016].

Bebbington, A. and Riddell, R. (1995). The Direct Funding of Southern NGOs by Donors: New Agendas and Old Problems. *Journal of International Development*, 7, pp. 879–893.

Beichelt, T., Hahn, I., Schimmelfennig, F. and Worschech, S. (2014). *Civil Society and Democracy Promotion*. Basingstoke: Palgrave Macmillan.

Beichelt, T. and Merkel, W. (2014). Democracy Promotion and Civil Society: Regime Types, Transitions Modes and Effects. In: T. Beichelt, I. Hahn, F. Schimmelfennig and S. Worschech, eds., *Civil Society and Democracy Promotion*. Basingstoke: Palgrave Macmillan, pp. 42–64.

Beichelt, T. and Minkenberg, M. (2002). *Explaining the Radical Right in Transition: Theories of Right-wing Radicalism and Opportunity Structures in Postsocialist Europe*. Frankfurt (Oder): FIT.

Belloni, R. (2001). Civil Society and Peace Building in Bosnia and Herzegovina. *Journal of Peace Research*, 38(2), pp. 163–180.

Bennett, W. and Segerberg, A. (2013). *The Logic of Connective Action: Digital Media and the Personalization of Contentious Politics*. New York: Cambridge University Press.

Bermeo, N. (2009). Does Electoral Democracy Boost Economic Equality? *Journal of Democracy*, 20(4), pp. 21–35.

Bermeo, S. (2011). Foreign Aid and Regime Change: A Role for Donor Intent. *World Development*, 39(11), pp. 2021–2031.

Bermeo, S. (2016). Aid Is Not Oil: Donor Utility, Heterogeneous Aid, and the Aid-Democratization Relationship. *International Organization*, 70(1), pp. 1–32.

Bernhagen, P. and Marsh, M. (2007). Voting and Protesting: Explaining Citizen Participation in Old and New European Democracies. *Democratization*, 14(1), pp. 44–72.

Bernhard, M. (1993a). Civil Society and Democratic Transition in East Central Europe. *Political Science Quarterly*, 108(2), pp. 307–326.

Bernhard, M. (1993b). *The Origins of Democratization in Poland: Workers, Intellectuals, and Opposition Politics, 1976–1980*. New York: Columbia University Press.

Bernhard, M. (1996). Civil Society after the First Transition: Dilemmas of Post-Communist Democratization in Poland and Beyond. *Communist and Post-Communist Studies*, 29(3), pp. 309–330.

Bieber, F. (2003). The Serbian Transition and Civil Society: Roots of the Delayed Transition in Serbia. *International Journal of Politics, Culture and Society*, 17(1), pp. 73–90.

Biesta, G. (2009). Good Education in an Age of Measurement: On the Need to Reconnect with the Question of Purpose in Education. *Educational Assessment, Evaluation and Accountability*, 21(1), pp. 33–46.

Biesta, G. (2011). *Learning Democracy in School and Society. Education, Lifelong Learning, and the Politics of Citizenship*. Rotterdam: Sense Publishers.

Biesta, G. and Lawy, R. (2006). From Teaching Citizenship to Learning Democracy. Overcoming Individualism in Research, Policy and Practice. *Cambridge Journal of Education*, 36(1), pp. 63–79.

Birch, S. (2002). The 2000 Elections in Yugoslavia: The "Bulldozer" Revolution. *Electoral Studies*, 21(3), pp. 499–511.

Birzea, C., Kerr, D., Mikkelsen, R., Pol, M., Froumin, I., Losito, B. and Sardoc, M. (2004). *All European Study on Education for Democratic Citizenship Policies*. Strasbourg: Council of Europe.

Björkman, M. and Svensson, J. (2009). Power to the People: Evidence from a Randomized Field Experiment of a Community-Based Monitoring Project in Uganda. *The Quarterly Journal of Economics*, 124(2), pp. 735–769.

Bobel, C. (2007). "I'm Not an Activist, Though I've Done a Lot of It": Doing Activism, Being Activist and the "Perfect Standard" in a Contemporary Movement. *Social Movement Studies*, 6, pp. 147–159.

Bollen, K., Paxton, P. and Morishima, R. (2005). Assessing International Evaluations: An Example from USAID's Democracy and Governance Programs. *American Journal of Evaluation*, 26, pp. 189–203.

Bolzendahl, C. and Coffé, H. (2009). Citizenship Beyond Politics: The Importance of Political, Civil and Social Rights and Responsibilities Among Women and Men. *The British Journal of Sociology*, 60, pp. 763–791.

Bolzendahl, C. and Coffé, H. (2013). Are "Good" Citizens "Good" Participants? Testing Citizenship Norms and Political Participation Across 25 Nations. *Political Studies*, 61, pp. 45–65.

Börzel, T. (2010). Why You Don't Always Get What You Want: EU Enlargement and Civil Society in Central and Eastern Europe. *Acta Politica*, 45(1–2), pp. 1–10.Börzel, T. and Buzogány, A. (2010). Governing EU Accession in Transition Countries: The Role of Non-state Actors. *Acta Politica*, 45(1–2), pp. 158–182.

Boulding, C. (2014). *NGOs, Political Protest, and Civil Society*. New York: Cambridge University Press.

Brady, H. (1999). Political Participation. In: J. Robinson, P. Shaver and L. Wrightsman, eds., *Measures of Political Attitudes*, 1st ed. San Diego, CA: Academic Press.

Brady, H., Verba, S. and Schlozman, K. (1995). Beyond SES: A Resource Model of Political Participation. *American Political Science Review*, 89(2), pp. 274–291.

Bratton, M., Mattes, R. and Gyimah-Boadi, E. (2005). *Public Opinion, Democracy, and Market Reform in Africa*. Cambridge: Cambridge University Press.

Bratton, M. and van de Walle, N. (1997). *Democratic Experiments in Africa: Regime Transitions in Comparative Perspective*. New York: Cambridge University Press.

Brinks, D. and Coppedge, M. (2006). Diffusion is No Illusion: Neighbor Emulation in the Third Wave of Democracy. *Comparative Political Studies*, 39(7), pp. 1–23.

Brown, W. (2015). *Undoing the Demos: Neoliberalism's Stealth Revolution*. Cambridge, MA: MIT Press.

Bruter, M., Banaji, S., Harrison, S., Cammaerts, B. and Anstead, N. (2016). *Youth Participation in Democratic Life: Stories of Hope and Disillusion*. London: Palgrave Macmillan.

Buckingham, D. (2000). *The Making of Citizens: Young People, News, and Politics*. London: Routledge.

Bunce, V. and Wolchik, S. (2006a). Favorable Conditions and Electoral Revolutions. *Journal of Democracy*, 17(4), pp. 5–18.

Bunce, V. and Wolchik, S. (2006b). International Diffusion and Postcommunist Electoral Revolutions. *Communist and Post-Communist Studies*, 39(3), pp. 283–304.

Bunce, V. and Wolchik, S. (2007). Youth and Postcommunist Electoral Revolutions: Never Trust Anyone over 30? In: J. Forbrig and P. Demeš, eds., *Reclaiming Democracy. Civil Society and Electoral Change in Central and Eastern Europe*, 1st ed. Washington: The German Marshall Fund of the United States, pp. 191–204.

Burnell, P. (2000). *Democracy Assistance: International Cooperation for Democratization*. London: Frank Cass.

Burnell, P. and Calvert, P. (2004). *Civil Society in Democratization*. Abingdon and New York: Routledge.

Burnell, P. and Calvert, P. (2005). Promoting Democracy Abroad. *Democratization*, 12(4), pp. 433–438.

Burnell, P. and Youngs, R. (2010). *New Challenges to Democratization.* Abingdon and New York: Routledge.

Burrows, M. and Stephan, M. (2015). *Is Authoritarianism Staging a Comeback?* Washington, DC: Atlantic Council.

Burtless, G. (1995). The Case for Randomized Field Trials in Economic and Policy Research. *The Journal of Economic Perspectives*, 9(2), pp. 63–84.

Bush, S. (2015). *The Taming of Democracy Assistance: Why Democracy Promotion Does Not Confront Dictators.* Cambridge: Cambridge University Press.

Bútora, M. (2007). OK '98: A Campaign of Slovak NGOs for Free and Fair Elections. In: J. Forbrig and P. Demeš, eds., *Reclaiming Democracy. Civil Society and Electoral Change in Central and Eastern Europe*, 1st ed. Washington:, DC The German Marshall Fund of the United States, pp. 21–52.

Bútora, M. and Bútorová, Z. (1999). Slovakia's Democratic Awakening. *Journal of Democracy*, 10(1), pp. 80–95.

Cammaerts, B., Bruter, M., Banaji, S., Harrison, S., Anstead, N. and Whitwell, B. (2016). *Youth Participation in Democratic Life Stories of Hope and Disillusion.* Basingstoke: Palgrave Macmillan.

Campbell, D. (2007). Sticking Together: Classroom Diversity and Civic Education. *American Politics Research*, 35(1), pp. 57–78.

Campbell, D. (2008a). Voice in the Classroom: How an Open Classroom Climate Fosters Political Engagement Among Adolescents. *Political Behaviour*, 30(4), pp. 437–454.

Campbell, D. (2008b). *Why We Vote: How Schools and Communities Shape Our Civic Life*. Princeton, NJ: Princeton University Press.

Campbell, D. (2009). Civic Engagement and Education: An Empirical Test of the Sorting Model. *American Journal of Political Science*, 53(4), pp. 771–786.

Campbell, D. and Niemi, R. (2016). Testing Civics: State-Level Civic Education Requirements and Political Knowledge. *American Political Science Review*, 110(3), pp. 495–511.

Canache, D. (2006). Measuring Variance and Complexity in Citizens' Understanding of Democracy. In *The LAPOP-UNDP Workshop: Candidate Indicators for the UNDP Democracy Support Index (DSI)*. Nashville, TN: Vanderbilt University. Available at www.researchgate.net/profile/Damarys_Canache/publication/267429762_Measuring_Variance_and_Complexity_in_Citizens%27_Understanding_of_Democracy/links/546b7d9e0cf2397f7831c1f3/Measuring-Variance-and-Complexity-in-Citizens-Understanding-of-Democracy.pdf [Accessed November 18, 2014].

Canache, D. (2012). Citizens Conceptualization of Democracy Structural Complexity, Substantive Content, and Political Significance. *Comparative Political Studies*, 45(9), pp. 1132–1158.

Canache, D., Mondak, J. and Seligson, M. (2001). Meaning and Measurement in Cross-National Research on Satisfaction with Democracy. *Public Opinion Quarterly*, 65(4), pp. 506–528.

Canovan, M. (1999). Trust the People! Populism and the Two Faces of Democracy. *Political Studies*, 47(1), pp. 2–16.

Cammaerts, B., Bruter, M., Banaji, S., Harrison, S., Anstead, N. and Whitwell, B. (2016). *Youth Participation in Democratic Life: Stories of Hope and Disillusion.* Palgrave Macmillan.

Carothers, T. (1999). *Aiding Democracy Abroad: The Learning Curve*. Washington, DC: Carnegie Endowment for International Peace.

Carothers, T. (2002). The End of the Transition Paradigm. *Journal of Democracy*, 13(1), pp. 5–21.

Carothers, T. (2004). *Critical Mission: Essays on Democracy Promotion*. Washington, DC: Carnegie Endowment for International Peace.

Carothers, T. (2006). The Backlash against Democracy Promotion. *Foreign Affairs*, 85(2), pp. 55–68.

Carothers, T. (2016). Closing Space for International Democracy and Human Rights Support. *Journal of Human Rights Practice*, 8(3), pp. 358–377.

Carothers, T. and Brandt, W. (1999/2000). Civil Society. *Foreign Policy*, Winter (117), pp. 18–29.

Carothers, T. and Brechenmacher, S. (2014). *Closing Space. Democracy and Human Rights Support under Fire*. Washington, DC: Carnegie Endowment for International Peace.

Ceka, B. and Magalhães, P. (2016). How People Understand Democracy: A Social Dominance Approach. In: M. Ferrin and H. Kriesi, eds., *How European View and Evaluate Democracy*, 1st ed. Oxford: Oxford University Press.

Centola, D. (2010). The Spread of Behavior in an Online Social Network Experiment. *Science*, 329(5996), pp. 1194–1197.

Challand, B. (2006). Civil Society, Autonomy and Donors: International Aid to Palestinian NGOs. *EUI Working Papers*, 20.

Checkoway, B. (2010). What is Youth Participation? *Children and Youth Services Review*, 33(2011), pp. 340–345.

Chimiak, G. (2016). *The Growth of Non-Governmental Development Organizations in Poland and Their Cooperation with Polish Aid*. Warsaw: IFiS PAN Publishers.

chnm.gmu.edu, (1989). Declaration of Charter 77. [online] Roy Rosenzweig Center for History and New Media. Available at: http://chnm.gmu.edu/1989/archive/files/declaration-of-charter-77_4346bae392.pdf [accessed December 10, 2017].

Christensen, D. and Weinstein, J. M. (2013). "Defunding Dissent: Restrictions on Aid to NGOs," *Journal of Democracy*, 24(2), p. 83.

citizensobservatory.pl, (2017). *Opinion on the Draft act on the National Freedom Institute—National Centre for the Development of Civil Society of Poland, Opinion-Nr.: NGO-POL/303/2017*. [online] Obserwatorium demokracji. Available at: http://citizensobservatory.pl/ustawa/osceodihr-opinion-on-the-draft-act-on-the-national-freedom-institute-national-centre-for-the-development-of-civil-society-of-poland/ [accessed August 22, 2017].

civicus.org, (2015). *CIVICUS State of Civil Society Report 2015*. [online] CIVICUS. Available at https://civicus.org/images/StateOfCivilSocietyFullReport2015.pdf.

Clark, A. (1995). Non-Governmental Organization and Their Influence on International Society. *Journal of International Affairs*, 48(2), pp. 507–525.

Clark, J. (1991). *Democratizing Development. The Role of Voluntary Organizations*. West Hartford, CT.

Clarke, R. and Mehtta, A. (2015). *5 Trends that Explain Why Civil Society Space is Under Assault Around the World*. [online] Oxfam Blogs. [Available at: https://oxfamblogs.org/fp2p/5-trends-that-explain-why-civil-society-space-is-under-assault-around-the-world/ [accessed August 25, 2015].

Cohen, J. and Arato, A. (1992). *Civil Society and Political Theory*. Cambridge, MA: MIT Press.

Cohen, J. and Rogers, J. (1992). Secondary Associations and Democratic Governance. *Politics and Society*, 20(4), pp. 393–472.

Cole, M., Dabelstein, N., Faint, T., Kliest, T. and Lavizzari, L. (2005). *Peer Assessment of Evaluation in Multilateral Organizations*. United Nations Development Programme, Copenhagen: Danish Ministry of Foreign Affairs, [available at http://web.undp.org/evaluation/documents/DAC-PeerReview.pdf]

Coleman, J. (1990). Metatheory: Explanation in Social Science. In: J. Coleman, ed., *Foundations of Social Theory*, 1st ed. Cambridge, MA: Harvard University Press, pp. 1–23.

Connolly, K. (2017). *Poland's President to Veto Controversial Laws Amid Protests*. [online] Guardian. Available at: www.theguardian.com/world/2017/jul/24/poland-president-to-veto-controversial-laws-amid-protests [accessed July 24, 2017].

Cooley, A. (2015). Authoritarianism Goes Global: Countering Democratic Norms. *Journal of Democracy*, 26(3), pp. 49–63.

Cooley, A. and Ron, J. (2002). The NGO Scramble: Organizational Insecurity and the Political Economy of Transnational Action. *International Security*, 27(1), pp. 5–39.

Coppedge, M., Gerring, J., Altman, D., Bernhard, M., Fish, S., Hicken, A, Kroenig, M., Lindberg, S., McMann, K., Paxton, P., Semetko, H., Skaaning, S., Staton, J. and Teorell, J. (2011). Conceptualizing and Measuring Democracy: A New Approach. *Perspectives on Politics*, 9(2), pp. 247–267.

Cox, R. (1997). *The New Realism: Perspectives on Multilateralism and World Order*. New York: St. Martin's/United Nations University Press.

Craig, S. and Maggiotto, M. (1982). Measuring Political Efficacy. *Political Methodology*, 8(3), pp. 85–109.

Crawford, B. and Lijphart, A. (1995). Explaining Political and Economic Change in Post-Communist Eastern Europe: Old Legacies, New Institutions, Hegemonic, Norms, and International Pressures. *Comparative Politics Studies*, 28(2), pp. 171–199.

Crick, B. and Lockyer, A. (2010). *Active Citizenship: What Could it Achieve and How?* Edinburgh: Edinburgh University Press.

Cunningham, B. (2016). *5 Takeaways from Slovakia's Election: A Potentially Hung Parliament Fractured Among Eight Parties Could Bring Political Chaos*. [online] POLITICO. Available at: www.politico.eu/article/slovakia-fico-asylum-migrants-elections-nazi-nationalists/ [accessed June 3, 2016].

Dahl, R. (1971). *Polyarchy: Participation and Opposition*. New Haven, CT and London: Yale University Press.

Dahl, R. (1989). *Democracy and its Critics*. New Haven, CT: Yale University Press.

Dahl, R. (2000). *On Democracy*. New Haven, CT: Yale University Press.

Dalton, R. (1988). *Citizen Politics in Western Democracies. Public Opinion and Political Parties in the United States, Great Britain, West Germany, and France*. London: Chatham House.

Dalton, R. (2000). The Decline of Party Identification. In: R. Dalton and M. Wattenberg, eds., *Parties Without Partisans: Political Change in Advanced Industrial Democracies*. Oxford: Oxford University Press, pp. 19–36.

Dalton, R. (2006). *Citizen Politics: Public Opinion and Political Parties in Advanced Industrial Democracies*, 4th ed. Washington, DC: CQ Press.

Dalton, R. (2008). Citizenship Norms and the Expansion of Political Participation. *Political Studies* 56(1), pp. 76–98.

Dalton, R. (2011a). *Engaging Youth in Politics: Debating Democracy's Future*. New York: IDEBATE Press.

Dalton, R. (2011b). Introduction: The Debates over Youth Participation. In: R. Dalton, ed., *Engaging Youth in Politics: Debating Democracy's Future*, 1st ed. New York: IDEBATE Press, pp. 1–15.

Dalton, R. (2011c). Participation beyond Elections. In: R. Dalton, ed., *Engaging Youth in Politics: Debating Democracy's Future*, 1st ed. New York: IDEBATE Press, pp. 112–131.

Dalton, R. (2014). *Citizen Politics: Public Opinion and Political Parties in Advanced Industrial Democracies*, 1st ed. Thousand Oaks, CA: CQ Press.

Dalton, R., Shin, D. and Jou, W. (2007). Popular Conceptions of the Meaning of Democracy: Democratic Understanding in Unlikely Places. *UC Irvine: Center for the Study of Democracy*.

Dawson, J. and Hanley, S. (2016). East Central Europe: The Fading Mirage of the "Liberal Consensus." *Journal of Democracy*, 27(1), pp. 20–34.

de Mesquita, B. and Smith, A. (2007). Foreign Aid and Policy Concessions. *Journal of Conflict Resolution*, 51(2), pp. 251–284.

de Mesquita, B. and Smith, A. (2009). A Political Economy of Aid. *International Organization*, 63(2), pp. 309–340.

de Tocqueville, A. (2000). *Democracy in America*. Chicago, IL: University of Chicago Press.

De Weerd, M., Gemmeke, M., Rigter, J. and van Rij, C. (2005). *Indicators for Monitoring Active Citizenship and Citizenship Education. Final Report*. Amsterdam: Regioplan Beleidsonderzoek.

Delanty, G. (2000). *Citizenship in a Global Age. Society, Culture, Politics*. Buckingham: Open University Press.

Demeš, P. and Forbrig, J. (2007). Civic Action and Democratic Power Shifts: On Strategies and Resources. In: J. Forbrig and P. Demeš, eds., *Reclaiming Democracy. Civil Society and Electoral Change in Central and Eastern Europe*, 1st ed. Washington, DC: The German Marshall Fund of the United States, pp. 175–190.

Deutsch, F. and Welzel, C. (2016). The Diffusion of Values among and between Democracies and Autocracies. In: *International Political Science Association World Congress*. Poznań: IPSA, p. 225.

Diamond, L. (1996). Is the Third Wave Over? *Journal of Democracy*, 7(3), pp. 20–37.

Diamond, L. (1999). *Developing Democracy: Toward Consolidation*. Baltimore: Johns Hopkins University Press.

Diamond, L. (2002). Thinking About Hybrid Regimes. *Journal of Democracy*, 13(2), pp. 21–35.

Diamond, L. (2003). Defining and developing democracy. In: R. Dahl, I. Shapiro and J. Cheibub, eds., *The Democracy Sourcebook*. Cambridge, MA: MIT Press, pp. 29–39.

Diamond, L. (2008). *The Spirit of Democracy: The Struggle to Build Free Societies Throughout the World*. New York: Times Books.

Diamond, L. (2015). Facing Up to the Democratic Recession. *Journal of Democracy*, 26(1), pp. 141–155.

Diamond, L. (2017). Reviving the Global Democratic Momentum. In: A. Basora, A. Marczyk and M. Otarashvili, eds., *Does Democracy Matter? The United States and Global Democracy Support*, 1st ed. Lanham, MD: Rowman & Littlefield, pp. 119–134.

Diamond, L. and Morlino, L. (2005). *Assessing the Quality of Democracy*. Baltimore, MD: Johns Hopkins University Press.

Diani, M. (2003). Introduction: Social Movements, Contentious Actions, and Social Networks: "From Metaphor to Substance"? In: A. Diani and D. McAdam, eds., *Social Movements and Networks: Relational Approaches to Collective Action. Comparative politics*, 1st ed. New York: Oxford University Press, pp. 1–20.

Diani, M. and McAdam, D. (2003). *Social Movements and Networks: Relational Approaches to Collective Action: Relational Approaches to Collective Action*. New York: Oxford University Press.

Dietrich, S. (2013). Bypass or Engage? Explaining Donor Delivery Tactics in Foreign Aid Allocation. *International Studies Quarterly*, 57(4), pp. 698–712.

Dimitrova, A. and Pridham, G. (2004). International Actors and Democracy Promotion in Central and Esatern Europe: The Integration Model and its Limits. *Democratization*, 11(5), pp. 91–112.

Diuk, N. (2012). *The Next Generation in Russia, Ukraine, and Azerbaijan Youth, Politics, Identity, and Change*. Plymouth, MA: Rowman & Littlefield.

Diuk, N. (2013). Youth as an Agent for Change: The Next Generation in Ukraine, *Demokratizatsiya*, 21(2), pp. 179–196.

Diuk, N. (2014a). Euromaidan. Ukraine's Self-Organizing Revolution. *World Affairs*, 176(6), pp. 9–17.

Diuk, N. (2014b). The Maidan and Beyond: Finding Ukraine, *Journal of Democracy*, 25(3), pp. 83–89.

Dodsworth, S. (2016). How Does the Objective of Aid Affect Its Impact on Accountability? Evidence from Two Aid Programmes in Uganda, *The Journal of Development Studies*, 53(10), pp. 1600–1614.

Domber, G. (2008). Evaluating International Influences on Democratic Development: Poland 1980–1989. *Center on Democracy, Development and the Rule of Law Working Papers*, 88, pp. 1–66.

Dufek, P., Holzer, J. and Mares, M. (2016). Introductory Remarks. In: J. Holzer and M. Mareš, eds., *Challenges to Democracies in East Central Europe*, 1st ed. Abingdon and New York: Routledge, pp. 1–14.

Duflo, E., Glennerster, R. and Kremer, M. (2007). Using Randomization in Development Economics: A Toolkit. In: T. Schults and J. Strauss, eds., *Handbook of Development Economics Vol. 4*, North Holland: Elsevier Science Ltd, pp. 3895–3962.

Dunning, T. (2004). Conditioning the Effects of Aid: Cold War Politics, Donor Credibility, and Democracy in Africa. *International Organization*, 58(2), pp. 409–423.

Dupuy, K. and Prakash, A. (2018). Do Donors Reduce Bilateral Aid to Countries with Restrictive NGO Laws? A Panel Study, 1993–2012. *Non-profit and Voluntary Sector Quarterly*, 47(1), pp. 89–106.

Dutkiewicz, P. and Gorzelak, G. (2013). The 2008–2009 Economic Crisis; Consequences in Central and Eastern Europe. In: J. DeBardeleben and C. Viju, eds., *Economic Crisis in Europe: What it Means for the EU and Russia*, 1st ed. New York: Palgrave Macmillan.

Dwyer, P. (2000). *Responsibilities: Contesting Social Citizenship*. London: Policy Press.

eacea.ec.europa.eu, (2012). *Citizen Education in Europe*. [online] Eurydice. Available at: http://eacea.ec.europa.eu/education/eurydice/documents/thematic_reports/139EN.pdf [accessed May 2012].

Edwards, M. (1994). International NGOs and Southern Governments in the "New World Order": Lessons of Experience at the Program Level. In: A. Clayton, ed., *Governance, Democracy and Conditionality: What Role for NGOs?* 1st ed. London: INTRAC, pp. 65–84.

Edwards, M. (2000). *NGO Rights and Responsibilities: A New Deal for Global Governance*. London: The Foreign Policy Centre/NCVO.

Edwards, M. and Hulme, D. (1996). Too Close for Comfort? The Impact of Official Aid on Nongovernmental Organizations. *World Development*, 24(6), pp. 961–973.

Ekiert, G. (1996). *The State against Society. Political Crises and Their Aftermath in East Central Europe*. Princeton, NJ: Princeton University Press.

Ekiert, G. (2003). The State After State Socialism: Poland in Comparative Perspective. In: T. Paul, J. Ikenberry and J. Hall, eds., *The Nation-State in Question*, 1st ed. Princeton, NJ: Princeton University Press, pp. 291–320.

Ekiert., G. (2012). The Illiberal Challenge in Post-Communist Europe: Surprises and Puzzles. *Taiwan Journal of Democracy*, 8(2), pp. 63–77.

Ekiert, G. and Foa, R. (2012). The Weakness of Post-Communist Civil Society Reassessed. *CES Papers—Open Forum*, 11.

Ekiert, G. and Hanson, S. (2003). *Capitalism and Democracy in Central and Eastern Europe: Assessing the Legacy of Communist Rule*. Cambridge: Cambridge University Press.

Ekiert, G. and Kubik, J. (1999). *Rebellious Civil Society: Popular Protest and Democratic. Consolidation in Poland, 1989–1993*. Ann Arbor: The University of Michigan Press.

Ekiert, G., Kubik, J. and Vachudova, M. (2007). Democracy in the Post-Communist World: An Unending Quest? *East European Politics and Societies*, 21(1), pp. 7–30.

Ekiert, G. and Ziblatt, D. (2013). Democracy in Central and Eastern Europe one hundred years on. *East European Politics and Societies*, 27(1), pp. 90–107.

Eliasoph, N. (2013). *The Politics of Volunteering*. Cambridge: Polity Press.

Emirbayer, M. and Goodwin, J. (1994). Network Analysis, Culture, and the Problem of Agency, Source. *The American Journal of Sociology*, 99(6), pp. 1411–1454.

Emirbayer, M. and Mische, A. (1998). What is Agency? *The American Journal of Sociology*, 103(4), pp. 962–1023.

europa.eu (2012). *European Commission, World Bank Institute and UNDP Sharing Knowledge and Transition Experience for Development: The View of New European Donors*. [online] capacity4dev. Available at: https://europa.eu/capacity4dev/cbyoung donors/event/sharing-knowledge-and-transition-exerience-development-view-new-european-donors [accessed November 26, 2012].

europeanvaluesstudy.eu (2009). [online] European Value Study EVS. Available at: www.europeanvaluesstudy.eu/ [accessed March 27, 2018].

Eurydice (2012). Citizen Education in Europe. Brussels: Education, Audiovisual and Culture Executive Agency. Available at: http://eacea.ec.europa.eu/education/eurydice/documents/thematic_reports/139EN.pdf. [accessed May 15, 2014].

Fairbanks, C. (2004). Georgia's Rose Revolution. *Journal of Democracy*, 15(2), pp. 110–124.

Falkowski, M. (2016). *Marching Democracy: In the Last Few Years We Have Witnessed the Reapprearance of "Protesting Civil Society."* [online] Visegrád Insight. Available at: http://visegradinsight.eu/marching-democracy/ [accessed May 7, 2016].

Ferrin, M. and Kriesi, H. (2016). *How Europeans View and Evaluate Democracy*. Oxford: Oxford University Press.

Finkel, S. (2014). The Impact of Adult Civic Education Programmes in Developing Democracies. *Public Administration and Development*, 34, pp. 169–181.

Finkel, S., Horowitz, J. and Rojo-Mendoza, R. (2012). Civic Education and Democratic Backsliding in the Wake of Kenya's Post-2007 Election Violence. *Journal of Politics*, 74(01), pp. 52–65.

Finkel, S., Pérez-Liñán, A. and Seligson, M. (2007). The Effects of US Foreign Assistance on Democracy Building, 1990–2003. *World Politics*, 59, pp. 404–439.

Finkel, S. and Smith, A. (2011). Civic Education, Political Discussion and the Social Transmission of Democratic Knowledge and Values in a New Democracy: Kenya 2002. *American Journal of Political Science*, 55(2), pp. 417–435.

Finnemore, M. (1996). *National Interests in International Society*. In Series: Cornell Studies in Political Economy. Ithaca, NY: Cornell University Press.

Finnemore, M. and Sikkink, K. (1998). International Norm Dynamics and Political Change. *International Organization*, 52(4), pp. 887–917.

Fisher, J. (1998). *Nongovernment: NGOs and the Political Development of the Third World.* West Hartford, CT: Kumarian Press.

Flanagan, C. (2013). *Teenage Citizens. The Political Theories of the Young*. Cambridge, MA: Harvard University Press.

Flanagan, C. and Levine, P. (2010). Civic Engagement and The Transition to Adulthood. *The Future of Children*, 20(1), pp. 159–180.

Flockhart, T. (2005). Socialization and Democratization: A Tenuous but Intriguing Link. In: T. Flockhart, ed., *Socializing Democratic Norms. The Role of International Organization for the Construction of Europe*, 1st ed. London: Palgrave Macmillan, pp. 1–20.

Florini, A. (2000). *The Third Force. The Rise of Transnational Civil Society*. Washington, DC: Carnegie Endowment for International Peace.

Forbrig, J. (2005a). Introduction: Democratic Politics, Legitimacy and Youth Participation. In: J. Forbrig, ed., *Revisiting Youth Political Participation: Challenges for Research and Democratic Practices in Europe*, 1st ed. Strasbourg: Council of Europe Publishing, pp. 7–18.

Forbrig, J. (2005b). *Revisiting Youth Political Participation.* Strasbourg: Council of Europe Publishing.

Fuchs, D. and Roller, E. (2014). Learned Democracy? Support of Democracy in Central and Eastern Europe, *International Journal of Sociology*, 36(3), pp. 70–96.

Fukuyama, F. (1989). The End of History? *National Interest*, 16, pp. 3–18.

Fukuyama, F. (2006). America at the Crossroads: Democracy, Power, and the Neoconservative Legacy. New Haven, CT: Yale University Press.

Fukuyama, F. (2015). Why is Democracy Performing So Poorly? *Journal of Democracy*, 26(1), pp. 11–20.

Fung, A. (2003). Associations and Democracy: Between Theories, Hopes and Realities. *Annual Reviews of Sociology*, 29, pp. 515–539.

Galston, W. (2001). Political Knowledge, Political Engagement, and Civic Education. *Annual Review of Political Science*, 4 (2001): 217–234.

Garton, A. (1999). The Polish Revolution: Solidarity. New Haven, CT: Yale University Press.

Gellner, E. (1991). Civil Society in Historical Context. (Rethinking Democracy: Institutionalism, Majority versus Consensus, Civil Society, Religion, the Media). *International Social Science Journal*, 43(3), pp. 495–511.

George, C. (1950). *The Human Group*. New York: Harcourt, Brace and Company.

Gershman, C. (2017). Democracy Support: Global Challenges and the Importance of U.S. Leadership. In: A. Basora, A. Marczyk and M. Otarashvili, eds., *Does Democracy Matter? The United States and Global Democracy Support*. London: Rowman & Littlefield, pp. 1–6.

Gershman, C. and Allen, M. (2006). New Threats to Freedom: The Assault on Democracy Assistance. *Journal of Democracy*, 17(2), pp. 36–51.

Glasius, M. and Ishkanian, A. (2015). Surreptitious Symbiosis: The Relationship Between NGO's and Movement Activists. [online] *openDemocracy*. Available at: http://eprints.lse.ac.uk/id/eprint/63086 [accessed August 12, 2015].

Gleditsch, K. and Ward, M. (2006). Diffusion and the International Context of Democratization. *International Organization*, 60(4), pp. 911–933.

Glennerster, R. and Takavarasha, K. (2013). *Running Randomized Evaluations: A Practical Guide* Princeton, NJ: Princeton University Press.

Goldfarb, J. (2012). *Reinventing Political Culture*. Cambridge: Polity Press.

Goldsmith, A. (2001). Foreign Aid and Statehood in Africa. *International Organization*, 55(1), pp. 123–148.

Gräwingholt, J., Leininger, J. and Schlumberger, O. (2009). *The Three Cs of Democracy Promotion Policy: Context, Consistency and Credibility*. [online] DIE-GDI. Available at: www.die-gdi.de/en/briefing-paper/article/the-three-cs-of-democracy-promotion-policy-context-consistency-and-credibility/ [accessed January 2009].

Gray, J. (1995). *Liberalism*. London: Open University Press.

Green, A. and Kohl, R. (2007). Challenges of Evaluating Democracy Assistance: Perspectives from the Donor Side. *Democratization*, 14(1), pp. 151–165.

Grimm, S. and Leininger, J. (2012). Not All Good Things Go Together: Conflicting Objectives in Democracy Promotion. *Democratization*, 19(3), pp. 391–414.

Grugel, J. (1999). *Democracy Without Borders: Transnationalization and Conditionality in New Democracies*. London: Routledge.

Guasti, P. (2007). Development of Citizen Participation in Central and Eastern Europe after the EU Enlargement and Economic Crises. *Communist and Post-Communist Studies*, 49(3), pp. 219–231.

Gulrajani, N. (2014). Organising for Donor Effectiveness: An Analytical Framework for Improving Aid Effectiveness. *Development Policy Review*, 32(1), pp. 89–112.

Gvozdanović, A. (2016). Determinants of Young People's Readiness for Elite-Challenging Activities in Croatia. *East European Politics*, 32(1), pp. 28–45.

Hadenius, A. and Uggla, F. (1998). Shaping Civil Society. In: A. Bernard, H. Helmich and P. Lehning, eds., *Civil Society and International Development*. Paris: North-South Centre of the Council of Europe and Development Centre Studies of the Organization for Economic Co-operation and Development, pp. 43–56.

Haerpfer, C., Bernhagen, P., Inglehart, R. and Welzel, C. (2009). *Democratization*. New York: Oxford University Press.

Hart, S. 2009. The "Problem" with Youth: Young People, Citizenship and the Community. *Citizenship Studies*, 13(6), pp. 641–657.

Hartay, E. (2017). Legal Aspects of Civil Society Organisations and Their Relation with Government: Hungary. In: T. van der Ploeg, W. van Veen, and C. Versteegh, eds., *Civil Society in Europe. Minimum Norms and Optimum Conditions of its Regulation*, 1st ed. New York: Cambridge University Press, pp. 418–444.

Havel, V. (1985). Power of Powerless. In: V. Havel and J. Keane, eds., *Power of Powerless: Citizens against the State in Central-Eastern Europe*. New York: M.E. Sharpe, pp. 23–96.

Havel, V. (1995). Democracy's Forgotten Dimension. *Journal of Democracy*, 6(2), pp. 3–10.

Hayes, B. and Bean, C. (1993). Political Efficacy: A Comparative Study of the United States, West Germany, Great Britain and Australia. *European Journal of Political Research*, 23(3), pp. 261–280.

Held, D. (2006). Models of Democracy, 3rd ed. Cambridge: Polity Press.

Henderson, S. (2000). Importing Civil Society: Foreign Aid and the Women's Movement in Russia. *Demokratizatsiya*, 8(1), pp. 65–82.

Henderson, Sarah H. (2002). Selling Civil Society: Western Aid and the Non-governmental Organization Sector in Russia. *Comparative Political Studies* March, 35, pp. 139–167.

Henderson, S. (2003). *Building Democracy in Contemporary Russia: Western Support for Grassroots Organizations*. Ithaca, NY: Cornell University Press.

Hensby, A. (2017). *Participation and Non-Participation in Student Activism*. London: Rowman & Littlefield International.

Hernandez, E. (2016). Europeans' Views of Democracy: The Core Elements of Democracy. In M. Ferrin and H. Kriesi, eds., *How European View and Evaluate Democracy*. Oxford: Oxford University Press, pp. 43–63.

Himmelmann, G. (2013). Competences for Teaching, Learning and Living Democratic Citizenship. In: M. Print and D. Lange, eds., *Civic Education and Competences for Engaging Citizens in Democracies*. Rotterdam, Boston and Taipei: Sense Publishers, pp. 3–8.

Hinshaw, D. (2017). *Polish Nationalist Youth March Draws Thousands in Capital: Crowd of Mostly Young People Carries Banners that Read "Europe Will Be White" and "Clean Blood."* [online] The Wall Street Journal). Available at: www.wsj.com/articles/polish-nationalist-youth-march-draws-thousands-in-capital-1510429006?mod=e2tw [accessed November 11, 2017].

Hobson, C. and Kurki, M. (2012). *The Conceptual Politics of Democracy Promotion*. London and New York: Routledge.

Holzer, J. and Mareš, M. (2016). *Routledge Advances in European Politics. Challenges to Democracies in East Central Europe*. Abingdon and New York: Routledge.

Homans, G. (1950). *The Human Group*. New York: Harcourt, Brace.

Honwana, A. (2013). *Youth and Revolution in Tunisia*. London: Zed Books.

Hooghe, M. and Boonen, J. (2016). Youth Engagement in Politics. Generational Differences and Participation Inequalities. In: P. Thijssen, J. Siongers, J. Laer, J. Haers and S. Mels, eds., *Political Engagement of the Young in Europe: Youth in the Crucible*, Abingdon and New York: Routledge, pp. 13–28.

Hooghe, M. and Dejaeghere, Y. (2007). Does the "Monitorial Citizen" Exist? An Empirical Investigation into the Occurrence of Postmodern Forms of Citizenship in the Nordic countries. *Scandinavian Political Studies*, 30(2), pp. 249–271.

Hooghe, M. and Marien, S. (2012). How to Reach Members of Parliament? Citizens and Members of Parliament on the Effectiveness of Political Participation Repertoires. *Parliamentary Affairs*, 66, pp. 536–560.

Hooghe, M., Oser, J. and Marien, S. (2016). A Comparative Analysis of "Good citizenship": A Latent Class Analysis of Adolescents' Citizenship Norms in 38 Countries. *International Political Science Review*, 37(1), pp. 115–129.

Hooghe, M. and E. Quintelier. (2013). Political Participation in European Countries: The Effect of Authoritarian Rule, Corruption, Lack of Good Governance and Economic Downturn. *Comparative European Politics*, 12(2), pp. 209–232.

Horký-Hlucháň, O. (2012). The Transfer of the Central and Eastern European 'Transition Experience' to the South: Myth or Reality? *Perspectives on European Politics and Society*, 13(1), pp. 17–32.

Horký-Hlucháň, O. and Lightfoot, S. (2013). *Development Policies of Central and Eastern European States from Aid Recipients to Aid Donors*. London and New York: Routledge.

Horowitz, E., Wanstrom, J. and Parker, K. (2003). Inside or Outside of Democracy? Political Socialization of Adolescents Within the Culture of Poverty. In: *The Annual Conference of the Association for Education in Journalism and Mass Communication*. Kansas City.

Hoskins, B. (2006). *A Framework for the Creation of Indicators on Active Citizenship and Education and Training for Active Citizenship*. Ispra: Joint Research Centre.

Howard, M. (2002). The Weakness of Post-communist Civil Society. *Journal of Democracy* 13(1), pp. 157–169.

Howard, M. (2003). *The Weakness of Civil Society in Post-Communist Europe*. Cambridge: Cambridge University Press.

Howell, J. and Lind, J. (2009). *Counter-Terrorism, Aid and Civil Society. Before and After the War on Terror*. Basingstoke: Palgrave Macmillian.

Howell, J. and Pearce, J. (2001). *Civil Society and Development: A Critical Exploration.* Boulder, CO: Lynne Rienner.

Huntington, S. (1991). *The Third Wave: Democratization in the Late Twentieth Century.* Norman: University of Oklahoma Press.

Hurrell, A. (2002). Norms and Ethics in International Relations. In: W. Carlsnaes, T. Risse and B. Simmons, eds., *Handbook of International Relations*, 1st ed. Trowbridge: Cromwell Press, pp. 119–136.

Hyde, S. (2010). Experimenting in Democracy Promotion: International Observers and the 2004 Presidential Elections in Indonesia. *Perspectives on Politics*, 8, pp. 511–527.

Hyde, S. (2015). Experiments in International Relations: Lab, Survey, and Field. *Annual Review of Political Science*, 18, pp. 403–424.

Ilon, L. (1998). Can NGOs Provide Alternative Development in a Market-Based System of Global Economics? *Current Issues in Comparative Education*, 1(1), pp. 42–45.

Inglehart, R. (1990). *Culture Shift in Advanced Industrial Society.* Princeton, NJ: Princeton University Press.

Inglehart, R. (1997). *Modernization and Postmodernization Cultural, Economic, and Political Change in 43 Societies.* Princeton, NJ: Princeton University Press.

Inglehart, R. (1999). Postmodernization Erodes Respect for Authority but Increases Support for Democracy. In: P. Norris, ed., *Critical Citizens: Global Support for Democratic Government*, 1st ed. Oxford: Oxford University Press, pp. 236–256.

Inglehart, R. (2003). How Sold is Mass Support for Democracy: And How Can We Measure It? *Political Science and Politics*, 36(1), pp. 51–57.

Inglehart, R. and Baker, W. (2000). Modernization, Cultural Change, and the Persistence of Traditional Values. *American Sociological Review*, 65(1), pp. 19–51.

Inglehart, R. and Catterberg, G. (2002). Trends in Political Action: The Developmental Trend and the Post-honeymoon Decline. *International Journal of Comparative Sociology*, 43(3–5), pp. 300–316.

Inglehart, R. and Norris, P. (2003a). *Rising Tide: Gender Equality and Cultural Change Around the World.* New York and Cambridge: Cambridge University Press

Inglehart, R. and Norris, P. (2003b). The True Clash of Civilizations. *Foreign Policy*, 135, pp. 62–70.

Inglehart, R. and Welzel, C. (2003). Political Culture and Democracy: Analyzing Cross-Level Linkages. *Comparative Politics*, 36(1), pp. 61–79.

Inglehart, R. and Welzel, C. (2005). *Modernization, Cultural Change, and Democracy: The Human Development Sequence*. New York: Cambridge University Press.

Inglehart, R. and Welzel, C. (2009). How Development Leads to Democracy: What We Know About Modernization Today? *Foreign Affairs*, 88(2), pp. 33–48.

Jacobsson, K. and Korolczuk, E. (2017). *Civil Society Revisited. Lessons from Poland.* New York and Oxford: Berghahn Books.

Jacoby, W. (2006). Inspiration, Coalition, and Substitution: External Influences on Post-communist Transformations. *World Politics*, 58(4), pp. 623–651.

Jahn, B. (2012). Liberalism and Democracy Promotion. In: C Hobson and M. Kurki, eds., Conceptual Politics of Democracy Promotion. London: Routledge, pp. 53–67.

Jahn, D. (2006). Globalization as "Galton's Problem": The Missing Link in the Analysis of Diffusion Patterns in Welfare State Development. *International Organization*, 60(2), pp. 401–431.

James, E. (1989a). *The Nonprofit Sector in International Perspective: Studies in Comparative Culture and Policy.* New York: Oxford University Press.

James, E. (1989b). The Private Provision of Public Services: A Comparison of Sweden and Holland. In: E. James, ed., *The Nonprofit Sector in International Perspective: Studies in Comparative Culture and Policy*. New York: Oxford University Press, pp. 31–60.

Janiszewska, J. and Michałowski, J. (2010). *Region in Transition*. Warsaw: Fundacja Edukacja dla Demokracji.

Jarábik, B. (2006). International Democracy Assistance to Belarus: An Effective Tool? In: J. Forbrig, D. Marples and P. Demeš, eds., *Prospects for Democracy in Belarus*. Washington, DC: The German Marshall Fund of the United States and Heinrich Boll Stiftung.

Kalyvitis, S. and Vlachaki, I. (2012). When Does More Aid Imply Less Democracy? An Empirical Examination. *European Journal of Political Economy*, 28(1), pp. 132–146.

Kandelaki, G. and Meladze, G. (2007). Enough! Kmara and The Rose Revolution in Georgia. In: J. Forbrig and P. Demeš, eds., *Reclaiming Democracy. Civil Society and Electoral Change in Central and Eastern Europe*, 1st ed. Washington, DC: The German Marshall Fund of the United States, pp. 101–126.

Karatnycky, A. (2005). Ukraine's Orange Revolution. *Foreign Affairs*, 84(2), pp. 35–52.

Karnst, M. and Mingst, K. (2010). *International Organizations: The Politics and Processes of Global Governance*. Boulder, CO: Lynne Rienner.

Karolewski, I. (2016). Protest and Participation in Post-transformation Poland: The case of the Committee for the Defense of Democracy (KOD). *Communist and Post-Communist Studies*, 49(3), pp. 255–267.

Karumidze, Z. and Wertsch, J. (2005). *Enough: The Rose Revolution in the Republic of Georgia 2003*. New York: Nova Science Publications.

Kaskiv, V., Chupryna, I. and Zolotariov, Y. (2007). It's Time! Pora and The Orange Revolution in Ukraine. In: J. Forbrig and P. Demeš, eds., *Reclaiming Democracy. Civil Society and Electoral Change in Central and Eastern Europe*, 1st ed. Washington, DC: The German Marshall Fund of the United States, pp. 127–154.

Keane, J. (1997). *Civil Society and the State*. London: Verso Books.

Keck, M. and Sikkink, K. (1998). *Activists Beyond Borders: Advocacy Networks in Inter-National politics*. Ithaca, NY: Cornell University Press.

Keohane, R. and Nye Jr., J. (1998). Power and Interdependence in the Information Age. *Foreign Affairs*, 77(5), pp. 81–94.

Keohane, R. and Nye Jr., J. (2000). Globalization: What's New? What's Not? (and So What?). *Foreign Policy*, 118(Spring), pp. 104–119.

Kieżun W. (2011). *Patologia transformacji*. Warszawa: Wydawnictwo Poltext.

Kim, D. (2016). The Rise of European Right Radicalism: The Case of Jobbik" *Communist and Post-Communist Studies*, 49(4), pp. 345–357.

Kirbiš, A. (2013). Political Participation and Non-democratic Political Culture in Western Europe, East-Central Europe and Post-Yugoslav Countries. In: K. Demetriou ed., *Democracy in Transition Political Participation in the European Union*, 1st ed. Berlin and Heidelberg: Springer, pp. 225–251.

Kitschelt, H. (1994). *The Transformation of European Social Democracy*. New York: Cambridge University Press.

Klingemann, H. (1999). Mapping Political Support in the 1990s: A Global Analysis. In: P. Norris, ed., *Critical Citizens: Global Support for Democratic Governance*, 1st ed. Oxford: Oxford University Press.

Klingemann, H., Fuchs, D. and Zielonka, J. (2014). Dissatisfied Democrats. Democratic Maturation in Old and New Democracies. In: R. Dalton and C. Welzel, eds., *Civic*

Culture Transformed: From Allegiant to Assertive Citizens, reprint ed. New York: Cambridge University Press, pp. 116–172.

Klotz, A. (1995). Norms Reconstituting Interests: Global Racial Equality and U.S. Sanctions against South Africa. *International Organization*, 49(3), pp. 451–478.

Kluknavska, A. and Smolík, J. (2016). We Hate Them All? Issue Adaptation of Extreme Right Parties in Slovakia 1993–2016. *Communist and Post-Communist Studies*, 49(4), pp. 335–344.

Knack, S. (2004). Does Foreign Aid Promote Democracy? *International Studies Quarterly*, 48(1), pp. 251–266.

Knack, S. and Keefer, P. (1997). Does Social Capital Have an Economic Payoff? A Cross-Country Investigation. *The Quarterly Journal of Economics*, 112(4), pp. 1251–1288.

Kokot, M. (2017a). *Nowe "narodowe konsultacje" rządu Viktora Orbana. Wrogiem publicznym po raz kolejny George Soros (New "national consultations" of Viktor Orban's government. A Public Enemy One Again George Soros)*. [online] Wyborcza. Available at: http://wyborcza.pl/7,75399,22444658,nowe-narodowe-konsultacje-rzadu-viktora-orbana-wrogiem-publicznym.html [accessed September 30, 2017].

Kokot, M. (2017b). *Orban jak Putin. Bierze się za organizacje pozarządowe (Orban like Putin. Attacks Non-governmental Organizations)*. [online] Wyborcza. Available at: http://wyborcza.pl/7,75399,21658682,orban-jak-putin-bierze-sie-za-organizacje-pozarzadowe.html [accessed April 19, 2017].

Kokot, M. (2017c). *Orbán Hits Non-governmental Organizations. They Will Have to Explain the Adoption of Foreign Subsidies—as in Russia*. [online] Wyborcza. Available at: http://wyborcza.pl/7,75399,21980175,orban-uderza-w-organizacje-pozarzadowe-beda-musialy-tlumaczyc.html [accessed June 19, 2017].

Kokot, M. and Kośmiński, P. (2017c). *Orbán przykręca śrubę aktywnym obywatelom (Orbán Limits the Freedom of Active Citizens)*. [online] Wyborcza. Available at: http://wyborcza.pl/7,75399,22325134,orban-przykreca-srube-aktywnym-obywatelom.html [accessed September 5, 2017].

Kopecky, P. and Mudde, C. (2003). *Uncivil Society Contentious Politics in Post-Communist Europe*. London and New York: Routledge.

Kopstein, J. and Reilly, D. (2000). Geographic Diffusion and the Transformation of the Post-Communist World. *World Politics*, 53(1), pp. 1–37.

Kořan, M. (2017). Democratic Reset. In: A. Basora, A. Marczyk, and M. Otarashvili, eds., *Does Democracy Matter? The United States and Global Democracy Support*, 1st ed. Lanham, MD: Rowman & Littlefield, pp. 101–118.

kormany.hu, (2016). *Hungary is a Member of the OECD Development Assistance Committee*. [online] Website of the Hungarian Government, State Secretary for Security Policy and International Cooperation. Available at: www.kormany.hu/hu/kulgazdasagi-es-kulugyminiszterium/biztonsagpolitikai-es-nemzetkozi-egyuttmukodesert-felelos-allamtitkar/hirek/magyarorszag-az-oecd-fejlesztestamogatasi-bizottsag-tagja-lett [accessed December 6, 2016].

Kornai, J. (2015). Hungary's U-turn: Retreating from Democracy. *Journal of Democracy*, 26(3), pp. 34–48.

Kostelka, F. (2014). The State of Political Participation in Post-Communist Democracies: Low but Surprisingly Little Biased Citizen Engagement. *Europe-Asia Studies*, 66(6), pp. 945–968.

Kovacheva, S. (2005). Will Youth Rejuvenate the Patterns of Political Participation? In: *Revisiting Youth Political Participation: Challenges for Research and Democratic Practice in Europe*. Edited by Joerg Forbrig, Council of Europe: Council of Europe Publishing, pp. 19–29.

Kraemer, R. (2017). A Case for Democracy Assistance and Ways to Improve It. In: A. Basora, A. Marczyk and M. Otarashvili, eds., *Does Democracy Matter? The United States and Global Democracy Support*. Lanham, MD: Rowman & Littlefield Publishers, pp. 33–50.

Krajewska, A. and Makowski, G. (2017). Law Regarding Civil Society in Poland. In: T. van der Ploeg, W. van Veen, and C. Versteegh, *Civil Society in Europe: Minimum Norms and Optimum Conditions of its Regulation*, 1st ed. Cambridge: Cambridge University Press, pp. 486–507.

Krastev, I. (2006). Democracy's "Doubles." *Journal of Democracy*, 17(2), pp. 52–62.

Krastev, I. (2007). The Strange Death of the Liberal Consensus. *Journal of Democracy*, 18(4), pp. 56–63.

Kratochwil, F. (1989). *Rules Norms and Decisions: On the Conditions of Practical and Legal Reasoning in International Relations and Domestic Affairs*. Cambridge: Cambridge University Press.

Kremer, M. (2003). Randomized Evaluations of Educational Programs in Developing Countries: Some Lessons. *The American Economic Review*, 93(2), pp. 102–106.

Kubik, J. (1994). *The Power of Symbols against the Symbols of Power: The Rise of Solidarity and the Fall of State Socialism in Poland*. University Park, PA: The Pennsylvania State University Press.

Kugiel, P. (2011). V4 Development Cooperation: Challenges and Prospects for Common Actions. *PISM Bulletin*, 102(319), pp. 602–603.

Kuleta-Hulboj, M. (2016). *The Global Citizen as an Agent of Change: Ideals of the Global Citizen in the Narratives of Polish NGO Employees (PDF Download Available)*. [online] ResearchGate. Available at: www.researchgate.net/publication/311971260_The_global_citizen_as_an_agent_of_change_Ideals_of_the_global_citizen_in_the_narratives_of_Polish_NGO_employees [accessed March 3, 2018].

Kumar, C. (2000). Transnational Network and Campaigns for Democracy. In A. Florini, ed., *The Third Force the Rise of Transnational Civil Society*, 1st ed. Tokyo: Japan Center for International Exchange and Washington, DC: The Carnegie Endowment for International Peace, pp. 115–143.

Kuzio, T. (2005). From Kuchma to Yushchenko: Ukraine's 2004 Elections and "Orange Revolution." *Problems of Post-Communism*, 52(2), pp. 29–44.

Kuzio, T. (2015). *Ukraine: Democratisation, Corruption and the New Russian Imperialism*. Santa Barbara, CA: Praeger.

Langran, I. and Birk, T. (2016). *Globalization and Global Citizenship: Interdisciplinary Approaches*. London and New York: Routledge.

Lawy, R. and Biesta, G. (2009). *Citizenship Learning and Democracy in the Lives of Young People*. In: *Adult Education Research Conference*. Halifax: New Prairie Press. Available at: http://newprairiepress.org/cgi/viewcontent.cgi?article=2568&context=aerc.

Legro, J. (1997). Which Norms Matter? Revisiting the "Failure" of Internationalism, *International Organization*, 51(1), pp. 31–63.

Leighley, J. (1990). Social Interaction and Contextual Influences on Political Participation. *American Politics Quarterly*, 18, pp. 459–475.

Levitsky, S. and Way, L. (2002). The Rise of Competitive Authoritarianism. *Journal of Democracy* 13(2): 51–65.

Levitsky, S. and Way, L. (2010). *Competitive Authoritarianism: Hybrid Regimes after the Cold War*. New York: Cambridge University Press.

Levitsky, S. and Way, L. (2015). The Myth of Democratic Recession. *Journal of Democracy*, 26(1), pp. 45–58.

Lewis, D. (2010). Political Ideologies and Non-governmental Organizations: An Anthropological Perspective. *Journal of Political Ideologies*, 15, pp. 333–345.

Lewis, J. (2005). New Labour's Approach to the Voluntary Sector: Independence and the Meaning of Partnership', *Social Policy and Society*, 4(2), pp. 121–133.

Licht, A. (2010). Coming Into Money: The Impact of Foreign Aid on Leader Tenure. *Journal of Conflict Resolution*, 54(1), pp. 58–87.

Lijphart, A. (1999). *Patterns of Democracy: Government Forms and Performance in Thirty-Six Countries*. New Haven, CT and London: Yale University Press.

Lin, N. (1982). Social Resources and Instrumental Action. In: P. Marsden and N. Lin, eds., *Social Structure and Network Analysis*, 1st ed. Beverly Hills, CA: Sage, pp. 131–145.

Lin, N. (2001) *Social Capital: A Theory of Structure and Action*. London and New York: Cambridge University Press.

Linde, J. and Ekman, J. (2003). Satisfaction with Democracy: A Note on a Frequently Used Indicator in Comparative Politics. *European Journal of Political Research*, 51(3), pp. 410–434.

Linz, J. and Stepan, A. (1996). *Problems of Democratic Transition and Consolidation: Southern Europe, South America, and Post-Communist Europe*. Baltimore, MD: Johns Hopkins University Press.

Lipschutz, R. (1992). Reconstructing World Politics: The Emergence of Global Civil Society. *Millennium: Journal of International Studies*, 21(3), pp. 389–420.

Lipset, S. (1995). Introduction. In S. Lipset, ed., *The Encyclopedia of Democracy: Vol. 1*. London: Routledge.

Lührmann, A., McMann, K. and Van Ham, C. (2017). The Effectiveness of Democracy Aid to Different Regime Types and Democracy Sectors. *V-Dem Working Paper*, 40.

Lutsevych, O. (2013). *How to Finish a Revolution: Civil Society and Democracy in Georgia, Moldova and Ukraine*. London: Chatham House.

Madon, S. (1999). International NGOs: Networking, Information Flows and Learning. *Journal of Strategic Information Systems*, 8(3), pp. 251–261.

Magen, A. and Morlino, L. (2009a). Hybrid Regimes, The Rule of Law, and External Influence on Domestic Change. In: A. Magen and L. Morlino, eds., *International Actors, Democratization and the Rule of Law: Anchoring Democracy?*, 1st ed. Abingdon: Routledge.

Magen, A. and Morlino, L. (2009b). *International Actors, Democratization and the Rule of Law: Anchoring Democracy?* Abingdon: Routledge.

Malak-Minkiewicz, B. (2007). Civic Education in Times of Change: The Post-Communist Countries. *Citizenship Teaching and Learning Special Issue: Reflections on the IEA Civic Education Study (1995–2005)*, 3(2), pp. 58–70.

Mannheim, K. (1952). The Problem of Generations—(1927/28). In: P. Kecskemeti, ed., *Karl Mannheim: Essays*. London: Routledge.

Manning, N. and Edwards, K. (2014). Why Has Civic Education Failed to Increase Young People's Political Participation? *Sociological Research Online*, 19(1), pp. 1–12.

Marat, E. (2006). *The Tulip Revolution. Kyrgyzstan One Year after*. Washington, DC: The Jamestown Foundation.

Marchenko, A. (2016). Civic Activities in Eastern Europe: Links with Democratic Political Culture. *East European Politics*, 32(1), pp. 12–27.

Marczyk, A. (2017). Academic Conclusions Working Hypotheses and Areas for Further Research. In: A. Basora, A. Marczyk and M. Otarashvili, eds., *Does Democracy Matter? The United States and Global Democracy Support*. Lanham, MD: Rowman & Littlefield, pp. 135–174.

Mariyasin, D. (2013). *New EU Donors and the Western Balkans: Sharing Knowledge and Experience for Development. 10 Years of Slovak Aid. A Vision of Development Cooperation for a Changing World.* Bratislava: Pontis Foundation.
Maroshek-Klarman, U. (1996). *There Is No Such Thing as a Little Democracy. About Education to Democracy and Democracy in the School System [Nie ma czegoś takiego jak trochę demokracji. O kszałceniu ku demokracji i o demokracji w systemie oświaty]* Warsaw: Foundation for Education for Democracy.
Martens, A. and Gainous, J. (2012). Civic Education and Democratic Capacity: How Do Teachers Teach and What Works? *Social Science Quarterly*, 94(4), pp. 956–976.
Mathews, J. (1997). Power Shift. *Foreign Affairs*, 76(1), 50–66.
Matus, M. (2011). Aid Watch Report: Polish Development Cooperation 2010. Warsaw: Studio Oktopus.
McAdam, D. (1986). Recruitment to High-Risk Activism: The Case of Freedom Summer. *American Journal of Sociology*, 92(1), 64–90.
McAdam, D. (1998). On the International Origins of Domestic Political Opportunities. In: A. Contstain and A. McFarland, eds., *Social Movements and American Political Institutions*. Lanham, MD: Rowman & Littlefield Publishers, pp. 251–268.
McAdam, D. and Paulsen, R. (1993). Specifying the Relationship between Social Ties and Activism. *American Journal of Sociology*, 99(3), pp. 640–667.
McAdam, D. and Snow, D. (1996). *Social Movements: Readings on Their Emergence, Mobilization and Dynamics*. Los Angeles, CA: Roxbury Press.
McClurg, S. (2003). Social Networks and Political Participation: The Role of Social Interaction in Explaining Political Participation. *Political Research Quarterly*, 56(4), pp. 449–464.
McFaul, M. (2002). The Fourth Wave of Democracy and Dictatorship: Noncooperative Transitions in the Post-communist World. *World Politics*, 54(2), pp. 212–244.
McFaul, M. (2005). Transitions from Post-Communism. *Journal of Democracy*, 16(3), pp. 5–19.
McFaul, M. (2010). *Advancing Democracy Abroad. Why We Should and How We Can.* Lanham, MD: Rowman & Littlefield.
McLeod, J. (2000). Media and Civic Socialization of Youth. *Journal of Adolescent Health*, 27(2), Supplement 1, pp. 45–51.
McMahon, P. (2000). Building Civil Societies in East Central Europe: The Effect of American Non-governmental Organizations on Women's Groups. In: P. Burnell, ed., *Civil Society in Democratization, Democracy Assistance: International Co-operation for Democratization*, 1st ed. London: Frank Cass Co. Ltd.
McMahon, P. (2002). International Actors and Women's NGOs in Poland and Hungary. In: S. Mendelson and J. Glenn, eds., *The Power and Limits of NGOs: A Critical Look at Building Democracy in Eastern Europe and Eurasia.* New York: Columbia University Press.
McMahon, P. (2004). Building Civil Societies in East Central Europe: The Effect of American Non-governmental Organizations on Women's Groups. In: P. Burnell and P. Calvert, eds., *Civil Society in Democratization*, London: Routledge.
Mendelson, S. (2001). Democracy Assistance and Political Transition in Russia. *International Security*, 25(4), pp. 68–106.
Mendelson, S. (2015). *Why Governments Target Civil Society and What Can Be Done in Response: A New Agenda.* Washington, DC: Center for Strategic and International Studies.
Mendelson, S. and Glenn, J. (2002). *The Power and Limits of NGOs A Critical Look at Building Democracy in Eastern Europe and Eurasia*. New York: Columbia University Press.

Mitilin, D. (1998). The NGOs Sector and its Role in Strengthening Civil Society and Securing Good Governance. In: A. Bernard, H. Helmich and P. Lehning, eds., *Civil Society and International Development*. Paris: North-South Centre of the Council of Europe and Development Centre Studies of the Organization for Economic Co-operation and Development.

Moller, J. and Skaaning, S. (2013). Regime Types and Democratic Sequencing. *Journal of Democracy*, 24(1), pp. 142–156.

Morgan, W. and Streb, M. (2001). Building Citizenship: How Student Voice in Service-learning Develops Civic Values. *Social Science Quarterly*, 82(1), pp. 154–169.

Morrison, K. (2007). Natural Resources, Aid, and Democratization: A Best-Case Scenario. *Public Choice*, 131, pp. 365–386.

Mortensen, A., Sterling, J. and Dewan, A. (2017). Poles Outraged over Controversial Bill Take to the Streets. [online] CNN. Available at: https://edition.cnn.com/2017/07/23/europe/poland-judicial-bill-protests/index.html [accessed July 23, 2017].

Morton, R. and Williams, K. (2006). Experimentation in Political Science. In: Box-Steffensmeier, J., Collier, D. and Brady, H., eds., *The Oxford Handbook of Political Methodology*. Oxford: Oxford University Press, pp. 339–358.

Morton, R. and Williams, K. (2008). Experimentation in Political Science. In: J. Box-Steffensmeier, H. Brady and D. Collier, eds., *The Oxford Handbook of Political Methodology*, New York: Oxford University Press.

Mudde, C. (2004). The Populist Zeitgeist. *Government and Opposition*, 39(4) pp. 542–563.

Mudde, C. (2007). Civil Society. In: S. White, J. Batt and P. Lewis, eds., *Development in Central and East European Politics*, 4th ed. Durham, NC: Duke University Press and Basingstoke: Palgrave Macmillan, pp. 213–228.

Mudde, C. (2016). Europe's Populist Surge: A Long Time in the Making. *Foreign Affairs*, 95(6), pp. 25–30.

Mulderig, C. (2013). *An Uncertain Future. Youth Frustration and the Arab Spring*. Boston, MA: Boston University Creative Services.

Munck, G. and Verkuilen, J. (2002). Conceptualizing and Measuring Democracy–Evaluating Alternative Indices. *Comparative Political Studies*, 35(1), pp. 5–34.

Mvukiyehe, E. and Samii, C. (2017). Promoting Democracy in Fragile States: Field Experimental Evidence from Liberia. *World Development*, 95, pp. 254–267.

Mycock, A. and Tonge, J. (2014). *Beyond the Youth Citizenship Commission: Young People and Politics*. London: Political Studies Association.

Nadelmann, E. (1990). Global Prohibition Regimes: The Evolution of Norms in International Society. *International Organization*, 44(4), pp. 479–526.

Narozhna, T. (2004). Foreign Aid for a Post-euphoric Eastern Europe: The Limitations of Western Assistance in Developing Civil Society. *Journal of International Relations and Development*, 7(3), pp. 243–266.

National Research Council of the National Academies. (2008). *Improving Democracy Assistance: Building Knowledge through Evaluations and Research*. Washington, DC: National Research Council of the National Academies.

Newton, K. (1999). Social and Political Trust. In: P. Norris, ed., *Critical Citizens: Global Support for Democratic Government*. Oxford: Oxford University Press.

Newton, K. (2001). Trust, Social Capital, Civil Society, and Democracy. *International Political Science Review*, 22(2), pp. 201–214.

Newton, K. and Norris, P. (2000). Confidence in Public Institutions: Faith, Culture, or Performance. In: S. Pharr and R. Putnam, eds., *Disaffected Democracies. What's Troubling the Trilateral Countries?*, 1st ed. Princeton, NJ: Princeton University Press, pp. 52–73.

Nicholls, A. (2006). *Social Entrepreneurship: New Models of Sustainable Social Change*. New York: Oxford University Press.

Nielsen, N. (2017). *Hungary Rejects Criticism of NGO Crackdown*. [online] EUObserver. Available at: https://euobserver.com/migration/137046 [accessed February 27, 2017].

Nieuwelink, H., ten Dam, G. Geijsel, F. and Dekker, P. (2017). Growing into Politics? The Development of Adolescents' Views on Democracy Over Time. *Politics*, DOI: 10.1177/0263395717724295.

Norris, P. (2002). *Democratic Phoenix: Reinventing Political Activism*. Cambridge: Cambridge University Press.

Norris, P. (2011). *Democratic Deficit: Critical Citizens Revisited*. Cambridge and New York: Cambridge University Press.

Norris, P. (2017). *Strengthening Electoral Integrity: The Pragmatic Case for Electoral Assistance*. New York: Cambridge University Press.

Obydenkova, A. and Libman, A. (2015). *Autocratic and Democratic External Influences in Post-Soviet Eurasia*. London and New York: Routledge.

Ociepka, Beata. (2014). Public Diplomacy in the European Union: Models for Poland,. PISM Policy Paper, no 5 (88). [online] www.pism.pl/Publications/PISM-Policy-Paper-no-88 [accessed May 5, 2018]

O'Donnell, G. (1994). Delegative Democracy. *Journal of Democracy*, 5, pp. 55–69.

O'Donnell, G. (2007a). *Dissonances: Democratic Critiques of Democracy*. Notre Dame, IN: University of Notre Dame Press.

O'Donnell, G. (2007b). The Perpetual Crises of Democracy. *Journal of Democracy* 18(1): 5–11.

O'Donnell, G. and Schmitter, P. (1986). *Transitions from Authoritarian Rule: Tentative Conclusions about Uncertain Democracies*. Baltimore, MD: Johns Hopkins University Press.

Ofer, I. and Grove, T. (2016). *Performing Citizenship: Social Movements across the Globe*. Abingdon and New York: Routledge.

Ogris, G. and Westphal, S. (2005). *Political Participation of Young People in Europe—Development of Indicators for Comparative Research in the European Union (EUYOUPART). Deliverable 17: Final Comparative Report*. Vienna: Institute for Social Research and Analysis.

Oliver, P. and Myers, D. (2003). Networks, Diffusion, and Cycles of Collective Action. In: M. Diani and D. McAdam, eds., *Social Movements and Networks: Relational Approaches to Collective Action*, 1st ed. Oxford: Oxford University Press, pp. 173–202.

Olken, B. (2007a). Monitoring Corruption: Evidence from a Field Experiment in Indonesia. *Journal of Political Economy*, 115(2), pp. 200–249.

Olken, B. (2007b). *Political Institutions and Local Public Goods: Evidence from a Field Experiment*. Cambridge, MA; Harvard University.

O'Loughlin, J., Ward, M., Lofdahl, C., Cohen, J., Brown, D., Reilly, D., Gleditsch, K. and Shin, M. (1998). The Diffusion of Democracy, 1946–1994. *Annals of the Association of American Geographers*, 88(4), pp. 545–574.

O'Loughlin, J., Ward, M., Lofdahl, C. and Shin, M. (2007). The Diffusion of Democracy, 1946–1994. *Annals of the Association of American Geographers*, 88(4), pp. 545–574.

Orłowski, M. (2017a). *Orbán chwali rząd PiS. "Podważanie praworządności w Polsce to jakaś inkwizycja" (Orbán Praises the PiS Government. "Undermining the Rule of Law in Poland is an inquisition")*. [online] Wyborcza. Available at: http://wyborcza.pl/7,75398,22410396,orban-chwali-rzad-pis-podwazanie-praworzadnosci-w-polsce-to.html [accessed September 22, 2017].

Osa, M. (2003). *Solidarity and Contention Networks of Polish Opposition*. Minneapolis: University of Minnesota Press.

Osler, A. (2012). Citizenship Education and Diversity. In: J. Banks, ed., *Encyclopedia of Diversity in Education Vol. 1*, 1st ed. London and Los Angeles, CA: Sage, pp. 353–361.

Ost, D. (2005). *The Defeat of Solidarity: Anger and Politics in Postcommunist Europe.* Ithaca, NY: Cornell University Press.

Ost, D. (2011). The Decline of Civil Society after 'Post-Communism.' In: U. Liebert and H. Trenz, eds., *The New Politics of European Civil Society*, 1st ed. Abingdon and New York: Routledge, pp. 163–177.

Otarashvili, M. (2014). Hunger for Power in Hungary? The Alarming nature of Viktor Orbán's New "Manifesto." [online] Foreign Policy Research Institute. 2014. Available at: www.fpri.org/2014/07/hunger-for-power-in-hungary-the-alarming-nature-of-viktor-orbans-new-manifesto/ [accessed September 10, 2014].

O'Toole, T. (2004). Explaining Young People's Non-participation: Towards a Fuller Understanding of the Political. *ECPR Joint Sessions*. Uppsala: Uppsala Universitet. Available at: https://ecpr.eu/Filestore/PaperProposal/83555710-2738-4ff3-8cf8-2fece39c9599.pdf.

Ottaway, M. (2003). *Democracy Challenged: The Rise of Semi-Authoritarianism.* Washington, DC: Carnegie Endowment for International Peace.

Ottaway, M. and Carothers, T. (2000). *Funding Virtue: Civil Society Aid and Democracy Promotion.* Washington, DC: Carnegie Endowment for International Peace.

Ottaway, M. and Chung, T. (1999). Debating Democracy Assistance: Toward a New Paradigm. *Journal of Democracy*, 10(4), pp. 9–113.

Oxley, L. and Morris, P. (2013). Global Citizenship: A Typology for Distinguishing its Multiple Conceptions. *British Journal of Educational Studies*, 61(3), pp. 301–325.

Panke, D. and Petersohn, (2012). Why International Norms Disappear Sometimes. *Journal of International Relations*, 18(4), pp. 601–624.

Paris, R. and Sisk, T. (2009). *The Dilemmas of Statebuilding: Confronting the Contradictions of Postwar Peace Operations*. London: Routledge.

Parsons, T. and Shils, E. (1951). *Toward a General Theory of Action.* Cambridge, MA: Harvard University Press.

Pateman, C. (1970). *Participation and Democratic Theory*. Cambridge: Cambridge University Press.

Patomaki, H. (2012). Democracy Promotion: Neoliberal vs Social Democratic Telos. In: C. Hobson and M. Kurki, eds., *The Conceptual Politics of Democracy Promotion*, 1st ed. Abingdon and New York: Routledge, pp. 85–99.

Pennington, M. (2010). *Robust Political Economy Classical Liberalism and the Future of Public Policy*. Cheltenham: Edward Elgar Publishing.

Pérez-Liñán, A., Finkel, S. and Seligson, M. (2016). Under What Conditions Does Democracy Assistance Work? In: *American Political Science Association Annual Meeting.* Philadelphia: APSA.

Petrova, T. (2014). *From Solidarity to Geopolitics: Support for Democracy among Postcommunist States*. Cambridge: Cambridge University Press.

Petrova, T. and Tarrow, S. (2007). Transactional and Participatory Activism in the Emerging European Polity: The Puzzle of East-Central Europe. *Comparative Political Studies*, 40(1), pp. 74–94.

Platter, M. (2015). Is Democracy in Decline? *Journal of Democracy*, 26(1), pp. 5–10.

Plattner, M. (2008). *Democracy without Borders? Global Challenges to Liberal Democracy.* Lanham, MD: Rowman and Littlefield.

Pleines, H. and Bušková, K. (2007). *Czech Environmental NGOS: Actors or Agents in EU Multilateral Governance*. Olomouc: Filozofická fakulta.

Pop-Eleches, G. and Tucker, J. (2013). Associated With the Past? Communist Legacies and Civic Participation in Post-communist Countries. *East European Politics and Societies*, 27(1), pp. 45–68.

Pospieszna, P. (2010). When Recipients Become Donors: Polish Democracy Assistance in Belarus and Ukraine. *Problems of Post-Communism*, 57(4), pp. 3–15.

Pospieszna, P. (2014). *Democracy Assistance from the Third Wave: Polish Engagement in Belarus and Ukraine*. Pittsburgh, PA: University of Pittsburgh Press.

Pospieszna, P. and Galus, A. (2018). Promoting Active Youth: Evidence from Polish NGO's Civic Education Program in Eastern Europe. *Journal of International Relations & Development*, DOI: 10.1057/s41268-018-0134-4.

Pridham, G. (1991). International Influences and Democratic Transition: Problems of Theory and Practice in Linkage Politics. In: G. Pridham, ed., *Encouraging Democracy: The International Context of Regime Transition in Southern Europe*. New York: St. Martin's Press, pp. 1–29.

Pridham, G. (2005). *Designing Democracy: EU Enlargement and Regime Change in Post-Communist Europe*. Basingstoke: Palgrave Macmillan.

Pridham, G. (2006). European Union Accession Dynamics and Democratization in Central and Eastern Europe: Past and Future Perspectives. *Government and Opposition*, 41(3), pp. 373–400.

Pridham, G., Herring, E. and Sanford, G. (1997). *Building Democracy? The International Dimension of Democratization in Eastern Europe*. London: Leicester University Press.

Print, M. (2013). Competences for Democratic Citizenship in Europe. In: M. Print and D. Lange, eds., *Civic Education and Competences for Engaging Citizens in Democracies*, 1st ed. Rotterdam, Boston, MA and Taipei: Sense Publishers, pp. 37–49.

Print, M. and Lange, D. (2012). *Schools, Curriculum and Civic Education for Building Democratic Citizens*. Rotterdam, Boston, MA and Taipei: Sense Publishers.

Puddington, A. (2016). Hungary Fought for Freedom. Now it's Content with Tyranny. [online] Foreign Policy. Available at: http://foreignpolicy.com/2016/10/27/hungary-fought-for-freedom-now-its-content-with-tyranny/ [accessed October 27, 2016].

Punyanunt-Carter, N. and Nance, H. (2014). Activists and Activism, Digital Activism. In H. Kerric, ed., *Encyclopedia of Social Media and Politics*. Thousand Oaks, CA: Sage Publications, pp. 2–11.

Putnam, Robert D. (1993) What Makes Democracy Work? *National Civic Review* 82(2), pp. 101–107.

Putnam, R. (1995). Bowling Alone: America's Declining Social Capital. *Journal of Democracy*, 6(1), pp. 65–78.

Putnam, R. (2000). *Bowling Alone: The Collapse and Revival of American Community*. New York: Simon & Schuster.

Putnam, R., Leonardi, R. and Nanetti, R. (1993). *Making Democracy Work: Civic Traditions in Modern Italy*. Princeton, PA: Princeton University Press.

Quigley, K. (1997). *For Democracy Sake: Foundations and Democracy Assistance in Central Europe*. Washington, DC: Woodrow Wilson Center Special Studies.

Quigley, K. (2000). Lofty Goals, Modest Results: Assisting Civil Society. In: M. Ottaway and T. Carothers, eds., *Funding Virtue: Civil Society and Democracy Promotion*. Washington, DC: Carnegie Endowment for International Peace.

Raik, K. (2006). Making Civil Society Support Central to EU Democracy Assistance. In: J. Forbrig, D. Marples and P. Demeš, eds., *Prospects for Democracy in Belarus*. Washington, DC: The German Marshall Fund of the United States and Heinrich Boll Stiftung.

Raiser, M. (2001). Informal Institutions, Social Capital, and Economic Transition: Reflections on a Neglected Dimension. In: G. Cornia and V. Popov, eds., *Transition and Institutions. The Experience of Gradual and Late Reformers*. New York: Oxford University Press, pp. 218–226.

Regulska, J. (1999). NGOs and Their Vulnerabilities During the Times of Transition: The Case of Poland. *International Journal of Voluntary and Non-profit Organizations*, 10(1), pp. 61–67.

Richter, J. (2002). Promoting Civil Society? Democracy Assistance and Russian Women's Organizations. *Problems of Post-Communism*, 48(1), pp. 30–41.

Rieff, D. (1999). *The False Dawn of Civil Society*. [online] The Nation. Available at: www.thenation.com/article/false-dawn-civil-society [accessed February 4, 1999].

Risse, T. (2000). "Let's Argue!": Communicative Action in World Politics. *International Organization*, 54(1), pp. 1–39.

Risse, T. (2004). Global Governance and Communicative Action. *Government and Opposition*, 39(2), pp. 288–313.

Risse, T., Ropp, S. and Sikkink, K. (1999). *The Power of Human Rights: International Norms and Domestic Change*. New York: Cambridge University Press.

Roberts, K. (2009). *Youth in Transition: Eastern Europe and the West*. Basingstoke and New York: Palgrave Macmillan.

Robinson, J., Shaver, P. and Wrightsman, L. (1999). *Measures of Social Psychological Attitudes, Vol. 2. Measures of Political Attitudes*. San Diego, CA: Academic Press.

Rogers, E. (1962). *Diffusion of Innovations*. New York: Free Press of Glencoe.

Rogers, E. (1995). *Diffusion of Innovations*, 4th ed. New York: Free Press.

Ronovská, K. and Vitoul, V. (2017). Legal Framework for Civil Society in the Czech Republic. In: T. van der Ploeg, W. van Veen and C. Versteegh, eds., *Civil Society in Europe. Minimum Norms and Optimum Conditions of its Regulation*, 1st ed. New York: Cambridge University Press, pp. 344–362.

Rosanvallon, P. (2008). *Counter-Democracy. Politics in an Age of Distrust*. Cambridge: Cambridge University Press.

Rose, R. (2001). A diverging Europe. *Journal of Democracy*, 12(1), pp. 93–106.

Rose, R. and Haerpfer, C. (1995). Democracy and Enlarging the European Union Eastwards. *Journal of Common Market Studies* 33(3), pp. 427–450.

Rose-Ackerman, S. (2007). *From Elections to Democracy: Building Accountable Government in Hungary and Poland.* New York: Cambridge University Press.

Rosenau, J. (1997). The Complexities and Contradiction of Globalization. *Current History*, 96(616), pp. 360–364.

Rosenstone, S. and Hansen, J. (1993). *Mobilization, Participation and Democracy in America*. New York: Macmillan.Rothbauer, P. (2008). Triangulation. In: L. Given, ed., *The SAGE Encyclopedia of Qualitative Research Methods*, 1st ed. Thousand Oaks, CA: Sage Publications, pp. 892–894.

Rucht, D. (2003). Social Movements Challenging Neo-liberal Globalization. In: P. Ibarra Güell, ed., *Social Movement and Democracy*, 1st ed. New York: Palgrave Macmillan, pp. 211–228.

Rupnik, J. (1979). Dissent in Poland 1968–78: The End of Revisionism and the Rebirth of the Civil Society. In R. Tökés, ed., *Opposition in Eastern Europe*, 1st ed. London and Basingstoke: Palgrave Macmillan, pp. 60–112.

Rupnik, J. and Zielonka, J. (2013). Introduction: The State of Democracy 20 Years On: Domestic and External Factors. *East European Politics and Societies*, 27(1), pp. 3–25.

Russell, C. (2011). *Collective Decision Making: Applications from Public Choice Theory*. London and New York: Routledge.

Rutzen, D. (2015). Authoritarianism Goes Global (II): Civil Society under Assault. *Journal of Democracy*, 26(4), pp. 28–39.

Ruzza, C. (2011). Identifying Uncivil Society in Europe: Towards a 'New Politics of the Enemy'? In: U. Liebert and H. Trenz, eds., *The New Politics of European Civil Society*, 1st ed. London and New York: Routledge, pp. 143–163.

Rydgren, J. (2005). Is Extreme Right-wing Populism Contagious? Explaining the Emergence of a New Party Family. *European Journal of Political Research*, 44(3), pp. 413–437.

Sartori, G. (1995). How Far Can Free Government Travel? *Journal of Democracy*, 6(3), pp. 101–111.

Schimmelfennig, F. (2007). European Regional Organization, Political Conditionality, and Democratic Transformation in Eastern Europe. *East European Politics and Societies*, 21(1), pp. 126–141.

Schimmelfennig, F., Engert, S. and Knobel, H. (2006). *International Socialization in Europe: European Organizations, Political Conditionality, and Democratic Change*. Basingstoke: Palgrave Macmillan.

Schleifer, Y. (2014). *Hungary at the Turning Point*. [online] Slate, Moment Magazine. Available at: www.slate.com/articles/news_and_politics/moment/2014/10/viktor_orban_s_authoritarian_rule_the_hungarian_prime_minister_is_destroying.html [accessed October 3, 2014].

Schmitter, P. (1986). An Introduction to Southern European Transitions from Authoritarian Rule: Italy, Greece, Portugal, Spain, and Turkey. In: G. O'Donnell, P. Schmitter and L. Whitehead, eds., *Transitions from Authoritarian Rule: Prospects for Democracy*, 1st ed. Baltimore, MD: Johns Hopkins University Press, pp. 3–46.

Schulz, W., Fraillon, J., Ainley, J., Losito, B. and Kerr, D. (2008). *International Civic and Citizenship Education Study. Assessment Framework*. Amsterdam: International Association for the Evaluation of Educational Achievement (IEA).

Schumpeter, J. (1952). *Capitalism, Socialism and Democracy*. New York: Harper Perennial Modern Classics.

Schumpeter, J. (1976). *Capitalism, Socialism and Democracy*. New York: Harper Perennial Modern Thought.

Sedelmeier, U. (2014). Anchoring Democracy from Above? The European Union and Democratic Backsliding in Hungary and Romania after Accession. *Journal of Common Market Studies*, 52(1), pp. 105–121.

Siegel, D. and Yancey, J. (1992). *The Rebirth of Civil Society*. New York: Rockefeller Brothers Fund, Inc.

Siegel, D. and Yancey, J. (1995). *The Rebirth of Civil Society: The Development of the Nonprofit Sector in East Central Europe and the Role of Western Assistance*. New York: The Rockefeller Fund.

Sikkink, K. (2016). "Human Rights." Why Govern? Rethinking Demand, Purpose and Progress. In: A. Acharya, ed., *Global Governance*, 1st ed. New York: Cambridge University Press, 121–137.

Silander, D. (2005). Democracy from the Outside-In? The Conceptualization and Significance of Democracy Promotion. *Acta Wexionensia*, 73.

Silitski, V. (2007). Different Authoritarianisms, Distinct Patters of Electoral Change. In: J. Forbrig and P. Demeš, eds., *Reclaiming Democracy. Civil Society and Electoral Change in Central and Eastern Europe*, 1st ed. Washington, DC: The German Marshall Fund of the United States, pp. 155–174.

Simmons, B., Dobbin, F. and Garrett, G. (2008). *The Global Diffusion of Markets and Democracy*. New York: Cambridge University Press.

Simon, Z. (2014). *Orbán Says He Seeks to End Liberal Democracy in Hungary*. [online] Bloomberg. Available at: www.bloomberg.com/news/articles/2014-07-28/orban-says-he-seeks-to-end-liberal-democracy-in-hungary [accessed July 28, 2014].

Simon, Z. (2017). *Hungary Plans to Crack down on All Soros-Funded NGOs*. [online] Bloomberg. Available at: www.bloomberg.com/news/articles/2017-01-10/trump-s-win-prompts-hungarian-call-for-crackdown-on-soros-groups [accessed January 10, 2017].

Skilling, H. (1981). *Charter 77 and Human Rights in Czechoslovakia* London: George Allen & Unwin.

Sklair, L. (1997). Social Movement for Global Capitalism: The Transnational Capitalist Class in Action. *Review of International Political Economy*, 4(3), pp. 514–538.

Smith, I. and Keri, E. (2013). *Sociology of Globalization: Cultures, Economics, and Politics*. Boulder, CO: Westview Press.

Smith, K. (2012). *Sociology of Globalization: Cultures, Economies, and Politics*, 1st ed. London and New York: Routledge.

Solhaug, T. (2013). Trends and Dilemmas in Citizenship Education. Nordidactica. *Journal of Humanities and Social Science Education*, (1), 180–200.

Sprinz, P. (2007). *Populism and Nationalism in the V4: Temporary Setback*. [online] Visegrád Group. Available at: www.visegradgroup.eu/students-section/populism-and [accessed March 24, 2018].

Stanowski, K. (2002). Z kart historii współpracy polskich organizacji pozarządowych w III RP a partnerami zagranicznymi. In: G. Czubek, ed., *Międzynarodowa działalność polskich organizacji pozarządowych*. Warsaw: Fundacja im. Stefana Batorego.

Starr, H. (1991). Democratic Dominoes: Diffusion Approaches to the Spread of Democracy in the International System. *Journal of Conflict Resolution*, 35(2), pp. 356–381.

Starr, H. and Lindborg, C. (2003). Democratic Dominoes Revisited. The Hazards of Governmental Transitions, 1974–1996. *Journal of Conflict Resolution*, 47(4), pp. 490–519.

Stiles, K. (2000). Grassroots Empowerment. States, Non-state Actors and Global Policy Formulation. In: R. Higgot, G. Underhill and A. Bieler, eds., *Non-State Actors and Authority in Global Systems*. London: Routledge, pp. 32–48.

Stolle, D., and Hooghe, M. (2005). Inaccurate, Exceptional, One-Sided or Irrelevant? The Debate about the Alleged Decline of Social Capital and Civic Engagement in Western Societies. *British Journal of Political Science*, 35, pp. 149–167.

Stolle, D. and Hooghe, M. (2010). Shifting Inequalities, *European Societies*, 13(1), pp. 119–142.

Stromquist, N. (2002). NGOS in A New Paradigm of Civil Society. *Current Issues in Comparative Education*, 1(1), pp. 62–67.

Sullivan, J. and Transue, J. (1999). The Psychological Underpinning of Democracy: A Selective Review of Research on Political tolerance, Interpersonal Trust and Social Capital. *Annual Review of Psychology*, 50, pp. 625–650.

Sundstrom, L. (2006). *Funding Civil Society: Foreign Assistance and NGO Development in Russia*. Stanford, CA: Stanford University Press.

Sundstrom, S. (2015). *Why Governments Target Civil Society and What Can Be Done in Response: A New Agenda*. [online] United Nations Human Rights. Office of the High Commissioner. Available at: www.ohchr.org/Documents/AboutUs/CivilSociety/ReportHC/67_CSIS-MendelsonGovTargetCivilSocietyNewAgenda-2.pdf [accessed April 2015].

Svensson, J. (2000). Foreign Aid and Rent-seeking. *Journal of International Economics*, 51, pp. 437–461.

Swindler, A. (1986). Culture in Action: Symbols and Strategies. *American Sociological Review*, 51(5), pp. 273–286.
Szent-Iványi, B. (2012). Aid Allocation of the Emerging Central and Eastern European Donors. *Journal of International Relations and Development*, 15(1), pp. 65–89.
Szent-Iványi, B. (2014). The EU's Support for Democratic Governance in the Eastern Neighbourhood: The Role of Transition Experience from the New Member States. *Europe-Asia Studies*, 66(7), pp. 1102–1121.
Szent-Iványi, B. and Lightfoot, S. (2016). Central and Eastern European Transition Experience: A Depoliticisation of Democracy Aid? In: B. Berti, K. Mikulova, and N. Popescu, eds., *Democratization in EU Foreign Policy. New Member States as Drivers of Democracy Promotion*, 1st ed. Abingdon: Routledge.
Szent-Iványi, B. and Végh, Z. (2018). Is Transition Experience Enough? The Donor-side Effectiveness of Czech and Polish Democracy Aid to Georgia, *Democratization*, 25(4), pp. 614–632.
Szurovecz, I. (2014). *Civil Funds Awarded to NGOs Close to Hungary's Governing Fidesz-KDNP alliance*. [online] Budapest Beacon. Available at: https://budapest beacon.com/civil-funds-awarded-to-ngos-close-to-hungarys-govering-fidesz-kdnp-alliance/) [accessed November 18, 2014].
Tamkin, E. (2017). *The Force behind the Thousands Protesting Corruption in Slovakia? Teenagers. The Slovak Kids are Alright*. [online] Foreign Policy. Available at: http://foreignpolicy.com/2017/04/19/the-force-behind-the-thousands-protesting-corruption-in-slovakia-teenagers/ [accessed April 19, 2017].
Tarrow, S. (1998). Fishnets, Internets, and Catnets: Globalization and Transnational Collective Action. In: M. Hanagan, L. Moch and W. te Brake, eds., *Challenging Authority. The Historical Study of Contentious Politics. Social Movements, Protest, and Contention Volume 7*, 1st ed. Minneapolis and London: University of Minnesota Press, pp. 228–244.
Tarrow, S. (2005). *The New Transnational Activism*. Cambridge: Cambridge University Press.
Tarrow, S. (2010). The Strategy of Paired Comparison: Toward a Theory of Practice. *Comparative Political Studies*, 43(2), pp. 230–259.
Tarrow, S. and della Porta, D. (2005). *Transnational Protest and Global Activism*. Lanham, MD: Rowman & Littlefield.
Teorell, J. (2003). Linking Social Capital to Political Participation: Voluntary Associations and Networks of Recruitment in Sweden. *Scandinavian Political Studies*, 26(1), pp. 49–66.
Teorell, J., Torcal, M. and Montero, J. (2007). Political Participation: Mapping the Terrain. In: J. van Deth, J. Montero, and A. Westholm, eds., *Citizenship and Involvement in European Democracies: A Comparative Analysis*, 1st ed. New York: Routledge, pp. 334–357.
Thijssen, P., Siongers, J., Laer, J., Haers, J. and Mels, S. (2016). *Political Engagement of the Young in Europe: Youth in the Crucible*. Abington and New York: Routledge.
Thompson, M. and Kuntz, P. (2004). Stolen Elections: The Case of the Serbian October. *Journal of Democracy*, 15(4), pp. 159–172.
Tilly, C. (2007). *Democracy*. New York: Cambridge University Press.
Tolstrup, J. (2014). External Influence and Democratization: Gatekeepers and Linkages. *Journal of Democracy*, 25(4), pp. 126–138.
Tomini, L. (2015). *Democratizing Central and Eastern Europe: Successes and Failures of the European Union*. London and New York: Routledge.

Torney-Purta, J. (2007). *Citizenship Teaching and Learning Special Issue: Reflections on the IEA Civic Education Study (1995–2005)*, 3(2): 1-4.

Torney-Purta, J., Lehman, R., Oswald, H. and Schultz, W. (2001). *Citizenship and Education in Twenty-eight Countries: Civic Knowledge and Engagement at Age Fourteen.* Amsterdam: International Association for the Evaluation of Educational Achievement.

Torney-Purta, J., Oppenheim, A. and Farnen, R. (1975). *Civic Education in Ten Countries: An Empirical Study*. Oxford: Halstead.

Torney-Purta, J., Wilkenfeld, B. and Barber, C. (2008). How Adolescents in 27 Countries Understand Support and Practice Human Rights. *Journal of Social Issues*, 64(4); pp. 857–880.

Toth, O. (2001). Hungarian Adolescents' Attitudes Toward their Future, Peace, and the Environment. In: J. Myers-Walls, P. Somlai and R. Rapoport, eds., *Families as Educators for Global Citizenship*, 1st ed. Aldershot: Ashgate, pp. 131–138.

Tudoroiu, T. (2007). Rose, Orange, and Tulip: The Failed Post-Soviet Revolutions. *Communist and Post-Communist Studies*, 40(3), pp. 315–342.

Tupy, M. (2006). *The Rise of Populist Parties in Central Europe: Big Government, Corruption, and the Threat to Liberalism.* [online] Washington, DC: Cato Institute. Available at: www.cato.org/publications/development-policy-analysis/rise-populist-parties-central-europe-big-government-corruption-threat-liberalism?print [accessed November 8, 2006].

UN Security Council Report. (2004). *The Rule of Law and Transitional Justice in Conflict and Post-conflict societies.* [online] Relief Web. Available at: https://reliefweb.int/sites/reliefweb.int/files/resources/F248759F512E0EB7C125739B003DC473-un_aug2004.pdf [accessed August 23, 2004].

UNESCO (United Nations Educational, Scientific and Cultural Organization). 2014 *Global Citizenship Education. Preparing Learners for the Challenges of the 21st Century.*

unesdoc.unesco.org, (2014). *Global Citizenship Education. Preparing Learners for the Challenges of the Twenty-first Century.* [online] New York: UNESCO. Available at: http://unesdoc.unesco.org/images/0022/002277/227729E.pdf [accessed August 4, 2015].

USAID Mission to Poland Europe and Eurasia. (1989–1999). USAID and the Polish Decade.

Van der Eijk, C. and Franklin, M. (1996). *Choosing Europe? The European Electorate and National Politics in the Face of Union.* Ann Arbor: University of Michigan Press.

Van der Meer, T. W. G. and E. J. van Ingen. (2009). Schools of Democracy? Disentangling the Relationship Between Civic Participation and Political Action in 17 European Countries. *European Journal of Political Research*, 48, pp. 281–308.

van Deth, J. (1997). *Private Groups and Public Life: Social Participation and Political Involvement in Representative Democracies.* London and New York: Routledge.

van Deth, J. (2001). Studying Political Participation: Towards a Theory of Everything? In: *Workshop "Electronic Democracy: Mobilisation, Organisation and Participation via new ICTs."* [online] Grenoble: Joint Sessions of Workshops of the European Consortium for Political Research. Available at: https://s3.amazonaws.com/academia.edu.documents/30286486/partECPR2001.pdf?AWSAccessKeyId=AKIAIWOWYYGZ2Y53UL3A&Expires=1521766113&Signature=CMoCuxqVHnZLdYlgH9lwI3vsL%2F0%3D&response-content-disposition=inline%3B%20filename%3DSTUDYING_POLITICAL_PARTICIPATION_TOWARDS.pdf [accessed April 11, 2001].

van Deth, J. (2010). Is Creative Participation Good for Democracy? In: W. Micheletti and A. McFarland, eds., *Creative Participation: Responsibility-taking in the Political World*, 1st ed. Boulder, CO: Paradigm, pp. 146–170.

van Deth, J. (2014). A Conceptual Map of Political Participation. *Acta Politica*, 49(3), pp. 349–367.

van Deth, J., Montero, J. and Westholm, A. (2007). *Citizenship and Involvement in European Democracies: A Comparative Analysis*. New York: Routledge.

Vanderhill, R. (2017). Active Resistance to Democratic Diffusion. *Communist and Post-Communist Studies*, 50(1), pp. 41–51.

Verba, S. and Nie, N. (1972). *Participation in America: Political Democracy and Social Equality*. New York: Harper and Row.

Verba, S., Nie, N. and Kim, J. (1978). *Participation and Political Equality: A Seven-nation Comparison*. Cambridge: Cambridge University Press.

Verba, S., Schlozman, K. and Brady, H. (1995). *Voice and Equality: Civic Voluntarism in American Politics*. Cambridge, MA: Harvard University Press.

Verick, S. and Islam, I. (2010). The Great Recession of 2008–2009: Causes, Consequences and Policy Responses. *Institute for the Study of Labor Discussion Papers*, 4934.

Veugelers, W. (2011). *Theory and Practice of Citizenship Education. The Case of Policy, Science and Education in the Netherlands*. [online] Perú Ministerio de Educación. Available at: http://repositorio.minedu.gob.pe/handle/123456789/972 [accessed June 19, 2013].

Vráblíková, K. (2017). *What Kind of Democracy? Participation, Inclusiveness and Contestation*. New York: Routledge.

Walgrave, S. and Rucht, D. (2010). Introduction. In: S. Walgrave and D. Rucht, eds., *The World Says No to War: Demonstrations against the War on Iraq*, 1st ed. Minneapolis: University of Minnesota Press, pp. xiii–xxvi.

Walker, C. (2016). The Authoritarian Threat: The Hijacking of Soft Power. *Journal of Democracy*, 27(1), pp. 49–63.

Walzer, M. (2002). Equality and Civil Society. In: S. Chambers and W. Kylicka, eds., *Alternative Conceptions of Civil Society*, 1st ed. Princeton, NJ: Princeton University Press, pp. 34–49.

Way, L. (2005). Ukraine's Orange Revolution: Kuchma's Failed Authoritarianism. *Journal of Democracy*, 16(2), pp. 131–145.

Wedel, J. (1998). *Collision and Collusion. The Strange Case of Western Aid to Eastern Europe*. Basingstoke: Palgrave Macmillan.

Wedel, J. (2001). *Collision and Collusion: The Strange Case of Western Aid to Eastern Europe*. New York: Palgrave for St. Martin's Griffin.Weinstein, J. (2013). Defunding Dissent: Restrictions on Aid to NGOs D Christensen. *Journal of Democracy*, 24(2), pp. 77–91.

Wejnert, B. (2014). *Diffusion of Democracy: The Past and Future of Global Democracy*. New York: Cambridge University Press.

Welzel, C. (2009). Theories of Democratization. In: C. Haerpfer, P. Bernhagen, R. Inglehart and C. Welzel, eds., *Democratization*, 1st ed. New York: Oxford University Press, pp. 74–92.

Welzel, C. (2013). *Freedom Rising Human Empowerment and the Quest for Emancipation*. Cambridge: Cambridge University Press.

Welzel, C. and Deutsch, F. (2012). Emancipative Values and Nonviolent Protest: The Importance of "Ecological" Effects. *British Journal of Political Science*, 42(2), pp. 465–479.

Welzel, C. and Inglehart, R. (2008). Democratization as Human Empowerment. *Journal of Democracy*, 19(1), pp. 126–140.

Welzel C., Inglehart, R. and Deutsch, F. (2005). Social Capital, Voluntary Associations and Collective Action: Which Aspects of Social Capital Have the Greatest "Civic" Payoff?" *Journal of Civil Society*, 1(2), pp. 121–146.

Wendt, A. (1987). The Agent-Structure Problem in International Relations Theory. *International Organization*, 41(3), pp. 335–370.

Westholm, A., Montero, J. and van Deth, J. (2007). Introduction: Citizenship, Involvement, and Democracy in Europe. In: J. van Deth, J. Montero and A. Westholm, eds., *Citizenship and Involvement in European Democracies: A Comparative Analysis*, 1st ed. London: Routledge, pp. 1–32.

Wheatley, J. (2005). *Georgia from National Awakening to Rose Revolution: Delayed Transition in the Former Soviet Union.* New York: Ashgate.

Whitehead, L. (1986). International Aspects of Democratization. In: G. O'Donnell, P. Schmitter and L. Whitehead, eds., *Transitions from Authoritarian Rule: Prospects for Democracy*, 1st ed. Baltimore, MD: Johns Hopkins University Press, pp. 3–46.

Wilde, C. (2002). The Challenge of Using NGOs as a Strategy for Engagement. In: M. Balmaceda, J. Clem and L. Tarlow, eds., *Independent Belarus: Domestic Determinants Regional Dynamics, and Implications for the West.* Cambridge, MA: Harvard University Press.

Wolff, J. and Poppe, A. (2015). *From Closing Space to Contested Spaces Re-assessing Current Conflicts over International Civil Society Support.* [online] PRIF and HSFK. Available at: www.hsfk.de/fileadmin/HSFK/hsfk_downloads/prif137.pdf [accessed March 24, 2018].

Wright, J. and Winters, M. (2010). The Politics of Effective Foreign Aid. *Annual Review of Political Science*, 13, pp. 61–80.

Wyborcza. (2017). Orban przykręca śrubę aktywnym obywatelom article by Michał Kokot, Paweł Kośmiński September 5, 2017. Available at http://wyborcza.pl/7,75399,22325134,orban-przykreca-srube-aktywnym-obywatelom.html [accessed March 24, 2018].

Yasuda, Y. (2015). *Rules, Norms and NGO Advocacy Strategies: Hydropower development on the Mekong River*. Abingdon and New York: Routledge.

Youngs, R. (2006). *Survey of European Democracy Promotion Policies 2000–2006.* Madrid: FRIDE.

Youngs, R. (2012). Misunderstanding the Maladies of Liberal Democracy Promotion. In: C. Hobson and M. Kurki, eds., *The Conceptual Politics of Democracy Promotion*, 1st ed. London and New York: Routledge, pp. 100–116.

Youngs, R. (2015). *The Puzzle of Non-Western Democracy.* Washington: Carnegie Endowment for International Peace.

Zakaria, F. (1997). The Rise of Illiberal Democracy. *Foreign Affairs*, 76(6), pp. 22–43.

Zakaria, F. (2003). *The Future of Freedom: Illiberal Democracy at Home and Abroad.* London and New York: W.W. Norton & Company.

Zakrzewski, R. (2017). *Rządowe organizacje pozarządowe (Governmental Non-governmental Prganizations).* [online] Wyborcza. Available at: http://wyborcza.pl/7,75968,22419901,rzadowe-organizacje-pozarzadowe.html [accessed September 24, 2017].

Zalan, E. (2017). *New Polish PM visits Hungary in snub to Brussels.* [online] EUObserver. Available at: https://euobserver.com/political/140440 [accessed January 3, 2017].

Zalas-Kamińska, Katarzyna (2016). Polska pomoc rozwojowa—co dalej? [Polish development aid – what next?] Available at http://wiadomosci.ngo.pl/wiadomosc/1894856.html [accesssed May 15, 2018].

Zimmer, A. and Priller, E. (2004). *Future of Civil Society: Making Central European Non-Profit Organizations Work.* Wiesbaden: Springer Fachmedien.

Zimmermann, L. (2017). *Global Norms with a Local Face: Rule-of-Law Promotion and Norm Translation.* Cambridge: Cambridge University Press.

Zukin, C., Keeter, S., Andolina, M., Jenkins, K. and Carpini, M. (2006). *A New Engagement? Political Participation, Civic Life, and the Changing American Citizen.* Oxford: Oxford University Press.

Zürn, M. and Checkel, J. (2005). Getting Socialized to Build Bridges: Constructivism and Rationalism, Europe and the Nation-State. *International Organization*, 59(4), pp. 1045–1079.

Zwingel, S. (2012). How Do Norms Travel? Theorizing International Women's Rights in Transnational Perspective. *International Studies Quarterly*, 56(1), pp. 115–129.

Index

Page numbers in **bold** denote tables, those in *italics* denote figures.

BIOLOGICAL
CHEMISTRY